An Easy

COMPANY
AND
COMPENSATION LAWS

(In Accordance with the Latest Syllabus of B.Com)

An Easy Approach to

COMPANY
AND
COMPENSATION LAWS

(In Accordance with the Latest Syllabus of B.Com)

J.P. Sharma

M.Com, LL.B., Dip T&D, FCS, Ph.D.

Professor of Law & Corporate Governance
Department of Commerce
Faculty of Commerce and Business
Delhi School of Economics
University of Delhi

Ane Books Pvt. Ltd.

New Delhi ♦ Chennai ♦ Mumbai

Bengaluru ♦ Kolkata ♦ Thiruvananthapuram ♦ Lucknow

An Easy Approach to Company and Compensation Laws

J.P. Sharma

© Author, **2010**

Published by

Ane Books Pvt. Ltd.
4821, Parwana Bhawan, 1st Floor, 24 Ansari Road,
Darya Ganj, **New Delhi** - 110 002, India
Tel.: +91(011) 23276843-44, Fax: +91(011) 23276863
e-mail: kapoor@anebooks.com, Website: www.anebooks.com

Branches

▓ Avantika Niwas, 1st Floor, 19 Doraiswamy Road, T. Nagar,
 Chennai - 600 017, Tel.: +91(044) 28141554, 28141209
 e-mail: anebooks_tn@airtelmail.in

▓ Plot No. 59, Sector-1, Shirwane, Nerul, **Navi Mumbai** - 400 706,
 Tel.: +91(022) 27720842, 27720851
 e-mail: anebooksmum@mtnl.net.in

▓ 38/1, 1st Floor, Model House, First Street, Opp. Shamanna Park,
 Basavannagudi, **Bengaluru** - 560 004, Tel.: +91(080) 41681432, 26620045
 e-mail: anebang@airtelmail.in

▓ Flat No. 16A, 220 Vivekananda Road, Maniktalla,
 Kolkata - 700 006, Tel.: +91(033) 23547119, 23523639
 e-mail: anebooks_vsn@bsnl.in

▓ # 6, TC 25/2710, Kohinoor Flats, Lukes Lane, Ambujavilasam Road,
 Thiruvananthapuram - 01, Kerala, Tel.: +91(0471) 4068777, 4068333
 e-mail: anebookstvm@airtelmail.in

Representative Office

▓ C-26, Sector-A, Mahanagar, **Lucknow** - 226 006
 Mobile - +91 93352 29971

ISBN : 978-93-8015-674-3

Printed at : Gopaljee Enterprises, Delhi

PREFACE

I was tempted to write this book because hardly any quality book is available in the market that caters to the demand and need of B. Com students of Delhi University and the faculty teaching this paper. The foremost aim of writing this book is to state Company and Compensation Laws in a manner which is simple, readable, and up-to-date for the benefit, in particular, of over twenty thousand B. Com second year students of Delhi University. However, given the growing interest in the subject of Company and Compensation Laws in the country, I hope that a wide range of other readers may find the book of use.

Each law in the book has been preceded by its historical background to generate interest amongst the users about the periodic growth and development of the regulation in the country. To ensure clarity and easy understanding of the subject, many of the concepts have been supported by judicial interpretations and case examples at appropriate places. In order to keep the book to a manageable size and keeping in view the requirements of students, sections are not always reproduced in full and at places some sections have been omitted.

I wish to express my appreciation to all those who have helped shape this book and in particular to those hundreds of my M.Com students at the Delhi School of Economics, who tested in their classroom discussions the draft versions of the book. I must also thank my wife Rajesh for her understanding and patience throughout.

I am most grateful to M/s Ane Books Pvt. Ltd. for the remarkable efficiency and speed with which the first edition of this book has been brought to press.

I have made an effort to state the law as known to me on 25th September, 2009.

Professor J.P. Sharma
Delhi School of Economics

STUDENTS' FEEDBACK

Students of M.Com Final at the Delhi School of Economics and University of Delhi South Campus have rated Professor J.P. Sharma as an excellent teacher by giving him a score of 6.36 out of 6.45 and 6.17 out of 6.79, respectively, in the year 2002-2003, 2003-2004 and, also exceptional score in the year 2008-2009. The authorities conducted the student's evaluation of teachers by giving an evaluation perform to all the students at the end of the academic session, which was analyzed by independent evaluators.

Individual Observations of Students of M.Com Final at the Delhi School of Economics

2003-2004

• Enjoyable and interesting class	• Gives proper notes
• Good command over the subject	• Enthusiastic
• Good/effective communication skill	• Good explanation of cases efficient in explaining
• Takes up doubts and queries readily	• Cool and confident
• Comes prepared for lecture	• Well organized & systematic presentation
• Vast knowledge of the subject	• Makes the subject understandable/ simplified
• Participative	• Handles queries
• Regular	• Effectively manages the big class
• Good teacher/wonderful nature	• Ability to command the class very well

2002-2003

• Very regular and participative nature	• Good command over the subject, simple language used, audible. Though he was not in good health, he took pains to cover our course

• Well prepared notes, good communication skills	• Good personality, effective communication, well behaved, well natured
• Enthusiastic, good lecture to attend	• He sets the example of perfection
• Provides understanding of subject	• He does not dictate, but gives notes.
• He has vast knowledge about his subject	• Best teacher, after coming from serious health problem he is very regular in taking his classes
• Wonderful teacher	• Very good professor, good knowledge, explains everything very nicely
• Enthusiastic, good teacher, clear understanding, experience	• Very good teacher, teaches confidently, very cooperative person
• In spite of being unwell, has managed to efficiently complete the course, makes us understand the technicalities of the subject.	• Ideal for the students, kind, affectionate, hardworking and honest, perfection in his field, interactive and participative classes
• Was very regular, very participative, gives comprehensive lectures	• Qualitative teaching, interactive classes
• Good teacher, good command over subject and efficiency	• Command over the subject, complicated topics explained easily, makes topics interesting, makes effective use of blackboard, updated with recent events
• An ideal teacher, good communication skill, perfection in all types of law	• Really interesting & informative classes
• Good command over subject, friendly nature and interacts well with the students	

Sd/-	**Sd/-**
Professor Sanjay K. Jain	Professor Sri Ram Khanna
Faculty of Commerce & Business	Head & Dean
Delhi School of Economics	Faculty of Commerce & Business
Delhi University	Delhi School of Economics, Delhi University

SYLLABUS

B.Com – Part II

Paper – VIII: Company and Compensation Laws

Duration: 3 hrs.   **Max. Marks: 75**

Unit–I
Company: Definition, Characteristics, Lifting of Corporate Veil. Types of Companies, Formation of a Company: Promoters, Pre-incorporation Contracts, Provisional Contracts, Memorandum of Association, Articles of Association.

Unit–II
Prospectus: Contents, Abridged Prospectus, Red-herring Prospectus, Shelf Prospectus, Statement in lieu of Prospectus. Misrepresentation of Prospectus, Share Capital: Issue and allotment of shares, SEBI guidelines on allotment, Issue of Shares at Premium and at Discount, Buy Back of Shares, Rights Issue, Book Building, Concept of Bonus, Shares, Share Certificate, Demat System.

Unit–III
Calls on Shares, Forfeiture and Surrender of Shares, Transfer & Transmission of Shares, Provisions relating to Payment of Dividend, Investor's Education and Protection Fund.

Unit–IV
Directors: Appointment, Share Qualification and Legal Position. Meetings: Meeting of Board of Directors, Meeting of Shareholders, and Requisites of a valid Meeting: Notice, Agenda, Quorum, Chairman, Resolutions and Minutes, Proxy. Compulsory Winding up (Sec. 433)
Emerging Issues in Company Law

Unit–V
Employees State Insurance Act, 1948
Definitions: Personal Injury, Factory, Manufacturing Process, Wages, Partial and Permanent Disablement. ESI Corporation, Standing Committee and Medical Benefit Council, Contributions, Adjudication of Dispute and Claims, Benefits

Unit–VI
Workmen's Compensation Act, 1923
Definitions: Dependent, Employer, Partial and Total Disablement, Workmen, Injury, Accident, Payment of Compensation, Contracting, Commissioner.

CONTENTS

Part-I   Company Law

Part-II Compensation Laws

Part-I Company Law

Historical Background

Historical Development of Company Law

The Company Law in India is conceived and developed in UK. It is a cherished child of English parents born and brought up in England. The history and development of Company Law in India is closely linked with that of United Kingdom (UK). The Companies Acts passed from time to time in India have been following the English Company laws with minor changes here and there. Therefore, a brief resume of the origin and growth of company law in England is essential for logical understanding of company law in India.

Origin and Growth of Company Law in England

The origin of company form of organization in England dates back to centuries and its glimpses can be traced from 11th Century. A century-wise discussion about the growth and development of Company Law in England is given in the succeeding paragraphs:

11 to 13th Century : Period of Merchant Guilds

- The earliest business associations in England during 11th to 13th Centuries were called the Merchant Guilds.
- Such Guilds which were prevalent in England obtained Charter from the King Queen to establish a body corporate.
- Purpose of establishing such Guilds was to secure monopoly in a particular trade.
- Gradually members of Guilds started trading on joint account subject to Guilds rules.

Two Types of Guilds Prevalent

(i) *Commendas*
- Characteristics of the present day companies were visible in such guilds,
- Trader lent money to another and got share profit,

    ❑   Had limited liability to money financed,

    ❑   Lender was a sleeping partner

(ii) Societas

    ❑   Characteristics of the present day partnerships were visible in such guilds,

    ❑   All members took active part,

    ❑   Had unlimited liability,

    ❑   There was mutual agency on the lines of present day partnership.

14th Century : Guilds Extended to Foreign Trade

    ❑   By Royal Charter, such Guilds were given special privileges,

    ❑   Guilds were extended to foreign trade,

    ❑   The word "company" was adopted by some traders for trading with foreign countries.

16th Century : Period of Regulated Companies

    ❑   Guilds during this period were called Regulated Companies.

    ❑   During this period joint trading started growing,

    ❑   Separate trading or private trading by members of Guilds/Joint Trading Companies was allowed.

17th Century : Period of Joint Stock Companies

    ❑   Companies during this period were called as Joint Stock Companies.

1600 : East India Company Established

The Royal Charter of Queen Elizabeth I established East India Company in the year 1600. The object was to share profits of each voyage from its monopoly trade in Far East[1]. The characteristics of modern corporate bodies were clearly visible in the constitution and working of East India Company. In the charter of the Company were named a Governor of the Company, who was not different from modern day chairman of the Board of Directors and several committee members equivalent of present day directors. The successors of the committeemen were to be elected annually by the shareholders. The Governor and the committeemen were required to submit frequent reports on their important decisions for confirmation of General Courts of all subscribers of the Company corresponding to the general meetings of the shareholders in the present day[2].

---

1. *The Hutchison Encyclopaedia* (1990), *Random Century Group, p.*367.
2. *E S Srinivasachari (European Settlements), "History and Culture of the Indian People" Vol 7, the Mughal Empire* (1994) *end note 5 to chapter* XVI (*p* 518) *Bhartiya Vidya Bhawan.*

1670 : The Harts and Bay Company was founded by the Royal Charter.

1692 : Separate trading/private trading by members of East India Company was prohibited.

1694 : Bank of England was founded by the Royal Charter.

18th Century : Enactment of the Bubble Act, 1719

- ❑ Bubble Act was passed in 1719,
- ❑ The Act prohibited formation of Joint Stock Companies except by the Royal Charter,
- ❑ The aim was to put check on the growth of unregistered companies,
- ❑ With the passing of this Act, companies disappeared like the bursting of the bubble,
- ❑ The Act had led to widespread panic amongst unregistered companies.

19th Century : Repealment of the Bubble Act and Growth of Company Law

1825 : The Bubble Act was ultimately repealed in 1825.

- ❑ Again, both the companies formed by Royal Charter and unregistered companies started growing.
- ❑ It was during this period that the Royal Charter incorporated trading companies like Peninsular and Oriental Stream Navigation Company (in 1840) that still operates in England,
- ❑ Non-trading concerns incorporated by Charter and that still operate include BBC, public schools, colleges and universities and some learned professional bodies like:
  - The Institute of Chartered Accountant in England and Wales,
  - The Chartered Institute of Secretaries and Administrators,
  - The Chartered Institute of Management Accountants,
  - The Chartered Association of Certified Accountants
- ❑ Now a day the trading concerns prefer incorporation under Companies Act than by a Charter.

1844 Joint Stock Companies Act, 1844 (*Joint Stock Companies Act, 1850 in India*)

- ❑ First enactment to bear the title of "Joint Stock Companies Act",
- ❑ Provision for the registration of companies was there,
- ❑ The office of the Registrar of Joint Stock Companies was created.

1855 Limited Liability Act, 1855 (*Joint Stock Companies Act, 1857 in India*)

- ❑ English Parliament in 1855 passed the Act providing for limited liability to the members of a registered company.

1856 : Joint Stock Companies Act, 1856

- ❑ A Comprehensive Act of 1856 superseded Act of 1844.
- ❑ This Act introduced the mode of formation of companies by Memorandum of Association and Articles of Association.

1862 : Companies Act, 1862 (*Companies Act,* 1862 *in India*)

- ❑ First enactment to bear the title of "Companies Act",
- ❑ Memorandum and Articles were made compulsory,
- ❑ Any alteration in the object clause of Memorandum of Association was prohibited,
- ❑ A company could be formed with liability limited by guarantee, Provisions of winding up were also introduced.

1890 : Companies (Memorandum of Association) Act, 1890

This Act made relaxation with regard to change in the object clause of Memorandum of Association. The change was allowed by passing special resolution in the general meeting.

20th Century : Development of Modern Company Law

1900 : Companies Act, 1900

- ❑ Compulsory audit of the company's accounts was enforced.

1908 : Companies Act, 1908 (*Indian Companies Act,* 1913)

- ❑ It was called as Companies (Consolidation) Act, 1908.
- ❑ The Concept of private company was introduced.

1948 : Companies Act, 1948

- ❑ It was the Principal Act in force in England,
- ❑ It was based on the report of a Committee under Lord Cohen,
- ❑ New form of company known as Exempt Private Company was introduced,
- ❑ Emphasis was on the public accountability of the company,
- ❑ Protection of minority was the highlight.
- ❑ Investigation of Company's affairs was also incorporated.
- ❑ Shareholders in general meeting were given power to remove a director before the expiration of his period of office.

1967 : Companies (Amendment) Act, 1967

- ❑ It was based upon the Jenkins Committee recommendations presented in 1962.

- ❏ The Amendment Act abolished the concept of exempt private company.
- ❏ Stringent provisions were introduced in relation to director's interests in the company and disclosures thereof.

1976 : Companies Act, 1976

- ❏ Strengthened the requirements of public accountability and relating to disclosures of interests in the shares of the company.

1980 : Companies Act, 1980: Reforms Process Started

- ❏ The Act was a major step towards Company Law reforms in UK.
- ❏ The Act fundamentally changed the structure of company law in England.
- ❏ Insider dealing was made a criminal offence.
- ❏ Shareholders were given a right of pre-emption in the case of new issues of shares.
- ❏ Dealings between directors and their companies became greatly restricted and maximum financial limits were introduced for such dealings.

1981 : Companies Act, 1981

- ❏ For the purposes of accounting and disclosures, companies were divided as small, medium sized and other companies. Their disclosures requirements were differentiated accordingly.
- ❏ Law relating to names of companies was simplified by the abolition of the approval of the name by the Department of Trade.
- ❏ The Act further abolished the register of business names, which had to be kept under the Registration of Business Names Act, 1916.
- ❏ Company was authorised to issue redeemable equity shares.
- ❏ Company was authorised to purchase its own shares.

1985 : Companies Act, 1985

- ❏ Whole of the existing Statute relating exclusively to companies has been consolidated in the Companies Act, 1985.
- ❏ The contents of the Companies Act,1985 have been derived from sources going back to the Act of 1956 which enacted the Prevention of Fraud (investigation) Act, 1958, the Stock Transfer Act, 1963, the Banking Act,1979 and the Insurance Companies Act, 1982. These Statutes remain in force and have not been consolidated into the Companies Act, 1985.

1989 : Companies (Amendment) Act, 1989

- ❏ Many sections and schedules were revised and reinserted in the Companies Act, 1985 by amending Act in 1989.

2006 : Companies Act, 2006

- An Act (46 chapters, 1300 sections, 16 schedules) to reform company law and restate the greater part of the enactments relating to companies; to make other provision relating to companies and for connected purposes. It was enacted by the Queen's most Excellent Majesty on 8th other forms of business organization; to make provision about directors' disqualification, business names, auditors and actuaries; to amend Part 9 of the Enterprise Act, 2002; November, 2006, by and with the advice and consent of the Lords Spiritual and Temporal, and Commons, in this present Parliament assembled, and by the authority of the same.

Growth of Company Law in India

The following paragraphs provide a year-wise growth of company in law in the India:

1850 : Joint Stock Companies Act, 1850

- This Act was based on the Joint Stock Companies Act, 1844 of England.
- The Act provided for the registration of Joint Stock Companies in India.
- Under this Act, the office of Registrar of Companies was created and the Supreme Courts of Bombay, Calcultta and Madras were authorised to order the registration of companies and to act as a Registrar of Companies.

1857 : Joint Stock Companies Act, 1857

- Limited liability was introduced. The Act conferred right of registration with or without limited liability.
- This benefit was not extended to the banking and insurance companies. Subsequently, by an Act of 1860, this right was granted to the banking and insurance companies also following the similar principles in Great Britain.

1866 : Companies Act 1866

- 1st *enactment to bear the title of Companies Act.*
- It was a comprehensive Companies Act, which consolidated the laws relating to incorporation, regulation and winding up of trading companies and other associations. This Act was recasted in 1882 embodying the amendments made in England up-to that period.

1913 : Indian Companies Act, 1913

- The Indian Companies Act, 1913 which was based on the UK Companies Act, 1908 recognised for the first time, the concept of Private Limited

Company. The object was to provide an alternative form of organisation to small traders and family concerns that did not invite public subscription. This helped them maintain some privacy about their business affairs, as is there in a partnership form of organisation and at the same time, get the benefit of limited liability and separate legal personality with perpetual succession.

- The Act was found highly unsatisfactory, as it did not take into account the peculiar features of Indian trade.
- Thus, it was amended in 1914, 1915, 1920, 1926, 1930, 1932, 1936 and then almost every year up-to 1951.

1950 : H.C. Bhaba Committee

- After the World War IInd and especially after the enactment of Comprehensive Companies Act in England in 1948, the need was felt for a similar comprehensive Companies Act in India.
- The Government of India on 25th October, 1950 appointed a 12-member committee under the chairmanship of Shri H.C. Bhaba.
- The Committee submitted its report on all the aspects of Companies Law in April, 1952.
- Government accepted recommendations of the committee and the Companies Act, 1956, which was modeled on the Companies Act of 1948 of UK, was enacted.

1956 : Companies Act, 1956

- This Act repealed all earlier Companies Acts.
- It is effective from 1st April, 1956 and extends to whole of India.
- It is the biggest of all procedural laws in country. It is in XIII Parts with 658 sections, 6 tables and 15 schedules.

Radical Changes in the Indian Company Laws

- Corporate Governance has received focused attention in the recent years world over and many countries have amended their company laws to keep pace with the changed world.
- A serious effort in India was made in the years 1999, 2000, 2002 and 2006 when certain corporate governance reforms were announced by amending the Companies Act. It was a comprehensive amendment of the Companies Act of 1956. Most of the proposals of the Bill of 1993 and 1997 were incorporated in these amendments.
- By amending the Companies Act in 2002, mismanaged manufacturing co-operative societies in the country were brought under the purview

of the Act as Producers Companies by adding Part IXA contained in 12 chapters.

□ The Companies (2nd) Amendment Act, 2002 provided for the replacement of the Company Law Board (CLB) by the mechanism of Tribunal, though the Notification to dissolve the CLB under section 10 FA has not yet been issued by the Central Government.

□ Based on the recommendations of the JJ Irani Committee, the Companies Act was amended in May, 2006 to provide for the filing of company returns online by a simple click on *www.mca.gov.in* and to make payment of fees by using credit card and electronically. The electronic filing has been made mandatory from September 16, 2006. The amendment also has a provision for the mandatory allotment of Director Identification Number (DIN) to all existing and future directors on company boards and online registration of companies.

□ To have LLP form of entity in the country, LLP Act, 2008 was passed and notified in January, 2009.

□ The Companies (Amendment) Bill, 2009 has been re-introduced in the Lok Sabha on 3rd August, 2009. The Bill has been forwarded to a Parliamentary Standing Committee, but since the committee is loaded with no deadline, it may take roughly a year to get it enacted. Only the time will tell whether this time the proposal to completely overhaul the company law gets through? Government's earlier attempt in 1993 and 1997 did not see the light of the day.

Proposed Reforms

Companies (Amendment) Bill, 2009

□ The Companies (Amendment) Bill, 2009, re-introduced in the Lok Sabha on 3rd August, 2009, is similar in content to the one introduced in the Lok Sabha on 24th October, 2008, which lapsed with the change in government. Earlier, the Ministry of Finance locked horns with the Ministry of Corporate Affairs (MCA) over certain provisions of the new company law. Finance Ministry wanted the Investor's Education and Protection Fund, now at the disposal of Ministry of Corporate Affairs (MCA), to be transferred to SEBI as the capital market regulator SEBI does not have access to public funds to protect the interests of investors. The Ministry of Corporate Affairs (MCA) has not accepted this view arguing that use of this fund is not restricted to only listed companies. Besides, the source of this fund (unclaimed dividends/deposits) is also not restricted to listed companies. The Ministry of Finance has also said that new company law need not mandate that every listed company should reserve 1/3rd of its board seats to independent directors. Finance

Ministry has also proposed to remove the cap of 50 members for a private company.

❑ The Ministry of Corporate Affairs (MCA) took up a comprehensive revision of the Companies Act, 1956 in 2004 keeping in view that not only had the number of companies in India expanded from about 30,000 in 1956 to nearly 9.5 lakhs, Indian companies were also mobilizing resources at a scale unimaginable even a decade ago, continuously entering into and bringing new activities into the fold of the Indian economy. In doing so, they were emerging internationally as efficient providers of a wide range of goods and services while increasing employment opportunities at home. At the same time, the increasing number of options and avenues for international business, trade and capital flows had imposed a requirement not only for harnessing entrepreneurial and economic resources efficiently but also to be competitive in attracting investment for growth. These developments necessitated modernization of the regulatory structure for the corporate sector in a comprehensive manner.

❑ The review and redrafting of the Companies Act, 1956 was taken up by the Ministry of Corporate Affairs on the basis of a detailed consultative process. A 'Concept Paper on New Company Law' was placed on the website of the Ministry of Corporate Affairs (www.mca.gov.in) on 4th August, 2004. The inputs received were put to a detailed examination in the Ministry. The Government also constituted an Expert Committee on Company Law under the Chairmanship of Dr. J.J. Irani on 2nd December, 2004 to advice on new Companies Bill. The Committee submitted its report to the Government on 31st May, 2005. Detailed consultations were also taken up with various Ministries, Departments and Government Regulators. The Bill was thereafter drafted in consultation with the Legislative Department of the Central Government.

❑ The re-introduced Companies Bill, 2009 seeks to enable the corporate sector in India to operate in a regulatory environment of best international practices that fosters entrepreneurship, investment and growth and provides for:

  • The basic principles for all aspects of internal governance of corporate entities and a framework for their regulation, irrespective of their area of operation, from incorporation to liquidation and winding up, in a single, comprehensive, legal framework administered by the Central Government. In doing so, the Bill also harmonizes the Company law framework with the imperative of specialized sectoral regulation.

- Articulation of shareholders democracy with protection of the rights of minority stakeholders, responsible self-regulation with disclosures and accountability, substitution of government control over internal corporate processes and decisions by shareholder control.
- A new entity in the form of One-Person Company (OPC) while empowering Government to provide a simpler compliance regime for small companies.
- Retains the concept of Producer Companies, while providing a more stringent regime for not-for–profit companies to check misuse.
- Speedy incorporation process, with detailed declarations disclosures about the promoters, directors etc. at the time of incorporation itself.
- Every company director would be required to acquire a unique Directors identification number.
- Every company to have at least one director resident in India.
- A provision for independent directors to be appointed on the Boards of such companies as may be prescribed, along with attributes determining independence. The requirement to appoint an independent director, where applicable, is a minimum of 33% of the total number of directors.
- Statutory recognition to audit, remuneration and stakeholders grievances committees of the Board
- Recognizes the Chief Executive Officer (CEO), the Chief Financial Officer (CFO) and the Company Secretary as Key Managerial Personnel (KMP).
- The role, rights and duties of the auditors defined as to maintain integrity and independence of the audit process.
- It also provides for shares with differential voting rights to be done away with.
- Valuation of non-cash considerations for allotment of shares through independent valuers.
- Easy transition of companies operating under the Companies Act, 1956, to the new framework as also from one type of company to another.
- No restriction proposed on the number of subsidiary companies that a company may have, subject to disclosure in respect of their relationship and transactions/dealings between them.
- Application of the successful e-Governance initiative of the Ministry of Corporate Affairs (MCA-21) to all the processes involved in meeting compliance obligations. Company processes, also to be

enabled to be carried out through electronic mode. The proposed e-Governance regime is intended to provide for ease of operation for filing and access to corporate data over the internet to all stakeholders, on round the clock basis.

- Facilitates joint ventures and relaxes restrictions limiting the number of partners in entities such as partnership firms, banking companies etc. to a maximum 100 with no ceiling as to professions regulated by Special Acts.
- Companies not to be allowed to raise deposits from the public except on the basis of permission available to them through other Special Acts.
- The Bill recognizes insider trading by company directors/KMPs as an offence with criminal liability.
- Recognition of both accounting and auditing standards.
- Consolidation of financial statements of subsidiaries with those of holding companies is proposed to be made mandatory.
- A single forum for approval of mergers and acquisitions, along with concept of deemed approval in certain situations.
- A separate framework for enabling fair valuations in companies for various purposes. Appointment of valuers is proposed to be made by audit committees.
- Claim of an investor over a dividend or a security not claimed for more than a period of seven years not being extinguished, and Investor Education and Protection Fund (IEPF) to be administered by a statutory Authority.
- Shareholders Associations/Group of Shareholders to be enabled to take legal action in case of any fraudulent action on the part of company and to take part in investor protection activities and 'Class Action Suits'.
- A revised framework for regulation of insolvency, including rehabilitation, winding up and liquidation of companies with the process to be completed in a time bound manner.
- Incorporates international best practices based on the models suggested by the United Nations Commission on International Trade Law (UNCITRAL).
- Consolidation of fora for dealing with rehabilitation of companies, their liquidation and winding up in the single forum of National Company Law Tribunal with appeal to National Company Law Appellate Tribunal.
- The nature of the Rehabilitation and Revival Fund proposed in the Companies (Second Amendment) Act, 2002 to b; replaced by

Insolvency Fund with voluntary contributions linked to entitlements to draw money in a situation of insolvency.

- Company is identified as a separate entity for imposition of monetary penalties from the officers in default.
- A more effective regime for inspections and investigations of companies.
- Laying down the maximum as well as minimum quantum of penalty for each offence with suitable deterrence for repeat offences.
- In case of fraudulent activities/actions, provisions for recovery and disgorgement have been included.
- Levy of additional fee in a non-discretionary manner for procedural offences, such as late filing of statutory documents, to be enabled through rules.
- Defaults of procedural nature to be penalized by levy of monetary penalties by the Registrars of Companies. The appeals against such orders of Registrars of Companies to lie with suitably designated higher authorities.
- Special Courts to deal with offences under the Bill.
- Company matters such as mergers and amalgamations, reduction of capital, insolvency including rehabilitation, liquidations and winding up are proposed to be addressed by the National Company Law Tribunal/ National Company Law Appellate Tribunal.

Review Questions

1. Trace out in brief the history of company law in India and explain briefly the various reforms in the area of company laws after 2000.
2. Do you agree that the Indian company law is modelled on English provisions?
3. During the last ten years, by way of amendments, some major changes have been incorporated in the Companies Act. Explain briefly important amendments and those are in the pipelines.

2

Company

What is a Company?

- ❏ There is no single, accepted definition of company. Different persons at different times, under different situations and circumstances have defined the word company in their own different ways. Dictionary has a different meaning, Judges have defined in their own ways and authors on the subject have taken altogether a different meaning.
- ❏ The term 'company' is derived from the two Latin words *'Com + Pany'* which means

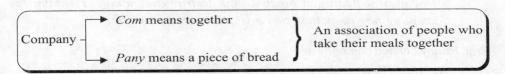

Company
- *Com* means together
- *Pany* means a piece of bread
} An association of people who take their meals together

Definitions

The word company has strictly

- No technical meaning and
- No legal meaning

As held in Smith v Anderson (1880)

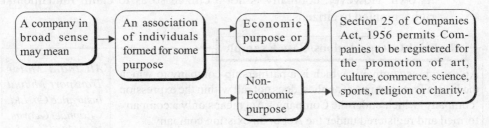

A company in broad sense may mean → An association of individuals formed for some purpose → Economic purpose or / Non-Economic purpose → Section 25 of Companies Act, 1956 permits Companies to be registered for the promotion of art, culture, commerce, science, sports, religion or charity.

As per Justice Lindley

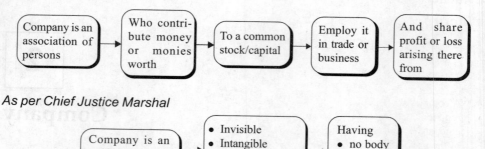

As per Chief Justice Marshal

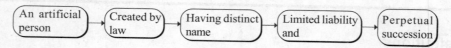

Prof. L C B Gower in his Modern Company (1957) while equating company with the river Thames of UK observes as follows:

- *'Company is like river Thames'*— *member may come and go but company can go for ever,*
- *'King is dead, long live the king'* *meaning the company never dies like a kingdom.*
- *'Not even a hydrogen bomb could destroy a company'* *meaning the company has perpetual succession or permanent life.*

Prof. Haney defined company as

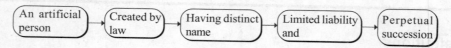

- Company is thus a voluntary association of persons formed for some purpose. It is a juristic person having a separate legal entity distinct from the memberswho constitute it. It is created by law having a distinct name, common seal, common capital divided into shares (transferable) with limited liability and perpetual succession. It is capable of having rights and duties of its own. However, company is not a citizen so as to claim fundamental rights granted to citizens.

Judicial Interpretations/Case Example	
An insurance company, which is a partnership company to which the Indian Partnership Act applies, does not fall within the expression 'company' which under the Companies Act means only a company formed and registered under the Act or an existing company.	*All India Motor Transport Mutual Insurance Co. Ltd.* v *Raphael George,* 1963, 33 Comp Cas 1166 (Bom).

Characteristics of a Company

■ *Incorporated/Registered Body*

❑ Under Section 3 (*i*) of the Companies Act, 1956:

A company means a company formed and registered under this Act or an existing company formed and registered under any of the previous company laws.

→

Previous Company Laws:
- Law prevalent before 1866
- Indian Companies Act, 1866
- Indian Companies Act, 1882
- Indian Companies Act, 1913
- Registration of Transferred Companies' Ordinance, 1942
- Portugese Commercial Code

❑ A company therefore cannot be formed unless it is registered under the Companies Act.

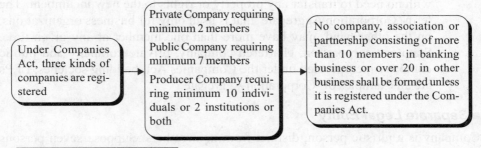

Under Companies Act, three kinds of companies are registered

→

Private Company requiring minimum 2 members

Public Company requiring minimum 7 members

Producer Company requiring minimum 10 individuals or 2 institutions or both

→

No company, association or partnership consisting of more than 10 members in banking business or over 20 in other business shall be formed unless it is registered under the Companies Act.

Judicial Interpretations	
An incorporated company is a body corporate but many bodies corporate are not incorporate companies.	*Madras Central Urban Bank Ltd.* v *Corporation of Madras,* 1932, 2 Comp Cas 328 (Mad).

■ *An Artificial Juristic Person*

(*a*) A Company is an artificial juristic person

Invisible
Intangible
Having

→

No body
No mind
No soul

→

Exists only in the eyes of law, and, depends upon natural persons who are called directors

(*b*)

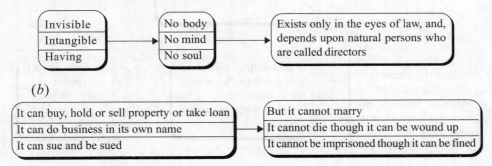

It can buy, hold or sell property or take loan

It can do business in its own name

It can sue and be sued

→

But it cannot marry

It cannot die though it can be wound up

It cannot be imprisoned though it can be fined

❑ An expression 'person' includes not only a natural person but also juristic persons. Since a company is a juristic person having no body, no mind, no limbs and no soul, it depends upon natural persons who are competent to represent it before a Court of law or any other place. Such representatives are called directors.

Company v Corporation

❑ The term 'person' is used to include both natural and artificial person. Every artificial person or juristic person is corporation, which may include Corporation Sole and Corporation Aggregate. The term 'Corporation Sole' is often attached as an incident of an office and is limited by law to one member at any given time. Mayor of Delhi Municipal Corporation is an example of 'Corporation Sole'. The Corporation Sole is distinct in law from the individual who occupies the post at any point in time. The individual office-holder may change over time, but the Corporation Sole continues with no need to transfer any property or rights to the new incumbent. The term 'Corporation Aggregate' that is used only for business organizations, on the other hand, may have more than one member at any given time. Statutory corporation, chartered company, private company and public company incorporated under the Companies Act, building societies, LLPs are all examples of 'Corporation Aggregate'.

■ Separate Legal Entity

Company is a juristic person, distinct from its members. Suppose seven persons have formed a public company ABC Ltd. The group now has eight persons, seven natural persons who are promoters and eighth, the company an artificial person that has separate legal entity to its promoters.

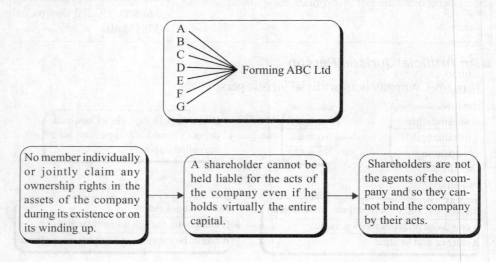

A
B
C
D → Forming ABC Ltd
E
F
G

| No member individually or jointly claim any ownership rights in the assets of the company during its existence or on its winding up. | A shareholder cannot be held liable for the acts of the company even if he holds virtually the entire capital. | Shareholders are not the agents of the company and so they cannot bind the company by their acts. |

Judicial Interpretations/Case Example	
Merely because there is only one shareholder, the entities, which are otherwise distinct, one is a natural person and the other is an artificial juristic person, it cannot be contended that the said entities merge and one can act for and on behalf of other.	*Floating Services Ltd. v MV 'San Fransceo Dipalola'* 2004, 52 SCL 762 (Guj).
Solomon was running prosperous leather business (leather merchant and wholesale boot manufacturing) as an unincorporated proprietorship. He converted business into a registered limited company called Solomon and Co Ltd. He, his wife, daughter, and four sons were the seven promoters. All of them subscribed for one shares each and actual cash paid by them was just pound 7. The entire issued share capital was held by Solomon. Solomon becomes managing director and his two sons were directors. Solomon sold the business to newly formed company for £38782 (nominal capital of the Company was £ 40,000) and charged consideration as follows:	*Solomon* v *Solomon and Co Ltd.,* 1897 AC (HL) 22: (1895-99), All. ER 33 (HL).

£ 10,000 debentures	Taken by Solomon
£ 20,000 shares	Taken by Solomon
£ 8,782	Paid in cash to Solomon

The business was solvent when it was taken over. But, the company had a brief career; it fell upon evil days. Shortly after it was started there seems to have come a period of great depression in the boot and shoe business. There were strikes of workmen too. And then Solomon got his debentures cancelled and reissued to one Mr. Broderip who advanced him 5000 pound money which Solomon immediately handed over to the company on loan. Solomon defaulted on payment of interest on debentures and Mr. Broderip then sued to enforce his security against the company. The company was put into liquidation at the instance of unsecured creditors. If Mr. Broderip claim were accepted, there would be nothing left for the unsecured creditors. The Receiver was appointed. The balance sheet had Assets: £ 6050, Liabilities (Debentures): £ 10,000 and Creditors: £ 8000. In the Court of first instance, Solomon was asked to indemnify the liquidator against the whole unsecured debts of the company and the company was held to be the agent of Solomon himself. The case was appealed to the Court of Appeal which dismissed the appeal. A further appeal was made to the House of Lords. By this time Mr. Broderip had been paid off and therefore ceased to be a party to the action. Held, the company once incorporated was an entirely separate legal person and though it may be that after incorporation the business is precisely the same as it was before, and the same persons receive the profits, the company in not in law the agent of subscribers or trustee for them. Held,

Contd..

Solomon was not liable to indemnify the company against the creditor's claim; that there had been no fraud committed on the creditors or shareholders. The House of Lords thus disagreed with lower courts and revised order of Appellate Court. Whatever available in the company was not paid to the ordinary creditors but was paid to Solomon himself being the debenture holders (secured creditors).	
Lee had formed a company 'Lee's Air Farming Ltd' for the purpose of carrying out top-dressing of crops from the air. The company that operated in New Zealand held insurance against liability to pay compensation to Lee. Lee, a qualified pilot held all but one of the shares (out of share capital of £ 3000) in the company. He voted himself as managing director and got himself appointed as chief pilot officer at a salary. He was thus the controlling shareholder, governing director of the company and its chief pilot. While carrying out his duties, the aeroplane crashed and Lee was killed. His widow claimed compensation for death on the plea that he was a worker employed by the company within the meaning of New Zealand Workers Compensation Act, 1922. Company opposed the claim on the ground that same person cannot be an employer as well as employee. The case was appealed to the Privy Council. The substantial question involved in the case is whether the deceased was a 'worker'? The Privy Council held that Lee and the company were distinct legal persons. The mere fact that someone is a director of a company is no impediment to his entering into a contract to serve the company. Held, the relationship between Lee and the company were that of master and servant and in his capacity as managing director he could give orders to himself as pilot officer (on behalf of the company). Wife could thus claim the compensation.	*Lee* v *Lee's Air Farming Ltd.,* 1961 AC 12; (1960) 3 All. ER 420 (PC).
A lease was executed by the directors of the company without the Seal of the company. Later a suit was filed by the directors and not by the company to avoid lease on the ground that a new term had been fraudulently included in the lease deed by the defendants. Suit was held to be non maintainable as the case was not made by the company but some of the directors.	*Rajendra Nath Dutta* v *Shibendra Nath Mukherjee Calcutta,* 1982, 52 Comp. Cos. 293 (Cal).

■ *Separate Property*

- ❑ Company being a legal person is distinct from its members.
- ❑ It is capable of owing, enjoying and disposing property in its own name.
- ❑ Shareholders are not the part owners of the company or its property. They are only given certain rights by the law *e.g.*, to receive dividend, attend and vote at the meeting.

Judicial Interpretations/Case Example	
The property of the company is not the property of the shareholders. But, it is the property of the company so much so that even if a shareholder acquires all shares of a company, business of the Company does not become his business.	*Gramophone and Typewriters Company* v *Stanley,* (1908-1910) All. ER 833, 2 KB 89 (CA).
The company may own property; its assets belong to the company itself and not to its members. However, member has a right to participate in the assets of the company, which would be left over after winding up but not in the assets as a whole.	*Bacha F. Guzdar* v *CIT,* 1955, 25 Comp Cas 1 (SC).
A shareholder has no right to intervene or object in suit pending against company in respect of some of its assets independently of company.	*Purna Investment Ltd.* v *Bank of India Ltd.,* 1984, 55 Comp Cas 737 (Cal).
Macaura (M), the owner of a timber estate sold all the timber to a registered company, the Irish Canadian Sawmills Ltd, in exchange for shares in the company. The timber continued to be insured in Macaura's name personally, rather than in the name of the company. He held all except one share of the company. He also advanced substantial loan to the company and thus was the company's largest unsecured creditors. Bulk of timber on the estate was destroyed by fire. Macaura sued the insurance companies which refused to pay on the plea that Macaura had no insurable interest in the timber as the timber belongs to the company and not him. The matter was referred to arbitrator who also rules that Macaura had Ireland to the House of Lords. Held, neither as shareholder no insurable interest in the property that he insured. The case was appealed from the Court of Appeal in Northern nor as creditor Macaura have an insurable interest in the timber that belonged to the Irish Canadian Sawmills Ltd being a separate entity. Though Macaura owned almost all the shares in the company, and the company owed him a good deal of money, but, neither as creditor nor as shareholder, could he insure the company's property.	*Macaura* v *Northern Assurance Co Ltd.,* (1925) AC 619; 1925 ALL ER 51.
No member can claim himself to be the owner of company's property during its existence or in its winding up.	*R.F.Perumal* v *H John Deavin,* AIR 1960, Madras.

■ *Limited Liability*

❏   The liability of members of a company is limited either by shares or guarantee.

One of the principal advantages of trading through a company is that it has limited liability. Limited liability was first introduced in 1850 in England and 1857 in India.	Company may be • Limited by shares • Limited by guarantee • Unlimited company	25 g of Partnership Act, 1932 states that each partner is liable jointly and also severally.

Exception:

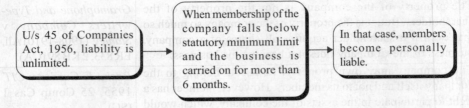

| U/s 45 of Companies Act, 1956, liability is unlimited. | → | When membership of the company falls below statutory minimum limit and the business is carried on for more than 6 months. | → | In that case, members become personally liable. |

■ Transferability of Shares

❑ Shares of a company are transferable. They can be sold or bought in a market called stock exchange.

❑ Shares are movable property. On transfer, the transferee steps in to the shoes of transferor.

■ Perpetual Succession

❑ Members may come and go but company can go forever. As observed by Prof. LCB Gower in the Modern Company Law (1957), company is like river Thames in London, whether flooded or dried up, river Thames called Thames always.

❑ A registered company never dies except when wound up. Once formed, a company will continue until such time as it is wound up.

❑ The life of a company is either perpetual or it may continue for specified period to carry on an object given in the memorandum.

❑ Death, insolvency, retirement of members does not affect the life of a company.

Judicial Interpretations/Case Example	
A member, even one holding 90 per cent of the shares in the company, dies has no effect on the legal existence of the company. A company once brought into existence by incorporation cannot be brought to an end except by winding-up, even if the incorporation was an abuse of, or fraud upon, the Act of the legislature.	*Princess Reuss* v *Bos,* 1871 LR 5 HR 176.
In this case it was observed that "King is dead, long live the King". The first king here refers to the individual monarch and the second king refers to the office of king *i.e.*, the institution. During the war, all the members of a private company, while in general meeting were killed by a bomb. But the company survived. Held, not even a hydrogen bomb could destroy a company. (Prof. LCB Gower in Modern Company Law, 2nd edition 1957).	*Meat Suppliers Guild-ford Ltd.,* (1966) 1 WLR 1112 Re Common Seal.

■ *Common Seal*

Meaning and Purpose:

❑ Common Seal is used by a Corporation as the symbol of its registration incorporation.

❑ It provides evidence of authenticity of a document.

Contents: Company's name engraved in legible characters along with the place of the company and date of its incorporation.

Form: Common Seal should be made up of some metal (Department of Company Affairs circular No 8/70(147)/64-PR dated Dec 8, 1964) but no shape/ no form is laid down.

Documents to which Common Seal is Compulsorily Affixed

Section 48 (1)	:	Power of attorney (empowering any person as attorney).
Section 50 (2)	:	Documents authorizing any person outside India to affix Company Seal to a deed or other documents.
Section 84	:	Share Certificate.
Section 114	:	Share Warrant.

❑ Other documents need not be under Common Seal (Sec. 54) except to the extent provided in the Articles of Association. It is not statutorily required that the debenture certificate should be issued under the Common Seal.

Safe Custody of Common Seal: *According to Table A* 84 (2), common seal should be under the custody of some responsible duly authorized officer like a director or a company secretary.

Authorization for Affixing the Common Seal: Authorization by a resolution of board/committee of Board and the procedure for authorization for affixing seal may be given in the Articles of Association.

Manner of Affixing Common Seal: *According to Table A* 84 (2), common seal is affixed in the presence of atleast 2 directors and the company secretary or some other person authorized by the Board.

Common Seal Dispensed in England: *The possession and use of Common Seal by companies is dispensed and it is no longer required in England.*

Advantages of Incorporation

A company has following advantages over other forms of business organization:

1. A company is a legal entity, separate and independent from its member.
2. As the company is independent of its members, its members are not personally liable for any act or omission on the part of the company, unless the law expressly provides otherwise.

3. The liability of members is limited to the extent they have agreed to contribute towards the capital of the company and/or the amount of guarantee respectively undertaken by them.

4. The company being a juristic person, distinct from its members, it is capable of owing, enjoying and disposing property in its own name. Shareholders are not the part owners of the company or its property. They are only given certain rights by the law *e.g.*, to receive dividend, attend and vote at the meeting.

5. The company being a juristic person can sue and also be sued in its own name.

6. A registered company never dies except when wound up. Once formed, a company will continue until such time as it is wound up. Death, insolvency, retirement of members does not affect the life of a company.

7. Transferability of the shares in a company provides an element of liquidity to the investors in respect of their investment in the shares of the company.

8. Shares of small denomination provide an opportunity to the public at large to invest in company's shares.

9. In company, ownership and management is in separate hands. Therefore, it affords opportunity for professionalization of its management and entrusting the administration of its affairs to persons of professional competence and standing.

10. Company provides better borrowing facilities as compared to other forms of organizations. Banking and financial institutions prefer to render financial assistance to incorporated companies. The company can raise large amount, on comparatively easier terms, by issue of debentures, especially those secured by a floating charge or by accepting public deposits from the public.

11. A Company can only be dissolved with the provisions of the law.

Disadvantages of Incorporation

Disadvantages of a company form of organization include the following:

1. *Lot of Formalities and Expensive Formation:* Lot of formalities as regard to documents, returns and maintenance of books and registers and holding of meetings are to be complied with in the case of company. Formalities like obtaining Directors Identification Number (DIN), Digital Signature Certificate (DSC), expenses incurred on incorporation, payment of registration fee based on authorized share capital and day-to-day management and compliances by the company, such as holding meetings of the Board of directors and general meetings, preparation of accounts and auditing, passing of resolutions, preparation of statutory register and records, filing of on-line documents with the Registrar, etc, are required by a company which are not required by other forms of business, except LLPs.

2. *Loss of Privacy:* All the documents, resolutions passed, returns and other information are to be filed with the ROC, which is a public office. Any body can inspect after paying fees. Therefore, there is almost nil privacy.

3. *Control by Few:* Board is family managed with unchallenged powers of decisions making. Shareholders being ill-organised have little say in the management. Greater possibility of fraud is therefore in the case of a company, as the control is in few hands.

4. *Unlimited Liability:* While the members' liability is limited, the company itself is fully liable for its debts and thus has unlimited liability. But, under Section 45 of Companies Act, 1956, even the liability of members is unlimited when membership of the company falls below statutory minimum limit and the business is carried on for more than 6 months; when in any act or contract, the name of the company has been mis-described, those who have actually done the act or made the contract, shall be personally liable for it; and when in the course of winding up of a company, any business of the company has been carried out to defraud the creditors, persons who are knowingly parties to such conduct shall be personally liable for the debts of the company.

5. *Cumbersome Winding up Procedure:* As compared to a partnership firm, winding up of a company is very complicated, time-consuming and also a costly process.

6. *Not a Citizen:* Though a company is a person but it has no citizenship rights being not a citizen.

Doctrine of Lifting of Corporate Veil

❑ The basic principle of 'doctrine of corporate veil' protects members from the liability of company, which is a separate legal entity. As per this doctrine, there is a veil or a curtain between the company being separate legal entity and its members. If anything goes wrong in the company or if company incurs any liability, members may take the protection of this doctrine pleading that they are not empowered to look inside the curtain raised by company as to who is doing what and who is at fault, saying that it is the company's liability and not theirs as was held in a decided case '*Solomon* v *Solomon and Co Ltd*". As per this case, the company and its members/directors are treated as distinc and not one. Members started taking undue advantage of the decision held in Solomon case. Resultantly, the Courts had to intervene and started giving judgment against the 'doctrine of corporate veil'. The façade of corporate personality was to be removed or lifted to identify persons who were really guilty. In that case, the company and its members directors were treated as one and not distinct as was held in Solomon's case. It was observed by the Courts that there is every possibility that the corporate personality of the company might be used to commit frauds or improper or illegal acts as in reality business of a company which is an artificial person is always carried on by and for the benefit of some individuals who are the real beneficiaries, as held in *Gallaghar* v *Germania Brewing Co* (1893) 53 MINN. 214.

Circumstances when Corporate Veil has been Lifted

Judicial Pronouncements: The 'Corporate Veil' is said to have been lifted in certain circumstances, which have developed over a period of time through judicial pronouncements. These are:

To Determine whether Company is an Enemy: The Company being artificial person cannot have character *i.e.*, be a friend or an enemy. However, during war, it may become necessary to lift the corporate veil and see the persons behind as to whether they are enemies or friend. If persons who are in the de-facto control of company belong to some enemy country than the company should also be treated as enemy. And dealing with enemy company amounts to trading with enemy, which is against the public policy and interest of the country.

The court in the following case has lifted corporate veil of the company (*i.e.*, ignored the separate entity of the company) and examined the character of persons who are in real control.

Judicial Interpretations/Case Example	
Company was registered in England for the purpose of selling tyres manufactured in Germany by a German company. Bulks of shares in English company were held by German company. Remaining shares except one were held by Germans residing in Germany. All the directors of the English Company were also Germans residing in Germany. Real control of English company was thus in German hands. War was declaration in 1914 between England and Germany. The said English company brought legal action to recover trade debts from buyers (in England). Held, English company had assumed enemy character and it was not allowed to proceed with action. In this case, House of Lords made following observations, "Company is not a natural person with mind or conscience. It can be neither loyal nor disloyal. It can be neither friend nor enemy. But it may assume an enemy character when persons in the de facto control of its affairs are residents in any enemy country or whenever resident are acting under control of enemies."	*Daimler Company Ltd* v *Continental Tyre and Rubber Co.,* (Great Britain) Ltd., (1916) 2 AC 307.

Company is Used for Evasion or to Evade Tax Obligation: If corporate entity is used to evade tax, in that case, for protecting revenue, the court may lift the corporate veil (*i.e.*, ignore the separate entity) and fix the liability on members/directors. Company and members may be treated as one and income of company and members may be taxed as that of one person. The court in the following case has lifted corporate veil of the company and examined the liability of a member.

Judicial Interpretations/Case Example	
The Court applied the doctrine of lifting the corporate veil in regard to the prosecution of directors for alleged evasion of excise duty by the company.	*Santanu Ray* v *Union of India*, 1989, 65 Comp Cas 196.
The assessee was a wealthy man receiving huge dividend and interest income on his investments.	*Re: Sir Dinshaw Maneekjee Petit*, AIR 1927, Bombay, 371.
He formed four private companies to reduce tax liability.	
He transferred his investments to these four private companies in exchange of their shares.	
These companies did no business except receipt of dividends and interest (on the investments, which was transferred in company's account).	
Income received from investments was credited to the accounts of these four companies and each company handed back the same to Dinshaw as loan.	
In this way Dinshaw divided his income into four parts and reduced his tax liability.	
Held, the companies were formed by Dinshaw purely and simply to avoid tax and companies were nothing but assessee himself.	

Company is Formed to Defeat or Escape Law or Defraud Creditors or to Circumvent Legal Obligations: If it appears to the Court that company is formed to defraud creditors or for some fraudulent/ improper purpose or to defeat the provision of law then in such cases Court may ignore separate entity and look into the ownership of the company or the persons responsible. In the following case, the court has lifted corporate veil of the company and examined the liability of a director.

Judicial Interpretations/Case Example	
Where it is found that corporate character has been used for committing illegalities and for defrauding people, corporate veil can be lifted with a view to rendering full justice to affected parties.	*Life Insurance Corpn. of India* v *Escorts Ltd.*, 1986, 59 Comp Cas 548 (SC).
Horne was managing director of the company.	*Gilford Motors Company* v *Horne*, 1933, 1 CH 935.
As per the appointment conditions he could not during his service or afterwards entice the customers of the company.	
His employment was terminated and after some time he formed a company to carry on his own business.	
He started enticing or soliciting customers of his ex-company.	
He pleaded the separate entity protection stating that it is the company (formed by him) and not him who is enticing the customers.	

Contd..

> The Court restrained both him and his company. It was also held that company formed by Horne is a mere hoax/cloak/fraud. Held, both he and his company are one and the same.

Dummy Companies: The court would lift the corporate veil where the company is found to be a mere sham formed for some fraudulent purpose or so that the promoters of the company could exploit rules of law in an indecent manner or the company that exists only on paper. For example, A carries jewellery business and forms a private company with two members, himself and his wife. No business is transferred, only bank account is opened with small amount of money and the company practically has no assets. B a customer entrusts some jewellery with A for ornamentation which is suppose stolen. A's plead that he is only a managing director in the company and case may be filed against the company itself and not him, will not heard. In this case, the corporate façade shall be lifted and guilty A will be punished.

Judicial Interpretations/Case Example

The veil was lifted because the company was a sham formed for the sole purpose of defeating a claim for specific performance. The purpose of the company was to commit a fraud.	*Jones* v *Lipman,* 1962, 1 WLR 832.

If public Interest Requires: The court may also lift the corporate veil on the plea of public interest or public policy as was held in the following case.

Judicial Interpretations/Case Example

It was held in this case that lifting of corporate veil is permissible if public interest requires. If the company uses another concern (s) to facilitate evasion of its legal obligation like payment of taxes, direct or indirect, or denial of statutory benefits to workmen, the Court has to disregard its separate legal entity.	*Krishi Foundry Employees' Union* v *Krishi Engineers Ltd.,* 2003 CLC 546 (AP).

Statutory Provisions: The 'corporate veil' may be lifted in the following circumstances when statutory provisions have been violated:

S.N.	Provision	Section	Circumstances
1.	Reduction of membership	Sec. 45	• Members have been reduced below 2 or 7 in the case of private and public company and the statutory minimum of 2/10 limit in case of Producer Company. • Business is carried out for more than 6 months. • Members are aware of the fact that they have individual liability. • Director/member is liable.
2.	Misrepresentation in prospectus	Sec. 63	• Every director/ promoter or authorized person is liable. • Penalty up-to Rs 50,000 or 2 years or both.

S.N.	Provision	Section	Circumstances
3.	Failure to return application money	Sec. 69	• If no allotment within 60 days. • Return money within next 10 days or pay 15% interest p.a.
4.	Mis-description of name		• While signing on B/E, Cheque, D/D or PN, it may lead to personal liability, if the name of the company is not mentioned or improperly mentioned like LR Agencies Ltd in stead of L and R Agencies Ltd.
5.	Oppression and mis-management	Secs. 235, 239	• Appointment of inspector to investigate the affairs of the company • Unlimited liability of persons who are in the de-facto control.
6.	Oligarchy	Sec. 247	• Appointment of inspectors by central government to investigate the true person who are in actual control of the company.
7.	Winding up		• Fraudulent conduct, or • If business has been carried to defraud the creditors.

Kinds of Companies

Companies under the Companies Act, 1956 may be classified on the following grounds:

On the Basis of Incorporation

(*i*) Incorporated by a Charter *i.e.*, Chartered Company.

(*ii*) Incorporated by Parliament *i.e.*, Statutory Company.

(*iii*) Incorporated under the Companies Act.

   ❑ Private Company   ❑ Public Company

   ❑ Producer Company   ❑ Company Formed under Sec. 25

On the Basis of Liability

   ❑ Companies Limited by Shares.

   ❑ Companies Limited by Guarantee having Share Capital.

   ❑ Companies Limited by Guarantee not having Share Capital.

   ❑ Companies with unlimited Liability.

On the Basis of Control of Management

   ❑ Government Company   ❑ Holding Company

   ❑ Subsidiary Company

On the Basis of Place of Registration

   ❑ Indian Company   ❑ Foreign Company

On the Basis of Listing

   ❑ Listed Company   ❑ Unlisted Company

Incorporated by a Charter

■ *Chartered Company*

- ❑ Chartered companies are formed by grant of a Charter by the Crown and the companies draw their powers from the Charter.
- ❑ The very first companies were of this variety, for example, the East India Company (1600), Harts and Bay Company (1670), Bank of England (1694).
- ❑ Trading concerns for which the registration under Companies Act is a better choice do not now use this form of incorporation. Some trading companies still operate under Charters. One such company is Peninsular and Oriental Stream Navigation Company, which was formed by the Royal Charter in 1840.
- ❑ The non-trading concerns incorporated by the Charter include the BBC, public schools, colleges and universities. Some learned societies and professional bodies like The Institute of Chartered Accountants in England and Wales, The Chartered Association of Certified Accountants, The Chartered Institute of Secretaries and Administrators and The Chartered Institute of Management Accountants, have also been formed as chartered companies.

Judicial Interpretations/Case Example	
The Companies Act does not apply to chartered companies and they are governed by the Charter.	*Ranjeet Kumar Chatterjee* v *Union of India,* 1959, Calcutta.

Incorporated by the Parliament

■ *Statutory Company*

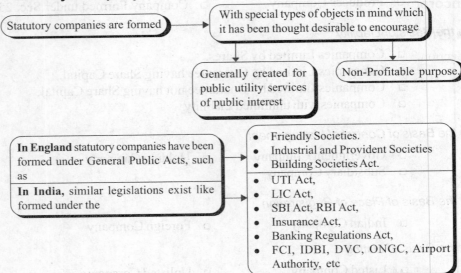

Statutory companies/corporations have the following characteristics:

- Statutory companies/statutory corporations are formed by the Special Act of Parliament or the State Legislature.
- Provisions of Companies Act, 1956 apply to statutory companies, in so far as the same are not inconsistent with the Special Act under which such companies have been formed like the Insurance Act, Banking Regulation Act and Electric Supply Act. [Sec 616].
- Such companies do not use 'ltd' as part of their name and are also known as corporations.
- Such companies do not necessarily require memorandum of association.
- Such companies/corporations are owned by the State.
- It is a body corporate, can sue and be sued and can enter into a contract and acquire property.
- Such companies/corporations have immunity from Parliament scrutiny for Parliamentary inquiry *i.e.*, the Parliament has a right to discuss and determine only major policy concerning nationalized industries; the day to day conduct of their business by public corporations should be immune from parliament scrutiny.
- The employees of such companies/corporations are not civil servants and are not governed by government regulations in r/o conditions of service.
- The audit of such companies/corporations has been entrusted to the Comptroller and Auditor General of India except in the case of banking companies, LIC and financial institution, where audit is done by chartered accountant.

Incorporated under the Companies Act

■ Private Limited Company

Section 3 (1) (*iii*) defines a private company as one which:

1. Has a minimum paid-up share capital of Rs. 1 Lakh or such higher capital as may be prescribed; and
2. By its Articles of Association:
    - (*i*) Restricts the right to transfer its shares;
    - (*ii*) Limits the number of its members to 50;
    - (*iii*) Prohibits any invitation to the public to subscribe for any shares or debentures of the company; and
    - (*iv*) Prohibits any invitation or acceptance of deposits from persons other than its members, directors or their relatives.

- Because the articles of a private company prohibit invitation or acceptance of deposits from persons other than its members, directors or their relatives, in such companies, public interest is not involved.

- ❏ The basic characteristics of a private company in terms of Section 3(1) (*iii*) of the Companies Act do not get changed just because it is a subsidiary of a public company in view of Section 3 (1) (*iv*) (*c*). All the provisions in the articles of a private company will continue to govern the affairs of the company even though it is a subsidiary of a public company.

Judicial Interpretations/Case Example	
One of the basic characteristics of a private company is restriction on the right to transfer and the same will apply even if a private company is a subsidiary of a public company.	*Hillcrest Realty SDN. BHD* v *Hotel Queen Road (P) Ltd,.* 2006, 72 CLA 245 (CLB).

Why Restrictions on Transferability?

- ❏ Promoting the company as a closely knit family or friendly affair.
- ❏ To enable the company to keep the number of members to 50.
- ❏ To prevent anybody or everybody acquiring shares of the company by transfer.

No Prohibition or Ban on Transfer

- ❏ Restriction on transfer should not be construed as a ban;
- ❏ Transfer in circumstances not covered by specific restrictions is possible;
- ❏ Restriction on transfer is relevant only in the case of private company having a share capital and therefore inapplicable to a private company incorporated as a pure guarantee company;
- ❏ Existing members of a private company have preferential right (called right of pre-emption) to purchase shares of other members as and when sold by them. In a private company, the shares are first offered to the existing members at a price to be determined by the articles or as determined by the auditors of the company. If shareholder fails to get acceptance of his offer, he would then be free to offer to any other person and directors will be obliged to affect transfer.

Limit on Membership

- ❏ It is only membership which is limited to 50 and not debentureholdership;
- ❏ Joint membership is treated as single member;
- ❏ Limits of members to 50 will not include members who are employees of the company; and members who are ex-employees of the company and were members while in such employment and who have continued to be members after ceasing to be employees;
- ❏ In 50, directors if members are counted as in that case they are not the employees. But if a director is also employed by the company in another capacity *e.g.*, as works manager or sales manager or chief accounts officer

or company secretary; he may be treated as an employee and excluded from counting 50.

Invitation to Public: Deposits from members, directors and their relatives are permitted as private company can only collect capital through private approach.

Special Privileges or Exemptions available to a Private Company

Why Exemptions? Privileges or exemptions are available to a private company because of its

- Small Character
- Public money is not involved in a private company and hence there is less government interference and company has less social accountability.

Scope of such Exemptions: Such exemptions are available to only an independent or pure private company and are not available to a private company which is a subsidiary of a public company or deemed company. A private company losses these exemptions the moment it becomes subsidiary of a public company or deemed public company.

Privileges or Exemptions of a Private Company

S.N.	Section	Privileges or Exemptions
1.	Sec. 3 (1) (iii)	Only 1 lakh minimum paid up capital required as compared to 5 lakh for public company.
2.	Sec. 12 (1)	Only 2 members are required for the formation of a private company.
3.	Sec. 70	Prospectus or statement in lieu of prospectus is not required.
4.	Sec. 81	Further issue need not be offered to the existing shareholders.
5.	Secs. 85 to 89	The share capital of a company limited by shares shall be of two kinds: • Equity share capital (*i*) With voting rights or (*ii*) With differential right as regards to dividend, etc. • Preference capital Private company can issue deferred shares carrying disproportionate rights. By amending Section 86, the Companies Amendment Act, 2000 has allowed even public company to issue equity shares with disproportional rights.
6.	Sec.111 (13)	Right of appeal to CLB against rejection of transfer of shares by the company is available to the members of a private company where the rejection is outside the company's articles of association.
7.	Sec. 149	No need of certificate of commencement.
8.	Sec. 165	No need to hold statutory meeting.
9.	Sec. 179	Only one member (if up-to 7 member) can demand polls. Where as in a public cor..pany poll can be demanded by 1/10 of the voting power

S.N.	Section	Privileges or Exemptions
		or on which an aggregate sum of not less than Rs. 50,000 has been paid-up.
10.	Sec. 198	Private company is exempted from the provisions of Sec. 198, which fix the overall limit to the managerial remuneration at 11% of net profits.
11.	Meetings	Quorum–only 2 members in a private company while it is 5 in the case of public company. Notice–shorter than 21 days allowed.
12.	Sec. 220	Annual accounts filed with the ROC are not to be made open to public for inspection, only members can inspect.
13.	Sec. 252	Minimum number of directors only 2 while in a public it is 3.
14.	Sec. 255	All directors are non-rotational.
15.	Sec. 263	Directors may be appointment enblock by a single resolution.
16.	Sec. 270	Director is not required to file with the ROC qualification shares for directorship at the time of incorporation.
17.	Sec. 275	No restriction in private company on number of directorship while in a public company it is 15.
18.	Sec. 284	Life director appointed by a private company on or before April 1952 cannot be removed in the AGM.
19.	Sec. 293	Restrictions on powers of directors do not apply to private company.
20.	Sec. 295	Provisions regarding loan to directors do not apply to a private company.
21.	Sec. 300	Provisions regarding interested directors' do not apply to a private company.

■ Public Limited Company

Section 3 (1) (iv) defines a public limited company as one which

- ❑ Is not a private company.
- ❑ Is a private company which is a subsidiary of a public company.
- ❑ Has a minimum paid up capital of 5 lakh rupees or such higher paid up capital, as may be prescribed

Conversion of a Private Company into Public Company

Conversion by Default [Sec. 43]

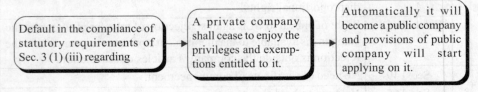

Default in the compliance of statutory requirements of Sec. 3 (1) (iii) regarding → A private company shall cease to enjoy the privileges and exemptions entitled to it. → Automatically it will become a public company and provisions of public company will start applying on it.

Exemptions: Provided that the Central Government may grant relief, on being satisfied that failure to comply with the conditions was:

- Accidental or
- Due to inadvertence/unintentional or
- To some other sufficient cause, or
- On the grounds of just and equitable.

Conversion by Operation of Law [Sec. 43 A]

❑ Deemed public company concept that was introduced in 1960, was strengthened in 1974 and 1988 to check misuse of private company status but finally in the year 2000, it was made inoperative by dropping Section 43 A from the Companies Act. The effect of this change is that on and after commencement of the amendment Act 2000, a private company will not automatically become a public company on account of shareholding or turnover.

Conversion by Choice [Sec. 44]

A Private Company may be converted into a Public Company by taking on the following procedure:

- Special resolution is to be passed deleting from Articles the conditions under Section 3 (1) (iii),
- Increase the membership up to at least 7,
- Increase directors from 2 to 3,
- Prospectus/statement in lieu of prospectus to be filed with ROC within 30 days.

Conversion of a Public Company into Private Company

No express provisions in this regard exist in the Companies Act except the reference or in the provision to Section 31 (1) and (2A) for converting public company into private company and the following process has to be followed:

- Passing of special resolution,
- Changing the name of the company,
- Obtaining central government approval [Sec. 31],
- Filing of printed copy of articles of association with the ROC within 1 month of central government approval.

■ Producer Company

❑ The Companies (Amendment) Act, 2002 has brought manufacturing types of cooperative societies in the country under the purview of Companies Act as Producer Companies. Part IX A with 12 chapters has been inserted in the Companies Act, 1956 (Sections 581A to 581 2T) that contains provisions on the formation, management, decision making, conversion of existing industrial cooperatives into producer companies and matters connected therewith. The conversion of co operatives into producer companies is purely voluntary. The conversion option by co-operative society can be exercised only if two-thirds of the members of the concerned society vote in favour of the resolution to that effect. The producer company indicate that only certain categories of persons can participate in the ownership of such companies, the members of the producer company have necessarily to be 'primary producers', that is persons engaged in an activity connected with, or relatable to, primary produce. A new Producer Company can be formed by any 10 or more individual producers or two or more producer institutions or combination of the two.

■ *Non-Profit Making or Charitable Company*

❑ Where it is proved to the satisfaction of the Central Government that an association:

  (a) Is about to be formed as a limited company for promoting commerce, art, science, religion, charity or any other useful object, and

  (b) Intends to apply its profits, if any, or other income in promoting its objects, and to prohibit the payment of any dividend to its members,

❑ The Central Government may, by license, direct that the association may be registered as a company with limited liability, without the addition to its name of the word "Limited" or the words "Private Limited". [Sec. 25 (1)]

❑ The association may thereupon be registered accordingly; and on registration shall enjoy all the privileges, and be subject to all the obligations, of limited companies. [Sec. 25 (2)]

❑ An association shall make an application electronically to the Central Government (powers have been delegated to the regional director) on behalf of the existing company/proposed company as the case may be, for grant of license under Section 25.

❑ The Central Government while granting license should be satisfied that:

  (a) The object for which the company is proposed to be formed or already formed is to promote commerce, art, science, religion, charity or any other useful objects;

  (b) Profits, if any, earned in carrying out the object and other income are proposed to be applied only for promoting its objects; and

  (c) The company intends to prohibit the payment of dividend to its members.

❑ Such license may be granted on such terms as central government thinks fit. The central government may require such terms and conditions to be included in company's memorandum and articles or in both.

❑ The central government may by an order, exempt such company (association) from such provision of the Companies Act as may be specified in the order.

- Such an association (company) cannot alter its object clause of memorandum without prior approval of central government.
- License granted by central government can also be revoked by the central government after giving written notice to the association (company).
- After revocation of license, the association loses exemptions granted by such license and the Association must add 'ltd' word in name.

Advantages

- The main advantage of incorporating such an association and dispensing with the word 'ltd' or 'private ltd' is that, it can adopt more suitable name without using the word company. Such association can use the word chamber, club, guild etc. and in the process; such an association obtain advantages of a body corporate such as separate entity, common seal, ltd liability, etc.
- Partnership firm may become member of such a company. However, the individual partners of such a firm cannot claim the status and privileges of membership for each of them. On dissolution of the firm, it will cease to be the members of the association.

Exemptions Available

(i)   Such a company is exempted from the provisions of Section 147 regarding the publication of name,

(ii)   AGM of such a company may be held on any day, including a holiday,

(iii) Notice of general meeting is 14 days as against 21 days,

(iv)   The annual return of such a company need not include particulars of members,

(v)   Books of accounts of such a company are preserved for 4 years instead of 8 years in the case of other companies,

(vi)   Election of directors by ballot does not apply,

(vii) Any increase in number of directors under Section 259 shall not require the approval of central government,

(viii) Provisions of Section 264 regarding the filing of consent of directors do not apply,

(ix)   At least one meeting within 6 months as against 3 months in the case of other companies applies.

(x)   Quorum of board meetings as per Section 287 is 8 or 1/4, whichever is less provided it is not less than 2, is applicable,

(xi)   Company secretary in such a company need not be a qualified CS under Section 2 (45),

■ Limited Companies

- In such kinds of companies, the liability of members is forever limited that may include companies limited by shares, limited by guarantee having share capital and limited by guarantee not having share capital. Companies, in which there is no limit to the liability is called as unlimited liability company.

❑ Liability of a company is never limited; it is the liability of members, which is limited.

Companies Limited by Shares

❑ Such kinds of companies are relatively common in business, trading and industrial sector. The authorized share capital of a certain amount in such kinds of companies is divided into units of distinct sum called shares. The share capital may comprise of ordinary or equity shares (voting and non voting) and preference shares.

❑ The liability of each member of such company is limited to the unpaid amount of shares and premium, if any, payable by him.

Companies Limited by Guarantee having Share Capital

❑ The liability of the members of such a company by way of undertaking in its Memorandum of Association is restricted to a certain fixed amount for payment in the event of winding up.

❑ The members are liable only for the amount contracted before he ceased to be a member or payment within one year after he ceased to be a member.

❑ Such companies may also have share capital and in that case, the members will be liable for the amount, if any, remaining unpaid on the shares subscribed by them, in addition to the said guaranteed amount.

Companies Limited by Guarantee not having Share Capital

❑ Such companies are similar in nature to the guarantee companies as referred above except that they do not have share capital. The members will be liable to contribute an amount not exceeding the sum specified in the Memorandum of Association.

Companies with Unlimited Liability

❑ Unlimited types of companies are similar to that of partnership firm where the liability of partners is unlimited. Liability of members in such companies extends to whole amount of company's debts.

❑ Every member in unlimited company is jointly and severally liable for all the debts and liabilities of the company.

❑ But unlike the liability of partners, the members of a company cannot be directly proceeded against. The claims can be enforced against the company (being separate entity). It is only afterwards, that official liquidator can call upon the members to pay.

❑ Unlimited company may or may not have share capital.

- Unlimited company is not subjected to any restrictions regarding purchase of its own shares.
- A company registered as unlimited company may subsequently convert itself into a limited company.

Government Company

Definition [Sec. 617]

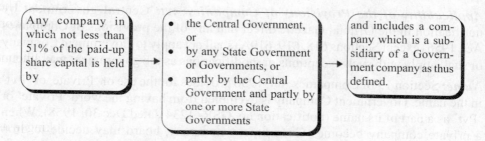

Any company in which not less than 51% of the paid-up share capital is held by → • the Central Government, or • by any State Government or Governments, or • partly by the Central Government and partly by one or more State Governments → and includes a company which is a subsidiary of a Government company as thus defined.

- Company here means a company as defined under Section 3 (1) (i) of the Companies Act, 1956 and two types of companies are formed and registered under Section 3 that is private company and public company.
- A statutory corporation or company formed under a statute or (Special Act) is not a company under Section 3 (1) (i) of the Companies Act, 1956 and hence cannot called or become a Government Company.
- Paid up capital here means
  - ➢ Equity
  - ➢ Preference carrying voting rights
  - ➢ Preference shares carrying no voting rights
- Legal status of a Government Company is not different from any other kind of company formed under Section 3 of the Companies Act having separate entity, separate property, perpetual existence, etc. Thus, even if entire capital or majority of capital of a Government Company is held by central or state government, it cannot be said that company is owned by government.
  Therefore, a government company can sue the government in its own name.
- Employees of Government Company are not the employees of central government or state government but they are the employees of the Government Company.
- Winding up or dissolution or insolvency of a Government Company does not mean that government has become bankrupt.
- A nationalized bank has been equated with a government company as held in *State of Gujarat* v *Central Bank of India,* (1988).

Government Company whether Initially be formed as Private or Public Company?

❏ The Companies Act in this respect is silent; as a result the Government Company may be incorporated either as a private or public company.

❏ Actually, incorporating a government company as a private company is more convenient; as a result, originally, almost all Government Companies are formed as private company.

Special Provisions Applicable to Government Companies

Applicability of the Provisions of Companies Act: Central government by notification in the Official Gazette direct that any of the provisions of Companies Act, 1956 (except Sections 618, 619, 619A) shall not apply to Government Company or shall apply with such exceptions or modifications as the government may like.

Name: Section 13 of Companies Act, 1956 provides for the use of 'Private' or 'Pvt' in the name. Government Company is exempted from having the word 'Private' or 'Pvt' as a part of its name (notification no. GSR- 1234 dated Dec 30, 1958). When a private company becomes Government Company, board may decide to drop 'Private' or 'Pvt' word, and the passing of special resolution in that case is not necessary if it is the deletion of 'Private' or 'Pvt' word from name (notification no. GSR 1649 dated Nov. 13, 1965).

AGM: For availing extension of 3 months time for holding the AGM, approval of central government instead of the Registrar of Companies (ROC) is required. The AGM in the case of Government Company may be held at a place as the central government may approve while in the case of private and public companies it is held in the city or town where the registered office of the company is situated.

Approving Authority: The approving authority in the case of Government Company is central government instead of Court under the Companies Act.

Audit of Government Company: The auditor of a Government Company shall be appointed or re-appointed by the Comptroller and Auditor-General of India [Sec. 619 (2)]. The auditor shall submit a copy of his audit report to the Comptroller and Auditor-General of India who shall have the right to comment upon, or supplement, the audit report in such manner as he may think fit. [Sec. 619 (4)]. Any such comments upon, or supplement, to the audit report shall be placed before the annual general meeting of the company at the same time and in the same manner as the audit report. [Sec. 619 (5)]

Annual report on Government Companies: Where the Central Government is a member of a Government Company, the Central Government shall cause an annual report on the working and affairs of that company to be prepared within three months of its annual general meeting (AGM) before which the audit report is placed; and as soon as may be, laid before both Houses of Parliament together with a copy of the audit report and any comments upon, or supplement to, the audit report, made by the Comptroller, and Auditor-General of India. [Sec. 619A (1)]

■ *Holding Company and Subsidiary Company*

❑ A Company shall be deemed to be subsidiary of another if the other company

(*a*) Controls the composition of the Board of directors of the former; or

(*b*) Exercises or controls more than half of the total voting power of the former or

(*c*) The former company is a subsidiary of any other company which is the subsidiary of the other. [Sec. 4 (1)]

❑ An agreement that provides authority to the lenders to appoint directors in the company may be deemed to be considered as control over the composition of the Board of directors of the borrowing company. This right would be sufficient to constitute the lending company as holding company and the borrowing company as subsidiary.

❑ An Indian private company will be deemed to be a subsidiary of body corporate incorporated outside India if the entire share capital in a private company is not held by that body corporate whether alone or together with one or more other bodies corporate incorporated outside India. [Sec. 4 (7)]

Judicial Interpretations/Case Example

The case summarizes holding subsidiary arrangement of a company in an impressive way.

Control over the Composition of Board: A company has powers to appoint or remove all or majority of directors of other company when:

- A person cannot be appointed as a director without the consent of that company,
- A person's appointment as a director in another company follows necessarily from his appointment as a director manager or any other office in that company.
- The person holding the office of director is the person nominated by the company or its subsidiary." It is not material if the majority of directors remain on the board only up to next AGM. The relationship of holding and subsidiary is established atleast for the time being.

Holding of Majority Shares: Means holding more than half of nominal value of equity shares. Majority of shares may be held by the holding company itself or by a nominee for the holding company or by another subsidiary of the holding company. However, the shares of the subsidiary company held in a fiduciary capacity are discarded.

Velayudhan v *Registrar of Companies,* 1980, 50 Comp Cas 33 (Ker).

Nominal value denotes face value and equity share denote issued and not authorized capital. If other company is an existing company and its preference shares were issued before commencement of Act 1956, than equity included preference shares also.

■ *Indian Company*

- ❑ Indian company is registered in India by following the procedure given in the Companies Act.

■ *Foreign Company*

- ❑ Foreign Company means a company incorporated outside India but having place of business in India.
- ❑ No formality required for establishing placing business in India except filing of document with the ROC and RBI.
- ❑ Foreign companies may include the following two classes of companies, namely: companies incorporated outside India which, after the commencement of the Companies Act, 1956 established a place of business within India; and companies incorporated outside India which have, before the commencement of this Act, established a place of business within India and continue to have an established place of business within India at the commencement of this Act. [Sections 592 to 602]

Foreign Controlled Company v *Foreign Company:* A foreign controlled company means a company (Indian or foreign) in which the majority shareholdings and voting power is in the hands of foreign individuals and foreign body corporate. A foreign company whereas means a company registered outside India having a place of business in India.

Judicial Interpretations/Case Example	
A company shall be said to have a place of business in India, if it has a specified identifiable place at which it carries on business such as an office, store house, go-down.	*Deverall* v *Grand Advertisement Inc.,* 1954, 3 ALL ER 389.
Where representatives of company incorporated outside country frequently visited and stayed in a hotel for looking after purchase of machinery and other articles, it was held that the company had a place of business in hotel.	*Re: Tovarishestvo Manufacture Ludvig Rebenek,* 1944, Ch 404.
Where the company delivered to the ROC at Mumbai documents under Section 592 which are to be delivered within 30 days of the establishment of place of business, it was held that by delivering the documents the defendants had admitted that the company had established place of business with in India.	*Framroze Rustomji Paymaster* v *British Burmah Petroleum Co Ltd.,* 1976, 46 Comp. Cas. 597 Bombay.
Having a share transfer office or share registration office will constitute a place of business.	*Employees Liability Assurance Corporation* v *Sedgwick, Collins and Co.,* 1927, AC 95
Mere holding of property cannot amount to having place of business. The fact that the directors of a company had a residence in England from where they acted on behalf of the company did not constitute an established place of business.	*Re: Oriel Ltd,* 1985, 3 ALL ER 216.

Special Provisions relating to Foreign Company

Documents, etc. to be Delivered to Registrar by Foreign Companies: A foreign Company has to furnish following documents to the ROC for registration within 30 days of establishment of business in India:

(a) Certified copy of its charter/statute/memorandum and articles and if the instrument is not in the English language, a certified translation thereof;

(b) The full address of the registered or principal office of the company;

(c) A list of the directors and secretary of the company, with details of name, address, occupation, etc;

(d) The name and address or the names and addresses of some one or more persons resident in India, authorised to accept on behalf of the company service of process and any notices or other documents required to be served on the company; and

(e) The full address of the office of the company in India which is to be deemed its principal place of business in India.

> Any change in the above particulars should be intimated to the ROC. [Section 593]

> The documents are to be filed at two places, the ROC of the State and the ROC at New Delhi. [Section 597]

Obligation Regarding Accounts [Section 594]

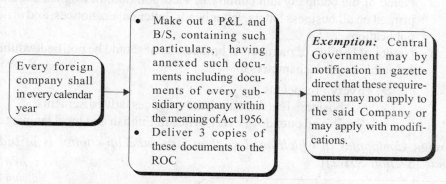

| Every foreign company shall in every calendar year | • Make out a P&L and B/S, containing such particulars, having annexed such documents including documents of every subsidiary company within the meaning of Act 1956.
 • Deliver 3 copies of these documents to the ROC | *Exemption:* Central Government may by notification in gazette direct that these requirements may not apply to the said Company or may apply with modifications. |

❑ Indian Accounts have to be drawn up in Indian Rupees.

Position Regarding Global Accounts

| Three copies of P&L a/c and B/S including documents relating to its subsidiaries, as submitted to foreign authorities called global accounts | Shall be filed with the ROC (both at New Delhi and the State) within 9 months from the closing of financial year of the foreign company. ROC at New Delhi may exten⁺ period of filing by 3 months | Global a/c's should be delivered with the principal ROC at New Delhi and also at concerned ROC in the State. |

Position Regarding Indian Business Accounts

Three copies of P&L a/c and B/S of Indian Business Accounts duly audited by CA in the form prescribed in Schedule IV	Shall be filed with the ROC (both at New Delhi and the State) within 9 months of closure of financial year. ROC at New Delhi may extended by 3 months.	Then accounts have to be file with the principal ROC at New Delhi and also at concerned ROC.

- ❑ P&L a/c of Indian business of a foreign company, (if incorporated under this Act, would be a Private company), shall not be open to inspection by any person other than members.
- ❑ If foreign company establishes any branch of its business in India, the company should deliver along with the annual accounts 3 copies of a list of its places of business in India, with reference to which the accounts are made out. [Section 594 (3)]

Other Obligations: [*Section* 595]

- ❑ Prospectus inviting subscription to share/debentures should state the country of its incorporation.
- ❑ Display of its name and country of incorporations to be exhibited on outside of every office in English and in local language.
- ❑ Name of the company and country of incorporation, in English should be printed on all business letters, letter heads, letter papers notices, and official publications.
- ❑ Nature of liability of members if limited than it should be notified/exhibited in legible English characters in.
    - ➢ Every prospectus
    - ➢ All business letters, letter heads, notices, advertisements
    - ➢ Exhibit on outside of every office in English and local language.

Foreign Companies in which not less than 50% paid up capital is in Indian hands [*Section* 591(2)]

Where not less than fifty per cent, of the paid-up share capital (whether equity or preference or partly equity and partly preference) of a company incorporated outside India and having an established place of business in India, is held by one or more citizens of India or by one or more bodies corporate incorporated in India, or by one or more citizens of India and one or more bodies corporate incorporated in India, whether singly or in the aggregate,	→	Such foreign company shall be treated for business conducted in India, as if it were a company incorporated in India or India Company.

Penalty [Section 598]

- ❑ Company and every officer in default shall pay a fine of up to Rs. 10,000 and in the case of a continuing offence, with an additional fine which may extend to Rs 1,000 per day during which the default continues and such company loses the right to sue.

Winding up a Foreign Company [Section 584]

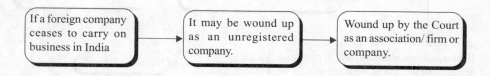

| If a foreign company ceases to carry on business in India | It may be wound up as an unregistered company. | Wound up by the Court as an association/ firm or company. |

■ *Listed Company*

- ❑ Listed Company is that company which lists its securities in the list of one or more recognised stock exchanges in the country.
- ❑ These companies are required to comply with the requirements of the Listing Agreement, Security Contracts and Regulations Act, Depository Rules and SEBI guidelines as may be amended from time to time.

■ *Unlisted Company*

- ❑ Unlisted Company is that company which has not listed its securities in the list of one or more recognised stock exchanges in the country.
- ❑ Such company is not required to comply with any requirements of the stock exchange and other regulatory authorities.

■ *Unregistered Company [Section 582]*

- ❑ The expression 'unregistered company' shall not include:
    - (*i*) A railway company incorporated by any Act of Parliament or other Indian law or any Act of Parliament of the United Kingdom;
    - (*ii*) A company registered under the Companies Act; or
    - (*iii*) A company registered under any previous companies law and not being a company the registered office whereof was in Burma, Aden or Pakistan immediately before the separation of that country from India; and
    - (*iv*) Shall include any partnership, association or company consisting of more than seven members at the time when the petition for winding up the partnership, association or company, as the case may be, is presented before the Court/Tribunal.

■ *Illegal Association [Section 11]*

Prohibition of Associations and Partnerships Exceeding Certain Number

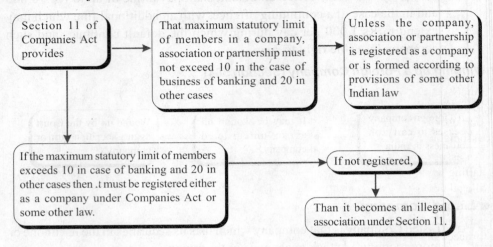

Exemptions: Section 11 does not apply to stock exchanges (as it is not formed to carry on any business), and association not for profit. Section 11 also does not apply to a joint family. When two or more joint families carry on business, then both the male and female members shall be taken into account, but the minor members of such families shall be excluded for reckoning the number of persons, which is maximum 10/20 as the case may be.

- ❑ An illegal association under Section 11 is not an association for illegal purpose.
- ❑ If an association becomes illegal it remains illegal until it is registered under the Companies Act or formed as per some other Indian Law.
- ❑ The illegality of association cannot be cured by subsequent reduction in the number of members.
- ❑ Profits made by an illegal association are however liable to be assessed under the Income Tax.

■ *Consequences*

- ❑ It has no legal existence.
- ❑ It cannot enter into any binding contract.
- ❑ It cannot bring any legal action against its members or outsiders also cannot bring action against such an association.
- ❑ It cannot be wound up (dissolved) under the provisions of Companies Act not even under the provisions relating to unregistered companies (u/s 584).
- ❑ Every member of a company, association or partnership carrying on business in contravention of this section shall be personally liable for all liabilities incurred in such business. [Section 11 (4)].

❑ Every person who is a member of a company, association or partnership formed in contravention of this section shali be punishable with fine which may extend to ten thousand rupees. [Section 11 (5)].

❑ The offence under Section 11 is compoundable by the Regional Director under the provisions of Section 621A of the Companies Act, 1956.

Judicial Interpretations/Case Example	
An association consisting of more than the maximum number of members prescribed by this section and formed for the purpose of carrying on business with a view of gain is an illegal association.	*Kumaraswami Chettiar (S.N.T.)* v *Chinnathambi Chettiar (M.S.M.)*, 1950, 20 Comp Cas 286 (Mad).
An association of more than 20 persons must be registered, failing which it would be an illegal body and any suit by such illegal body would be incompetent.	*Dayal Singh* v *Des Raj* 1963 (1) *Comp,* LJ 100 (P and H).
An illegal association of more than twenty persons carrying on any such business will not be able to initiate any legal proceedings against a person to recover debts due to the said association.	*Madras Hindu Mutual Benefit Fund* v *Raghava Chetti*, 1895, ILR 29 Mad 200.
Where an association that is compulsorily registrable under Section 11, is not registered, one member of the association cannot sue another member in respect of any matter connected with the association, nor can a member or an outsider maintain a suit against the association, for it cannot contract any debt, or enter into any contract.	*Ram Kishun* v *Baij Nath* 1911, 8 ALJ 32: 9 IC 25; *Re, London Marine Association* 1869, 8 Eq 176.

Review Questions

1. Define company. What are its essential characteristics? Distinguish it from partnership firm.
2. "A joint stock company is an artificial person created by law with a perpetual succession and a common seal." Comment.
3. "A company having no natural existence cannot sue and be sued." Explain.
4. "The term 'body corporate' connotes a wider meaning than the term 'company'". Explain.
5. "A company has a nationality but not a citizenship." Comment.
6. "No owner can claim himself to be the owner of the company's property during its existence or in its winding up". Comment.
7. A and B were the only two members of a private limited company. Both of them were killed in bomb blast. Does the company cease to exist? Explain.
8. Enumerate the advantages that a business organization enjoys through incorporation under the Companies Act, 1956.

9. "A company is a legal person distinct from its members taken individually or collectively." In what cases does court ignore this principle?

10. Discuss the concept of corporate personality in the light of decision given in Salomon v Salomon and Co. Ltd.

11. What is meant by corporate veil? When it is lifted?

12. "A company exists even after the number of members falls below the statutory limit." Comment.

13. Directors of a public limited company accepted a bill of exchange on behalf of the company. But the word 'limited' was omitted from the name of the company at the time of the acceptance. Who can be held liable for the payment of the bill?

14. Explain in brief the different types of companies on the basis of incorporation.

15. What is a private company? Describe briefly the procedure for effecting the conversion of a private company into a public company.

16. What is a private company? How does a private company differ from public company?

17. "A private company cannot issue debentures to the public." Explain.

18. Define a public company. State the procedure for the conversion of public company into a private company and from private company to public company.

19. Explain what is meant by a holding company and a subsidiary company. Give examples.

20. State the circumstances when a company can be formed without using the word 'Limited' or the words 'Private Limited', at the end of the name.

21. What is a Government Company? State its special features. How farit is governed by Companies Act, 1956?

22. What is foreign company? What are the provisions of Companies Act ,1956 relating to foreign companies?

23. A representative of a foreign company in India was only receiving orders from customers. State whether the place where the orders so received from customers is a 'place of business' of the foreign company.

24. State the law regarding compulsory registration of an association formed for the purpose of carrying on business. What are legal consequences where an association must be registered under Companies Act, 1956 is not registered?

25. Can a company with 'unlimited liability' be formed under the Companies Act, 1956?

26. Attempt the following giving reasons. Credit will be given for the answers supported by relevant provisions and case laws, if any.

   (a) S was running prosperous leather (boot and shoe) business. He converted his business in o a limited company with himself, wife, daughter, and four sons as founding members. S and his two sons became directors. All of them subscribed for one share each so that actual cash paid by them was just pound 7. S sold the business to newly formed company for pound £ 38782 (a nominal capital of £ 40,000) and took 10,000 debenture, £ 20,000 shares and £ 8,782 in cash. Company went into liquidation and a Receiver was appointed by debenture holders. The balance sheet of the company had assets amounting £ 6050, liabilities (debenture): £ 10,000 and ordinary creditors: £ 8000. Decide, if the available assets and money is payable to creditors or S being debenture holder?

(b) M held all except one share of the company. He also advanced substantial loan to the company. He insured company property in his own name. Timber was destroyed by fire and his claim was rejected for want of insurable interest. Decide.

(c) During the war, all the members of a private company, while in general meeting were killed by a bomb. Decide if the company survived.

(d) A company was registered in England for the purpose of selling types manufactured in Germany by a German company. Bulk shares in the English company were held by Germans residing in Germany. All the directors of the company were also Germans residing in Germany. Real control of English company was in German hands. War declared in 1914 between England and Germany. English company brought legal action to recover trade debts. Decide.

(e) The assessee, a wealthy man receiving huge dividends and interest income on his investments, formed four private companies to reduce his tax liability. He transferred his investments to these four private companies in exchange of their shares. These companies did no business except receipt of dividends and interest on the investments of him, which was transferred in companies account. Income received from his investments was credited to the accounts of these four companies and each company handed back the same to him as loan. In this way he divided his income into four parts and reduced his tax liability. Decide if the income of company and member is taxed as that of one person.

(f) A was managing director of the company. His appointment condition was that he shall not during his service or afterwards entice the customers of the company. His employment was terminated and after some time he formed a company to carry his own business that enticed the customers. He wanted the separate entity protection that it is the company and not him who is enticing the customers. Decide, if he and his company are one and the same.

27. Write short notes on:

 (*i*) Perpetual Succession
 (*ii*) One-Man Company
 (*iii*) Investment Companies
 (*iv*) Finance Companies
 (*v*) Defunct Companies

3

Formation of
A Company

Promoter

- ❏ The term promoter has not been defined under Companies Act, even though the term has been explicitly given in Sections 62, 69, 76, 478 and 519. Even under the English Laws no definition is available.

Palmer defined Promoter as

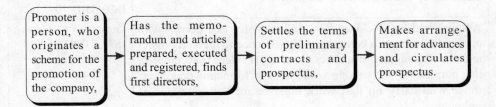

Promoter is a person, who originates a scheme for the promotion of the company, → Has the memorandum and articles prepared, executed and registered, finds first directors, → Settles the terms of preliminary contracts and prospectus, → Makes arrangement for advances and circulates prospectus.

Securities Exchange Commission of USA, Rule 405 (a) defines Promoter as

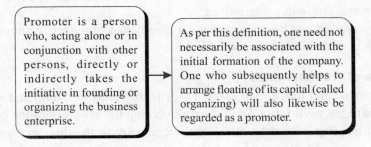

Promoter is a person who, acting alone or in conjunction with other persons, directly or indirectly takes the initiative in founding or organizing the business enterprise. → As per this definition, one need not necessarily be associated with the initial formation of the company. One who subsequently helps to arrange floating of its capital (called organizing) will also likewise be regarded as a promoter.

Promoter is used in common phrasing to denote

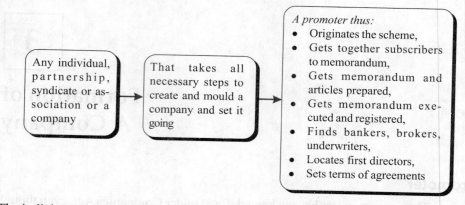

The judiciary while pronouncing judgments has defined the term promoter as follows:

Judicial Interpretations/Case Example	
The term promoter is a term not of law but of business usefully summing up in a single word 'promotion'	*Whaley Bridge Printing Company* v *Green,* 1880, 5 BD, 109.
As observed by Cockburn C.J, 'A promoter is a person who undertakes to form a company with reference to a given project and to set it going and who takes the necessary steps to accomplish that purpose-----and so long as the work of formation continues, those who carry on that work must retain the character of promoters.'	*Twycross* v *Grant,* 1877, 2 CPD, 469.

Not a Promoter

- ❑ Persons assisting the promoters by acting in a professional capacity like a solicitor who drafts articles, accountant who values assets, do not thereby become promoters themselves.
- ❑ A person cannot become a promoter merely by signing the memorandum as a subscriber for one or more shares.

When Role of Promoter Ends?

- ❑ The role and function of promoter generally ends or terminated when the Board has been formed that starts governing the activities of the company.
- ❑ On handing over the control of the company to the directors, promoters fiduciary and common law duties cease.
- ❑ Where there has been no board independent of the promoters, the promoters needed to make disclosures to the shareholders and secure their consent. But this does not work if the shareholders are not independent of the promoters.

❑ A number of sections under the Companies Act impose civil as well as criminal liabilities on promoters for misrepresentation in prospectus or statement in lieu of prospectus and that is why the date of handing over the control of the company to the directors is a matter of great importance to the promoter and the company.

Judicial Interpretations/Case Example	
A syndicate of bankers headed by Erlanger acquired the lease of West Indies island for £ 55,000 that was sold for £ 110,000, through a nominee company, to a company promoted by Erlanger. The purchase of lease was ratified without enquiry at a board meeting of the newly formed company at which not all directors were present and only one director was independent of Erlanger. The public subscribed for shares without the real circumstances of the sale being disclosed to them. The sale of the lease was approved without proper disclosures at the first shareholder's meeting. Company's business went badly, the original directors were removed, and new directors brought legal proceedings to have the sale of the lease to the company rescinded. Held, the contract should be set aside with an order for members of the syndicate to repay the purchase money. Lord Cairns giving order observed, 'it is —— —— incumbent on the promoters to take care that in forming the company they provide it with an executive, that is, to say, with a board of directors, who shall both be aware that the property which they are asked to buy is the property of the promoters, and who shall be competent and impartial judges as to whether the purchase ought or ought not to be made.'	*Erlanger v New Sombrero Phosphate Company,* 1878, 3 App Cas 1218 (HL); 39, LT 269.

■ *Legal Position, Status and Duties of Promoter*

❑ Promoters occupy an important place in a company and have wide powers relating its formation. But, they are neither an agent nor a trusty of the company since there is no company yet in existence.

❑ Promoter in relation to the company stands in fiduciary relationship of trust and confidence.

❑ Promoter is supposed to make full disclosures of all material facts relating to the formation of the company.

❑ A promoter is not prohibited to make profits but he should not make any secret profits at the expense of the company he promotes.

Judicial Interpretations/Case Example	
Although not an agent for the company, nor a trusty for it before its formation, the old familiar principles of law of agency and of trusteeship have been extended and very properly	*Lidney and Wigpool Iron Ore company* v *Bird,* 1866, 33 Ch. D 85.

Contd...

extended to meet such cases. It is perfectly well settled that a prompter of a company is accountable to it (company) for all monies secretly obtained by him from it, just as the relationship of the principal and agent or the trustee and the trust had really existed between him and the company when the money was obtained.	
The promoters of a company stand undoubtedly in a fiduciary position. They have in their hands the creation and the moulding of the company. They have the power of defining how and when and in what shape and under whose supervision it shall come into existence and begins to act as a trading corporation. It was further held that the disclosures by the promoters should be made to an independent and competent Board. Where it is not possible to constitute an independent Board, the disclosures should be made to the whole body of persons who are invited to become shareholders through prospectus or mentioned in the articles.	*Erlanger* v *New Sombrero Phosphate Company,* 1878, 3 App Cas 1218 (HL); 39, LT 269.

■ Liabilities of Promoters

For non-disclosure	Company may either • Rescind the contract and recover purchase price where promoter sold his own property to the company, • Recover profit made, • Claim damages for breach of fiduciary duties.
Under Companies Act, 1956	**1.** For misrepresentation in prospectus: • Under Sections 62 and 63, promoter is liable to the original allottee only, • Penalty upto Rs. 50,000 or 2 years imprisonment or both. **2.** In the course of winding up: • Promoter is liable for misfeasance or breach of trust, • Court may also order for public examination of promoters (Section 478). The court may order for public examination of the promoter on the report of liquidator that in his opinion a fraud has been committed by the promoter in the formation of the company. • Death of a promoter does not relieve his estate from liability arising out of abuse of fiduciary position.

■ Remuneration of Promoters

- ❑ Promoter cannot claim remuneration from the company as a matter of right rather he can claim that only if there is a valid contract between him and the company.
- ❑ In practice, however, there is no risk to them as their nominees are usually the first directors and they are handsomely rewarded provided they make proper disclosers.
- ❑ Form of remuneration can be:
  - ➢ Cash or by allotment of shares or both,
  - ➢ Commission on shares sold by the company,
  - ➢ Commission on purchase price of business or property acquired by the company.

Judicial Interpretations/Case Example	
In the absence of contract, promoter is not even entitled to recover his preliminary expenses or the registration fees and stamp duty.	*Re: English and Colonial Produce Company,* 1906, 2 Ch. 435 CA.
The articles generally contain a provision authorizing the directors to pay the *i.e.,* the promoters.	*Touche* v *Metropolitan Railways Warehousing Company,* 1871, LR 6 Ch. 671.

Incorporation of a Company

■ Process of Formation

- ❑ Persons desirous of forming a company must stick to the step-by-step procedure as discussed below:

■ Selection of the Type of Company

The first task before the promoters is to select the type of company they want to incorporate. They are to define and decide the objects and various other matters proposed like scale of operations, capital involved, etc. for the company proposed to be incorporated. They are decide the type of company as they wish to form themselves into *viz.* private company, public company, non-profit making company, producer company, etc.

■ Precondition for having DIN

Before submission of e-Form 1A all the directors of the proposed company must ensure that they are having DIN. However, 'he provisional DIN allotted on-line will serve the purpose for filing of e-Form 1A. The Amendment Act, 2006 provides for the allotment of mandatory Director Identification Number (DIN) f'r all existing and future directors on company boards. Only a single DIN is required for an individual irrespective of number of directorships held by him. DIN is also mandatory for directors of Indian companies who are not citizens of India (foreigner). But, DIN is not mandatory for directors of foreign company having branch offices in India. Every director is to intimate his/her DIN in form DIN-2 to all companies where he/she is a director. All companies are now required to inform the DIN of its directors to the Registrar of Companies (ROC). Specific care should be taken that a person cannot have more than one DIN; therefore, a DIN once obtained shall serve the requirement for all the companies in which he/she is director or intended to be a director. The following forms have been notified for the purpose:

DIN Form 1: Application for allotment of DIN.

DIN Form 2: Director is to intimate his DIN to the company or all companies.

DIN Form 3: Company is to intimate DIN to Registrar within one week of receipt from the Director.

DIN Form 4: Changes in the particulars of a Director are to be filed within 30 days of change.

■ Requirement for having Digital Signatures

With effect from September 16, 2006, every e-form or application or document or declaration required to filed or delivered under the Companies Act and rules made there under, shall be filed in computer readable electronic form, in portable document format (pdf) and authenticated by a managing director, director, or company secretary or person specif.ed in the Act for such purpose by the use of a valid digital signatures. Every such MD, director or secretary or specified person shall obtain a digital signature certificate from the Certifying Authority for the purpose of such authentication. The central government has set up and maintains a secure electronic registry in which all the documents filed electronically shall be stored. Every document, application or certificate or notice, etc, required to be signed by the registrar (ROC) or an officer of the central government, shall be authenticated through a valid digital signature of such person or a system generated digital signature. It is therefore, compulsorily required to obtain digital signatures of at least one director to sign the e-Form 1A and other documents.

■ Requirement for having Corporate Identity Number (CIN)

Beginning with about 30,000 companies in 1956 when the Companies Act was enacted, India now has the largest corporate base with over 9 lakh companies at work, which are spread through out the country, and larger numbers of new companies are being incorporated every year. But, the administrative mechanism to administer company law has not been developed at such a fast speed. Resultantly, limited numbers of 20 Registrars of Companies (ROC) in the country with little infrastructure feel handicapped administering such number of companies. In order to provide prompt and efficient service to companies, the Ministry has networked electronically all the offices of ROCs under its MCA 21 Programme. Keeping in view the administrative aspect of company law, the MCA 21 has made it mandatory for all companies including private companies to obtain a Corporate Identity Number (CIN).

Based on the recommendations of E-Corporate Business Working Group to synergic the provisions of Companies Act with the Information Technology Act of 2000, Corporate Identity Number were introduced in the country with effect from November 1st, 2000. The purpose of introducing CIN is to make Corporate Governance investors friendly, corporate friendly and compatible with the provisions of Information Technology Act, 2000. All companies registered under Companies Act 1956, prior to November 1st, 2000, were to be allotted a Corporate Identity Number (CIN) within a year in a phased manner. In the case of companies registered w.e.f. November 1st, 2000, the Registrars of Companies were asked to provide CIN to such companies at the time of registration.

■ Requirement for having Name

The name of the limited company must be ended by the word 'limited' in case of a public limited company and 'private limited' in case of a private company, though, company formed under section 25 of the Companies Act does not require any such suffixes to the name. The promoters may select any appropriate name provided it is not forbidden or undesirable. A panel of six names is required to be selected and submitted to the Registrar in order of preference. The promoters shall make an application in an e-Form 1A as notified by the Ministry of Corporate Affairs along-with fee of Rs. 500 to be filed electronically with the Registrar of Companies. On receipt of the application in e-Form 1A, the Registrar shall provide a letter for his confirmation or observations regarding availability of name as the case may be. The confirmation of the name made available shall be valid for a period of sixty days (the period of six months has been reduced to sixty days w.e.f. 19th November, 2007 *vide* notification No. GSR 720 (E), 16th November, 2007). If the promoters fail to file all the required documents for incorporation within that period, or if the existing name of a company is not changed within sixty days of availability of name so allowed, the promoters may apply for extension for retention of such name for a further period of thirty days on payment of fifty per cent of the fee prescribed for the application at the initial stage. No further extension will be granted after expiry of ninety days from the date the name is allowed in the first instance. The name allowed shall lapse after expiry of sixty or ninety days, as the case may be, from the date it is allowed first.

■ Preparation of the Memorandum (MOA) and Articles (AOA)

Subsequent to the availability of name made by the Registrar, drafting of the Memorandum (MOA) and Articles (AOA) is generally a step to be taken by the promoters. These two documents are fundamentally the charter and internal rules of the company; therefore, they must be drafted with utmost care and with the expert's advice. Memorandum is to be signed by each subscriber with address, occupation and other basic details in the presence of one witness, who shall attest the signatures and thumb impression in case of illiterate subscriber. The subscriber should clearly state number of shares subscribed. A duly authorized agent through power of attorney may sign the memorandum on behalf of subscriber.

■ *Vetting of Memorandum and Articles, Printing, Stamping and Signing*

It is not advisable to print the Memorandum (MOA) and Articles (AOA) unless the same have been vetted by the ROC/Regional Director. ROC/Regional Director may suggest some changes in these documents before issuing the license.

■ *Filing of Documents*

The promoters are to file the following documents with the Registrar for incorporation of the company, along-with the required filing fees as applicable for registration within a period of sixty days and/or within the further extended period of 30 days from the date of intimation of availability of name:

(i) Memorandum of Association, duly signed by the subscribers and witnessed, showing the number of shares against their names electronically attached in PDF file, properly stamped as per the stamp duty applicable in the State.

(ii) Articles of Association duly signed by the subscribers and witnessed, showing the number of shares against their names electronically, properly stamped according to the authorized share capital as per the stamp duty applicable in the state.

(iii) Copy of the agreement, if any that the company proposes to enter into with any individual for appointment as its managing director or whole time director or manager shall be attached in the PDF file.

(iv) Declaration by either company secretary or chartered accountant engaged in whole time practice in India or by a person named in the Articles as a director, manager or secretary of the company in e-Form 1, that all the requirements of the Companies Act, 1956 and the rules made there-under have been complied with, which may be accepted by the Registrar as sufficient evidence of such compliance. Details of all the companies in which directors are also director should as well be given. The names, addresses and other particulars of directors and promoters should be matched with the information provided in the DIN application Form and e-Form 1A.

(v) Power of Attorney given on Non-Judicial stamp paper of appropriate value should be furnished by all the subscribers in favour of any one subscriber or any other person authorizing him to file these documents with the Registrar and to obtain certificate of incorporation.

(*vi*) Any other agreement, which has been stated in the Memorandum of Association or Articles of Association, shall also be filed in the PDF file with the Registrar.

(*vii*) Notice of registered address is to be filed with the Registrar (ROC) in form No 18 (electronically with the digital signatures in e-Form 18), as from the day on which it begins to carry on business, or as from the thirtieth day after the date of its incorporation whichever is earlier. The E Form 18 shall be certified by the company secretary or chartered accountant or cost accountant in whole-time practice.

(*viii*) Particulars of directors in form No. 32 to be filed with Registrar (ROC) within 30 days of registration or appointment of first directors. E-Form 32 with the adequate filing fee as prescribed under Schedule XIII is required to be filed with the Registrar electronically for filing particulars of directors and the personal details should match with the information provided in the DIN. E-Form 32 is also required to be certified by the company secretary or chartered accountant or cost accountant in practice digitally before filing with the Registrar.

(*ix*) Consent to act as director (Sec. 266) in form No. 29 of Companies (Central Government) General Rules and Forms, 1956 on plain paper (in case of a public limited company) is to be attached.

■ Registration Fees for a New Company

The fees payable to the Registrar (ROC) at the time of registration of a new company differs according to the authorised capital of a company proposed to be registered as per Schedule X to the Act. The fees payable for registration can be calculated on the MCA portal. (www.mca.gov.in)

■ Certificate of Incorporation

If the Registrar is satisfied that all the requirements aforesaid have been complied with by the company and that it is authorised to be registered, under the Companies Act, he shall retain and register the Memorandum, the Articles, if any, and the agreement, if any. On the registration of the Memorandum of a company, the Registrar shall certify under his hand that the company is incorporated and, in the case of a limited company, that the company is limited. The Registrar shall issue a Certificate of Incorporation normally within 7 days of the receipt of documents. The Certificate of Incorporation is treated as conclusive evidence that all requirements of the Companies Act have been complied with and that the association is a legal company. Any defect in the process (Memorandum was not signed by adequate number of subscribers or signatures were forged) will not affect status of the company.

Judicial Interpretations/Case Example	
The date of registration of a company is the date mentioned in the certificate and not that on which the signature of the Registrar was written. The ROC in this case issued certificate of registration on Jan 8 but dated it Jan 6 which was the date he received documents. The company made allotment of shares on Jan 6. Further held, the date mentioned in the certificate is the first day of the company's corporate existence. The corporate person is to be treated as having been in existence for the whole of the day on which it was incorporated.	*Jublee Cotton Mills ltd* v *Lewis,* 1924, 1923, 1 Ch 1, 1924, AC 958.
Memorandum was signed by two adults and guardian of other five members who were minors. ROC issued certificate of registration. Held, the certificate prevents any one from alleging that the company does not exist.	*Moose* vs *Ibrahim,* ILR 1913, 40 Cal. 1.

▣ Commencement of Business

A Private Limited Company and a Company not having share capital may commence its business activities from the date of its incorporation for the reason that a private company is prohibited from inviting public for raising funds and it obtains capital from its own sources. Therefore, a private company need not wait for the issue of Certificate of Commencement by the Registrar. However, a Public Limited Company having share capital is also required to obtain a additional Certificate of Commencement of Business as per Section 149 (2A) of the Companies Act, 1956.

▣ Restrictions on Commencement of Business [Sec. 149]

1. Where a company having a share capital has issued a prospectus inviting the public to subscribe for its shares, the company shall not commence any business or exercise any borrowing powers, unless:

    (*a*) Shares held subject to the payment of the whole amount thereof in cash have been allotted to an amount not less in the whole than the minimum subscription;

    (*b*) Every director of the company has paid to the company, on each of the shares taken or contracted to be taken by him and for which he is liable to pay in cash, a proportion equal to the proportion payable on application and allotment on the shares offered for public subscription;

    (*c*) No money is, or may become, liable to be repaid to applicants for any shares or debentures which have been offered for public subscription by reason of any failure to apply for, or to obtain, permission for the shares or debentures to be dealt in on any recognised stock exchange; and

    (*d*) There has been filed with the Registrar a duly verified declaration by one of the directors or the secretary or, where the company has not appointed a secretary, a secretary in whole-time practice, in the prescribed form, that clauses (*a*), (*b*) and (*c*) of this sub-section, have been complied with.

2. Where a company having a share capital has not issued a prospectus inviting the public to subscribe for its shares, the company shall not commence any business or exercise any borrowing powers, unless:

   (*a*) There has been filed with the Registrar a statement in lieu of prospectus;

   (*b*) Every director of the company has paid to the company, on each of the shares taken or contracted to be taken by him and for which he is liable to pay in cash, a proportion equal to the proportion payable on application and allotment on the shares payable in cash; and

   (*c*) There has been filed with Registrar a duly verified declaration by one of the directors or the secretary or, where the company has not appointed a secretary, a secretary in whole-time practice, in the prescribed form, that clause (*b*) of this sub-section has been complied with.

3. The Registrar shall, on the filing of a duly verified declaration in accordance with the provisions, and, in the case of a company which is required by sub section (2) to file a statement in lieu of prospectus, also of such a statement, certify that the company is entitled to commence business, and that certificate shall be conclusive evidence that the company is so entitled.

4. Any contract made by a company before the date at which it is entitled to commence business shall be provisional only, and shall not be binding on the company until that date, and on that date it shall become binding.

5. Nothing in this section shall prevent the simultaneous offer for subscription or allotment of any shares and debentures or the receipt of any money payable on application for debentures.

6. If any company commences business or exercises borrowing powers in contravention of this section, every person who is responsible for the contravention shall, without prejudice to any other liability, be punishable with fine which may extend to five thousand rupees for every day during which the contravention continues.

7. Nothing in this section shall apply to:

   (*a*) A private company; or

   (*b*) A company registered before the first day of April, 1914, which has not issued a prospectus inviting the public to subscribe for its shares.

Pre-Incorporation Contracts

❑ Contracts entered prior to the incorporation of a company are called as Pre-Incorporation Contracts.

❑ Since company before incorporation is non entity, Pre–Incorporation contracts are not binding on the company.

Position of Pre-Incorporation Contracts before the Passing of Specific Relief Act, 1963

❑ Pre-incorporation contract never binds a company, since a person who is not born, cannot contract. (*Parke* v *Modern Woodman,* 181 All 214 and 234)

❑ Ratification of such contracts is not possible. (*Kelner* v *Baxter,* 1866, 15 LT 213)

❑ The company is not entitled to sue on a pre-incorporation contract (*Natal Land and Colonization Company* v *Pauline Colliery Syndicate,* 1904, AC 120).

Position of Pre-Incorporation Contracts after Passing of Special Relief Act, 1963

❑ Until of passing of Specific Relief Act, 1963, the promoters in India found it difficult to carry out the work of incorporation as the contract prior to incorporation were considered as void and could not be ratified. People therefore were to hesitate to either supply any goods or service for the cause of incorporation. Promoters also felt shy/ risky of accepting personal liability. Specific Relief Act, 1963 was a relief to promoter.

❑ Section 15 (h) of the Specific Relief Act, 1963 provides that where promoters have made a contract before incorporation for the purpose of the company and if such contract is within the scope of company's objects stated in the Memorandum, the company may enforce it.

❑ Section 19 of the Specific Relief Act, 1963 allows the other party to enforce contract if company had adopted it after its incorporation.

Liability of Promoter vis-à-vis Pre-Incorporation Contract

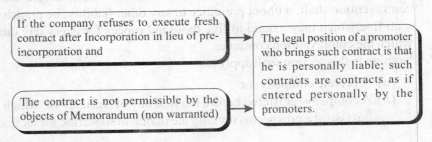

If the company refuses to execute fresh contract after Incorporation in lieu of pre-incorporation and

The contract is not permissible by the objects of Memorandum (non warranted)

The legal position of a promoter who brings such contract is that he is personally liable; such contracts are contracts as if entered personally by the promoters.

Provisional Contracts

❑ Contracts entered after the Incorporation but before commencement are called as Provisional Contracts.

- Such contracts are binding only when the company receives certificate of commencement.
- Such contracts are automatically binding and there is no need of further ratification.
- However, the contract should be otherwise valid.

Review Questions

1. Who is a promoter of a company? Discuss citing legal cases, his legal position in relation to the company he promotes.
2. "A promoter stands in a fiduciary relation towards the company he promotes." Explain.
3. What are the duties and liabilities of a promoter? How he is remunerated?
4. Can a company ratify the acts of promoters who acted on behalf the company before its incorporation? What remedy are available to third party in case of such contracts?
5. What are the main rules applicable to pre-incorporation contracts in case of a public company? Describe the legal effects of pre incorporation contracts.
6. "A private company requires no provisional contracts." Comment.
7. Distinguish between 'Preliminary Contracts' and 'Provisional Contracts'.
8. How a Company is formed under Companies Act, 1956? Enumerate the various documents to be filed with the Registrar in this connection.
9. What are the consequences of incorporation of a company? Briefly describe the documents to be filed with the Registrar of Companies prior to incorporation.
10. A company was formed on the basis of certificate of incorporation obtained by threatening the Registrar of Companies. Is the company legally formed?
11. A company can enter into contracts and sue and be sued in its own name.
12. A certificate of incorporation is conclusive evidence that all the requirements of the Companies Act have been complied with.
13. State the steps you would take to obtain certificate of incorporation. A certificate of incorporation cannot be challenged on any grounds whatsoever. Explain.
14. "A company having share capital which has not issued prospectus inviting public to subscribe for its shares can commence business immediately." Comment.
15. When can a company, which has issued a prospectus inviting the public to subscribe for its shares, commences business or exercise borrowing powers?
16. Explain the steps required to be taken for formation of a private limited company and the documents required to be filed with the Registrar of Companies.
17. "Unlike a private company, a public company cannot commence business immediately after incorporation." Comment.

18. Distinguish between a certificate of incorporation and certificate of commencement of business.

19. Write short notes on the following:

    (*a*) Commencement of Business

    (*b*) Remuneration of Promoters

    (*c*) Provisional Contracts

☐☐☐

4

Memorandum of Association

Meaning

❏ Memorandum means memorandum of association of a company as originally framed or altered from time to time in pursuance of any previous company laws or of this Act. This definition is incomplete as it does not contain meaning, nature or importance of the document. [Section 2 (28)]

> *"Modify" and "modification" shall include the making of additions and omissions.*

❏ According to Palmer 'Memorandum contains objects for which the company is formed and therefore identifies the possible scope of its operation beyond which its actions cannot go. It defines as well as confines the powers of the company. Any thing done beyond the powers is *'ultra vires'* and therefore void. Memorandum is considered the charter or constitution of the company and defines the relationship of the company with the outside world.'

Judicial Interpretations/Case Example	
Lord Cairns observed, 'Memorandum defines the limitations on powers of the company and it contains in it both, that which is affirmative and that which is negative. It enables shareholders, creditors, suppliers to know what the powers are, what the range of activities is, otherwise the acts are *ultra vires*.'	*Ashbury Railway Carriage and Iron Co. Ltd* v *Riche,* (1875), LR 7 HL 653.
The company has no power to do any act not authorised expressly or impliedly by its memorandum and any act so done is *ultra vires* and incapable of ratification, even if every member of the company assents to it.	*Pacific Coast Coal Mines Ltd.* v *Arbuthnot,* 1917, AC 607 (PC).
Any provision of memorandum or articles of association would be void if it is repugnant not only to express provisions of the Companies Act, but also to those provisions which have to be read in the Act by necessary implication.	*Cricket Club of India Ltd.* v *Madhav L. Apte,* 1975, 45 Comp Cas 574.

Forms of Memorandum

- Section 14 requires that the Memorandum shall be drawn up in such a form as given in Tables B, C, D and E in the Schedule I.
- A company may either adopt any of the above models of form or may prepare it in other form.

> **Table B** : MOA of a company limited by shares,
> **Table C** : MOA of a company limited by guarantee and not having a share capital,
> **Table D** : MOA of a company limited by guarantee and having a share capital,
> **Table E** : MOA of an unlimited company

Requirements with Respect to Memorandum

- The Memorandum of every company shall state the clauses, which are compulsory and are designated by the Act as "conditions" on the basis of which alone the company is incorporated. In addition to the compulsory conditions clauses, the Memorandum may contain any other provisions. [Section 13]

> *These conditions or clauses are termed as contents of Memorandum.*

- The Memorandum of every company shall state:

  (*a*) The name of the company with "Limited" as the last word of the name in the case of a public limited company, and with "Private Limited" as the last words of the name in the case of a private limited company;

  (*b*) The State in which the registered office of the company is to be situated;

  (*c*) In the case of a company in existence immediately before the commencement of the Companies (Amendment) Act, 1965, the objects of the company;

  (*d*) In the case of a company formed after such commencement,—

      (*i*) The main objects of the company to be pursued by the company on its incorporation and objects incidental or ancillary to the attainment of the main objects;

      (*ii*) Other objects of the company not included in sub-clause (*i*); and

  (*e*) In the case of companies (other than trading corporations), with objects not confined to one State, the States to whose territories the objects extend.

  (*f*) The Memorandum of a company limited by shares or by guarantee shall also state that the liability of its members is limited. [Section 13 (2)]

❑ The Memorandum of a company limited by guarantee shall also state that each member undertakes to contribute to the assets of the company in the event of its being wound up while he is a member or within one year after he ceases to be a member, for payment of the debts and liabilities of the company, or of such debts and liabilities of the company as may have been contracted before he ceases to be a member, as the case may be, and of the costs, charges and expenses of winding up, and for adjustment of the rights of the contributories among themselves, such amount as may be required, not exceeding a specified amount. [Section 13 (3)]

❑ In the case of a company having a share capital:

   (a) Unless the company is an unlimited company, the Memorandum shall also state the amount of share capital with which the company is to be registered and the division thereof into shares of a fixed amount;

   (b) No subscriber of the Memorandum shall take less than one share; and

   (c) Each subscriber of the Memorandum shall write opposite to his name the number of shares he takes. [Section 13 (4)]

Additional Clauses

❑ In addition to above compulsory clauses, the Memorandum may contain other information, for example, rights attached to various classes of shares.

❑ Memorandum cannot contain any thing contrary to the Companies Act. If it does, the same shall be devoid of any legal effect. [Section 9]

Contents of Memorandum

Name Clause

This clause shall state name of the company to establish its separate identity. Name of a company is the symbol of its independent existence should be followed by the word "Limited" in the case of a public company and "Private Limited" if the company is proposed to be registered as a private company. On the other hand, companies formed under Section 25 of the Company Act for promoting art, culture, religion or charity not for profit have been exempted from this requirement. Proper care should be taken in selection of name and confirmation of name must be obtained from the Registrar of Companies.

Undesirable Name: The name of a company may be undesirable under the following circumstances:

1. A company cannot have a name by which a company has already been registered and is in existence;

2. The name of a company cannot be identical or too closely or nearly resembles with the name of some existing company in the country;

3. The name of a company should not be prohibited under the Emblems and Names (Prevention of Improper Use) Act, 1950.

Guidelines for Availability of Name: As per the guidelines formulated that will be taken into account for deciding availability of names, the proposed name should not be:

1. Identical or too nearly resembles with the name of some existing company,
2. Identical or too nearly resembles the name of the company in the process of liquidation,
3. Identical or too closely resembles the name of the company liquidated or dissolved. In such a case name is not allowed for two years, as it may lead to problems, if the dissolution is declared void within the period by court under Section 559,
4. Closely resembles a popular or abbreviated description or names of important companies like TISCO or ICICI or WIMCO etc. such words are not allowed even though they have not been registered as trademarks,
5. Merely addition/ subtraction of word like New/ Modern, etc is not allowed, like New Bata Shoes Co. Ltd/Nav/New Bharat Electronics, etc is not allowed,
6. If it connotes government participation or patronage unless circumstances justify. *e.g.*, National, Union, Central, President, *Rashtrapati*, etc,
7. If it includes the word cooperative/regional or *sehkari* in English or regional translation,
8. If it includes the word bank/banking/insurance or trust unless the circumstances of a particular case justify,
9. If it intends to produce a misleading impression which would be beyond the resources at its disposal as universal/ world/Engineering Co (P) Ltd., which runs a small business with limited range of products and finance but by name it looks like a big company,
10. If name suggests a business which is not proposed to be undertaken.
11. If it is exact Hindi translation of existing name like Birla Industries to Birla Udyog,
12. If it includes the name of registered trademark unless consent of owner of trademark has been produced.
13. If it implies association/connection with/patronage of a national hero (*e.g.*, Mahatama Gandhi),
14. If it is not in consonance with the proper objects of the company,
15. If the company is only general one like 'Y2K Ltd.' 'Silk Manufacturing Ltd.',
16. If it includes word (s) which are offensive to any section of public,
17. If the proposed name has a close phonetic resemblance to name of existing company like JK Industries Ltd. and Jay Kay Industries Ltd.

18. If only difference to the extent of name of place within brackets Indian Press (Delhi) Ltd./Indian Press Ltd.

19. If it attracts the provisions of Emblem and Names (Prevention of Improper Use Act, 1950), for example:

    (*i*)   Name, emblem or seal of UNO, WHO, WTO, INTERPOL, UNESCO etc,

    (*ii*)   Indian national flag,

    (*iii*)   Name, emblem, seal of Government of India, state government, government departments,

    (*iv*)   Name, emblem, seal of the President, Governor, Union of India,

    (*v*)   Name of Mahatama Gandhi, Jawahar Lal Nehru, Shivaji, Prime Minister, Ashok charka,

    (*vi*)   Name of International Olympic Committees.

Department of Company Affairs (now MCA) circular dated 7th *March,* dated 13th *May,* **1999:** Names starting with small letters / having small letters have been allowed by the ROC's *e.g.,* names stating with small alphabets like 2 technologies ltd. However, the name should not have any phonetic resemblances. Similarly, the companies having the word 'insurance' or 'risk corporation' as part of their name should be registered after consulting RBI and Insurance Regulatory Authority. This circular has also advised the ROCs that the use of words like 'Infosys', Software, System, Infosystem, Cyber, Cyberspace, Computers, etc should be allowed by them or allow change of names to companies to reflect business position of their income (reflected by audited a/c's) is derived from software business.

Department of Company Affairs (now MCA) circular dated 7th *March,* **1989:** If a company uses any of the following words in its name it must have a minimum authorized capital as follows:

Key Words	Required Capital
Corporation	5 crores
International, global, universal, continental, intercontinental, asiatic, asia being first word	1 crore
If any of the above words used within the name with or without brackets	50 lakhs
Hindustan, India, Bharat being the first word of name	50 lakhs
If any of the above words used within the name ie Hindustan, India, Bharat	5 lakhs
Industries/ Udyog	1 crore
Enterprises, Products, Business, Manufacturing	10 lakhs

Judicial Interpretations/Case Example	
The former secretary of existing company informed the ROC that the company has not functioned since 1970, no annual report /minutes have been filed with the ROC since 1970 and some directors died and some left. Court held since the company is practically defunct, it is not a bar to the registration of a new company with a similar. Further held, if name of a company gives such misleading indication of its activities as to cause harm to public, it should not be registered. Held, the Registrar cannot ask an authorized association to obtain no objection certificate from a company registered with a similar name, which it has, no right to use.	*Executive Board of the Methodist Church in India* v *Union of India*, 1985, 57 Comp Cas 443 (Bom).
Plaintiff was carrying on business "Buttercup Dairy Co". Defendant formed new company "Buttercup Margarine Co Ltd". Plaintiff bought action against new company that it should be restrained from using the name of existing company and pleaded that name used by new company created an impression that the two companies were closely connected. Court restrained the new company from using that name.	*Ewing* v *Buttercup Margarine Co Ltd*, 1917, 2 Ch. 1.
Existing company 'Society of Motor Manufacturers and Traders Ltd' brought an action to restrain the new company 'Motor Manufacturers and Traders Mutual Assurance Ltd.' to register with the said name. Court held that the new company (defendant) is an insurance company and the existing company (plaintiff) was a trade protection society. Names of company do not suggest that both companies are connected/ associated. Court held the name of new company could not be regarded as one calculated to deceive and thus allowed the new company with the new name.	*Society of Motor Manufacturers and Traders Ltd* v *Motor Manufacturers and Traders Mutual Assurance Ltd.*, 1925, 1 Ch. 675.
Kothari Product Ltd. was marketing edible items under registered trade mark under the Registered Trade Mark Act 1986 "Parag". Parag International (KNP) P Ltd. was registered without the consent of M/s Kothari Product Ltd; Allahabad High Court held the name was undesirable and disallowed.	*Kothari Product ltd* v *ROC*, 2000, 26, SCL 156 (ALL).

Publication of Name

- Every company shall paint or affix its name and address of its registered office and keep it painted or affixed on outside of every office or place of business in letters easily legible and language in general use in locality both in English and in local language. Outside office does not mean outside premises in which the office is situated, where the office is situated within a compound, the display outside the office room though inside the building is sufficient.
- Have its name engraved in legible characters on its seal,
- Have its name and address of its registered office in legible characters on all its

> Business Letters
> Bill Heads
> Negotiable Instruments
> Invoices
> Receipts, etc.

Penalty: Both company and every officer is liable for violating rules regarding publication of name and to pay penalty upto Rs. 500 per day till the default continues.

Personal Liability: If any contract is made on behalf of the company by misdescription of its name *i.e.*, by using incorrect name then officers of the company who made the contract are personally liable. However, the word 'limited' may not be used in full.

Judicial Interpretations/Case Example	
'A' director of "AB & Co ltd." accepted a B/E on behalf of the company and signed his name as director of "AB & Co". In this case the word limited is omitted. The director is personally liable to pay the amount of B/E.	*Basudeo Lal* v *Madan Lal,* (1969).
No personal liability, if the word 'limited' is accidentally omitted *e.g.*, stamp was longer than paper, impression of stamp was not clear. Association not for profit under Section 25 of the Companies Act are exempted from the word 'ltd'.	*Dermatine Co* v *Ashworth,* 1905, 21 TIR 510.

Registered Office or Domicile Clause

❑ The registered office clause shall state the State in which the registered office of the company is situated and there is no requirement to mention here the address of the registered office.

❑ Registered office is the address where company's statutory books are kept and correspondence is dealt and communications are received.

❑ Registered office establishes domicile of the company to decide the court jurisdiction.

❑ The notice of exact situation (address) of registered office is given to the Registrar of Companies (ROC) in Form 18 (e-Form 18) within 30 days of incorporation, which is required to be filed simultaneously along with the e-Form 1 with the ROC at the time of registration.

❑ Section 147 (1) (a) makes provisions regarding publication of registered address of office.

Object Clause

This clause sets out the objects and is the most important of all clauses. It informs the shareholders (members) kind of business in which their money may be used.

❑ It informs the persons dealing with the company, the powers of the company. Thus, it provides certain degree of protection to the creditors.

❑ It defines the limit of operations to be carried on by the company.

❑ It serves the public interest by restricting the company's activities to defined objects.

❑ It is required to state separately the main objects, which the company will basically undertake on incorporation and the incidental or ancillary objects for the attainment of the main objects. The objects should be stated in the following manner:

> (*a*) The main objects of the company to be pursued by the company on its incorporation,
>
> (*b*) Objects incidental or ancillary to the attainment of the main objects,
>
> (*c*) Other objects not included in (*a*) or (*b*) above.

❑ No business given in other objects clause can, however, be commenced unless prior approval of shareholders is obtained by passing special resolution.

❑ When company is not able to pass special resolution, the central government, may on an application made by Board, allow a company to commence business given in 'other objects' provided decision is taken by majority (ordinary resolution).

❑ The objects must not be illegal, immoral or against public policy and against the provisions of Companies Act.

❑ Choice of objects rests with the subscribers to the memorandum.

Judicial Interpretations/Case Example

The statement of objects should be clear. It must not be too vague and too general, and too wide, for in that case it will defeat its very purpose and object.	*Ref: Bhutoria Bros. (P) Ltd.,* 1958, 28 Comp Cas 122 (Cal).
The acts incidental or naturally conducive to the main object are those, which have a reasonably proximate connection with the object. Where the primary object of the company was to carry on life insurance business in all its branches, the donations of the company's funds for the benefit of a trust for charitable purposes could not be said to be incidental to or naturally conducive to that object.	*Lakshmanaswami Mudaliar* v *Life Insurance Corp. of India.,* 1963, 33 Comp Cas 420 (SC).
The 'incidental or conducive' clause in objects clause refers to main object of company and not to any ancillary objects.	*Evans* v *Brunner, Mond. and Co. Ltd.,* 1921, 1 Ch. 359 (Ch. D).

Liability Clause [Section 13 (2)]

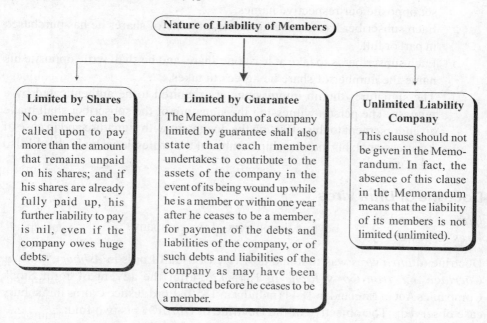

Nature of Liability of Members

Limited by Shares

No member can be called upon to pay more than the amount that remains unpaid on his shares; and if his shares are already fully paid up, his further liability to pay is nil, even if the company owes huge debts.

Limited by Guarantee

The Memorandum of a company limited by guarantee shall also state that each member undertakes to contribute to the assets of the company in the event of its being wound up while he is a member or within one year after he ceases to be a member, for payment of the debts and liabilities of the company, or of such debts and liabilities of the company as may have been contracted before he ceases to be a member.

Unlimited Liability Company

This clause should not be given in the Memorandum. In fact, the absence of this clause in the Memorandum means that the liability of its members is not limited (unlimited).

Directors, etc., with Unlimited Liability in Limited Company: In a limited company, the liability of the directors or of any director or manager may, if so provided by the Memorandum, be unlimited. [Section 322 (1)]

Capital Clause [Section 13 (4)]

❑ This clause is required to state the authorized or nominal capital with which the company having a share capital is to be registered and the division thereof into shares of a fix amount.

❑ The authorized capital should not be less than the minimum paid-up capital required Rs. 5,00,000 for public company and Rs. 1,00,000 for private limited company.

❑ If the company has both equity and preference shares than division of capital is to be under these two heads.

❑ It lays down the limit beyond which the company cannot issue shares without altering the Memorandum as provided by Section 94 of the Companies Act.

Association or Subscription Clause [Section 13 (4) (C)]

❑ This clause is a sort of declaration given by all the subscribers of the Memorandum in a following way: "We the several persons, whose names and addresses and occupations are subscribed, are desirous of being formed into a company in pursuance of this memorandum of association and we respectively agree to take the number of shares in the capital of the company set opposite our respective names."

❑ Each subscriber has to state his name, number of shares he has purchased in part or full,

❑ Each subscriber is to take at least one share, and he shall write opposite his name the number of share he agrees to takes,

❑ The signatures/thumb impressions are required to be authenticated by a witness. The person witnessing the signature of the subscriber shall make an endorsement to this effect on the document with signature and in case of a professional; his membership number of the professional body should also be stated.

Doctrine of *Ultra vires*

$Ultra$ = beyond
$Vires$ = powers $\Big\}$ beyond the powers of the company.

Doctrine of *ultra vires* was first laid down by House of Lords in *Ashbury Railway Carriage and Iron Co.* v *Riche* in 1875 *i.e.*, after the advent of Joint Stock Companies Act in England in 1844 (in India in 1850). Lord Justice Cairns in Ashbury case observed: 'The objective of the Doctrine of *Ultravires* is two fold:

(*a*) To protect the investors of the company so that they may know the objects in which their money is to be employed, and.

(*b*) To protect the creditors by ensuring that the company funds to which they must look for the payment, are not wasted in unauthorized activities.

Judicial Interpretations/Case Example	
The company has no power to do any act not authorized expressly or impliedly by its Memorandum and any act so done is *ultra vires* and incapable of ratification, even if every member of the company assents to it.	*Pacific Coast Coal Mines Ltd.* v *Arbuthnot* ,1917, AC 607 (PC).

■ *Types of Ultra vires Acts*

Ultra vires acts may be categorized as:

An Act Ultra vires the Directors: The act is not altogether void. It can be ratified by the general body meeting of shareholders.

An Act Ultra vires the Articles: Also not altogether void and inoperative. It can be ratified by amending articles accordingly.

An Act Ultra vires the Memorandum: It is *ultra vires* the company and such an act cannot be ratified by the whole body of shareholders.

Ultra vires Contract: A contract which is *ultra vires* the company is void and is no contract at all.

Ultra Vires Borrowings: The *ultra vires* borrowings do not create the relationship of debtor and creditor and it gives rise to no rights at law or in equity.

Ultra Vires Grants: The Directors cannot make any grant unless it is authorized and the object is to promote prosperity of the company or the grant is incidental to carrying out of the object of the company.

Position under the Indian Companies Act: Under the Companies Act in India, a company can pursue any object not covered by its Memorandum by getting the approval of the shareholders by a special resolution in a general meeting subject to the condition that such objects will enable the company to achieve any of the purposes specified in sub-section (1) of Section 17. Also, under sub-section (2A) of Section 149, such powers are available.

Judicial Interpretations/Case Example	
Where a railway company was authorised by its Special Act to acquire land for the purposes of the railway and the company acquired a strip of land on which it constructed a railway carried over series of arches and the interiors of the arches were let for shops and other business purposes, it was held that the company's act of letting out the interiors of arches for shops and other business purposes was *intra vires.*	*Foster* v *London, Chatham and Dover Railway Co.,* 1891, 1 QB 711 (CA).

Position under the UK Companies Act: Cohen Committee (1945) in England recommended the abolition of doctrine of *ultra vires*. Finally in 1989, the doctrine of *ultra vires* has been given a go bye by the English Companies Amendment Act, 1989. Any documents signed or contract entered by any officer on behalf of the company, is now binding against the company in England. The company may, of course, proceed against the erring officer. The strict interpretation of the Doctrine of *ultra vires* caused great harm to third parties who have contracted with the company in good faith. However, if one were to examine the facts of the decided cases, it would become evident that the principle was strictly interpreted on the basis of the object contained in the Memorandum and objects incidental and consequential thereto. Extraordinary powers have been vested with the Directors that has come as a great relief to outsiders and creditors who have suffered under the *ultra vires* doctrine.

Judicial Interpretations/Case Example	
The object of the company was "to make and sell, or lend on hire, railway carriages and wagons and all kinds of railway plant, fittings, machinery and rolling stock and to carry on the business of mechanical engineers and general contractors; to purchase, lease, work and sell mines, minerals, lands and buildings; to purchase and sell any such materials on commission or as agents; to acquire, purchase, hire, construct or erect works or buildings for the purpose of the company and to do all such other things as are necessary, contingent or	*Ashbury Railway Carriage and Iron Co.* v *Riche,* 1875, LR 7 HL 653.

Contd..

conducive to all or any of such objects." The company entered into a contract with the plaintiff for the financing of the construction of a railway line in Belgium. This contract was also ratified by special resolution of the company. Later the company repudiated the contract being *ultra vires* its powers and the firm of railway brought an action against the company for damages or breach. Contentions of railway contractor firm was that the contract was well within the word 'general contractors' as used in objects clause, and that the contract was also ratified by majority shareholders by passing special resolution. The company defended its action of repudiation of contract on the ground of ultravires. The question that came up before the court was whether the contract was valid. The House of Lords held the contract was *ultra vires* the company and thus void and observed that the Memorandum of Association "states affirmatively the ambit and extent of vitality and power which by law are given to the corporation and it states negatively that nothing shall be done beyond that ambit and that no attempt shall be made to use the corporate life for any other purpose than that which is so specified. Held, the contract was entirely beyond the objects in the Memorandum and thus void. The contract could not be validated even by the unanimous consent of the shareholders.

■ Implied Powers of a Company

Powers exercisable by a company are to be confined to objects clause in Memorandum. Such powers are inferred from the powers expressed in the object clause of the Memorandum. These powers given in Memorandum may be express or implied.

Implied Powers of a company by virtue of its being incorporate body.	❑ Power to appoint and act through agents(*e.g.*, directors)
	❑ In case of trading company ➢ Power to borrow, ➢ Power to give security for the purpose of its business, ➢ Power to sell.
Powers which are not implied, such powers should be expressly provided in object clause of the Memorandum.	➢ To acquire any business similar to company's own, ➢ Entering into an agreement with other persons companies for carrying on business in partnership joint venture, ➢ Taking share in other companies having similar objects, ➢ Promoting other companies or helping them financially, ➢ Power to use funds for political purpose, *Contd..*

	➤ A power to give gifts and make donations or contributions for charities not relating to objects stated in the Memorandum, ➤ Power to sell or dispose whole of a company undertaking, ➤ To enter into contract of surety ship or guarantee.

■ Effects of Ultravires Transactions

Void *ab initio*

Judicial Interpretations/Case Example	
The company not bound by such acts, the company cannot sue and be sued.	*Ashbury Railway Carriage and Iron Company* v *Riche*, 1875, LR 7 HL 653.
However, the complaint that the company is indulging into activities not mentioned in the objects clause is to be filed within 6 months of date of knowledge.	*NEPC India ltd* v *ROC*, 1999, 22 SCI, 94 (Madras HC).
Though the *ultra vires* acts are void but the company is entitled to bring legal action for the protection of its property even if it is acquired by unauthorized acts or expenditure.	*National Telephone Co* v *St. Peter Part Constables*, 1990.

Injunction

Judicial Interpretations/Case Example	
Even a single member can get an order of injunction from the court.	*Attorney General* v *G R Eastern Railway Company*, 1880, 5 AC 473.

Personal Liability of Directors to Third Parties: The agents are personally liable if they exceed their authority by doing ultravires acts. Directors being agents of the company are therefore personally liable. If the directors induce anybody to contract with the company in a manner in which the company has no power to act, the directors are personally liable.

Judicial Interpretations/Case Example	
It is one of the foremost duties of directors to ensure that the corporate capital is used for legitimate purpose/ business given in the Memorandum. In this case, the directors were held liable. Held, acts *ultra vires* the directors can be ratified.	*Jahangir R. Modi* v *Shamji Ladha*, 1866-67, 4 Bom HCR 1855.

Doctrine of Ultra vires, an Illusory Protection: The purpose of ultravires is to protect the interest of shareholders and creditors. But, HC Bhaba Committee on

Company Law Reforms (1952) criticized it as this doctrine has not proved effective in protecting shareholders and creditors. The Company in India may do any business which has not been expressly provided under its object clause but which is covered by Section 17 (1) of Companies Act. This may also be against the interest of shareholders as they never know, at what time and what new business, the company may start. Further, the shareholders may not all the time approach the court (for many reasons) and thus the directors may think that all their activities are within their powers until they are challenged in the court.

Alteration of Memorandum

❑ Until the year 1890, Memorandum was regarded as unalterable charter. However, in the present day context, it does not appear to be wholly true. The unalterable charter (nature) of the Memorandum led to a number of difficulties in the working of the companies. Consequently, the Companies Act, 1844 (Indian 1850) was amended to provide for the alteration of various clauses of the Memorandum of Association.

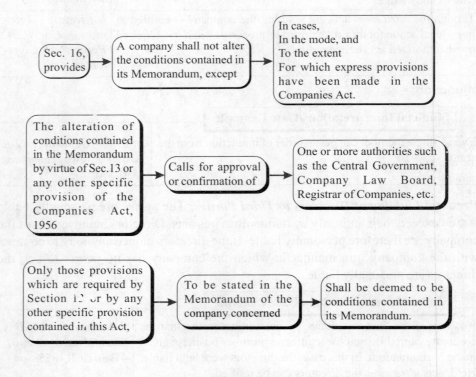

■ *Change of Name*[1]

- A company may, by *special resolution and with the approval of the Central Government (pow*ers now delegated to the Registrar of Companies) signified in writing, change its name,
- Provided that no such approval shall be required where the only change in the name of a company is the addition thereto or, as the case may be, the deletion there from, of the word "Private", consequent on the conversion in accordance with the provisions of this Act of a public company into a private company or of a private company into a public company. [Section 21]
- A copy of special resolution and duly filled Form no. 23 of Companies (Central Government) General Rules and Form, 1956 have to filed with the Registrar of Companies (ROC) within 30 days........
- ***Rectification of name of Company:*** If through inadvertence company has got registered with an undesirable name, it can by passing an ordinary resolution and with the previous approval of the Central Government signified in writing, change that name within a period of three months from the date of the direction or such longer period as the Central Government may think fit to allow. [Section 22]
- If a company makes default in complying with any direction given above, the company, and every officer who is in default, shall be punishable with fine which may extend to one thousand rupees for every day during which the default continues. [Section 22(2)]

Judicial Interpretations/Case Example	
Where a company is registered with a name that is identical with the name of some existing company, the petition for change of name made to the central government by aggrieved company after 12 months was not entertained.	*Sidhvi Construction (India) Ltd* v *ROC,* 1997,24 CLA 207.

Registration of Change of Name and Effect Thereof

- Where a company changes its name in pursuance of Section 21 or 22, the Registrar shall enter the new name on the register in the place of the former name, and shall issue a fresh certificate of incorporation with the necessary alterations embodied therein; and the change of name shall be complete and effective only on the issue of such a certificate. [Section 23 (1)]
- The Registrar shall also make the necessary alteration in the Memorandum of association of the company. [Section 23 (2)]
- The change of name shall not effect any rights or obligations of the company, or render defective any legal proceedings by or against it; and any legal

---

1. *Rule 4A of the Companies (Central Governments) General Rules and Forms, 1956 has prescribed e-Form 1A and fees of Rs. 500.*

proceedings which might have been continued or commenced by or against the company by its former name may be continued by or against the company by its new name. [Section 23 (3)]

Judicial Interpretations/Case Example	
Where a company changes its name and new name has been registered by the ROC the commencement of legal proceedings in former (old) name is not competent.	*Malhati Tea Syndicate Ltd* v *Revenue Officer,* 1973.
By change of name the constitution of company does not change. *Held*: All the rights and obligations of old company pass to new company, and it is not similar to reconstitution of a partnership firm which means creation of a new entity. Further held, change of name does not bring into existence a new company even though a new certificate of incorporation has been issued after change in name.	*Economic Investment Corporation Ltd* v *CIT,* 1970, Calcutta.

Change of Name of Existing Private Limited Company

❑ In the case of a company which was a private limited company immediately before the commencement of the Companies Act, 1956, the Registrar shall enter the word "Private" before the word "Limited" in the name of the company upon the register and shall also make the necessary alterations in the certificate of incorporation issued to the company and in its Memorandum of Association. The change of name shall not effect any rights or obligations of the company, or render defective any legal proceedings by or against it; and any legal proceedings which might have been continued or commenced by or against the company by its former name may be continued by or against the company by its new name. [Section 24]

Power to Dispense with "Limited" in Name of Charitable or other Company

❑ Where it is proved to the satisfaction of the Central Government that an association:

   (*a*) Is about to be formed as a limited company for promoting commerce, art, science, religion, charity or any other useful object, and

   (*b*) Intends to apply its profits, if any, or other income in promoting its objects, and to prohibit the payment of any dividend to its members,

❑ The Central Government may, by license, direct that the association may be registered as a company with limited liability, without the addition to its name of the word "Limited" or the words "Private Limited". [Section 25 (1)]

❑ A license may be granted by the Central Government under this section on such conditions and subject to such regulations as it thinks fit, and those conditions and regulations shall be binding on the body to which the license is granted. [Section 25 (5)]

- It shall not be necessary for a body to which a license is so granted to use the word "Limited" or the words "Private Limited" as any part of its name and, unless its articles otherwise provide, such body shall, if the Central Government by general or special order so directs and to the extent specified in the directions, be exempt from such of the provisions of this Act as may be specified therein. [Section 25 (6)]

- The license may at any time be revoked by the Central Government, and upon revocation, the Registrar shall enter the word "Limited" or the words "Private Limited" at the end of the name upon the register of the body to which it was granted; and the body shall cease to enjoy the exemption granted by this section: Provided that, before a license is so revoked, the Central Government shall give notice in writing of its intention to the body, and shall afford it an opportunity of being heard in opposition to the revocation. [Section 25 (7)]

- Upon the revocation of a license granted under this section to a body the name of which contains the words "Chamber of Commerce", that body shall, within a period of three months from the date of revocation or such longer period as the Central Government may think fit to allow, change its name to a name which does not contain those words; and:

  (*a*) The notice to be given under the proviso to sub-section (7) to that body shall include a statement of the effect of the foregoing provisions of this sub-section; and

  (*b*) Section 23 shall apply to a change of name under this sub-section as it applies to a change of name under Section 21. [Section 25 (9)]

- If the body makes default in complying with the requirements of Section 25 (9), it shall be punishable with fine which may extend to [five thousand rupees for every day during which the default continues. [Section 25 (10)]

■ *Change of Registered Office*

Change in the registered office may include the following:

Change within the City, Town or Village

1. *Board Resolution:* A company may change its registered office from the local limit of one place to another within the same town, city or village, by passing a resolution of the Board.

2. *Intimation to Registrar:* Notice of such change should be filled in Form 18 with the Registrar within 30 days of the change.

Change within the State

1. *Special Resolution:* Except on the authority of a special resolution passed by the company, the registered office of the company shall not be removed:

(*a*) In the case of an existing company, outside the local limits of any city, town or village where such office is situated at the commencement of this Act, or where it may be situated later by virtue of a special resolution passed by the company; and

(*b*) In the case of any other company, outside the local limits of any city, town or village where such office is first situated, or where it may be situated later by virtue of a special resolution passed by the company. [Section 146]

> **Default:** *If default is made in complying with the requirements of this section, the company, and every officer of the company who is in default, shall be punishable with fine which may extend to five hundred rupees for every day during which the default continues.* [*Section* 146 (4)]

2. ***Confirmed by the Regional Director:*** No company shall change the place of its registered office from the jurisdiction of one Registrar (ROC) to another ROC within a State unless such change is confirmed by the Regional Director. This provision will have applicability only to companies situated in Tamilnadu and Maharashtra which have two ROCs. Since the State shall remain the same and registered office clause of Memorandum contains only the name of State, there seems to be no question of alteration of Memorandum in this case. The company shall make an application in the prescribed form to the Regional Director for confirmation in this connection. [Section 17A[2] (1) (2)]

> **Explanation:** *The provisions of this section shall apply only to the companies which change the registered office from the jurisdiction of one Registrar of Companies to the jurisdiction of another Registrar of Companies within the same State.*

3. ***Intimation to the Registrar:*** The company shall file, with the Registrar a certified copy of the confirmation by the Regional Director for change of its registered office under this section, within two months from the date of confirmation, together with a printed copy of the Memorandum as altered and the Registrar shall register the same and certify the registration under his hand within one month from the date of filing of such document. The certificate shall be conclusive evidence that all the requirements of this Act with respect to the alteration and confirmation have been complied with and henceforth the Memorandum as altered shall be the Memorandum of the company. [Section 17 A (4)]

---

2. *Companies (Amendment) Act,* 2000, *notified on* 1/3/2001.

Change from one State to another State

1. **Special Resolution:** A company may, by special resolution, alter the provisions of its Memorandum so as to change the place of its registered office from one State to another, so far as may be required to enable it:

    (a) To carry on its business more economically or more efficiently; or

    (b) To attain its main purpose by new or improved means; or

    (c) To enlarge or change the local area of its operations; or

    (d) To carry on some business which under existing circumstances may conveniently or advantageously be combined with the business of the company; or

    (e) To restrict or abandon any of the objects specified in the memorandum; or

    (f) To sell or dispose of the whole or any part of the undertaking or of any of the undertakings, of the company; or

    (g) To amalgamate with any other company or body of persons. [Section 17]

2. **Confirmation by the Central Government:** The alteration of the provisions of Memorandum relating to the change of the place of its registered office from one State to another shall not take effect unless it is confirmed by the Central Government on petition. [Section 17]

    ❑ Before confirming the alteration, the Central Government must be satisfied:

    (a) That sufficient notice has been given to every holder of the debentures of the company, and to every other person or class of persons whose interests will, in the opinion of the Central Government, be affected by the alteration; and

    (b) That, with respect to every creditor who, in the opinion of the Central Government, is entitled to object to the alteration, and who signifies his objection in the manner directed by the Central Government, either his consent to the alteration has been obtained or his debt or claim has been discharged or has been determined, or has been secured: Provided that the Central Government may, in the case of any person or class of persons, for special reasons, dispense with the notice required. [Section 17 (3)]

    ❑ The Central Government shall cause notice of the petition for confirmation of the alteration to be served on the Registrar who shall also be given a reasonable opportunity of appearing before the Central Government and state his objections and suggestions, if any, with respect to the confirmation of the alteration. [Section 17 (4)]

    ❑ The Central Government may make an order confirming the alteration on such terms and conditions, if any, as it thinks fit, and make such order as to costs as it thinks proper. [Section 17 (5)]

❏ The Central Government shall, in exercising its powers under this section, have regard to the rights and interests of the members of the company and of every class of them, as well as to the rights and interests of the creditors of the company and of every class of them. [Section 17 (6)]

3. *Intimation to the Registrar:* A company shall file with the Registrar:

   (*a*) A special resolution passed by a company in relation to clauses (a) to (g) of sub-section (1) of Section 17, within one month from the date of such resolution;or

   (*b*) A certified copy of the order of the Central Government made under sub-section (5) of that section confirming the alteration, within three months from the date of order, as the case may be, together with a printed copy of the Memorandum as altered and the Registrar shall register the same and certify the registration under his hand within one month from the date of filing of such documents. [Section 18 (1)]

❏ The certificate shall be conclusive evidence that all the requirements of this Act with respect to the alteration and the confirmation thereof have been complied with, and thenceforth the Memorandum as so altered shall be the Memorandum of the company. [Section 18 (2)]

❏ Where the alteration involves a transfer of the registered office from one State to another, a certified copy of the order confirming the alteration shall be filed by the company with the Registrar of each of the States, and the Registrar of each such State shall register the same, and shall certify under his hand the registration thereof; and the Registrar of the State from which such office is transferred shall send to the Registrar of the other State all documents relating to the company registered, recorded or filed in his office. [Section 18 (3)]

❏ The Central Government may, at any time, by order, extend the time for the filing of documents or for the registration of the alteration under this section by such period as it thinks proper. [Section 18 (4)]

Effect of Failure to Register

❏ No such alteration as is referred to in Section 17 shall have any effect until it has been duly registered in accordance with the provisions of Section 18. [Section 19(1)]

❏ If the documents required to be filed with the Registrar under Section 18 are not filed within the time allowed under that section, such alteration and the order of the Central Government made under sub-section (5) of Section 17

and all proceedings connected therewith, shall, at the expiry of such period, become void and inoperative: provided that the Central Government may, on sufficient cause shown, revive the order on application made within a further period of one month. [Section 19(2)]

Loss of Revenue or Employment

Judicial Interpretations/Case Example	
Orissa High Court declined to confirm change of registered office from Orissa to West Bengal *inter alia* on the ground that in Federal Constitution, every State has right to protect its revenue and therefore the interest of the state must be taken into account.	*Orient Paper Mills Ltd* v *State,* AIR 1957, Orissa, 232.
Bombay High Court had given decision opposite to the above. The court held that the question of loss of revenue is to be considered in the prospects of total revenue for the Republic of India. The court held that Company Law Board cannot refuse confirmation on the ground that change would cause revenue loss to a State or would have adverse affect.	*Minerva Mills Ltd* v *Govt of Maharashtra,* 1975, 45, Comp Cas. 1 Bombay.
The State has no statutory right under Section 17 to oppose shifting of registered office from one State to another.	*Rank Film Distributors of India* v *Registrar of Companies,* AIR 1969, Cal 32.

■ Change of Object

Purposes for Alteration: A company may, by special resolution, alter the provisions of its Memorandum so as to change the objects of the company so far as may be required to enable it:

   (*a*) To carry on its business more economically or more efficiently; or
   (*b*) To attain its main purpose by new or improved means; or
   (*c*) To enlarge or change the local area of its operations; or
   (*d*) To carry on some business which under existing circumstances may conveniently or advantageously be combined with the business of the company; or
   (*e*) To restrict or abandon any of the objects specified in the memorandum; or
   (*f*) To sell or dispose of the whole or any part of the undertaking or of any of the undertakings, of the company; or
   (*g*) To amalgamate with any other company or body of persons. [Section 17]

Procedure

   1. *Special Resolution:* The alteration of object clause requires passing of a special resolution.
   2. *Intimation to Registrar:* The alteration of object clause requires confirmation by the Registrar of Companies.

■ Change of Liability

   ❑   Generally the company as per Section 38 cannot alter its liability clause of Memorandum so as to increase the liability of members. Liability of members can be increased only.

> When concerned members agrees in writing *e.g.*, alteration to compel the member to buy additional shares,

> To make the liability of directors or managers unlimited, provided articles authorize so and directors give their consent,

> In case the company is a club or similar association and alteration requires members to pay periodical subscription or changes at higher rate, although he does not agree in writing to be bound by alteration, it shall be binding on him,

> In case of unlimited company the liability may be made limited or reduced by re-registration of the company. The alteration will, however, not affect any debts, liability, obligations or contracts entered into by or with the company before the registration of the unlimited company as a limited company. [Section 32]

1. ***Special Resolution:*** The liability of members can be increased only with their consent in writing. However, the limited liability of directors can be converted into unlimited liability, only by passing special resolution.

2. ***Intimation to Registrar:*** The alteration of liability clause requires confirmation by the Registrar of Companies.

■ *Change of Capital*

Kinds of Change: A limited company having a share capital, may, if so authorized by its articles, alter the conditions of its Memorandum as per Section 94 (1) as follows, that is to say, it may:

(*a*) Increase its share capital by such amount as it thinks expedient by issuing new shares;

(*b*) Consolidate and divide all or any of its share capital into shares of larger amount than its existing shares;

(*c*) Convert all or any of its fully paid up shares into stock, and reconvert that stock into fully paid-up shares of any denomination;

(*d*) Sub-divide its shares, or any of them, into shares of smaller amount than is fixed by the Memorandum, so, however, that in the sub-division the proportion between the amount paid and the amount, if any, unpaid on each reduced share shall be the same as it was in the case of the share from which the reduced share is derived;

(*e*) Cancel shares which, at the date of the passing of the resolution in that behalf, have not been taken or agreed to be taken by any person, and diminish the amount of its share capital by the amount of the shares so cancelled. [Section 94]

> ➤ *The powers conferred by this section shall be exercised by the company in general meeting and shall not require to be confirmed by the Court.*
>
> ➤ *A cancellation of shares in pursuance of this section shall not be deemed to be a reduction of share capital within the meaning of this Act.*

Notice to Registrar: If a company having a share capital has consolidated and divided its share capital into shares of larger amount than its existing shares; converted any shares into stock; reconverted any stock into shares; sub-divided its shares or any of them; redeemed any redeemable preference shares; or cancelled any shares, otherwise than in connection with a reduction of share capital under sections 100 to 104; the company shall within thirty days after doing so, give notice thereof to the Registrar specifying, as the case may be, the shares consolidated, divided, converted, sub-divided, redeemed or cancelled, or the stock reconverted. The Registrar shall thereupon record the notice, and make any alterations which may be necessary in the company's Memorandum or Articles or both. [Section 95(1)]

> *Default: If default is made in complying with the provisions, the company, and every officer of the company who is in default, shall be punishable with fine which may extend to five hundred rupees for every day during which the default continues.*

Effect of Conversion of Shares into Stock: Where a company having a share capital has converted any of its shares into stock, and given notice of the conver-sion to the Registrar, all the provisions of this Act which are applicable to shares only, shall cease to apply as to so much of the share capital as is converted into stock. [Section 96]

Notice of Increase of Share Capital or of Members: Where a company having a share capital, whether its shares have or have not been converted into stock, has increased its share capital beyond the authorized capital, and where a company, not being a company limited by shares, has increased the number of its members beyond the registered number, it shall file with the Registrar, notice of the increase of capital or of members within thirty days after the passing of the resolution authorizing the increase; and the Registrar shall record the increase and also make any alterations which may be necessary in the company's memorandum or articles or both. The notice to be given as aforesaid shall include particulars of the classes of shares affected and the conditions, if any, subject to which the new shares have been or are to be issued. [Section 97]

> *Default: If default is made in complying with this section, the company, and every officer of the company who is in default, shall be punishable with fine which may extend to five hundred rupees for every day during which the default continues.*

Reduction of Share Capital: Following procedure is adopted for the reduction of share capital:

Special Resolution for Reduction of Share Capital: A company limited by shares or a company limited by guarantee and having a share capital, may, if so authorized by its articles, by special resolution, reduce its share capital in any way; and in particular and without prejudice to the generality of the foregoing power, may:

(*a*) Extinguish or reduce the liability on any of its shares in respect of share capital not paid-up;

(*b*) Either with or without extinguishing or reducing liability on any of its shares, cancel any paid-up share capital which is lost, or is unrepresented by available assets; or

(*c*) Either with or without extinguishing or reducing liability on any of its shares, pay off any paid-up share capital which is in excess of the wants of the company;

(*d*) And may, if and so far as is necessary, alter its memorandum by reducing the amount of its share capital and of its shares accordingly. [Section 100]

Application to Tribunal for Confirming Order, Objections by Creditors, and Settlement of list of Objecting Creditors: Where a company has passed a resolution for reducing share capital, it may apply, by petition, to the Tribunal for an order confirming the reduction. [Section 101(1)]

Order Confirming Reduction and Powers of Tribunal on Making Such Order: The Tribunal, if satisfied with respect to every creditor of the company who under Section 101 is entitled to object to the reduction, that either his consent to the reduction has been obtained or his debt or claim has been discharged, or has determined, or has been secured, may make an order confirming the reduction on such terms and conditions as it thinks fit. [Section 102(1)]

Registration of Order and Minute of Reduction: The Registrar on production to him of an order of the Tribunal confirming the reduction of the share capital of a company; and on the delivery to him of a certified copy of the order and of a minute approved by the Tribunal showing, with respect to the share capital of the company as altered by the order, (*i*) the amount of the share capital, (*ii*) the number of shares into which it is to be divided, (*iii*) the amount of each share, and (*iv*) the amount, if any, at the date of the registration deemed to be paid-up on each share; shall register the order and minute. On the registration of the order and minute and not before the resolution for reducing share capital as confirmed by the order shall take effect. [Section 103(1) (2)]

Liability of Members in respect of Reduced Shares: A member of the company, past or present, shall not be liable, in respect of any share, to any call or contribution exceeding in amount the difference, if any, between the amount paid on the share, or reduced amount, if any, which is to be deemed to have been paid thereon, as the case may be, and the amount of the share as fixed by the minute of reduction: [Section 104(1)]

Diminution* v *Reduction of Share Capital: Diminution means cancellation of such shares which have been issued by the company but are not taken up by the public.

- ❑ This results in diminish of amount of capital by the amount of the shares so cancelled,
- ❑ It is different from reduction of capital,
- ❑ Diminution requires passing of shareholders resolution,
- ❑ Diminution requires only resolution while reduction requires Tribunal approval also.

Review Questions

1. "The Memorandum of Association is the fundamental law or a charter defining the objects and limiting the powers of a company." Explain.
2. "Memorandum of Association is a charter of the company." Comment upon the statement and explain the clauses which are included in a Memorandum of Association of a company.
3. What is registered office of a company? Within what period a company must have a registered office?
4. "A company cannot undertake any business not stated in the object clause." Comment.
5. Discuss the doctrine of *ultra vires vis-à-vis* a company, the directors and the articles. What is the legal effect of *ultra vires* acts?
6. "The doctrine of *Ultra Vires* is a dark cloud for adventurous directors and careless creditors." Discuss this statement.
7. "The doctrine of *'ultra vires'* is an illusionary protection to the shareholders and a pitfall to outsiders." Discuss.
8. What is a Memorandum of Association? What are its contents? When and how it may be altered? What is the effect of failure to register the alteration?
9. What are the compulsory clauses in Memorandum of Association? In what cases, in what mode and to what extent a company can alter these clauses?
10. "A company cannot alter the conditions contained in its Memorandum of Association except in cases, in the mode and to the extent for which express provision is made in the Act." Amplify.
11. "The intention of the legislature is to prevent too easy an alteration of the conditions in the Memorandum of Association." Comment.
12. "Alteration of any provisions of the Memorandum of Association invariably involves passing of special resolution." Comment
13. Set out the restrictions imposed on the choice of a name for a company. What are the requirements on 'Publication of Name?' How a company can change its name?

14. State the circumstances under which the limit within which the Central Government, under the provisions of the Companies Act, 1956, directs a company to rectify its name by which the company is already registered with the Registrar of Companies.
15. Why it is necessary for a company to have a registered office? How can the registered office of a company be changed?
16. "The location of the registered office may not be given at the time of registration of the company." Comment.
17. What is the procedure for shifting of registered office of a company from one state to another? Can State Government oppose such shifting?
18. Explain the necessity of clearly setting out the objects in Memorandum. By what method and within what limits may the objects be altered? To what extent may a company lawfully undertake business and perform acts not expressly set out in the objects clause?
19. A company was formed with mining as its object. Can it alter its objects clause to sell goods on hire-purchase basis?
20. The object clause of the Memorandum of Association of a company empowers it to carry on distillery business and any other business that is allied to it. The company wants to alter its Memorandum of Association so as to include the cinema business in its object clause. Advise the company.
21. Advise Asiatic Government Security Life Insurance Co. Ltd. whether it can seek an injunction against The New Asiatic Insurance Co. Ltd. which was subsequently formed restraining it from having its name the words 'Asiatic' on the ground that it has caused confusion and can deceive public.
22. Can the liability clause of Memorandum of Association be altered?

5

Articles of Association

Meaning

- There are two important documents in relation to every company, which are Memorandum of Association and Articles of Association. These documents are infact the life giving documents to a company because the birth of a company is not possible unless these two documents are prepared, filed and registered with the Registrar of Companies. The Articles of Association is subordinate to the Memorandum of Association that is a primary and a public document.

- "Articles of Association" means the Articles of a company as is originally framed or as altered from time to time in pursuance of any previous companies law or of this Act, including, so far as they apply to the company, the regulations contained, as the case may be, in Table B in the Schedule annexed to Act No. 19 of 1857 or in Table A in the First Schedule annexed to the Indian Companies Act, 1882 (6 of 1882), or in Table A in the First Schedule annexed to the Indian Companies Act, 1913 (7 of 1913), or in Table A in Schedule I annexed to this Act. [Section 2(2)]

- The Articles of Association of a company lays down the rules and regulations for the internal management of a company.

- This document provides powers to the company for its management by the Board and authority of the members to regulate the conduct of the company.

- It establishes a contract between the company and its members and between the members *inter se* and regulates their relationship.

- The Article is subsidiary, both to the Companies Act and Memorandum. It is controlled by the Memorandum which is the dominant instrument and contains the general constitution of the company.

- The Articles of the company are 'not law' and do not have the force of law.

- Contents of Articles of different companies may vary substantially.

Judicial Interpretations/Case Example	
The Articles of Association merely govern the internal management, business or administration of a company. They may be binding between the persons affected by them but they do not have the force of statute.	*Irrigation Development Employees' Association* v *Government of Andhra Pradesh,* 2005, 55 SCL 459 (AP).
Articles are regulations of the company binding on the company and on its shareholders.	*Rangaraj (V.B.)* v *Gopala-krishnan (V.B.),* 1992, 73 Comp Cas 201 (SC).
Since the Articles constitute a contract between the members *inter se*, any contract entered into between them subsequent to their joining the company must inevitably be subject to the provisions of the Articles.	*First National Bank Ltd* v *Seth Sant Lal,* 1958, 28 Comp Cas 402.
Articles do not constitute contracts with strangers or members in other capacities.	*Browne* v *La Trinidad,* 1887, 37 Ch D 1.

Registration of Articles

Mandatory for Companies to have Articles: According to Section 26, a company is required to register along-with the Memorandum, the Articles of Association. It is mandatory in the case of a private company limited by shares, a company limited by guarantee, a company under Section 25 or an unlimited company to prepare and register their Articles. However, public limited companies have option either to frame and register their own Articles or abide by Table A given in the Schedule I.

Judicial Interpretations/Case Example	
The Registrar will decline registration if he considers them to be improperly stamped.	*Queen* v *Registrar* 1888, (21) QBD 131.
The registration of a company takes place when the Memorandum and Articles are accepted and retained by the Registrar, and not on the date on which his signature is written.	*Jubilee Cotton Mills* 1923, (1) Ch 1.

Adoption and Application of Table A in the case of Companies Limited by Shares [*Section* 28]: The Articles of a company limited by shares may adopt all or any of the regulations contained in Table 'A' in Schedule I. If a public company does not register Articles of its own, the provisions in Table 'A' of Schedule I to the Act will automatically apply to such company. Generally, a public company formulates its own Articles and registers it along with Memorandum.

There are three alternatives available to a public company limited by shares:

(*a*) It may adopt 'Table A' in full as its Articles or
(*b*) It may wholly exclude 'Table A' and frame its own articles.
(*c*) It may partly frame its own articles and adopt part of 'Table A'.

Judicial Interpretations/Case Example	
If a company has not expressly or by implication excluded any regulation in Table A, regulation will be deemed to be incorporated in its articles.	*Sagar Automotives (P) Ltd.* v *CIT,* 1984, 56 Comp Cas 141 (MP).

Private Company Limited by Shares, Company Limited by Guarantee or an Unlimited Company [Section 27]

(*a*) In the case of a private company having a share capital, the articles shall contain provisions relating to the matters specified in sub-clauses (*a*), (*b*) and (*c*) of clause (*iii*) of sub-section (1) of Section 3; and in the case of any other private company, the articles shall contain provisions relating to the matters specified in the said sub-clauses (*b*) and (*c*).

> *A private limited company must have articles of its own which must contain the four restrictions as provided in Section 3 (1) (iii) of the Companies Act, 1956. The restrictions are: (a) restrict the right to transfer its share/s in the company; (b) limitation of the number of members to fifty (c) prohibitions on invitation to the public to subscribe for any shares in, or debentures of the company; and (d) prohibitions on invitation or acceptance of deposits from the persons other than its members, directors or their relatives. With these restrictions the private limited companies are having liberty to adopt all or any of the regulations contained in Table 'A'. Private limited company can adopt Table A with or without modification or exclusion of all or some of the provisions contained in Table A.*

(*b*) In the case of a company limited by guarantee, the articles shall state the number of members with which the company is to be registered.

(*c*) In the case of an unlimited company, the articles shall state the number of members with which the company is to be registered and, if the company has a share capital, the amount of share capital with which the company is to be registered.

Forms of Articles

Articles of a company not being a company limited by shares *i.e.* a guarantee/ unlimited company shall be in such one form as given in Tables C, D and E. However, a company may include any additional matters in its articles, so far they are not consistent with provisions contained in Tables C, D and E. [Section 29]

Model forms of Memorandum and Articles: Schedule I to Act provides model forms of memorandum and articles:

Table A	Regulations for management of company limited by shares
Table B	Memorandum of a company limited by shares
Table C	Memorandum and Articles of a company limited by guarantee and not having a share capital

Contd...

Table D	Memorandum and Articles of a guarantee company limited by guarantee and having a share capital
Table E	Memorandum and Articles of an unlimited company
Table F	Form of statement to be published by limited banking companies, insurance companies and deposit, provident or benefit societies

Judicial Interpretations/Case Example

Held that the provisions in the articles of a guarantee company that prevented its members from participating in the AGM was illegal and void and also inconsistent with or contrary to Table C.	*P.C. Arvindhan* v *M.A. Kesavan,* 1973, Tax LR 1844 (Ker).
In case of guarantee company not having share capital such as club or library or society, an article giving power to board (BOD) or managing committee, to expel a member is not invalid being not inconsistent with Table C in articles.	*Gaiman* v *National Association for Mental Health,* 1971, 41 Comp. Cas 929 (Ch D).

Signing of Articles [Section 30]

Articles shall be

(*a*) Printed

Department of Company Affairs press note dated 22 June 1993 provides that articles printed on computer shall be accepted by the ROC for registration, provided they are neatly and legibly printed.

(*b*) Divided into paragraphs numbered consecutively; and

(*c*) Signed by each subscriber of the Memorandum (who shall add his address, description and occupation, if any), in the presence of at least one witness who shall attest the signatures and shall likewise add his address, description and occupation, if any.

Contents of Articles

While drafting the Articles, the following important clauses should be incorporated:

(*a*) Share capital
(*b*) Lien on shares
(*c*) Calls on shares
(*d*) Transfer of shares
(*e*) Transmission of shares
(*f*) Surrender of shares
(*g*) Forfeiture of shares
(*h*) Conversion of shares into stock
(*i*) Share warrants
(*j*) Alteration of capital

(*k*) General meetings and proceedings there of

(*l*) Voting rights of members, voting by polls, proxies

(*m*) Directors including first directors/directors for life, their appointment, remuneration, qualifications, powers and proceedings of board of directors meetings

(*n*) Dividend and reserves

(*o*) Accounts and audit

(*p*) Borrowing powers

(*q*) Winding up

Alteration of Articles

It is the fundamental right of members to alter the Articles. The regulations contained in the Articles that they are unalterable, will be illegal and bad in law and shall render void the statutory powers as conferred upon a company by Section 31.

Judicial Interpretations/Case Example	
Any thing contained in the Articles or Memorandum of Association or by any separate contract, which bans alteration of the Articles of Association is void and is inoperative and the provisions of the Act will prevail. The Articles must be altered in good faith and not so as to give an unfair advantage to a majority of the shareholders.	*Neal* v *City of Birmingham Tramways*, 1910, 2 Ch D 464.

Procedure Required

Alteration is far Easy: Alteration of Articles of Association is far easy as compared to the alteration of Memorandum of Association of the company.

Passing of Special Resolution: As per Section 31 of the Companies Act, a company may, subject to the provisions of the Companies Act, 1956 and to the conditions given in the Memorandum, alter its Articles by passing of special resolution in the meeting of the shareholders.

No Approval of the Registrar: No approval of the Registrar of Companies for alteration of Articles of Association is required.

Approval of the Central Government: However, where the alteration relates to change of a public company into a private company shall have no effect unless the approval of the Central Government has been obtained (powers have been delegated to the Registrar of Companies).

Printed Copy filed with the Registrar: Where any alteration had been approved by the Central Government, a printed copy of the Articles as altered shall be filed by the company with the Registrar within one month of the date of receipt of the order of approval. [Section 31 (2A)]

Filing of Form **23:** Form 23 (e-Form 23) is required to be filed electronically with the digital signature of managing director or whole-time director or director or manager or secretary of the company together with the certified copy of the amended Articles, special resolution and explanatory statement within a period of 30 days from the date of special resolution passed by the company in its general meeting. E-Form 23 is also required to be certified by chartered accountant or company secretary or cost accountant in practice before filing.

> *The Department of Company Affairs (now Ministry) has clarified vide circular No 8/32 (31) 63-PR, dated 23-10-1963 that a company can never replace its Articles, it is only the regulations contained therein which may be changed.*

■ *Restrictions/Limitation on Alteration*

There are certain restrictions on the powers of a company to alter its Articles as stated below:

(a) **Alteration should not be Inconsistent with the Provisions of Companies Act, 1956:** The alteration should not be inconsistent with the provisions of Companies Act, 1956, or other Statute. The alterations in Articles to provide payment of dividends out of capital in case of insufficient profit, is violative of Section 205 of the Companies Act.

(b) **Alteration should not be Inconsistent with the Provisions of Memorandum of Association:** The alteration should not be inconsistent with the provisions of Memorandum of Association. In the event of conflict between Memorandum and Articles, Memorandum will prevail.

(c) **Alteration must be Bonafide for the Benefit of the Company:** The alteration should be in the interest of the company as a whole and must be bonafide for the benefit of the company as a whole.

(d) **Alteration should not be Oppressive to Minority:** The alteration should not be oppressive to minority and must not constitute a fraud on the minority. No provision be added which discriminates between the majority and minority or to give some advantage to the majority of which the minority is deprived.

(e) **Alteration must not allow anything which is Illegal or Unlawful:** Alteration must not allow anything which is illegal or unlawful or opposed to public policy. Alteration to allow gambling in the office building after business hours and to earn commission on that is unlawful.

(f) **Alteration must not Increase the Liability of Existing Members:** By alteration of articles, shareholders cannot be asked to pay more than their liability, unless they agree in writing. However, written consent of members is not necessary where the company is a club or association and the alteration requires a member to pay recurring or periodical subscription or changes at a higher rate.

(g) *Alteration must not cause a Breach of Contract:* An alteration which enables the company to commit a breach of contract with a third party is not justified and the company has to pay damages. Sometimes, it is expressly provided in an independent contract with a third party that the company shall not alter its articles so as to cause a breach of contract. In such cases the court may restrain the company from committing breach.

Judicial Interpretations/Case Example	
A company cannot deprive itself of the statutory power to alter its Articles of Association, either by a statement in Articles, or by a contract that they shall not be altered.	*Chithambaram* v *Krishna* ILR 1910, 33 *Mad* 36; *All India Railway Men's Benefit Fund* v *Basheshwarnath,* AIR 1945 Nag 187.
A court would not restrain a company from altering its Articles of Association unless it is ultra vires the Act, Memorandum or is unlawful and especially not if it merely causes a breach of contract by the company with an individual.	*Southern Foundries* (1926) *Limited* v *Shirlow,* 1940, 10 Comp Cas 255.
Company wanted to issue preference shares but there was no express provision either in Memorandum or Articles regarding issue of preference shares. Company altered Articles by passing special resolution to issue preference shares and directors issued preference shares. Held, the alteration in Articles to issue preference shares was valid as issue of preference shares were not expressly forbidden by the Memorandum.	*Andrew* v *Gasmeter Co. Ltd,* 1897, Chennai.
An alteration, which though injurious to an individual shareholder but is bona fide and for benefit of company, is valid.	*Sidebottom* v *Kershaw, Lease and Co.* 1920, 1 Ch D 154 (CA).
Power conferred on the company under Section 31 to alter the articles by special resolution, shall not be abused by the majority of shareholders so as to oppress the minority. No majority of shareholders can, by altering the Articles retrospectively, affect, to the prejudice of the non-consenting owners of shares, the right already existing under a contract, nor take away the right already accrued, *e.g.*, after a transfer of shares is lodged, the company cannot have a right of lien so as to defeat the transfer.	*Mathrubhumi Printing and Publishing Co. Ltd.* v *Vardhaman Publishers Ltd.,* 1992, 73 Comp Cas 80 (Ker).
The ordinary rule relating to alteration of articles is that everything in the Articles, which is not provided for by the Memorandum may be altered by a special resolution.	*King Emperor* v *Mathura Thakur,* (1902) WN 78.

Relationship between Memorandum and Articles

Ashbury Railway Carriage and Iron Company Ltd. v *Riche,* (1875) asserts the relationship between Memorandum and Articles as following:

- The Memorandum is the area beyond which the actions of the company cannot go; inside that area, shareholders may make such regulations, for their own governance as they think fit.
- Memorandum defines the company's object and various powers it possess; Articles provide that how these objects and powers shall be achieved and those powers exercised.
- Though Articles are subordinate and controlled by the Memorandum, yet if there be any doubt in the Memorandum, the Articles may be used to explain it but not so as to extend the objects.
- Memorandum and Articles are contemporaneous documents; they must be read together and ambiguity or uncertainty in one may be removed by reference to the other.
- If the Memorandum is perfectly clear, a doubt as to its meaning cannot be raised by reference to the Articles. In such a case, the Articles are simply inconsistent with the Memorandum and are disregarded.

Binding Effect of the Memorandum and Articles

The Memorandum and Articles when registered, bind the company and its members thereof to the same extent as if they respectively have been signed by the company and by each member. They create a contract between the company and its members, members company and members and members. But, they are not binding on the company and members in their relation to outsiders and an outsider (non- member) therefore, cannot take advantage of the provisions contained in Articles. [Section 36]

Judicial Interpretations/Case Example	
It is Memorandum and Articles that constitute a contract between company and each member of company; prospectus is not a contract and does not prevail over Articles.	*Globe Motors Ltd.* v *Globe United Engg. and Foundary Co. Ltd.* (1975) 45 Comp Cas 429 (Del).
Articles constitute a contract between members *inter se* even though there is no express contract between them.	*Re: Shiv Omkar Maheshwan* v *Bansidhar Jaganath,* 1957, Mumbai.
Any private agreements between shareholders are not binding and cannot be enforced by the company, as long as it is not incorporated in Articles.	*Rangraj (V B)* v *Gopal akrishnan (V B)*, 1992, 73 Comp Cas 201 (SC).
The Memorandum of a trading company is empowered to do all things incidental to achieving the object. Articles provided to lend money. Held, provision in the Articles empowering the company to lend money merely exemplifies the general words of the Memorandum and the company was therefore entitled to lend money to its employees.	*Rainford* v *James Keith and Blackman Company Ltd.,* 1905, 2 Ch. 147.

Whether Directors are bound by the Articles?

- ❑ Directors derive their powers from the Articles, subject to some limitations. If they contravene any provision of Articles, two parties may be affected *i.e.*, company and the outsiders.
- ❑ For any contravention of Articles, directors render themselves liable to an action at the instance of the members.
- ❑ However, members may ratify the acts of directors if they desire.
- ❑ But if as a result of breach of duty on the part of directors, any loss has resulted to the company, the directors are liable to reimburse the company, any loss so suffered.

Doctrine of Constructive Notice

- ❑ The office of the Registrar of Companies (ROC) is a public office and documents filed or registered therewith are public documents. These documents are open and accessible to all for inspection, etc., subject to rules framed in this regard under different sections of the Companies Act, 1956. [Section 610]
- ❑ Any outsider *i.e.*, every person who is dealing with the company, is presumed to have read the documents at ROC and presumed to know their content and understand them in their true perspective and sense. This is termed as 'Constructive Notice of Memorandum and Articles' or the 'Doctrine of Constructive Notice' that seeks to protect the company against outsiders. Likewise, anyone entering into a contract with a company must confirm that the proposed contracts are within the powers of the company concerned and its directors. If he does not do so then he will be entering into a contract with the company at his own risk.
- ❑ Following documents are of the importance for that purpose:
  - (*a*) Memorandum of Association,
  - (*b*) Articles of Association,
  - (*c*) Special resolution under Section 192,
  - (*d*) Particulars of Charges as per Section 125.

Judicial Interpretations/Case Example	
Outsiders dealing with the company are presumed to have constructive notice of contents of the Memorandum and the Articles. Held in *Venkatswami* v *Ramamurthy,* AIR 1934 Mad 579; *Charnock Collieries Co.* v *Bholanath,* ILR (1912) 39 Cal 810.	*Ernest* v *Nicholls,* 1857, 6 HLC 401, 419.
Outsiders are not bound to make enquiries and may assume that the company's internal management has been regular.	*Premier Industrial Bank* v *Carlton Manufacturing Co.,* 1909, 1 KB 106.

Contd...

The articles require that all documents should be signed by the MD, Secretary and the working director on behalf of the company. A deed of mortgage was executed by the secretary and working director only. Court held that no claim would lie under such a deed. The mortgager should have consulted the articles before the deed was executed. Even though mortgager acted in good faith and the money borrowed was applied for the purpose of the company, the mortgage was nevertheless invalid.	*Kotla Venkat Swamy* v *Chinta Rama Murthy,* AIR 1934, 579, Madras.

Doctrine of Indoor Management

The 'Doctrine of Indoor Management' also termed as 'Turquand Rule' pronounced in the famous and leading case of *Royal British Bank* v *Turquand* in 1856, restricts the application and scope of the 'Doctrine of Constructive Notices'. This Doctrine provides a shelter to the outsiders dealing with the company. A person, who has satisfied himself that a proposed dealing is not contradictory with the Memorandum and Articles of Association of the company is not bound to make a further enquiries and is entitled to assume that all the due internal procedures have been followed. It is none of the business of outsiders to look inside the doors of the company and conduct an inquiry and make sure that internal procedures have been duly and timely adhered to by the company. Therefore, the 'Doctrine of Indoor Management' is just reverse of the 'Doctrine of Constructive Notice'.

Doctrine of Indoor Management v *Doctrine of Constructive Notices:* In case of Doctrine of Indoor Management the outsider is protected against the company whereas in case of Doctrine of Constructive Notice, the company is protected from the outsiders.

Judicial Interpretations/Case Example	
The persons dealing with company need not enquire into regularity of internal proceedings.	*Varkey Souriar* v *Keraleeya Banking Co. Ltd.* 1957, 27 Comp Cas 591 (Ker).
Persons dealing with a director have to look to Articles to know only whether directors are having power, which they are purporting to exercise.	*Bigger Staff* v *Rowatt's Wharf Ltd.* 1896, 2 Ch. 93 (CA).
The strangers dealing with a company are entitled to assume that provisions contained in Memorandum and Articles have been complied with.	*Sree Meenakshi Mills Ltd.* v *Callianjee and Sons,* 1935, 5 Comp Cas 103 (Mad).

■ *Exceptions to the Doctrine of Indoor Management*

The Doctrine of Indoor Management has its own exceptions as stated hereunder:

(*i*) The rule cannot be invoked in favour of a person who did not in fact consult the Memorandum and Articles of Association.

(*ii*) The rule does not protect a person actually having actual or constructive knowledge of the irregularity.

(*iii*) The rule will not apply in favour of a person who does not make inquiry regarding the transaction being made under suspicious circumstances or where the circumstances so warrant, which, may be considered as negligence on his part.

(*iv*) The rule does not protect void or *ab initio* transactions.

(*v*) If the actions are outside the scope of the apparent authority, rule will not apply.

(*vi*) The rule does not apply if a person relies upon a document that is forged.

(*vii*) The rule does not render protection where the transaction requires special resolution, which has not been passed as it may be inspected at the office of the Registrar as enclosure of Form 23 or may verify the same with the Minutes of the General Meeting at the registered office of the company.

(*viii*) If an officer is purporting to exercise an authority exceeding his actual authority, the outsider cannot claim the protection of Doctrine of Indoor Management.

(*ix*) Doctrine of Indoor Management is not applicable where a precondition is to be fulfilled before company can exercise a particular power.

Review Questions

1. What are Articles of Association? How they can be altered? Discuss the limit upon the powers of a Company to alter or add to the Articles of Association.

2. "Is it mandatory for every company to register its own Articles of Association?" Comment.

3. What special provisions should the Articles of Association of (*i*) private limited company with shares; (*ii*) an unlimited company; and (*iii*) a guarantee company, contain?

4. What is the legal effect of the Articles of Association between Members and the company, Members *inter se*, Company and outsiders?

5. Can the shareholders enter into agreement amongst themselves which is inconsistent with the articles of association of the company?

6. Memorandum and Articles bind individual members *inter se* and the company to the members. Comment.

7. "The Articles of Association play a subordinate role to the Memorandum of Association." Comment.

8. Discuss the relationship between the Articles and Memorandum of Association of a company.

9. Subject to what limits imposed by either the general law or the Companies Act, 1956, may a company alter its Articles of Association?

10. "The power of altering the Articles of Association is wide, yet it is subject to a large number of limitations." Examine this statement.

11. The doctrine of constructive notice relating to Memorandum and Articles of Association is not a positive doctrine but a negative one. Discuss.

12. Explain the 'Doctrine of constructive notice' and 'doctrine of indoor management' as applicable in case of companies. State the circumstances in which the doctrine of indoor management is not applicable.

13. Discuss the scope of doctrine of indoor management. To what extent has the doctrine been incorporated by the Companies Act, 1956?

14. Explain and discuss the rule that the person dealing with a registered company need not enquire into the regularity of indoor management.

15. The doctrine of indoor management is silver lining to strangers dealing with the company. Comment.

16. Outline the rule in *Royal British Bank* v. *Turquand.* What are the exceptions to this rule?

17. The authorized signatory of a company issued a share certificate in favour of X, which apparently complied with the company's articles as it was purported to be signed by two directors and the secretary and it had the company's common seal affixed to it. In fact the secretary had forged the signatures of the directors, affixed the seal without any authority. Will the certificate be binding upon the company?

6

Prospectus

Meaning

The term 'Prospectus' under Section 2 (36) means any document described or issued as a prospectus and includes any notice, circular, advertisement or other document inviting deposits from the public or inviting offers from the public for the subscrip-tion or purchase of any shares in, or debentures of, a body corporate. A private company under Section 3 (1) (*iii*) is prohibited from inviting the public to subscribe for its shares or debentures; and also prohibited to invite or accept deposits from persons other than its members, directors or their relatives. Accordingly, a private company has no power to issue prospectus. Only a public company has power and privilege to issue prospectus to public for subscription of shares in or debentures of the company or for inviting public deposits. If a public company is able to raise funds from its own resources and does not issue a prospectus with reference to its formation then it has to file a statement in lieu of prospectus with the concerned Registrar of Companies.

Elements of a Prospectus

(*a*) There must be an invitation to the public,

(*b*) The invitation must be made by or on behalf of the company,

(*c*) The invitation must to subscribe or purchase, and

(*d*) The invitation must relate to securities.

Explanation

(*a*) Any oral or TV/film advertisement is not regarded as a prospectus, it should be in writing.

(*b*) The word subscription here means "taking" or "agreeing to take" securities for cash or to pay cash.

(*c*) Invitation to public means an invitation to public to subscribe for shares or debentures and shall include an invitation to any section of the public, whether selected as members or debenture holders of the company concerned or as clients of the person issuing the prospectus or in any other manner.

> *It's difficult to say exactly how many people constitute public. Public is general word and does not mean public at large–even section of public is considered public. Shares issued to all advocates, to all doctors, or to all foreigners living in India or to all citizens and to all shareholders in a particular company is considered as issued to public.*

(*d*) It is opposed to 'private communication' *e.g.*, invitation to friends, relatives of directors.

Requirements of a Prospectus

1. *It must be Dated:* The date so stated in the prospectus shall be taken as the date of its publication unless contrary is proved.

2. *Signed:* It must be signed by every Director or Proposed Director.

3. *It must be Registered with the Registrar:* The date of its filing with the Registrar (ROC) is taken to be the date of its issue (it can be issued up to 90 days) and the date of issue can be different from the date of its publication. The Registrar shall not register a prospectus unless the requirements of Sections 55, 56, 57 and 58 and sub-sections 1 and 2 of Section 60 have been complied with and the prospectus is accompanied by the consent in writing of the person, if any, named therein as the auditor, legal adviser, attorney, solicitor, banker or broker of the company or intended company, to act in that capacity.

4. *Terms of Prospectus not to be Varied or Changed:* After registration, terms mentioned in the prospectus cannot be changed except with the approval of shareholders in general meeting, so also with statement *in lieu of* prospectus.

5. *Alterations in Prospectus:* If the prospectus delivered for registration to the Registrar is not in conformity with the law or does not furnish required information, necessary corrections, alterations are made by companies as desired by the Registrar.

6. *Printed copies of the Prospectus Delivered to Regulatory Authorities:* Printed copies of the prospectus as registered by the Registrar, should be delivered to the SEBI, Stock Exchange and all the concerning authorities as true copy of the prospectus registered by the Registrar.

7. *Time of Issue:* Generally prospectus is issued after registration but there is no ban as such on its issue before the registration.

8. *It must be Issued within 90 Days from the Date on which a Copy was Delivered to the Registrar (ROC)* and facts be mentioned on the face of it. It is not necessary that a prospectus should be issued by a company. It may be issued on behalf of a company by its agents like an 'issuing house'.

9. *Application form to Accompany Prospectus:* Application form for shares debentures must accompany abridged (brief) form of prospectus. In the Companies Amendment Act, 1998, word 'prospectus' has been substituted

by "memorandum containing such salient features of prospectus as may be presented". Such memorandum is the abridged form of prospectus. Now companies are not required to issue full prospectus along with application form, which may be issued only on the request of the applicant. The purpose of issuing abridged prospectus (prospectus in brief) is to reduce the cost of issue by giving only the relevant and meaningful information. Non-compliance may lead to a fine of Rs 50,000.

10. *Furnishing of a Copy of Prospectus on Demand:* A copy of prospectus shall be furnished to a person who makes request in this regard before the closing of the subscription list. Any person who acts in contravention of provisions cited above shall be punishable with fine, which may extend to fifty thousand rupees. [Section 56(3]

11. **It must be Accompanied by:**

   (*i*)   Consent of expert if the report of the expert is to be published.

   (*ii*) Written consent of all those whose names are mentioned *e.g.*, the auditors, bankers, solicitors, etc.

   (*iii*) A copy of agreement for the appointment of managerial personnel and their consent.

   (*iv*) Copy of material contracts.

Judicial Interpretations/Case Example	
An offer of shares limited to the members of an existing company appears to be not an offer to the public.	*Booth* v *New Api Kander* (*B*), 1903, 1 Ch 295.
Any offer of shares or securities to the general public must be made by issuance of the prospectus. What is an offer to the public depends upon the circumstances of each particular case. It appears that an offer to the public means an offer by the company to anyone who chooses to come in and take shares.	*Sherwell* v *Combined I.M.Syndicates,* 1907, WN 110.
In this case 3000 of prospectus were sent out and distributed amongst the members of a certain gas company only. It is not considered to be an issue to public as it was directed to a specified person or a group of persons and it does not result in becoming available to others.	*Re: South of England Natural Gas and Petroleum Company Ltd,* 1911, 1 Ch., 573.
Public is a general word and no particular number are prescribed. Single private communication does not amount to issue to public. In this case, several copies of prospectus marked 'strictly confidential' containing particulars of the issue, accompanied by appropriate forms (not containing all material facts) and prepared by the managing director (MD) were given to company director who gave to a solicitor, who further gave them to a client and who to his brother-in-law, who induced 'L' to become director which	*Nash* v *Lynde,* 1929, A.C., 158.

Contd..

he did. L also took some shares in the company. *Held:* the document had not been issued as a prospectus, as the document was passed on privately through a small circle of friends of the MD.	
An offer to kith and kin of a director is not an invitation to the public.	*Rattan Singh* v *Moga Transport Company Ltd.,* 1959, 29 Comp. Cas. 165.

Where Prospectus is not Required to be Issued

1. A private company need not issue a prospectus.
2. Even a public company need not issue a prospectus when shares or debentures are not offered to public and money is being raised privately. In such a situation, a public company is to file 'Statement *in lieu of* Prospectus'.
3. Where shares or debentures are offered to the existing members by way of right issue.
4. Where shares or debentures are quoted on stock exchange and are uniform in all respects with shares/debentures previously issued.
5. Where an offer is made in connection with a *bona fide* invitation to a person to enter into an underwriting agreement with respect to shares or debentures.
6. Where any prospectus is published as a newspaper advertisement, it shall not be necessary in the advertisement to specify the contents of the memorandum or the signatories thereto, or the number of shares subscribed for by them. [Section 66]

Statement in Lieu of Prospectus

❑ As per Section 70 (1), a company (excluding a private company) having a share capital, which does not issue a prospectus on or with reference to its formation, or which has issued such a prospectus but has not proceeded to allot any of the shares offered to the public for subscription, shall not allot any of its shares or debentures unless at least three days before the first allotment of either shares or debentures, there has been delivered to the Registrar of Companies (ROC) for registration a statement in lieu of prospectus signed by every person who is named therein as a director or proposed director of the company or by his agent authorised in writing, in the form and containing the particulars set out in Part I of Schedule III and, in the cases mentioned in Part II of that Schedule, setting out the reports specified therein, and the said Parts I and II shall have effect subject to the provisions contained in Part III of that Schedule. [Section 70 (1)] If a company acts in contravention of this sub-section, the company, and every director of the company who willfully authorises or permits the contravention, shall be punishable with fine which may extend to ten thousand rupees. [Section 70 (4)]

Abridge Prospectus

❑ Prospectus is a bulky document and it is not economically feasible to supply full-fledged prospectus to the prospective investors. Therefore, as a cost saving measure, provision has been made to issue prospectus in abridged form.

❑ The dictionary meaning of 'Abridged Prospectus' is a condensed prospectus, reduced prospectus, abbreviated prospectus or shortened prospectus. Thus, it means a prospectus in brief where the company need not provide information in the prospectus in detail under several sub-headings as required by the Schedule II, but, the information is given in condensed form.

❑ Under Section 2 (1), 'Abridged Prospectus' means a memorandum containing such salient features of a prospectus as may be prescribed.

❑ In the Companies Amendment Act, 1988, word 'prospectus' has been substituted by "memorandum containing such salient features of prospectus as may be presented". Such memorandum is the abridged form of prospectus. After this amendment, companies are not required to issue full/detailed prospectus along with application form, which may be issued only on the request of the applicant.

❑ New rule 4cc has been inserted in the Companies (Central Govt) Rules and Forms 1956 and as per this rule, the salient features should be given in Form 2A which requires information to be given under nine heads:

1. General Information
2. Capital Structure
3. Terms of Present Issue
4. Particulars of the Issue
5. Company Management and Project
6. Financial Performance during 5 years
7. Payments/Refunds
8. Companies under same Management
9. Risk Factors

❑ The Department of Company Affairs (now Ministry of Corporate Affairs) circular no 1/92 dated 9th January, 1992 provides that

(i) Share application form should be a part of the abridged prospectus.

(ii) Abridged prospectus and application form (attached with) are allowed to bea same printed numbers.

After the issue of this circular, representation were made to government that only one application form attached to abridged prospectus might increase the printing charges and thus two forms to be attached. The government accepted suggestion and vide circular 10th April, 1992, two forms are now attached to abridged prospectus with separate printed numbers.

❑ SEBI requirements in respect of abridged prospectus will also have to be fulfilled.

Red-Herring Prospectus

❑ The red-herring process is useful when the issuer company wants to test market before finalizing issue size and or issue price.

❑ 'Red-herring Prospectus' means a prospectus which does not have complete particulars on the price of the securities offered and the quantum of securities offered. [explanation to Section 60B]

❑ A prospectus that does not have information of either number of shares being offered or the amount of issue or the issue price is called red-herring prospectus.

❑ Since the price is not disclosed, only the upper and lower price bands are disclosed in such a prospectus.

❑ When the red-herring prospectus and the draft offer document are filled with the Registrar without price band, the issuer company in that case will notify the floor price or a price band by way of advertisement one day prior to the opening of the issue.

❑ Only on completion of bidding process, the details of final price are included in the offer document that is filled with the Registrar and is called a prospectus.

Shelf Prospectus

Introduced in the Companies (Amendment) Act, 2000: As the issue of shares is a time consuming process with too many negotiations involved with various bodies of banks, underwriters and brokers and there are large number of matters which are highly informative to be published, repeating the procedures every time of issue is time consuming and costly too. Therefore, the provisions of shelf prospectus and information memorandum were inserted in the Companies (Amendment) Act, 2000 by inserting Sections 60A and 60B.

Need: Under the Companies Act, a company must issue a complete prospectus every time it approaches the capital market. It certainly leads to needless repetition more so when a company takes recourse to capital markets more than once in a given year. Newly inserted Section 60A provides relief to such a company (financial institution) that may issue a 'shelf prospectus' which will remain valid for a period of one year from the date of opening of the first issue. Such a prospectus has a limited life during which it remains on the "shelf", and is updated for any changes that may have occurred between two successive offerings.

Meaning: 'Shelf Prospectus' means a prospectus issued by any financial institution or bank for one or more issues of the securities or class of securities specified in that prospectus.

Requirements of a Shelf Prospectus

1. Any public financial institution, public sector bank or scheduled bank whose main object is financing shall file a shelf prospectus. [Section 60 A (1)]

2. A company filing a shelf prospectus with the Registrar shall not be required to file prospectus afresh at every stage of offer of securities by it within a period of validity of such shelf prospectus. [Section 60 A (2)]

3. A company filing a shelf prospectus shall be required to file an information memorandum on all material facts relating to new charges created, changes in the financial position as have occurred between the first offer of securities, previous offer of securities and the succeeding offer of securities within such time as may be prescribed by the Central Government (one year), prior to making of a second or subsequent offer of securities under the shelf prospectus. [Section 60 A (3)]

4. An information memorandum shall be issued to the public along with shelf prospectus filed at the stage of the first offer of securities and such prospectus shall be valid for a period of one year from the date of opening of the first issue of securities under that prospectus: provided that where an update of information memorandum is filed every time an offer of securities is made, such memorandum together with the shelf prospectus shall constitute the prospectus. [Section 60 A (4)]

Explanation: For the purpose of this section, 'financing' means making loans to or subscribing in the capital of, a private industrial enterprise engaged in infrastructural financing or, such other company as the Central Government may notify in this behalf.

Information Memorandum [Section 60B]

Requirements

1. A public company making an issue of securities may circulate information memorandum to the public prior to filing of a prospectus. [Section 60 B (1)]

2. A company inviting subscription by an information memorandum shall be bound to file a prospectus prior to the opening of the subscription lists and the offer as a red-herring prospectus, at least three days before the opening of the offer. [Section 60 B (2)]

3. The information memorandum and red-herring prospectus shall carry same obligations as are applicable in the case of a prospectus. [Sect: n 60 B (3)]

4. Any variation between the information memorandum and the red-herring prospectus shall be highlighted as variations by the issuing company. [Section 60 B (4)]

> *Explanation:* *'Red-Herring Prospectus' means a prospectus which does not have complete particulars on the price of the securities offered and the quantum of securities offered.*

5. Every variation as made and highlighted above shall be individually intimated to the persons invited to subscribe to the issue of securities. [Section 60 B (5)]
6. In the event of the issuing company or the underwriters to the issue have invited or received advance subscription by way of cash or post-dated cheques or stock-invest, the company or such underwriters or bankers to the issue shall not encash such subscription moneys or post-dated cheques or stockinvest before the date of opening of the issue, without having individually intimated the prospective subscribers of the variation and without having offered an opportunity to such prospective subscribers to withdraw their application and cancel their post-dated cheques or stock-invest or return of subscription paid. [Section 60 B (6)]
7. The applicant or proposed subscriber shall exercise his right to withdraw from the application on any intimation of variation within seven days from the date of such intimation and shall indicate such withdrawal in writing to the company and the underwriters. [Section 60 B (7)]
8. Any application for subscription which is acted upon by the company or underwriters or bankers to the issue without having given enough information of any variations, or the particulars of withdrawing the offer or opportunity for canceling the post-dated cheques or stock invest or stop payments for such payments shall be void and the applicants shall be entitled to receive a refund or return of its post-dated cheques or stock-invest or subscription moneys or cancellation of its application, as if the said application had never been made and the applicants are entitled to receive back their original application and interest at the rate of fifteen per cent from the date of encashment till payment of realisation. [Section 60 B (8)]
9. Upon the closing of the offer of securities, a final prospectus stating therein the total capital raised, whether by way of debt or share capital and the closing price of the securities and any other details as were not complete in the red-herring prospectus shall be filed in a case of a listed public company with the Securities and Exchange Board and Registrar, and in any other case with the Registrar only. [Section 60 B (9)]

Deemed Prospectus

❑ Since requirements of prospectus are very rigorous, in order to avoid the issue of prospectus, there is a practice to issue securities to another person called 'Issue House' who would then make further offer of sale of these securities to public by advertisements. Section 64 contains provisions as regards any document containing offer of shares in or debentures for sale shall be deemed to be prospectus. Following are the provisions in this regard:

❑ Where a company allots or agrees to allot any shares in or debentures of the company with a view to all or any of those shares or debentures being offered for sale to the public, any document by which the offer for sale to the public is made shall, for all purposes, be deemed to be a prospectus issued by the company; and all enactments and rules of law as to the contents of prospectuses and as to liability in respect of statements in and omissions from prospectuses, or otherwise relating to prospectuses, shall apply with the modifications specified in and have effect accordingly, as if the shares or debentures had been offered to the public for subscription and as if persons accepting the offer in respect of any shares or debentures were subscribers for those shares or debentures, but without prejudice to the liability, if any, of the persons by whom the offer is made in respect of mis-statements contained in the document or otherwise in respect thereof. [Section 64(1)]

❑ For the purposes of this Act, it shall, unless the contrary is proved, be evidence that an allotment of, or an agreement to allot, shares or debentures was made with a view to the shares or debentures being offered for sale to the public if it is shown:

(*a*) That an offer of the shares or debentures or of any of them for sale to the public was made within six months after the allotment or agreement to allot; or

(*b*) That at the date when the offer was made, the whole consideration to be received by the company in respect of the shares or debentures had not been received by it.

Misrepresentation in Prospectus

It is exclusively on the basis of the prospectus that prospective investors get the information about the company and based on that information take decision whether to invest or not? Therefore, the prospectus of the company must not suppress or omit any material fact about the company. Whatever given in the prospectus must be correct and whatever should have been given is not be concealed. The misrepresentation or concealment of facts in the prospectus may lead to both the civil liability as provided under Section 62 and the criminal liability prescribed under Section 63 of the Act.

Civil Liability for Mis-Statements in Prospectus [Section 62]

1. Where a prospectus invites persons to subscribe for shares in or debentures of a company, the following persons shall be liable to pay compensation to

every person who subscribes for any shares or debentures on the faith of the prospectus for any loss or damage he may have sustained by reason of any untrue statement included therein, that is to say:

(a) Every person who is a director of the company at the time of the issue of the prospectus;

(b) Every person who has authorised himself to be named and is named in the prospectus either as a director, or as having agreed to become a director, either immediately or after an interval of time;

(c) Every person who is a promoter of the company; and

(d) Every person who has authorised the issue of the prospectus:

Provided that where, under Section 58, the consent of a person is required to the issue of a prospectus and he has given that consent, or where under sub-section (3) of Section 60, the consent of a person named in a prospectus is required and he has given that consent, he shall not, by reason of having given such consent, be liable under this sub-section as a person who has authorised the issue of the prospectus except in respect of an untrue statement, if any purporting to be made by him as an expert.

2. No person shall be liable under sub-section (1), if he proves:

(a) That, having consented to become a director of the company, he withdrew his consent before the issue of the prospectus, and that it was issued without his authority or consent;

(b) That the prospectus was issued without his knowledge or consent, and that on becoming aware of its issue, he forthwith gave reasonable public notice that it was issued without his knowledge or consent;

(c) That, after the issue of the prospectus and before allotment there under, he, on becoming aware of any untrue statement therein, withdrew his consent to the prospectus and gave reasonable public notice of the withdrawal and of the reason therefore; or

(d) That—

   (i) As regards every untrue statement not purporting to be made on the authority of an expert or of a public official document or statement, he had reasonable ground to believe, and did up to the time of the allotment of the shares or debentures, as the case may be, believe, that the statement was true; and

   (ii) As regards every untrue statement purporting to be a statement by an expert or contained in what purports to be a copy of or an extract from a report or valuation of an expert, it was a correct and fair representation of the statement, or a correct copy of, or a correct and fair extract from, the report or valuation; and he had reasonable ground to believe, and did up to the time of the issue of the prospectus believe, that the person making the statement was competent to make it and that that person had given the consent required by Section 58 to the issue of the prospectus and had not withdrawn that consent before delivery of a copy of the prospectus for registration or, to the defendant's knowledge, before allotment there-under; and

(*iii*) As regards every untrue statement purporting to be a statement made by an official person or contained in what purports to be a copy of or extract from a public official document, it was a correct and fair representation of the statement, or a correct copy of or a correct and fair extract from, the document:

Provided that this sub-section shall not apply in the case of a person liable, by reason of his having given a consent required of him by Section 58, as a person who has authorised the issue of the prospectus in respect of an untrue statement, purporting to be made by him as an expert.

3. A person who, apart from this sub-section, would, under sub-section (1), be liable by reason of his having given a consent required of him by Section 58 as a person who has authorised the issue of a prospectus in respect of an untrue statement, purporting to be made by him as an expert, shall not be so liable, if he proves:

(*a*) That, having given his consent under Section 58 to the issue of the prospectus, he withdrew it in writing before delivery of a copy of the prospectus for registration;

(*b*) That, after delivery of a copy of the prospectus for registration and before allotment there-under, he, on becoming aware of the untrue statement, withdrew his consent in writing and gave reasonable public notice of the withdrawal and of the reason therefore; or

(*c*) That he was competent to make the statement and that he had reasonable ground to believe, and did up to the time of the allotment of the shares or debentures, believe, that the statement was true.

4. Where:

(*a*) The prospectus specifies the name of a person as a director of the company, or as having agreed to become a director thereof, and he has not consented to become a director, or has withdrawn his consent before the issue of the prospectus, and has not authorised or consented to the issue thereof; or

(*b*) The consent of a person is required under Section 58 to the issue of the prospectus and he either has not given that consent or has withdrawn it before the issue of the prospectus;

- The directors of the company excluding those without whose knowledge or consent the prospectus was issued, and every other person who authorised the issue thereof, shall be liable to indemnify the person referred to in clause (*a*) or clause (*b*), as the case may be, against all damages, costs and expenses to which he may be made liable by reason of his name having been inserted in the prospectus or of the inclusion therein of a statement purporting to be made by him as an expert, as the case may be, or in defending himself against any suit or legal proceeding brought against him in respect thereof: Provided that a person shall not be deemed for the purposes of this sub section to have authorised the issue of a prospectus by reason only of his having given the consent required by Section 58 to the inclusion therein of a statement purporting to be made by him as an expert.

5. Every person who, becomes liable to make any payment by virtue of this section, may recover contribution, as in cases of contract, from any other person who, if sued separately, would have been liable to make the same payment, unless the former person was, and the latter person was not, guilty of fraudulent misrepresentation.

Criminal Liability for Mis-Statements in Prospectus [Section 63]

1. Where a prospectus issued includes any untrue statement, every person who authorised the issue of the prospectus shall be punishable with imprisonment for a term which may extend to two years, or with fine which may extend to fifty thousand rupees, or with both, unless he proves either that the statement was immaterial or that he had reasonable ground to believe, and did up to the time of the issue of the prospectus believe, that the statement was true. [Section 63 (1)]

2. A person shall not be deemed for the purposes of this section to have authorised the issue of a prospectus by reason only of his having given:

    (*a*) The consent required by Section 58 to the inclusion therein of a statement purporting to be made by him as an expert, or

    (*b*) The consent required by sub-section (3) of Section 60

Contents of Prospectus [Section 56]

1. Every prospectus issued by or on behalf of a company, or by or on behalf of any person who is or has been engaged or interested in the formation of a company, shall state the matters specified in Part I of Schedule II and set out the reports specified in Part II of that Schedule; and the said Parts I and II shall have effect subject to the provisions contained in Part III of that Schedule.

2. A condition requiring or binding an applicant for shares in or debentures of a company to waive compliance with any of the requirements of this section, or purporting to affect him with notice of any contract, document or matter not specifically referred to in the prospectus, shall be void.

3. No one shall issue any form of application for shares in or debentures of a company, unless the form is accompanied by a memorandum containing such salient features of a prospectus as may be prescribed which complies with the requirements of this section: provided that a copy of the prospectus shall, on a request being made by any person before the closing of the subscription list, be furnished to him: provided further that this sub-section shall not apply if it is shown that the form of application was issued either—

    (*a*) In connection with a *bona fide* invitation to a person to enter into an underwriting agreement with respect to the shares or debentures; or

    (*b*) In relation to shares or debentures which were not offered to the public.

Non-Compliance: If any person acts in contravention of the provisions of this sub-section, he shall be punishable with fine which may extend to fifty thousand rupees.

4. A director or other person responsible for the prospectus shall not incur any liability by reason of any non-compliance with, or contravention of, any of the requirements of this section, if:

    (*a*) As regards any matter not disclosed, he proves that he had no knowledge thereof; or

    (*b*) He proves that the non-compliance or contravention arose from an honest mistake of fact on his part; or

    (*c*) The non-compliance or contravention was in respect of matters which, in the opinion of the Court dealing with the case, were immaterial, or was otherwise such as ought, in the opinion of that Court, having regard to all the circumstances of the case, reasonably to be excused: provided that no director or other person shall incur any liability in respect of the failure to include in a prospectus a statement with respect to the matters specified in clause 18 of Schedule II, unless it is proved that he had knowledge of the matters not disclosed.

5. This section shall not apply:

    (*a*) To the issue to existing members or debenture holders of a company of a prospectus or form of application relating to shares in or debentures of the company, whether an applicant for shares or debentures will or will not have the right to renounce in favour of other persons; or

    (*b*) To the issue of a prospectus or form of application relating to shares or debentures which are, or are to be, in all respects uniform with shares or debentures previously issued and for the time being dealt in or quoted on a recognised stock exchange;

but subject as aforesaid, this section shall apply to a prospectus or a form of application, whether issued on or with reference to the formation of a company or subsequently.

6. Nothing in this section shall limit or diminish any liability which any person may incur under the general law or under this Act apart from this section.

Matters Specified in Schedule II: Central government *vide* note no. 666 (E) dated 3/10/91 amended Schedule II and matters to be disclosed under revised Schedule II are given in 3 parts.

Part I

1. *General Information:* Declaration of the following items should be disclosed in prospectus.

- Registered office of the Company
- Consent of Central Government for the Present Issue
- Industrial Licence
- Details of Stock Exchange for Listing Purpose
- Refund if minimum subscription of 90% not received within 90 days from closure of list.
- Allotment letters/refund within 10 weeks
- Details of schedule–opening and closing
- Auditors and lead managers
- Underwriters

2. *Capital Structure of the Company:* Each and every pertinent detail about

- Authorised capital,
- Paid up capital and
- Size of present issue.

3. *Terms of Present Issue:* Information regarding payment schedule and procedure to apply.

4. *Company, its Management and Projects:* Information about history, subsidiary, promoters, details of directors, location of project, collaborations, P & M assets, products, marketing, future projects, capacity utilisation.

5. *Details of public issue made by companies under the same management.*

6. *Litigation, criminal proceedings and defaults launched against the company and against its directors.*

7. *Management perception of risk factors e.g., difficulty in availability of raw material, marketing, etc.*

Part II

1. *General Information*

- Consent of Directors, auditors, bankers, solicitors.
- Expert opinion obtained, if any

- Change if any, in directors/auditors-during 3 years
- Authority for the issue and resolution passed for issue
- Time schedule for allotment and issue of share certificate
- Details of company secretary- name and addresses of solicitors, auditors, bankers, underwriters.

2. *Financial Information*

- *Report by Auditors*: for 5 years preceding the issue of prospectus-Dividend, P&L a/c, B/S if business is less than 5 years than actual.
- *Report of Accountants* (CA): P&L a/c, B/S, 5 years.

3. *Statutory Information*

- Minimum subscription
- Expenses of the issue on experts, managers
- Underwriting commission
- Previous public issue details (of past 5 years)
- Premium
- Otherwise than in cash
- Purchase of property
- Details of management
- Rights of members
- Restriction on transfer
- Material contracts

Part III

- Any report by a chartered accountant under Part II must be by a qualified chartered accountant.
- Time and place where all P&L and B/S, contracts, documents etc can be inspected should be specified under Part III.
- Prospectus must end by the declaration by the directors that provisions/ guidelines have been complied with.

Review Questions

1. What steps are to be taken before a company is entitled to commence its business?
2. Define Prospectus. When a company is not required to issue prospectus? Briefly enumerate the statutory requirements in relation to a prospectus.
3. What is a prospectus? What are its contents?
4. What are the consequences that follow in case of issue of prospectus containing false statements on the strength of which shares are subscribed for?

5. What is an untrue statement in the prospectus? How to prove a mis-statement in a prospectus?

6. Who are liable for misstatements in a prospectus? Explain the extent of civil and criminal liability for such misstatements.

7. What are the remedies open to an allottee of shares who has applied for them on the faith of a false and misleading prospectus, and what are the defenses available to the directors of a company who have issued such a prospectus?

8. When and by whom can the allotment of shares be rescinding on the grounds of a false and misleading prospectus under Companies Act 1956?

9. Discuss the provisions about the liability of an expert for untrue statements given by him in the prospectus of a company. Under what circumstances is an expert not liable for such untrue statements in the prospectus?

10. Under what circumstances a document containing an offer for sale of shares or debentures shall be not deemed to be a prospectus?

11. State the provisions relating to 'prospectus' on the following specific matters:

> (*i*) Statement in lieu of Prospectus
> (*ii*) Dating of Prospectus
> (*iii*) Registration of Prospectus
> (*iv*) Shelf Prospectus
> (*v*) Information Memorandum
> (*vi*) Minimum Subscription
> (*vii*) Red-herring Prospectus
> (*viii*) 'Prospectus by Implication' or 'Deemed Prospectus'.

□□□

Share and Share Capital

Share

■ *Meaning*

❑ Section 2 (46) of the Companies Act defines a share as "Share in the share capital of a company, and includes stock except where a distinction between stock and shares is expressed or implied." Thus, a share represents a unit into which the share capital of a company is divided. For example, if the share capital of a company is rupees 5 crore divided into 5, 00,000 units of rupees 10, each unit of rupees 10 shall be termed a share of the company.

❑ Section 82 of the Companies Act instead portrays share as a movable property, transferable in the manner provided by the articles of the company. It is considered as 'goods' under the Indian Contract Act, 1872 or 'property' under the Sale of Goods Act, 1930 and therefore, it can be bought or sold like other goods or property are bought or sold.

❑ Each share in a company having a share capital shall be distinguished by its appropriate number: provided that nothing in this section shall apply to the shares held with a depository. [Section 83]

Judicial Interpretations/Case Example	
Share represents the interest of the shareholder in the company, measured by a sum of money for the purposes of liability and dividend.	*Borland's Trustee* v *Steel Bros,* 1901, 1 Ch. 279.
Shares are "goods" within the meaning of Section 76 of the Indian Contract Act.	*Maneckji* v *Wadilal Sarabhai and Co.,* 1926, ILR 50 Bom 360: 30 CWN 890.
Shares are goods under the Sale of Goods Act, 1930 (Section 2 (7) of that Act).	*Karunakaran* v *Krishna,* AIR, 1943, Mad 74.
Share are movable property in India and they can be transferred in the manner provided in the articles of the company.	*Arjun Prasad* v *Central Bank of India,* AIR, 1956, Pat 32.

■ *Share v Stock*

1. A 'share' represents a unit into which the share capital of a company is divided whereas 'stock' is an aggregate of fully paid-up shares of a member put together into one fund of equal value expressed in terms of money and not as number of shares.

2. A limited company having a share capital, may, if so authorised by its articles, convert all or any of its fully paid up shares into stock, and reconvert that stock into fully paid-up shares of any denomination. The conversion will not affect the rights of member in any way. [Section 94 (1) (c)]

3. Originally only shares are issued, whereas a company cannot make an original issue of the stock.

4. A share has a distinct number, whereas a stock has no such number.

5. A share may be either partly paid-up or fully paid-up, whereas a stock can never be partly paid up.

6. All shares of a class are of equal denominations, whereas stock may be of different denominations.

7. A share can only be transferred in one piece and not in fractions, whereas a stock may be transferred in any fractions.

■ *Share v Share Certificate*

❑ To a layman, both the share and share certificate mean one and the same thing. But, in the eyes of lay both have different meaning. Section 82 of the Companies Act considers 'share' as a movable property, transferable in the manner provided by the articles of the company. Section 84 (1), on the other hand, explain a 'share certificate' to mean a certificate, under the common seal of the company, specifying any shares held by any member which shall be *prima facie* evidence of the title of the member to such shares. Thus, 'share' represents movable property, whereas 'share certificate' is a conclusive evidence of title of the member to such property.

Judicial Interpretations/Case Example	
Under Section 84, a 'share certificate' is issued under the common seal of the company, specifying any shares held by any member which shall be *prima facie* evidence of the title of the member to such shares. Hence, a 'share certificate' is not the shares; it is only a *prima facie* evidence of the title to the shares. Each share bears a distinctive number and it is not the same as share certificate number, the two are different.	*Shree Gopal Paper Mills Ltd* v *CIT*, 1967, 37 Comp. Cas. 240 (Calcutta).

■ *Kinds of Share or Share Capital*

❑ As per Section 86 of the Companies Act as amended in 2000, the share capital of a company limited by shares shall be of two kinds only, namely:

1. Equity Share Capital:
   (*a*) With voting rights; or
   (*b*) With differential rights as to dividend, voting or otherwise in accordance with such rules and subject to such conditions as may be prescribed.
2. Preference Share Capital.

■ *Equity Share or Share Capital*

- ❑ Equity share or share capital means all such shares, which is not preference share or share capital. Thus, a share or share capital which does not satisfy the condition of preference share capital is equity share capital.
- ❑ Equity share shareholders have right to participate in the decision making of the company. They are entitled to voting rights in proportion to the paid-up equity capital.
- ❑ Equity share shareholders receive dividends out of profits as declared by the shareholders in annual general meeting only after preference shares, if any, have been paid their fixed dividend. If company is left with no funds after payments to the preference shareholders, equity shareholders in that case may not receive dividend.
- ❑ In case if a company has equity and preferential capital, both, the holder of equity shares does not have the following rights:
   (*a*) Preferential right in respect of payment of dividend;
   (*b*) Preferential right in respect of payment of capital in the event of liquidation of a company. In such cases the preferential shareholders shall get preferential rights in the payment of dividend, if any and payment of capital if company goes into liquidation.

■ *Equity Share with Differential Rights*

- ❑ 'Equity share with differential voting rights' includes rights as to dividend or voting. The word 'otherwise' in the view of Department of Company Affairs (now Ministry of Corporate Affairs) may include, inter alia rights as to participating in surplus in the events of winding up, mode of repayment, etc.

Conditions as to the Issue of Equity Shares with Differential Rights: The Central Government in has prescribed rules namely Companies (Issue of Share Capital with Differential Voting Rights) Rules, 2001 *vide* Notification No. GSR 167 (E), dated 9th March ,2001. Every company limited by shares may issue shares with differential rights as to dividend, voting or otherwise, if—

1. The company has distributable profits in terms of Section 205 of the Companies Act, 1956 for three financial years preceding the year in which it was decided to issue such shares;

2. The company has not defaulted in filing annual accounts and annual returns for three financial years immediately preceding the financial year in which it was decided to issue such share;

3. The company has not failed to repay its deposits or interest thereon on due date or redeem its debentures on due date or pay dividend;

4. The Articles of Association of the company authorizes the issue of shares with differential voting rights;

5. The company has not been convicted of any offence arising under Securities and Exchange Board of India Act, 1992, Securities Contracts (Regulation) Act, 1956, Foreign Exchange Management Act, 1999;

6. The company has not defaulted in meeting investors' grievances;

7. The company has obtained the approval of shareholders in general meeting by passing resolution as required under the provision of sub-clause (a) of sub-section (1) of Section 94 read with sub-section (2) of the said section;

8. The listed public company obtained approval of shareholders through Postal Ballot;

9. The notice of the meeting at which resolution is proposed to be passed is accompanied by an explanatory statement stating:

    (a) The rate of voting right which the equity share capital with differential voting right shall carry;

    (b) The scale or in proportion to which the voting rights of such class or type of shares will vary;

    (c) The company shall not convert its equity capital with voting rights into equity share capital with differential voting rights and the shares with differential voting rights into equity share capital with voting rights;

    (d) The shares with differential voting rights shall not exceed 25% of the total share capital issued;

    (e) That a member of the company holding any equity share with differential voting rights shall be entitled to bonus shares, right shares of the same class;

    (f) The holders of the equity shares with differential voting rights shall enjoy all other rights to which the holder is entitled to excepting right to vote as indicated in (a) above.

10. Every company referred above shall maintain a register as required under Section 150 of the Act containing the particulars of differential rights to which the holder is entitled to.

■ Sweat Equity Share

❑   The concept of Sweat Equity Share was introduced by inserting Section 79A in the Companies Act in 1999.

❑ The expression 'Sweat Equity Shares' means equity shares issued by the company to employees or directors at a discount or for consideration other than cash for providing know-how or making available rights in the nature of intellectual property rights or value additions, by whatever name called.

❑ According to Section 79A, a company may issue sweat equity shares of a class of shares already issued if the following conditions are fulfilled, namely:

(*a*) The issue of sweat equity shares is authorised by a special resolution passed by the company in the general meeting;

(*b*) The resolution specifies the number of shares, current market price, consideration, if any, and the class or classes of directors or employees to whom such equity shares are to be issued;

(*c*) Not less than one year has, at the date of the issue elapsed since the date on which the company was entitled to commence business;

(*d*) The sweat equity shares of a company whose equity shares are listed on a recognised stock exchange are issued in accordance with the regulations made by the Securities and Exchange Board of India in this behalf: provided that in the case of a company whose equity shares are not listed on any recognised stock exchange, the sweat equity shares are issued in accordance with the Unlisted Companies (Issue of Sweat Equity Shares) Rules, 2003.

(*e*) The following persons may be issued the sweat equity shares:

(*i*) **The Class or Classes of Directors or Employees:** The whole time director, executive director and the permanent employees working in India or abroad are considered as employees;

(*ii*) **Promoters:** There is no specific mention about the promoter being eligible for sweat equity shares in Section 79A, but both in SEBI Guidelines and the Unlisted Companies (Issue of Sweat Equity Shares) Rules, 2003, promoters have been given the right to get the sweat equity shares allotted.

(*iii*) Manager;

(*iv*) Non-employee;

■ Voting Rights of Equity Shareholders

❑ Section 87 of the Companies Act, 1956 gives the provisions as follows:

(*a*) Every member of a company limited by shares and holding any equity share capital therein shall have a right to vote, in respect of such capital, on every resolution placed before the company; and

(*b*) His voting right on a poll shall be in proportion to his share of the paid-up equity capital of the company.

Section 87 is not applicable in case of an independent private company.

■ Preference Share

- ❏ Section 85 (1) of the Companies Act provides that a preference share or preference share capital is that part of the share capital of the company which fulfils both the following requirements, namely:

  (a) That as respects dividends it carries or will carry a preferential right to be paid a fixed amount or an amount calculated at a fixed rate, which may be either free of or subject to income-tax; and

  (b) That as respect capital, it carries or will carry, on a winding up or repayment of capital, a preferential right to be repaid the amount of the capital paid-up or deemed to have been paid up, whether or not there is a preferential right to the payment of either or both of the following amounts, namely—

      (i) Any money remaining unpaid, in respect of the amounts specified in clause (a), up to the date of the winding up or repayment of capital; and

      (ii) Any fixed premium or premium on any fixed scale, specified in the memorandum or articles of the company.

- ❏ Thus, during the life time of the company, preference shareholders must be assured of a preferential dividend and on its winding up, preference share must carry a preferential right to be paid ie preference shareholders amount must be paid back before anything is paid to the equity shareholders.

Judicial Interpretations/Case Example	
Held, the effect of section 85 read with section 86 is that all share capital which is not preference share capital is equity share capital and, for the purpose of being brought within the purview of preference share capital, the conditions to be satisfied are that as respects dividends, it carries or will carry a preferential right to be paid a fixed amount or at a fixed rate and as respects capital, it carries or will carry, on a winding up or repayment of capital, a preferential right to be repaid the amount of the capital paid.	*Bihar State Financial Corporation* v *CIT,* 1976, 46 Comp Cas 155 (Pat)

■ Types of Preference Shares

Preference shares may be classified into the categories as follows:

1. *Participating Preference Shares:* These types of shares are entitlement to fixed preferential dividend or dividend at fixed rate and in addition are entitled to participate in the surplus profit/dividend after dividend at certain rate has been paid to equity shareholders.

2. *Non-Participating Preference Shares:* These types of shares are entitled to receive fixed amount of dividend or dividend at fixed rate but do not have

right to participate in surplus profits left after dividend at certain rate has been paid to equity shareholders.

3. *Cumulative Preference Shares:* A cumulative preference shareholder confers a right to claim fixed dividend of the past and the current year and out of future profits. Dividend in this case keeps on accumulating until it is paid.

4. *Non-Cumulative Preference Shares:* In the case of non-cumulative preference shares, if dividend on such shares is not paid in any year on account of losses or inadequate profits or otherwise, then the right to dividend for that year is lost and cannot be carried over in subsequent years.

5. *Redeemable Preference Shares:* As per section 80 (1), a company limited by shares may, if so authorised by its Articles, issue preference shares which are to be redeemed at the option of the company either at a fixed date or after a certain period of time during the life time of the company.

6. *Irredeemable Preference Shares:* Section 80 (5A) on the other hand provides that a company shall not issue preference shares which are either irredeemable or redeemable after the expiry of a period of 20 years from the date of its issue.

7. *Convertible Preference Shares:* These shares may be converted into equity shares as per the terms and conditions of their issue.

8. *Non-Convertible Preference Shares:* These shares have the preferential rights to payment of capital in the event of liquidation of the company or otherwise, but, are not convertible into equity shares.

Judicial Interpretations/Case Example	
Dividends can be paid to cumulative preference shareholders in winding up whilst assets of the company are being distributed, and they rank in priority to other shareholders both as regards dividend and capital.	*Re: Bombay Chlorine Products Ltd.,* 1965, 35 Comp Cas 282 (Bom)
Where cumulative preference shareholders are entitled to share in surplus of assets on winding up, they are not entitled to preference for arrears of dividend unless there is specific provision for priority to such arrears. Where the preference shareholders are entitled to participate in surplus assets on winding up, surplus assets will include undistributed profits on the date of liquidation.	*Dimbula Valley* (*Ceylon*) *Tea Co. Ltd.* v *Laurie,* 1961, 31 Comp Cas 655 (Ch. D)

■ *Voting Rights of Preference Shareholders*

❑ Every member of a company limited by shares and holding any preference share capital therein shall, in respect of such capital, have a right to vote only on resolutions placed before the company which directly affect the rights attached to his preference shares. The meaning of this is that a preference shareholder cannot vote on matters that do not directly affect their interest. Any resolution for winding up the company or for the repayment or reduction of its share capital shall be deemed directly to affect the rights attached to preference shares within the meaning of this clause. [Section 87 (2) (a)].

Judicial Interpretations/Case Example	
Section 87(2) (*a*) provides that every member of a company limited by shares and holding any preference share capital therein shall have a right to vote in respect of such share capital, on every resolutions placed before the company which directly affect the rights attached to his preference shares. It is only if the dividend due on cumulative preference shares remains unpaid for an aggregate period of not less than two years preceding the date of commencement of meeting that a cumulative preference shareholder gets the right to vote on all resolutions.	*Hotel Queen Road (P) Ltd.* v *Hill Crest Reality,* 2006, 68 SCL 197 (Del).
Variation of rights of a class of shareholders can be effected either by consent or by special resolution; it is not necessary that the consent given should be further confirmed by a special resolution. Accordingly, where there are equity shares and preference shares in a company, the rights attached to the preference shares, namely the rate of dividend payable on such shares or the period of redemption can be varied by passing a special resolution at a meeting of the holders of the preference shares.	*Rampuria Cotton Mills Ltd.,* In re (1959) 29 Comp Cas 85 (Cal).

■ *Equity* v *Preference Share*

Particulars	Equity Share	Preference Share
Rate of Dividend	The rate of dividend on equity shares depends upon the availability of profits.	Preference shares are more like debentures than like equity shares, as they are entitled to a fixed rate of dividend like fixed interest payable on debentures.
Order of Payment of Dividend	Dividend on equity shares is paid only after the payment of dividend to preference shares.	Dividend on preference shares is paid in preference to the equity shares.
Payment of Capital	Payment of capital on winding up in the case of equity shares is only after the payment of capital to preference shares.	Preference shares have preference to equity shares with regard to payment of capital.
Voting Right	An equity shareholder can vote on all matters concerning the company.	Preference shareholders have restricted voting rights. They can vote only on matters that concern their interest.

Particulars	Equity Share	Preference Share
Right Share or Bonus Shares	Right Shares or Bonus Shares may be issued to the existing equity shareholders.	Right Shares or Bonus Shares can not be issued to the existing preference share-holders.
Redemption	Equity shares can not be redeemed unless it is case of buy back of shares or reduction of capital.	Redeemable preference shares can be redeemed.

Judicial Interpretations/Case Example	
Where the equity shares are sought to be converted into redeemable preference shares, it was necessary to adopt the process of reduction of capital under section 100 to 104 of the Companies Act, 1956. Case referred *Chowgule and Co (P) Ltd* 1972 *Tax LR* 2163.	*St. James Court Estates Ltd.* 1994, Ch 6

Classification of Share Capital

Share capital may be classified into the categories as follows:

1. *Nominal or Authorised or Registered Capital:* This is the capital with which a company is to be registered originally or the increased authorised share capital as the case may be. The description of the authorised share capital is given in the capital clause of the Memorandum of Association of a company.
2. *Issued Capital:* Issued capital is a part of the authorised capital that is issued for subscription for the time being.
3. *Subscribed Capital:* It is a part of the issued share capital, which has been subscribed by the public in case of a public limited company.
4. *Called up Capital:* It is that portion of subscribed capital, which has been called up on the shares by the company. If the full value of the shares is called up on application then the subscribed capital and called up capital will be the same.
5. *Paid up Capital:* This consists of the amount actually paid up or credited as paid up on the shares subscribed.
6. *Reserved Capital:* It is that part of uncalled capital which company has decided to call on liquidation of the company and is termed as reserved capital.

Issue and Allotment of Shares

■ Meaning of Issue

□ The term 'issue' has not been defined under the Companies Act, 1956. In the case of a public limited company issue of shares/securities means offering them through the prospectus to public.

■ *Only Public Limited Company can Issue Shares*

❑ The document prospectus acts as an invitation to offer and not an offer. It does not create a binding contract between the applicant and the company because it is an invitation to the public to subscribe for shares/securities. Only an allotment of shares/securities to the applicant gives rise to a binding contract and is enforceable by law.

❑ Only a public company having a share capital can issue shares that can be issued either to general public or to persons comprising friends, relatives, associates, etc. A private company under section 3 (1) (*iii*) of the Act is prohibited from inviting public to subscribe for any shares in, or debentures of the company.

■ *Categories of Issue*

Share issue may be classified into the categories as:

Initial Public Offering (IPO): When an unlisted company makes either a fresh issue of securities or an offer for sale of its existing securities or both for the first time to the public, the issue is called as an Initial Public Offer (IPO).

Follow on Public Offering (FPO): When an already listed company makes either a fresh issue of securities to the public or an offer for sale to the public, through an offer document, it is called as a follow on public offering (FPO).

Rights Issue (RI): When a listed company proposes to issue fresh securities to its existing shareholders as on a record date, the issue is called a rights issue (RI). The right shares are normally offered in a particular ratio to the number of securities held prior to the issue.

Further Issue (FI): Where at any time after the expiry of two years the formation of a company or at any time after the expiry of one year from the allotment of shares in that company made for the first time after its formation, whichever is earlier, it is proposed to increase the subscribed capital of the company by allotment of further shares, then, such further shares shall be offered to the persons who, at the date of the offer, are holders of the equity shares of the company, in proportion, as nearly as circumstances admit, to the capital paid-up on those shares at that date. This is a faster way for a company to raise equity capital [Section 81]

Qualified Institutions Placement (QIP): Qualified institutions placement (QIP) is a private placement of equity shares or securities convertible in to equity shares by a listed company to qualified institutions buyers.

Eligibility Norms for Companies Issuing Securities

Conditions for Issue of Securities

❑ The companies issuing securities offered through an offer document, shall, satisfy the following at the time of filing draft offer document with SEBI

(Board), and also at the time of filing the final offer document with the Registrar of Companies/Designated Stock Exchange.

Filing of Offer Document: No issuer company shall make any public issue of securities, unless a draft prospectus has been filed with the Board through a Merchant Banker, at least 30 days prior to the filing of the prospectus with the Registrar of Companies (ROC).

Fast Track Issues: Nothing contained in above clauses shall apply to a public issue of securities by a listed issuer company or a rights issue of securities by a listed issuer company, where the aggregate value of such securities, including premium, if any, exceeds Rs. 50 lacs, if the following conditions are satisfied:

(a) The shares of the company have been listed on any stock exchange having nationwide terminals for a period of at least three years immediately preceding the reference date;

(b) The "average market capitalisation of public shareholding" of the company is at least Rs. 10,000 crores for a period of one year up to the end of the quarter preceding the month in which the proposed issue is approved by the Board of Directors/shareholders of the issuer;

(c) The annualized trading turnover of the shares of the company during six calendar months immediately preceding the month of the reference date has been at least two per cent of the weighted average number of shares listed during the said six months period;

(d) The company has redressed at least 95% of the total shareholder/investor grievances or complaints received till the end of the quarter immediately preceding the month of the reference date;

(e) The company has complied with the listing agreement for a period of at least three years immediately preceding the reference date;

(f) The impact of auditors' qualifications, if any, on the audited accounts of the company in respect of the financial years for which such accounts are disclosed in the offer document does not exceed 5% of the net profit/loss after tax of the company for the respective years.

(g) No prosecution proceedings or show cause notices issued by the Board are pending against the company or its promoters or whole time directors as on the reference date; and

(h) The entire shareholding of the promoter group is held in dematerialised form as on the reference date.

❑ A listed issuer company satisfying all the requirements specified above and filing a red herring prospectus (in case of a book built issue) or prospectus (in case of a fixed price issue) with ROC or letter of offer with designated stock exchange, as the case may be, shall simultaneously with such filing or as soon thereafter as reasonably practicable, but in any case not later than the opening of the issue, file a copy thereof with the Board.

Companies Barred not to Issue Security: No company shall make an issue of securities if the company has been prohibited from accessing the capital market under any order or direction passed by the Board.

Application for Listing: No company shall make any public issue of securities unless it has made an application for listing of those securities in the stock exchange (s).

Issue of Securities in Dematerialised Form: No company shall make public or rights issue or an offer for sale of securities, unless:

(*a*) The company enters into an agreement with a depository for dematerialisation of securities already issued or proposed to be issued to the public or existing shareholders; and

(*b*) The company gives an option to subscribers/shareholders/investors to receive the security certificates or hold securities in dematerialised form with a depository.

> ***Explanation:*** *A 'depository' shall mean a depository registered with the Board under the Securities and Exchange Board of India (Depositories and Participants) Regulations,* 1996.

Initial Public Offerings by Unlisted Companies: An unlisted company may make an initial public offering (IPO) of equity shares or any other security which may be converted into or exchanged with equity shares at a later date, only if it meets all the following conditions:

(*a*) The company has net tangible assets of at least Rs. 3 crore in each of the preceding 3 full years (of 12 months each), of which not more than 50% is held in monetary assets: provided that if more than 50% of the net tangible assets are held in monetary assets, the company has made firm commitments to deploy such excess monetary assets in its business/project;

(*b*) The company has a track record of distributable profits in terms of section 205 of the Companies Act, 1956, for at least three (3) out of immediately preceding five (5) years: provided further that extraordinary items shall not be considered for calculating distributable profits in terms of section 205 of Companies Act, 1956;

(*c*) The company has a net worth of at least Rs. 1 crore in each of the preceding 3 full years (of 12 months each);

(*d*) In case the company has changed its name within the last one year, at least 50% of the revenue for the preceding 1 full year is earned by the company from the activity suggested by the new name; and

(*e*) The aggregate of the proposed issue and all previous issues made in the same financial year in terms of size (*i.e.,* offer through offer document + firm allotment + promoters' contribution through the offer document), does not exceed five (5) times its pre-issue net worth as per the audited balance sheet of the last financial year.

- ❑ An unlisted company not complying with any of the conditions specified above may make an initial public offering (IPO) of equity shares or any other security which may be converted into or exchanged with equity shares at a later date, only if it meets both the conditions (a) and (b) given below:

  - (*a*) (*i*) The issue is made through the book-building process, with at least 50% of net offer to public being allotted to the Qualified Institutional Buyers (QIBs), failing which the full subscription monies shall be refunded.

    or

  - (*ii*) The "project" has at least 15% participation by Financial Institutions/Scheduled Commercial Banks, of which at least 10% comes from the appraiser (s). In addition to this, at least 10% of the issue size shall be allotted to QIBs, failing which the full subscription monies shall be refunded.

    and

  - (*b*) (*i*) The minimum post-issue face value capital of the company shall be Rs. 10 crores.

    or

  - (*ii*) There shall be a compulsory market-making for at least 2 years from the date of listing of the shares, subject to the following:

    - (*a*) Market makers undertake to offer buy and sell quotes for a minimum depth of 300 shares;

    - (*b*) Market makers undertake to ensure that the bid-ask spread (difference between quotations for sale and purchase) for their quotes shall not at any time exceed 10%;

    - (*c*) The inventory of the market makers on each of such stock exchanges, as on the date of allotment of securities, shall be at least 5% of the proposed issue of the company.

- ❑ An unlisted public company shall not make an allotment pursuant to a public issue or offer for sale of equity shares or any security convertible into equity shares unless, in addition to satisfying the conditions mentioned above as the case may be, the prospective allottees are not less than one thousand (1000) in number.

Public Issue by Listed Companies: A listed company shall be eligible to make a public issue of equity shares or any other security which may be converted into or exchanged with equity shares at a later date: provided that the aggregate of the proposed issue and all previous issues made in the same financial year in terms of size (*i.e.*, offer through offer document + firm allotment + promoters' contribution through the offer document), issue size does not exceed 5 times its pre-issue net worth as per the audited balance sheet of the last financial year: provided further that in case there is a change in the name of the issuer company within the last 1 year (reckoned from the date of filing of the offer document), the revenue accounted for by the activity suggested by the new name is not less than 50% of its total revenue in the preceding 1 full-year period.

Exemption from Eligibility Norms: The above provisions of shall not be applicable in case of,—

- (*i*) A banking company including a Local Area Bank set up under clause (c) of section 5 of the Banking Regulation Act, 1949, and which has received license from the Reserve Bank of India;
- (*ii*) A corresponding new bank set up under the Banking Companies (Acquisition and Transfer of Undertakings) Act, 1970, Banking Companies (Acquisition and Transfer of Undertakings) Act, 1980, State Bank of India Act, 1955 and State Bank of India (Subsidiary Banks) Act, 1959 (referred to as "public sector banks");
- (*iii*) An infrastructure company:
    - (*a*) Whose project has been appraised by a Public Financial Institution (PFI) or Infrastructure Development Finance Corporation (IDFC) or Infrastructure Leasing and Financing Services Ltd. (IL&FS) or a bank which was earlier a PFI; and
    - (*b*) Not less than 5% of the project cost is financed by any of the institutions referred to in sub-clause (a), jointly or severally, irrespective of whether they appraise the project or not, by way of loan or subscription to equity or a combination of both; or
- (*iv*) Rights issue by a listed company.

IPO Grading: No unlisted company shall make an IPO of equity shares or any other security which may be converted into or exchanged with equity shares at a later date, unless the following conditions are satisfied as on the date of filing of Prospectus (in case of fixed price issue) or Red Herring Prospectus (in case of book built issue) with ROC:

- (*i*) The unlisted company has obtained grading for the IPO from at least one credit rating agency;
- (*ii*) Disclosures of all the grades obtained, along with the rationale/description furnished by the credit rating agency (ies) for each of the grades obtained, have been made in the Prospectus (in case of fixed price issue) or Red Herring Prospectus (in case of book built issue); and
- (*iii*) The expenses incurred for grading IPO have been borne by the unlisted company obtaining grading for IPO.

Outstanding Warrants or Financial Instruments: No unlisted company shall make a public issue of equity share or any security convertible at a later date into equity share, if there are any outstanding financial instruments or any other right which would entitle the existing promoters or shareholders any option to receive equity share capital after the initial public offering.

Partly Paid-Up Shares: No company shall make a public or rights issue of equity share or any security convertible at a later date into equity share, unless all the existing partly paid-up shares have been fully paid or forfeited in a manner specified.

Means of Finance: No company shall make a public or rights issue of securities unless firm arrangements of finance through verifiable means towards 75% of the stated means of finance, excluding the amount to be raised through proposed Public/Rights issue, have been made.

Post-Issue Guidelines

The post-issue obligations shall be as follows:

Post-Issue Monitoring Reports: Irrespective of the level of subscription, the post-issue Lead Merchant Banker shall ensure the submission of the post-issue monitoring reports as per formats specified in Schedule XVI. These reports shall be submitted within 3 working days from the due dates.

The due date for submitting post-issue monitoring report in case of public issues by listed and unlisted companies may be as follows:

(a) **3-Day Monitoring Report in Case of Issue through Book-Building Route, for Book-Built Portion:** The due date of the report shall be third day from the date of allocation in the book-built portion or one day prior to the opening of the fixed price portion whichever is earlier.

(b) **3-Day Monitoring Report in other Cases, Including Fixed Price Portion of Book-Built Issue:** The due date for the report shall be the third day from the date of closure of the issue.

(c) **Final Post-Issue Monitoring Report for all Issues:** The due date for this report shall be the third day from the date of listing or 78 days from the date of closure of the subscription of the issue, whichever is earlier.

The due dates for submitting post-issue monitoring report in case of rights issues may be as follows:

(a) **3-Day Post-Issue Monitoring Report:** The due date for this report shall be the 3rd day from the date of closure of subscription of the issue.

(b) **50-Day Post-Issue Monitoring Report:** The due date for this report shall be the 50th day from the date of closure of subscription of the issue.

Due Diligence Certificate to be Submitted with Final Post Issue Monitoring Report: The post issue lead merchant banker shall file a due diligence certificate in the format given in Schedule XVIA along with the final post-issue monitoring report.

Redressal of Investor Grievances: The post-issue lead merchant banker shall actively associate himself with post-issue activities namely; allotment, refund, dispatch and giving instructions to self certified syndicate banks and shall regularly monitor redressal of investor grievances arising therefrom.

Co-Ordination with Intermediaries: (*i*) The post-issue lead merchant banker shall maintain close co-ordination with the Registrars to the issue and arrange to depute its officers to the offices of various intermediaries at regular intervals after the closure of the issue to monitor the flow of applications from collecting bank branches, self certified syndicate banks, processing of the applications including application form for applications supported by blocked amount and other matters till the basis of allotment is finalised, dispatch security certificates and refund orders completed and securities listed. (*ii*) Any act of omission or commission on the part of any of the intermediaries noticed during such visits shall be duly reported to the Board.

Underwriters: (*a*) (*i*) If the issue is proposed to be closed at the earliest closing date, the lead merchant banker shall satisfy himself that the issue is fully subscribed before announcing closure of the issue. (*ii*) In case there is no definite information about subscription figures, the issue shall be kept open for the required number of days to take care of the underwriters' interests and to avoid any dispute, at a later date, by the underwriters in respect of their liability. (*b*) In case there is a devolvement on underwriters, the lead merchant banker shall ensure that the underwriters honour their commitments within 60 days from the date of closure of the issue. (*c*) In case of undersubscribed issues, the lead merchant banker shall furnish information in respect of underwriters who have failed to meet their underwriting devolvements to the Board in the format specified at Schedule XVII.

Bankers to an Issue: The post-issue lead merchant banker shall ensure that moneys received pursuant to the issue and kept in a separate bank (*i.e.*, bankers to an Issue), as per the provisions of section 73 (3) of the Companies Act, 1956, is released by the said bank only after the listing permission under the said section has been obtained from all the stock exchanges where the securities were proposed to be listed as per the offer document.

Post-Issue Advertisements: Post-issue lead merchant banker shall ensure that in all issues, advertisement giving details relating to oversubscription, basis of allotment, number, value and percentage of all applications including applications supported by blocked amount, number, value and percentage of successful allottees for all applications including applications supported by blocked amount, date of completion of dispatch of refund orders/instructions to self certified syndicate banks by the Registrar, date of dispatch of certificates and date of filing of listing application is released within 10 days from the date of completion of the various activities at least in an English national daily with wide circulation, one Hindi national paper and a regional language daily circulated at the place where registered office of the issuer company is situated. Post-issue lead merchant banker shall ensure that issuer company/advisors/brokers or any other agencies connected with the issue do not publish any advertisement stating that the issue has been oversubscribed or indicating investors' response to the issue, during the period when the public issue is still open for subscription by the public. Advertisement stating that "the subscription to the issue has been closed" may be issued after the actual closure of the issue.

Basis of Allotment: In a public issue of securities, the executive director/managing director of the designated stock exchange along with the post issue lead merchant banker and the Registrars to the issue shall be responsible to ensure that the basis of allotment is finalised in a fair and proper manner in accordance with the following guidelines:

Proportionate Allotment Procedure: Allotment shall be on proportionate basis within the specified categories, rounded off to the nearest integer subject to a minimum allotment being equal to the minimum application size as fixed and disclosed by the issuer.

Reservation for Retail Individual Investor: The above proportionate allotments of securities in an issue that is oversubscribed shall be subject to the reservation for retail individual investors as described below:

(*a*) A minimum 50% of the net offer of securities to the public shall initially be made available for allotment to retail individual investors, as the case may be.

(*b*) The balance net offer of securities to the public shall be made available for allotment to:

    (*i*) Individual applicants other than retail individual investors, and

    (*ii*) Other investors including corporate bodies/institutions irrespective of the number of shares, debentures, etc. applied for.

(*c*) The unsubscribed portion of the net offer to any one of the categories specified in (a) or (b) shall/may be made available for allotment to applicants in the other category, if so required.

> *Explanation:* It is clarified that the words "a minimum of 50% of the public offer" used in sub-clause (*a*) above means that if the category of retail individual investors was to be entitled to get 70% of the public offer in accordance with proportionate formula, the category should get 70%. If the category is entitled to get only 30% of the public offer in accordance with the proportionate allotment formula, there should be a reservation of a minimum of 50% of the net public offer.

❑ The drawal of lots (where required) to finalise the basis of allotment, shall be done in the presence of a public representative on the governing board of the designated stock exchange.

❑ The basis of allotment shall be signed as correct by the executive director managing director of the designated stock exchange and the public representative (where applicable) in addition to the lead merchant banker responsible for post issue activities and the Registrar to the Issue. The designated stock exchange shall invite the public representative on a rotation basis from out of the various public representatives on its governing board.

Other Responsibilities

- The lead merchant banker shall ensure that the dispatch of share certificates refund orders and demat credit is completed and the allotment and listing documents submitted to the stock exchanges within 2 working days of the date of allotment.
- The post-issue lead manager shall ensure that all steps for completion of the necessary formalities for listing and commencement of trading at all stock exchanges where the securities are to be listed are taken within 7 working days of finalisation of basis of allotment.
- Lead merchant banker shall ensure payment of interest to the applicants for delayed dispatch of allotment letters, refund orders, etc. as prescribed in the offer document.
- The post-issue lead merchant banker shall ensure that the dispatch of refund orders/allotment letters/share certificates is done by way of registered post certificate of posting as may be applicable.
- In case of all issues, advertisement giving details relating to oversubscription, basis of allotment, number, value and percentage of all applications received including applications supported by blocked amount, number, value and percentage of successful allottees for all applications including applications supported by blocked amount, date of completion of dispatch of refund orders/instructions to self certified syndicate banks by the Registrar, date of dispatch of certificates and date of filing of listing application.
- Such advertisement shall be released within 10 days from the date of completion of the various activities.
- The post-issue lead merchant banker shall continue to be responsible for post-issue activities till the subscribers have received the shares/debenture certificates or refund of application moneys and the listing agreement is entered into by the issuer company with the stock exchange and listing trading permission is obtained.

Allotment of Shares

- The term 'Allotment' has not been defined under the Companies Act.
- Allotment is construed to mean 'the act of allotting'. In simple words, 'Allotment' is the acceptance by the company of the offer to take shares. Offers for shares are made on application forms supplied by the company. When an application is accepted, it amounts to an allotment.

❏ When a company issues shares through the document of prospectus, the application for shares does not create a binding contract between the applicant and the company because it is offer in response to an invitation to the public by the company to subscribe for shares/securities. Only an acceptance by the company to the proposed offer gives rise to a binding contract of allotment that is enforceable by law.

Judicial Interpretations/Case Example	
An allotment of shares is an act of the company by which the applicant for shares becomes the holder of unappropriated shares; shares standing in the name of one person cannot be allotted to another person by the company even with the former's consent, though such shares may be transferred by the person in whose name they stand.	*Spitzel* v *Chinese Corporation,* 1899, 80 LT 347.
Where the allotment or agreement involves any future commitment, it will be void.	*Mohori Bibi* v *Dharmodas Ghose* 1903, 30 IA 11.
If the notice of allotment is sent by post, the acceptance is deemed to be notified when the notice is posted, even though it never reaches the applicant provided the offer is one which can be accepted by a letter sent through post. Persons to whom no notice of allotment is served cannot be put on the list of contributories at the time of liquidation.	*Changa Mal* v *Provincial Bank Ltd.* 1914, ILR 36 All 412: 25 IC 210.
The company cannot allot shares on applications not accompanied by application money.	*Mutual Bank of India Ltd.* v *Sohan Singh AIR,* 1936, Lahore 790 (DB)
It may be noted that allotment of fully paid-up shares to minors is not void.	*Dewan Singh* v *Minerva Films Ltd.,* AIR 1959, Punj 106.
Allotment means the appropriation out of the previously unappropriated capital of the company of a certain number of shares to a person.	*Sri Gopal Jalan and Company* v *Calcutta Stock Exchange Association Ltd.,* AIR 1964 SC 250.
A contract to purchase shares or debentures is concluded by allotment of shares.	*Larsen and Toubro Ltd.* v *Haresh Jagtiani.,* AIR 1991, SC 1420.

General Principles of Allotment

Proper Authority: The allotment should be made by proper authority. Board of directors or committee of board authorised to allot shares, is the proper authority to allot shares. An allotment by an authority not authorised is not valid.

Judicial Interpretations/Case Example	
Allotment of shares by an irregularly constituted board of directors shall *prima facie* be invalid.	*Changamal* v *Provincial Bank,* 1914, ILR 36, 412, Allahabad.

No Allotment without Written Application: No valid allotment can be made without written application for allotment. It cannot be done on oral request.

Judicial Interpretations/Case Example	
Application is to be made only on the form supplied by the company.	*H.H.Manabendra Shah* v *Official Liquidator,* 1977, 47 Comp. Cas. 356.

Allotment must be Communicated: Allotment must be communicated to the applicant like in the case of any other valid contract.

Judicial Interpretations/Case Example	
G applied for shares and remitted application money. He received no intimation/notice that shares have been allotted to him nor was made any demand on him for remittance of the money on allotment. However, it was recorded in the minutes book that it was resolved to allot shares to G and his name was already entered in member register. But, as the company was ordered to be wound up, the question was whether G's name had been properly put in the list of contributories? *Held,* no contract of allotment exists between him and the company. It was not his duty to search the register and his name was therefore, to be deleted from the list of contributories.	*Re: Universal Banking Corporation,* 1867, LR 3 CH APP 40 (CA).
Held, a person cannot be treated as shareholder unless a notice of allotment has been sent to him.	*Changamal* v *Provincial Bank,* 1914, ILR 36, 412, Allahabad.

Within Reasonable Period: Allotment must be made within a reasonable period of time. What is reasonable time depends upon facts of the case.

Judicial Interpretations/Case Example	
The interval of about six months between application and allotment has been held to be not reasonable.	*Ramsgate Victoria Hotel Co* v *Montefiore,* 1866, LRI EX, 109.
On the expiry of reasonable period of time, Section 6 of the Contract Act becomes applicable and the application must be deemed to have been revoked. *Held,* the allotment of shares made almost after one year after the date of application was ineffective.	*Karachi Oil Products Ltd* v *Kumarshree Narendrasingh ji,* 1948, 18 Comp. Cas. 215, Bombay

Absolute and Unconditional: The allotment must be absolute and unconditional and no fresh conditions be put while making allotment *i.e.* the allotment must be made on the same terms as were stated in application.

Judicial Interpretations/Case Example	
No fresh terms from the company's side should be attached to the acceptance of an offer to purchase shares; otherwise it would be considered a new offer by the company and not to be effective unless it is accepted by the applicant.	*Gackson* v *Turquand,* 1869, LR 4 HL 305.
The applicant applied for shares on the condition that he should be appointed as branch manager of the company. Shares were allotted to him but he was not appointed the branch manager. *Held*, he is not bound by the allotment.	*Ramanbhai* v *Ghasi Ram,* 1918, L.R. 595, Bombay.

Statutory Conditions of Allotment

Registration of Prospectus: No prospectus shall be issued by or on behalf of a company or in relation to an intended company unless, on or before the date of its publication, there has been delivered to the Registrar for registration a copy thereof signed by every person who is named therein as a director or proposed director of the company or by his agent authorised in writing. If a prospectus is issued without a copy thereof being delivered under this section to the Registrar or without the copy so delivered having endorsed thereon or attached thereto the required consent or documents, the company, and every person who is knowingly a party to the issue of the prospectus, shall be punishable with fine which may extend to fifty thousand rupees. [Section 60 (1) (5)]

Amount Payable on Application: The amount payable on application on each share shall not be less than five per cent of the nominal amount of the share. [Section 69 (3)]

Moneys Received from Aapplicants shall be kept Deposited in a Scheduled Bank: All moneys received from applicants for shares shall be deposited and kept deposited in a Scheduled Bank—until the certificate to commence business is obtained under Section 149, or where such certificate has already been obtained, until the entire amount payable on applications for shares in respect of the minimum subscription has been received by the company, and where such amount has not been received by the company within the time on the expiry of which the moneys received from the applicants for shares are required to be repaid without interest, all moneys received from applicants for shares shall be returned in accordance with the provisions of that sub-section. [Section 69 (4)]

Prohibition of Allotment Unless Minimum Subscription Received: No allotment shall be made of any share capital of a company offered to the public for subscription, unless the amount stated in the prospectus as the minimum amount which, in the opinion of the Board of Directors, must be raised by the issue of share capital, has been subscribed, and the sum payable on application for the amount so stated has been paid to and received by the company, whether in cash or by a cheque or other instrument which has been paid. [Section 69 (1)] If the minimum subscription has not been received on the expiry of one hundred and twenty days after the first issue of the prospectus, all moneys received from applicants for shares shall be forthwith repaid to them without interest; and if any such money is not so repaid within one hundred and thirty days after the issue of the prospectus, the directors of the company shall be jointly and severally liable to repay that money with interest at the rate of six per cent per annum from the expiry of the one hundred and thirtieth day: provided that a director shall not be so liable if he proves that the default in the repayment of the money was not due to any misconduct or negligence on his part [Section 69 (5)]. However, as per the SEBI guidelines, a company must receive a minimum of 90% subscription against the entire issue before making an allotment within 60 days of closure of issue, the amount of subscription received is required to be refunded to the applicants. If the delay is beyond 8 days, the company shall pay interest prescribed under Section 73 of the Companies Act, which is currently 4% to 15% p. a.

Prohibition of Allotment in Certain Cases Unless Statement in Lieu of Prospectus Delivered to Registrar: A company having a share capital, which does not issue a prospectus on or with reference to its formation, or which has issued such a prospectus but has not proceeded to allot any of the shares offered to the public for subscription, shall not allot any of its shares or debentures unless at least three days before the first allotment of either shares or debentures, there has been delivered to the Registrar for registration a statement in lieu of prospectus signed by every person who is named therein as a director or proposed director of the company or by his agent authorised in writing, in the form and containing the particulars set out in Part I of Schedule III and, in the cases mentioned in Part II of that Schedule, setting out the reports specified therein, and the said Parts I and II shall have effect subject to the provisions contained in Part III of that Schedule. This section shall not apply to a private company. [Section 70]

Opening of Subscription: No allotment shall be made of any shares in or debentures of a company in pursuance of a prospectus issued generally, and no proceedings shall be taken on applications made in pursuance of a prospectus so issued, until the beginning of the fifth day after that on which the prospectus is first so issued or such later time, if any, as may be specified in the prospectus. [Section 72]

Closing of Subscription: Even though the Act is silent on this matter, SEBI guidelines issued in June 1992 provide that the subscription list for public issue must remain open for at-least three working days and for not more than ten days (60 days in the case of right issue)

Permission of Recognised Stock Exchanges: Every company, intending to offer shares or debentures to the public for subscription by the issue of a prospectus shall, before such issue, make an application to one or more recognised stock exchanges for permission for the shares or debentures intending to be so offered to be dealt with in the stock exchange or each such stock exchange. Where a prospectus, whether issued generally or not, states that an application has been made for permission for the shares or debentures offered thereby to be dealt in one or more recognized stock exchanges, such prospectus shall state the name of the stock exchange or, as the case may be, each such stock exchange, and any allotment made on an application in pursuance of such prospectus shall, whenever made, be void, if the permission has not been granted by the stock exchange or each such stock exchange, as the case may be before the expiry of ten weeks from the date of the closing of the subscription lists: provided that where an appeal against the decision of any recognised stock exchange refusing permission for the shares or debentures to be dealt in on that stock exchange has been preferred under Section 22 of the Securities Contracts (Regulation) Act, 1956 (42 of 1956), such allotment shall not be void until the dismissal of the appeal. [Section 73 (1) (1A)]

Cancellation of Allotment

❑ Allotment gives rise to a binding and enforceable contract between the allottee and the company. When an allotment is made on a binding contract, it cannot be cancelled by the company.

Judicial Interpretations/Case Example	
Cancellation of allotment would be reducing the capital of the company.	*Sorabji Jamsetji* v *Ishwardas Jugjiwandas,* 1896, ILR 20 Bom 654.
Alteration of the Articles of Association between an application and their allotment was held to invalidate the allotment.	*English, etc Rolling Stock Co.,* 1886, 20 Bom 654.

Return of Allotment

❑ Whenever a company having a share capital makes any allotment of its shares, the company shall, within thirty days thereafter:

(*a*) File with the Registrar a return of the allotments, stating the number and nominal amount of the shares comprised in the allotment, the names, addresses and occupations of the allottees, and the amount, if any, paid or due and payable on each share: provided that the company shall not show in such return any shares as having been allotted for cash if cash has not actually been received in respect of such allotment;] [Section 75 (1) (a)]

(*b*) In the case of shares (not being bonus shares) allotted as fully or partly paid up otherwise than in cash, produce for the i .spection and examination of the Registrar a contract in writing constituting the title of the allottee to the allotment together with any contract of sale, or a contract for services or other consideration in respect of which that allotment was made, such contracts being duly stamped, and file with the Registrar copies verified in the prescribed manner of all such contracts and a return stating the number and nominal amount of shares so allotted, the extent to which they are to be treated as paid up, and the consideration for which they have been allotted; and [Section 75 (1) (b)]

(c) File with the Registrar—

(i) In the case of bonus shares, a return stating the number and nominal amount of such shares comprised in the allotment and the names, addresses and occupations of the allottees and a copy of the resolution authorising the issue of such shares;

(ii) In the case of issue of shares at a discount, a copy of the resolution passed by the company authorising such issue together with a copy of the order of the Tribunal sanctioning the issue and where the maximum rate of discount exceeds ten per cent, a copy of the order of the Central Government permitting the issue at the higher percentage. [Section 75(c)]

❑ Where a contract such as is mentioned above is not reduced to writing, the company shall, within thirty days after the allotment, file with the Registrar the prescribed particulars of the contract stamped with the same stamp duty as would have been payable if the contract had been reduced to writing; and those particulars shall be deemed to be an instrument within the meaning of the Indian Stamp Act, 1899, and the Registrar may, as a condition of filing the particulars, require that the duty payable thereon be adjudicated under Section 31 of that Act. [Section 75 (2)]

❑ If the Registrar is satisfied that in the circumstances of any particular case of the period of thirty days specified above for compliance with the requirements of this section is or was inadequate, he may, on application made in that behalf by the company, whether before or after the expiry of the said period, extend that period as he thinks fit; and if he does so, the provisions of Sections 75 (1) and (2) shall have effect in that particular case as if for the said period of thirty days, the extended period allowed by the Registrar were substituted. [Section 75 (3)]

❑ If default is made in complying with this section, every officer of the company who is in default shall be punishable with fine which may extend to five thousand rupees for every day during which the default continues: provided that in case of contravention of the proviso to clause 75 (1) (a), every such officer, and every promoter of the company who is guilty of the contravention shall be punishable with fine which may extend to fifty thousand rupees. [Section 75 (4)]

❑ Nothing in this section shall apply to the issue and allotment by a company of shares which under the provisions of its articles were forfeited for non payment of calls. [Section 75 (5)]

Effect of Irregular Allotment

❑ An allotment made by a company to an applicant in contravention of the provisions of section 69 (about minimum subscription) or 70 (about registration of a statement in lieu of prospectus) shall be voidable at the instance of the applicant:

(*a*) Within two months after the holding of the statutory meeting of the company, and not later, or

(*b*) In any case where the company is not required to hold a statutory meeting or where the allotment is made after the holding of the statutory meeting, within two months after the date of the allotment, and not later. [Section 71 (1)]

❑ The allotment shall be voidable as aforesaid, notwithstanding that the company is in course of being wound up. [Section 71 (2)]

❑ If any director of a company knowingly contravenes, or willfully authorises or permits the contravention of, any of the provisions of Section 69 or 70 with respect to allotment, he shall be liable to compensate the company and the allottee respectively for any loss, damages or costs which the company or the allottee may have sustained or incurred thereby: provided that proceedings to recover any such loss, damages or costs shall not be commenced after the expiration of two years from the date of the allotment. [Section 71 (3)]

Effect and Liability

Sl. No.	Statutory Conditions	Effect	Liability of Company/ Directors
1.	Registration of prospectus [Sec. 60 (1)]	Valid allotment	Rs 50000* fine
2.	Less than 5% of application money [Sec .69(3)]	Voidable allotment	Damages ** and Rs 5000 as fine*.
3.	Minimum subscription-90% of entire issue [Sec .69(1)]	Voidable	(*i*) Refund after 60 days (*ii*) If not refunded within next 10 days, pay interest @ 15% p. a., and (*iii*)Pay damages.

Sl. No.	Statutory Conditions	Effect	Liability of Company/ Directors
4.	Application money not kept deposited in scheduled bank [Sec. 69(4)]	Voidable	Rs 50,000 fine* and damages**.
5.	Statement in lieu of prospectus not delivered to the ROC within 3 days before the allotment [Sec. 70]	Voidable	Fine* of Rs 10,000 and damages**
6.	Time limit as to opening of subscription not observed [Sec. (72)]	Valid allotment	Fine* of Rs 50,000
7.	Condition as to listing not observed [73 (1)]. (Company making public issue for shares and debentures, an application for listing to one or more stock exchange including the NSE should be made.)	Void allotment	If permission is not granted before the expiry of ten weeks from the date of the closing of the subscription lists, entire money has to be refunded, if not refunded within 8 days 15% interest is payable.

*   Fine is paid by the company and every responsible officer.

**   Damages are paid by those directors who are willfully responsible for the contravention.

Issue of Shares at Premium

❑   When share/security of the face value of rupees ten each are issued at a price, which is greater than rupees ten per share, it will be said that the issue is at a premium.

❑   Company issues shares/securities at premium when it is a well established company and has a reputation and goodwill in the market, and it has a feeling that its shares/securities will be bought in adequate numbers.

❑   Where a company issues securities at a premium, whether for cash or otherwise, a sum equal to the aggregate amount or value of the premiums on those securities shall be transferred to an account, to be called 'the securities premium account', and the provisions of this Act relating to the reduction of the securities capital of a company shall, except as provided in this section, apply as if the securities premium account were paid-up securities capital of the company. [Section 78 (1)]

❑   Section 78 (2) of the Companies Act, deals with application of premium received on issue of shares. The premium credited in securities premium account may be applied by the company:

(*a*) In paying up un-issued securities of the company to be issued to members of the company as fully paid bonus securities;

(*b*) In writing off the preliminary expenses of the company;

(*c*) In writing off the expenses of, or the commission paid or discount allowed on, any issue of securities or debentures of the company; or

(*d*) In providing for the premium payable on the redemption of any redeemable preference securities or of any debentures of the company.

Judicial Interpretations/Case Example	
A company issuing shares at premium is bound to transfer to the share (securities) premium account a sum equal to the aggregate amount or value of the premiums.	*Henry Head and Co v Ropner Holdings Ltd.,* 1951, 2 All ER 994

Company Cannot Write off Loses against Securities Premium Account: Securities premium account though treated as paid-capital of company for a limited purpose, cannot be treated as reserve fund. Therefore, no company can be allowed to write off or adjust loss against securities premium account.

Judicial Interpretations/Case Example	
Where articles of association of petitioner company did not specifically permit utilization of securities premium account for purposes other than those mentioned in Section 78, securities premium account could not be utilized for setting off of loss incurred due to investment in another company and therefore, petition seeking approval of resolution to that effect was to be dismissed.	*Re: Hyderabad Industries Ltd.,* 2004, 53 SCL 376 (AP)

Issue of Shares at a Discount

❑ Under Section 79 (2) of the Companies Act, a company may issue shares at a discount, if the following conditions are fulfilled, namely:

(*a*) The shares must be of a class already issued by the company;

(*b*) The issue of the shares at a discount is authorised by a resolution passed by the company in general meeting and sanctioned by the Central Government;

(*c*) The resolution specifies the maximum rate of discount at which the shares are to be issued: Provided that no such resolution shall be sanctioned by the Central Government if the maximum rate of discount specified in the resolution exceeds ten per cent unless the Central Government is of opinion that a higher percentage of discount may be allowed in the special circumstances of the case;

(*d*) Not less than one year has at the date of the issue elapsed since the date on which the company was entitled to commence business; and

(e) The shares to be issued at a discount are issued within two months after the date on which the issue is sanctioned by the Central Government or within such extended time as the Central Government may allow.

(f) Where a company has passed a resolution authorising the issue of shares at a discount, it may apply to the Central Government for an order sanctioning the issue; and on any such application, the Central Government, if having regard to all the circumstances of the case, it thinks proper so to do, may make an order sanctioning the issue on such terms and conditions as it thinks fit: provided that in the case of revival and rehabilitation of sick industrial companies under Chapter VIA, the provisions of this section shall have effect as if for the words "Central Government", the word "Tribunal" had been substituted. [Section 79 (3)]

(g) Every prospectus relating to the issue of the shares shall contain particulars of the discount allowed on the issue of the shares or of so much of that discount as has not been written off at the date of the issue of the prospectus. If default is made in complying with this provision, the company and every officer of the company who is in default shall be punishable with fine which may extend to five hundred rupees. [Section 79 (4)]

Judicial Interpretations/Case Example	
Reissue of forfeited shares at a discount (as fully paid) attracts the section.	*Biochemical and Synthetic Products Ltd.* v *Registrar of Companies,* 1962, AIR 1962, AP 459.

Buy-Back of Shares

❑ Buy back of shares was allowed by inserting new Sections 77A, 77AA and 77B in the Companies (Amendment) Act, 1999. Section 77 has provisions about restrictions on purchase by company, or loans by company for purchase, of its own or its holding company's shares; Section 77A empowers a company to purchase its own shares or other specified securities in certain cases from specified sources; Section 77AA is about transfer of certain sums to capital redemption reserve account; and Section 77B provides prohibition for buy-back in certain circumstances. After the amendment, a company may purchase its own shares or other specified securities (including employees' stock option) referred to as 'buyback' in the manner provided in Sections 77A, 77AA and 77B.

■ Sources of Buy-back

❑ As per provisions of Section 77A of the Act, the buy-back of shares and securities can be made out of:

(*i*) Its free reserves; or

(*ii*) The securities premium account; or

(*iii*) The proceeds of any shares or other specified securities: provided that no buy-back of any kind of shares or other specified securities shall be made out of the proceeds of an earlier issue of the same kind of shares or same kind of other specified securities.

■ Conditions for Buy-back

❑ As per provisions of Section 77A (2) of the Companies Act, no company shall purchase its own shares or other specified securities unless:

(*a*) The buy-back is authorised by its articles;

(*b*) A special resolution has been passed in general meeting of the company authorising the buy-back: provided that nothing contained in this clause shall apply in any case where:

(*i*) The buy-back is or less than ten per cent of the total paid up equity capital and free reserves of the company; and

(*ii*) Such buy-back has been authorised by the Board by means of a resolution passed at its meeting: provided further that no offer of buy-back shall be made within a period of three hundred and sixty-five days reckoned from the date of the preceding offer of buy-back, if any. The expression "offer of buy-back" means the offer of such buy-back made in pursuance of the resolution of the Board referred to above.

(*c*) The buy-back is or less than twenty-five per cent of the total paid-up capital and free reserves of the company: provided that the buy-back of equity shares in any financial year shall not exceed twenty-five per cent of its total paid-up equity capital in that financial year;

(*d*) The ratio of the debt owed by the company is not more than twice the capital and its free reserves after such buy-back: Provided that the Central Government may prescribe a higher ratio of the debt than that specified under this clause for a class or classes of companies.

(*e*) All the shares or other specified securities for buy-back are fully paid-up;

(*f*) The buy-back of the shares or other specified securities listed on any recognised stock exchange is in accordance with the regulations made by the Securities and Exchange Board of India in this behalf;

(*g*) The buy-back in respect of shares or other specified securities other than those specified in clause (*f*) is in accordance with the guidelines as may be prescribed.

❑ The notice of the meeting at which special resolution is proposed to be passed shall be accompanied by an explanatory statement stating— a full and complete disclosure of all material facts; the necessity for the buy back; the class of security intended to be purchased under the buy-back; the amount to be invested under the buy-back; and the time limit for completion of buy-back. [Section 77A (3)]

❑ Every buy-back shall be completed within twelve months from the date of passing the special resolution or a resolution passed by the board under clause (*b*) of sub-section (2). [Section 77A (4)].

❑ As per provisions of section 77A (5) of the Act, the buy-back may be:

(*a*) *From the Existing Security Holders on a Proportionate Basis:* It means a public offer to purchase by a company of its shares or other specified securities from its security holders at a certain price within a stated time limit, often in an effort to win control of the company. or

(*b*) *From the Open Market:* The buyback of shares or other specified securities from the open market may be in through stock exchange; or through Book Building process, or

(*c*) *From Odd Lots:* That is to say, where the lot of securities of a public company whose shares are listed on a recognised stock exchange, is smaller than such marketable lot, as may be specified by the stock exchange; or

(*d*) *By Purchasing the Securities Issued to Employees* of the company pursuant to a scheme of stock option or sweat equity.

❑ The Company shall, before making such buy-back, file with the Registrar and the Securities and Exchange Board of India a declaration of solvency in the form as may be prescribed, and verified by an affidavit to the effect that the Board has made a full inquiry into the affairs of the company as a result of which they have formed an opinion that it is capable of meeting its liabilities and will not be rendered insolvent within a period of one year of the date of declaration adopted by the Board, and signed by at least two directors of the company, one of whom shall be the managing director, if any: provided that no declaration of solvency shall be filed with the Securities and Exchange Board of India by a company whose shares are not listed on any recognised stock exchange. [Section 77A (6)]

❑ The company shall extinguish and physically destroy the securities so bought back within seven days of the last date of completion of buy-back. [Section 77A (7)]

❑ The company shall not make further issue of the same kind of shares (including allotment of further shares under clause (*a*) of sub-section (1) of Section 81) or other specified securities within a period of six months except by way of bonus issue or in the discharge of subsisting obligations such as conversion of warrants, stock option schemes, sweat equity or conversion of preference shares or debentures into equity shares. [Section 77A (8)]

❑ The company shall maintain a register of the securities so bought, the consideration paid for the securities bought-back, the date of cancellation of securities, the date of extinguishing and physically destroying of securities and such other particulars as may be prescribed. [Section 77A (9)]

❑ A company shall, after the completion of the buy-back under this section, file with the Registrar and the Securities and Exchange Board of India, a return containing such particulars relating to the buy-back within thirty days of such completion, as may be prescribed: provided that no return shall be filed with the Securities and Exchange Board of India by a company whose shares are not listed on any recognised stock exchange. [Section 77A (10)]

❑ If a company makes default in complying with the provisions of this section or any rules made there-under, or any regulations made under clause (*f*) of sub-section (2), the company or any officer of the company who is in default shall be punishable with imprisonment for a term which may extend to two years, or with fine which may extend to fifty thousand rupees, or with both. [Section 77A (11)]

Right Shares/Further Issue of Capital

❑ When the directors think there is need to have additional funds for expansion, diversification or modernization, they may go for the issue of further shares offered to the existing shareholders are called 'right shares'.

❑ Under Section 81 (1) of the Companies Act, 1956, where at any time after the expiry of two years of the formation of a company or at any time after the expiry of one year from the allotment of shares in that company made for the first time after its formation, whichever is earlier, it is proposed to increase the subscribed capital of the company by allotment of further shares, then:

(*a*) Such further shares shall be offered to the persons who, at the date of the offer, are holders of the equity shares of the company, in proportion, as nearly as circumstances admit, to the capital paid-up on those shares at that date;

(*b*) The offer aforesaid shall be made by notice specifying the number of shares offered and limiting a time not being less than fifteen days from the date of the offer within which the offer, if not accepted, will be deemed to have been declined;

(*c*) Unless the articles of the company otherwise provide, the offer aforesaid shall be deemed to include a right exercisable by the person concerned to renounce the shares offered to him or any of them in favour of any other person; and the notice referred to in clause (*b*) shall contain a statement of this right;

(*d*) After the expiry of the time specified in the notice aforesaid, or on receipt of earlier intimation from the person to whom such notice is given that he declines to accept the shares offered, the Board of Directors may dispose of them in such manner as they think most beneficial to the company.

Explanation: *In this sub-section, "equity share capital" and "equity shares" have the same meaning as in Section 85.*

❑ The further shares aforesaid may be offered to any persons whether or not those persons include the persons referred to in clause (*a*) above, in any manner whatsoever:

(*a*) If a special resolution to that effect is passed by the company in general meeting, or

(*b*) Where no such special resolution is passed, if the votes cast (whether on a show of hands, or on a poll, as the case may be) in favour of the proposal contained in the resolution moved in that general meeting (including the casting vote, if any of the Chairman) by members who, being entitled so to do, vote in person, or where proxies are allowed, by proxy, exceed the votes, if any, cast against the proposal by members so entitled and voting and the Central Government is satisfied, on an application made by the Board of Directors in this behalf, that the proposal is most beneficial to the company.

❑ Nothing in Section 81 shall apply:

(*a*) To a private company; or

(*b*) To the increase of the subscribed capital of a public company caused by the exercise of an option attached to debentures issued or loans raised by the company:

(*i*) To convert such debentures or loans into shares in the company, or

(*ii*) To subscribe for shares in the company:

Provided that the terms of issue of such debentures or the terms of such loans include a term providing for such option and such term

(*a*) Either has been approved by the Central Government before the issue of debentures or the raising of the loans, or is in conformity with the rules, if any, made by that Government in this behalf; and

(*b*) In the case of debentures or loans other than debentures issued to, or loans obtained from, the Government or any institution specified by the Central Government in this behalf, has also been approved by a special resolution passed by the company in general meeting before the issue of the debentures or the raising of the loans.

Judicial Interpretations/Case Example	
The power to issue further shares can be used to create a sufficient number of shareholders to enable a company to exercise statutory powers or to enable it to comply with statutory requirements.	*Needle Industries (India) Ltd* v *Needle Industries Newey (India) Holding Ltd.,* 1981, 51 Comp. Cas. 743.
Normally further shares are allotted either for mobilizing funds for the company or for meeting statutory requirements and requirements of financial institutions. In the allotment of shares the directors are in fiduciary position and cannot issue/allot shares with any ulterior motive like creation of a new majority. In a family company, even disturbance in the existing percentage of shareholding may be an act of oppression.	*Hansraj Gokuldas Ved* v *Nitin Dyeing and Bleaching Mills (P) Ltd.,* 2005, 64 CLA 64 (CLB).
Any issue of shares solely to gain control over the company is not permissible.	*S Varadarajan* v *Udhayem Leasings and Investments (P) Ltd.,* 2005, 125 Comp Cas 853
Allotment made to increase the shareholding so as to reduce a majority shareholder to minority, is not valid.	*Jabalpur Tea Co. Ltd.* v *Bengal Dooars National Tea Co. Ltd.,* 1984, 55 Comp Cas 160 (Cal).
If a member did not respond to offers made by company, it has to be necessarily held that he was not inclined to subscribe to additional shares, thereby impliedly consenting for allotment of shares to others.	*R. Khemka* v *Deccan Enterprises (P) Ltd.,* 1998, 16 SCL I (AP).
Even where it is proposed to issue shares to existing members (as distinguished from shareholders), it is desirable to pass the resolution.	*Kedarnath Agarwal* v *Jay Engineering Works Ltd.,* 1962, 66 CWN 1049
The Section 81 exempts private companies from the operation of the provisions of Section 81. However, a private company must comply with the provisions contained in its Articles.	*Sangramsingh P Gaekwad* v *Shantidevi P Gaekwad.,* 2005, 123 Comp Cas 566 (SC).
Though Section 81 requirements for further issue of capital do not apply to private limited company in terms of clause (a) of sub-section (3), the directors in a private limited company are expected to make a disclosure to the shareholders when further shares are issued. Any issue of shares solely to gain control over the company is not permissible.	*Varadarajan (S)* v *Udhayem Leasings and Investments (P) Ltd.,* 2005 65 CLA 21 (CLB).
Issue of preferential shares to promoters so as to strengthen promoters' hold in company would be valid so long as such issue does not violate guidelines issued by SEBI.	*Kothari Industrial Co. pn. Ltd.* v *Maxwell Dyes and Chemicals (P) Ltd.,* 1996 85 Comp Cas 79 (Mad).

Bonus Shares

- The Companies Act, 1956 though has made references to bonus shares issue in its Section 205; it does not contain a separate set of sections dealing with bonus shares. Section 205 (3) permits capitalization of profits or reserve of a company for the purpose of issuing fully paid-up bonus shares or paying up any amount for the time being unpaid on any shares held by the members of the company.
- Bonus shares are issued by capitalization of profits or reserve of a company by issuing fully paid bonus shares to the existing shareholders who are not required to pay anything in lieu of bonus shares they get. It is because; accumulated free reserves belong to them who are the ultimate owners of company.
- Thus, by the conversion of accumulated free reserves into paid up capital, issue of bonus shares in a way broadens the capital base of the company.
- Also, issue of bonus shares adds to the goodwill and image of the company.

■ Issue Governed by Articles or Table A

- A company cannot issue bonus shares, unless it is authorised by its articles. If the articles of a company contain no provisions for the issue of bonus shares, in that case, either the articles are to be altered or the regulations contained in Table A of the Act will automatically apply to the company if it is a public company limited by shares. Regulation numbers 96 and 97 deal with capitalisation of profits by issuance of bonus shares, which are reproduced hereunder:

■ Regulation 96 of Table A in Respect of Issuance of Bonus Shares

1. The company in general meeting may, upon the recommendation of the Board, resolve:

   (a) That it is desirable to capitalise any part of the amount for the time being standing to the credit of any of the company's reserve ccounts, or to the credit of the profit and loss account, or otherwise available for distribution; and

   (b) That such sum be accordingly set free for distribution in the manner specified in following clause (clause 2) amongst the members who would have been entitled thereto, if distributed by way of dividend and in the same proportions.

2. The sum aforesaid shall not be paid in cash but shall be applied, subject to the provision contained in the following clause (clause 3), either in or towards:

   (a) Paying up any amounts for the time being unpaid or any shares held by such members respectively;

(b) Paying up in full, unissued shares of the company to be allotted and distributed, credited as fully paid-up, to and amongst such members in the proportions aforesaid; or

(c) Partly in the way specified in sub-clause (a) and partly in that specified in sub-clause (b).

3. A share premium account and a capital redemption reserve account may, for the purposes of this regulation, only be applied in the paying up of unissued shares to be issued to members of the company as fully paid bonus shares.

4. The Board shall give effect to the resolution passed by the company in pursuance of this regulation

■ Regulation 97 of Table A in Respect of Issuance of Bonus Shares

1. Whenever such a resolution as aforesaid shall have been passed, the Board shall:

   (a) Make all appropriations and applications of the undivided profits resolved to be capitalised thereby, and all the allotments and issues of fully paid shares, if any; and

   (b) Generally do all acts and things required to give effect thereto.

2. The Board shall have full power:

   (a) To make such provision, by the issue of fractional certificates or by payment in cash or otherwise as it thinks fit, for the case of shares or debentures becoming distributable in fractions; and also

   (b) To authorise any person to enter, on behalf of all the members entitled thereto, into an agreement with the company providing for the allotment to them respectively, credited as fully paid up, of any further shares to which they may be entitled upon such capitalisation, or (as the case may require) for the payment up by the company on their behalf, by the application thereto of their respective proportions of the profits resolved to be capitalised, of the amounts or any part of the amounts remaining unpaid on their existing shares.

3. Any agreement made under such authority shall be effective and binding on all such members.

■ Guidelines for Bonus Issue

1. The articles of association of the company shall contain a provision for capitalisation of reserves, etc. If there is no such provision in the Articles the company shall pass a Resolution at its general body meeting making provisions in the Articles of Association for capitalisation.

2. A listed company proposing to issue bonus shares shall comply with the following:

(a) No company shall, pending conversion of FCDs/PCDs, issue any shares by way of bonus unless similar benefit is extended to the holders of such FCDs/PCDs, through reservation of shares in proportion to such convertible part of the FCDs or PCDs.

(b) The shares so reserved may be issued at the time of conversion (s) of such debentures on the same terms on which the bonus issues were made.

3. The bonus issue shall be made out of free reserves built out of the genuine profits or share premium collected in cash only.

4. Reserves created by revaluation of fixed assets are not capitalised.

5. The declaration of bonus issue, in lieu of dividend, is not made.

6. The bonus issue is not made unless the partly paid shares, if any existing, are made fully paid-up.

7. The Company:

(a) Has not defaulted in payment of interest or principal in respect of fixed deposits and interest on existing debentures or principal on redemption thereof; and

(b) Has sufficient reason to believe that it has not defaulted in respect of the payment of statutory dues of the employees such as contribution to provident fund, gratuity, bonus, etc.

8. A company which announces its bonus issue after the approval of the Board of Directors must implement the proposal within a period of six months from the date of such approval and shall not have the option of changing the decision.

9. Consequent to the issue of bonus shares if the subscribed and paid-up capital exceeds the authorised share capital, a resolution shall be passed by the company at its general body meeting for increasing the authorised capital.

10. A certificate duly signed by the issuer company and countersigned by statutory auditor or by Company Secretary in practice to the effect that the provision of the above mentioned clauses have been complied with shall be forwarded to the Board.

■ Procedure for Issuance of Bonus Shares

Following procedure is to be adopted for issuing bonus shares:

1. The Board of directors based on the report of auditors relating to the amount available for distribution as bonus shares, must consider the matter of issuance of bonus shares at their meeting. The Board should pass following necessary resolutions at their meeting:

(a) Approval of the bonus issue subject to the approval in General Meeting.

    (*b*) Approve the record date to determine the entitlement of bonus shares.

    (*c*) Approval of the date of the AGM/EGM.

2. Send intimation of such proposal to the stock exchanges where securities of the company are listed.

3. Pass the necessary resolution in the general meeting of the shareholders.

4. If shares have to be issued to NRIs/Non-residents, apply to the RBI for seeking its consent for such issue.

5. In case of listed companies:

    (*a*) The Board shall fix a record date for taking record of shareholders who would be entitled to receive bonus shares.

    (*b*) Intimation of such record in case of physical shares shall be given to the stock exchanges at least 21 days before the date and in case of D-mat, at least 15 days before the date.

    (*c*) General notice be published in the newspaper about issue of bonus shares; and

    (*d*) General notice be published in the newspaper about the record date in pursuance of Section 154.

6. Submit an application to the Stock Exchange for listing of bonus shares.

7. Submit Corporate Action Form to the CDSL and NSDL for admission of new capital.

8. After the record date, a complete list of all members, who are entitled to receive the bonus shares, is prepared.

9. A resolution in the meeting of Board of directors is to be passed for allotment of bonus shares.

10. Within 30 days of the allotment, a return of allotment is filed in e-Form 2 with the ROC.

11. e-Form 23 is filed with the Registrar within 30 days from the date of the general meeting.

12. Issue share certificates to the allottees in accordance with the Companies (Issue of Share Certificate) Rules, 1960 and credit to the Members DMat account through CDSL and/or NSDL in case of having shares in the electronic mode.

13. Suitable entries in the register of members are made.

14. In case of listed companies, application shall be made to stock exchanges for final listing and permission for trading of bonus shares and a compliance report be sent to the SEBI.

15. A certificate duly signed and counter signed by a statutory auditor or a company secretary in practice is filled to the SEBI that provisions of the SEBI Bonus Issues Guidelines have been complied with.

■ *Difference between Right Shares and Bonus Shares*

Right Shares	Bonus Shares
Right Shares are issued against payment and the shareholders are required to pay.	Bonus Shares are issued free of charge.
May be partly paid up	Always fully paid up.
Company will have to return the entire money received if the company fails to receive minimum subscription.	No such requirement.
Till the allotment is being approved by the stock exchange, the money received must be kept at a separate bank account.	Not relevant as no money is received.
Right to renounce is available and member may renounce in favour of his nominee. Right issue is regulated by the provisions of Companies Act and SEBI Guidelines.	No such facility is available.
	Bonus issue is regulated by the provisions of Company's Articles/Table A and the detailed SEBI Guidelines.

Judicial Interpretations/Case Example	
Bonus shares are capital in hands of shareholders and not dividend; bonus shares do not give them an immediate right to a larger amount of the existing assets but simply confer a title to a larger proportion of the surplus assets in the event of winding up.	*IRC* v *Blott.*, 1921, 2 AC 171 (HL).
By issue of bonus shares value of shares is likely to reduce proportionately, *i.e.*, in the ratio number of bonus shares bears to increased number of shares after bonus issue.	*Chandrakant Mulraj* v *Tata Engg. and Locomotive Co. Ltd.,* 1985, 58 Comp Cas 320 (Bom).

Book Building

❑ "Book Building" means a process undertaken by which a demand for the securities proposed to be issued by a body corporate is elicited and built up and the price for such securities is assessed for the determination of the quantum of such securities to be issued by means of a notice, circular, advertisement, document or information memoranda or offer document.

Offer to Public Through Book Building: An issuer company proposing to issue capital through book building shall comply with the following:

❑ An issuer company may make an issue of securities to the public through a prospectus in the following manner:

    (*a*) 100% of the net offer to the public through book building process, or

    (*b*) 75% of the net offer to the public through book building process and 25% at the price determined through book building.

❑ Book-Building shall be for the portion other than the promoters contribution and the allocation made to :

    (*a*) "Permanent employees of the issuer company and in the case of a new company the permanent employees of the promoting companies";

    (*b*) 'Shareholders of the promoting companies in the case of a new company and shareholders of group companies in the case of an existing company' either on a 'competitive basis' or on a 'firm allotment basis';

❑ The issuer company shall appoint an eligible Merchant Banker (s) as book runner (s) and their name (s) shall be mentioned in the draft prospectus.

❑ The issuer company shall enter into an agreement with one or more of the Stock Exchange (s) which have the requisite system of on-line offer of securities. The agreement shall specify inter alia, the rights, duties, responsibilities and obligations of the company and stock exchange (s) *inter se*. The agreement may also provide for a dispute resolution mechanism between the company and the stock exchange.

❑ The company may apply for listing of its securities on an exchange other than the exchange through which it offers its securities to public through the on-line system.

❑ The Lead Merchant Banker shall act as the Lead Book Runner.

❑ The Book Runner (s) may appoint those intermediaries who are registered with the Board and who are permitted to carry on activity as an 'Underwriter' as syndicate members.

❑ The Book Runner (s)/syndicate members shall appoint brokers of the exchange, who are registered with SEBI, for the purpose of accepting bids, applications and placing orders with the company and ensure that the brokers so appointed are financially capable of honouring their commitments arising out of defaults of their clients/investors, if any.

❑ The brokers and Self Certified Syndicate Banks accepting applications and application monies shall be considered as 'bidding/collection centres'.

❑ The broker/s so appointed, shall collect the money from his/their client for every order placed by him/them and in case the client/investors fails to pay for shares allocated as per the guidelines, the broker shall pay such amount.

❑ The company shall pay to the broker/s /Self Certified Syndicate Banks a commission/fee for the services rendered by him/them. The exchange shall ensure that the broker does not levy a service fee on his clients/investors *in lieu of* his services.

- ❑ The draft prospectus containing all the required disclosures except that of price and the number of securities to be offered to the public shall be filed by the Lead Merchant Banker with the Board.
- ❑ The red-herring prospectus shall disclose either the floor price of the securities offered through it or a price band along with the range within which the price can move, if any. provided that in case of a further public issue of a class of securities which is already listed on a recognised stock exchange, it shall not be necessary to disclose the floor price or price band in the red herring prospectus if the same is disclosed by way of an announcement made by the issuer or the merchant banker at least one day before the opening of the bid in all those newspapers where pre-issue advertisement was released.
- ❑ In case the red-herring prospectus discloses the price band, the lead book runner shall ensure compliance with the following conditions:

  (a) The cap of the price band should not be more than 20% of the floor of the band, *i.e.*, cap of the price band shall be less than or equal to 120% of the floor of the price band.

  (b) The price band can be revised during the bidding period in which case the maximum revision on either side shall not exceed 20% *i.e.*, floor of price band can move up or down to the extent of 20% of floor of the price band disclosed in the red-herring prospectus and the cap of the revised price band will be fixed in accordance with clause (a) above.

  (c) Any revision in the price band shall be widely disseminated by informing the stock exchanges, by issuing press release and also indicating the change on the relevant website and the terminals of the syndicate members.

  (d) In case the price band is revised, the bidding period shall be extended for a further period of three days, subject to the total bidding period not exceeding thirteen days.

  (e) The manner in which the shortfall, if any, in the project financing, arising on account of lowering of price band to the extent of 20% will be met shall be disclosed in the red-herring prospectus. It shall also be disclosed that the allotment shall not be made unless the financing is tied up.

Procedure for Bidding: The method and process of bidding shall be subject to the following:

- ❑ Bid shall be open for at least three working days and not more than seven working days, which may be extended to a maximum of ten working days in case the price band is revised.

- Bidding shall be permitted only if an electronically linked transparent facility is used.
- The 'syndicate members' shall be present at the bidding centres so that at least one electronically linked computer terminal at all the bidding centres is available for the purpose of bidding.
- The number of bidding centres, in case 75% of the net offer to the public is offered through the book building process, shall not be less than the number of mandatory collection centres as specified in these regulations. In case 100% of the net offer to the public is made through book building process, the bidding centres shall be at all the places, where the recognised stock exchanges are situated.
- The same norms as applicable for collection centres shall be applicable for the bidding centres also.
- Individual as well as qualified institutional buyers shall place their bids only through the "brokers" who shall have the right to vet the bids.
- During the period the issue is open to the public for bidding, the applicants may approach the brokers of the stock exchange/s through which the securities are offered under on-line system or Self Certified Syndicate Banks, as the case may be, to place an order for bidding for the securities. Every broker shall accept orders from all clients/investors who place orders through him and every Self Certified Syndicate Bank shall accept Applications Supported by Blocked Amount from ASBA investors.
- The investors shall have the right to revise their bids provided that Qualified Institutional Buyers shall not be allowed to withdraw their bids after the closure of the bidding.
- At the end of each day of the bidding period the demand shall be shown graphically on the terminals for information of the syndicate members as well as the investors.
- The identities of the Qualified Institutional Buyers making the bidding shall not be made public.
- The stock exchanges shall display data pertaining to book built issues in a uniform format, inter alia, giving category-wise details of bids received Indicative format is given in Schedule XXX. The data pertaining to an issue shall be displayed on the site for a period of at least three days after closure of bids.

■ Allocation/Allotment Procedure

- In case an issuer company makes an issue of 100% of the net offer to public through 100% book building process:

  (a) Not less than 35% of the net offer to the public shall be available for allocation to retail individual investors;

    (*b*) Not less than 15% of the net offer to the public shall be available for allocation to non-institutional investors *i.e.* investors other than retail individual investors and Qualified Institutional Buyers;

    (*c*) Not more than 50% of the net offer to the public shall be available for allocation to Qualified Institutional Buyers: provided that, 50% of net offer to public shall be mandatorily allotted to the Qualified Institutional Buyers, in case the issuer company is making a public issue: provided further that, in respect of issues made under rule 19 (2) (b) of Securities Contracts (Regulation) Rules, 1957, with 60% mandatory allocation to Qualified Institutional Buyers, the percentage allocation to retail individual investors and non-institutional investors shall be 30% and 10% respectively.

❑   In case an issuer company makes an issue of 75% of the net offer to public through book building process and 25% at the price determined through book building:

    (*a*) In the book built portion, not less than 25% of the net offer to the public,shall be available for non-qualified institutional buyers and not more than 50% of the net offer to the public shall be available for allocation to qualified institutional buyers. ,

    (*b*) The balance 25% of the net offer to the public, offered at a price determined through book building, shall be available only to retail individual investors who have either not participated or have not received any allocation, in the book built portion: provided that, 50% of net offer to public shall be mandatorily allotted to the Qualified Institutional Buyers, in case the issuer company is making a public.

    (*c*) Out of the portion available for allocation to Qualified Institutional Buyers, 5% shall be allocated proportionately to mutual funds. Mutual fund applicants shall also be eligible for proportionate allocation under the balance available for Qualified Institutional Buyers.

    (*d*) Allotment to retail individual investors, non-institutional investors and Qualified Institutional Buyers shall be made proportionately.

❑   After finalisation of basis of allocation, the Registrar to the Issue/company shall send the computer file containing the allocation details *i.e.*, the allocation numbers, allocated quantity of successful applicants, etc. along with broker wise funds pay-in obligation, to the Broker to the Issue and the stock exchange (s).

❑   The Company, Lead Manager/Book Runner shall announce the pay-in day and intimate the same to Brokers and stock exchange. It shall be responsibility of the broker to deposit the amount in the Escrow Account to the extent of allocation to his clients on the pay-in date.

- On receipt of the basis of allocation data, the brokers shall immediately intimate the fact of allocation to their client/applicant. The broker shall ensure that each successful client/applicant pays submits the duly filled-in and signed application form to him along with the amount payable towards the application money by the pay-in date. Amount already paid by the applicant as margin money shall be adjusted towards the total allocation money payable. The broker shall, thereafter, hand over the application forms of the successful applicants who have paid the application money, to the exchange, which shall submit the same to the Registrar to Issue/company for their records.
- The broker shall refund the margin money collected earlier, within 3 days of receipt of basis of allocation, to the applicants who did not receive allocation.
- The brokers shall give details of the amount received from each client investors and the names of clients/investors who have not paid the application money to Registrar/Book Runner the exchange. The brokers shall also give soft copy of this data to the exchange.
- In the event of the successful applicants failing to pay the application money, the broker through whom such client placed orders, shall bring in the funds to the extent of the client's default. If the broker does not bring in the funds, he shall be declared as a defaulter by the stock exchange and action as prescribed under the Bye-Laws of the stock exchange shall be initiated against him. In such an event, the Book Runners in case of issues through book building process, who have underwritten the issue, shall bring-in the shortfall.
- On pay-in date, the clearing house shall, without any instruction from the broker, debit the escrow account of each broker to the extent of allocation made to his clients/investors and credit the amount so collected from each broker to the 'Issue Account'.
- The concerned Exchange shall not use the Settlement/Trade Guarantee Fund of the Exchange for honouring brokers' commitments in case of failure of broker to bring in the funds.
- The broker shall open an "Escrow Securities Account" with any depository for the purpose of receiving credit of securities on behalf of the clients.
- On payment and receipt of the sum payable on application for the amount towards minimum subscription, the company shall allot the shares to the applicants as per these Guidelines.
- After the allotment, the Registrar to the issue shall post the share certificates to the investors or, instruct the depository to credit the Escrow Securities Account of each Broker, as the case may be.
- On receipt of the credit of securities to the Escrow Securities Account, the Broker shall transfer the shares to the clients'/applicants' depository account, after receipt of confirmation of full payment from the clients/applicants. For

this purpose broker shall be considered as Agent of the client/applicant. Broker shall confirm to the Book-runner/Registrar to the issue that shares have been credited to the account of clients/applicants not later than the day of commencement of trading, in case full payment had been received.

❑ Any cases of dispute, amongst the broker and the clients, would be referred to arbitration as per the bye-laws/regulations of the stock exchange.

❑ The Allotment details shall be put on the website (if available) of the Registrar to the issue and the issuer. Further, online messaging facility of NSDL CDSL or of stock exchanges may be used to communicate the Allotment details to Brokers, as an alternative of physical Confirmation of Allocation Note.

❑ Trading shall commence within 6 days from the closure of the issue failing which interest at the rate of 15% p.a. shall be paid to the investors.

❑ Schedule XX may be referred to for Clarificatory Examples for issue size and allocation has been specified in Schedule XX.

❑ Model Time Frame for Book Building is specified in Schedule XXI.

❑ In case the issuer company has made an issue of 75% of the net offer to public through book building process and 25% at the price determined through book building:

(a) The offer of 25% of the net offer to the public, made at a price determined through book building, shall open within 15 days from the date of closure of bidding;

(b) The offer for subscription to the public, shall remain open for a period of at least 3 working days after completing all the requirements of advertisement and dispatch of issue material to all the stock exchanges;

(c) During the time when the offer is open, the investors who have received an intimation of entitlement of securities, shall submit the application forms along with the application moneys;

(d) The other retail individual investors who had not participated in the bidding process or have not received intimation of entitlement of securities may also make an application.

Share Certificate

❑ Share certificate is a document issued under the common seal of the company, specifying any shares held by any member, which shall be *prima facie* evidence of the title of the member to such shares. [Section 84 (1)]

❑ This certificate may be renewed or a duplicate of a certificate may be issued if such certificate is proved to have been lost or destroyed, or having been defaced or mutilated or torn is surrendered to the company. [Section 84 (2)]

- If a company with intent to defraud renews a certificate or issues a duplicate thereof, the company shall be punishable with fine which may extend to one lakh rupees and every officer of the company who is in default shall be punishable with imprisonment for a term which may extend to six months, or with fine which may extend to one lakh rupees, or with both. [Section 84 (3)]

- Notwithstanding anything contained in the articles of association of a company, the manner of issue or renewal of a certificate or issue of a duplicate thereof, the form of a certificate (original or renewed) or of a duplicate thereof, the particulars to be entered in the register of members or in the register of renewed or duplicate certificates, the form of such registers, the fee on payment of which, the terms and conditions, if any (including terms and conditions as to evidence and indemnity and the payment of out of-pocket expenses incurred by a company in investigating evidence) on which a certificate may be renewed or a duplicate thereof may be issued, shall be such as may be prescribed. [Section 84 (4)]

- Every company, unless prohibited by any provision of law or of any order of any Court, Tribunal or other authority, shall, within three months after the allotment of any of its shares, and within two months after the application for the registration of the transfer of any such shares, deliver, in accordance with the procedure laid down in Section 53, the certificates of all shares allotted or transferred: provided that the Central Government may, on an application being made to it in this behalf by the company, extend any of the periods within which the certificates allotted or transferred shall be delivered, to a further period not exceeding nine months, if it is satisfied that it is not possible for the company to deliver such certificates within the said periods. [Section 113 (1)]

The expression "transfer", here means a transfer duly stamped and otherwise valid, and does not include any transfer which the company is for any reason entitled to refuse to register and does not register.

- If default is made in complying with the above provision, the company, and every officer of the company who is in default, shall be punishable with fine which may extend to five thousand rupees for every day during which the default continues. [Section 113 (2)]

- If any company on which a notice has been served requiring it to make good any default in complying with the above provisions, fails to make good the default within ten days after the service of the notice, the Central Government may, on the application of the person entitled to have the certificates or the debentures delivered to him, make an order directing the company and any officer of the company to make good the default within such time as may be specified in the order; and any such order may provide that all costs of and incidental to the application shall be borne by the company or by any officer of the company responsible for the default. [Section 113 (3)]

❑ Where the securities are dealt with in a depository, the company shall intimate the details of allotment of securities to depository immediately on allotment of such securities.[Section 113 (4)]

■ *Prima Facie Evidence of the Title and Payment*

Share certificate is issued under the common seal of the company, specifying any shares held by any member, and is a *prima facie* evidence of the title of the member to such shares. This certificate is a statement as against the company that the person, whose name appears on it, is the registered holder of the shares, and in the case of a *bona fide* purchaser for value without notice, that the amount certified as paid has been paid.

Judicial Interpretations/Case Example	
The share certificate is a statement as against the company that the person, whose name appears on it, is the registered holder of the shares, and in the case of a *bona fide* purchaser for value without notice, that the amount certified as paid has been paid.	*Re: Bahia and San Francisco Railway Co.,* 1868, LR 3 QB 584, 595.
If the company authorises issue of a certificate to a person, it is estopped from denying its title and if the company is unable to give him the shares, it will be liable to damages.	*Tomkinson* v *Balkis Consolidated Co.,* 1891, 2 QB 614.
The certificate of shares is the documentary evidence in the possession of a shareholder.	*Burkinshaw* v *Nicolls,* 1878, 3 App case 1004.
Share certificate is not a negotiable instrument or warranty of title by the company.	*Longman* v *Bath Electric Tramways,* 1905, 1 Ch 646 (CA).
Certificate obtained by fraud does not constitute estoppel against the company.	*Simm* v *Anglo American Telegraph Co.,* 1987, 5 QBD 188 (CA).
If an officer of the company issues certificates without authority, there will be estoppel.	*Ruben* v *Great Fingal Consolidated Co.,* 1906, AC 439.

■ *Format of Share Certificate*

Every share certificate shall specify the name (s) of the person (s) in whose favour it is issued, the number of shares allotted and the distinctive numbers. The reverse of the certificate contains the columns for transfers (namely date/transfer number, name (s) of the transferees, register folio, attestation by authorised signatory). In the case of a listed company, the format shall be approved by the stock exchange.

■ Sealing and Signing

Every share certificate is issued under the common seal of the company and be signed by two directors or by a duly registered power of attorney and by the company secretary or some other person appointed by the Board. One of the two directors mentioned above shall be other than the executive, if any. The directors may sign manually or their signature may be machine printed.

■ Stamping of Share Certificate

In terms of the Stamp Act applicable at the place of execution and issue, which is generally the place of registered office of the company, every shares certificate shall be stamped. Stamping in certificates individually can be avoided because the Stamp Rules allow payment of consolidated stamp duty for the whole lot of share certificates that may have to be issued at any time.

■ Entry in the Register of Members

Particulars of share certificates issued are entered in the register of members. The particulars of certificates issued in replacement of certificates sub-divided or consolidated or damaged or lost will be entered in the renewed and duplicate share certificates register.

■ Issue of Share Certificate

On the allotment of shares and the entry in the member's register, the person would become the shareholder of the company irrespective of whether the person had received the share certificate or not. Under Section 113, the company is bound to issue share certificate within a period of three months.

Judicial Interpretations/Case Example	
A share certificate is not a representation of continuing ownership as long as the certificate remains in existence. 'The only representation is that at the date of the certificate the person named therein was owner of the shares.'	*Rainford* v *James Keith and Blackman and Co Ltd.*, 1905, 2 Ch 147, 154 (CA).
If share certificate is not issued within the period of three months and if the company has not obtained the order of extension of period from the CLB for issuance of share certificates, the period of limitation commences for enforcement of rights for issuance of shares and consequently on completion of three months from allotment of shares by the company period of limitation for recovery of the amount shall commence under Article 47 of the Limitation Act, 1963.	*Gurdino Jiwatram Kukreja* v *Eastern Mining and Allied Industries Ltd.*, 2004, 121 Comp Cas 762 (Gau).

■ Service of Share Certificate

As the requirements of Section 53, a document may be served by a company on any member thereof either personally, or by sending it by post to him to his registered address, or if he has no registered address in India, to the address, if any, within India supplied by him to the company for the giving of notices to him. Where a document is sent by post, service thereof shall be deemed to be effected by properly addressing, prepaying and posting a letter containing the document, provided that where a member has intimated to the company in advance that documents should be sent to him under a certificate of posting or by registered post with or without acknowledgement due and has deposited with the company a sum sufficient to defray the expenses of doing so, service of the document shall not be deemed to be effected unless it is sent in the manner intimated by the member. Section 113 only requires company to keep certificates ready for delivery and does not impose an obligation on company to deliver them. What is punishable under Section 113 (2) is non-delivery in accordance with the provision laid down under Section 53 of the certificates of shares within prescribed time.

Judicial Interpretations/Case Example	
If the documents are posted within stipulated time, there would be compliance of Section 113 and there would not be any offence.	*Jayaram (H.V.)* v *Industrial Credit and Investment Corpn. of India Ltd.,* 2000, 99 Comp Cas 341 (SC).

■ *Issue of Duplicate Share Certificate*

- ❑ A share certificate may be renewed or a duplicate of a certificate may be issued if such certificate is proved to have been lost or destroyed, or having been defaced or mutilated or torn is surrendered to the company. [Section 84 (2)]
- ❑ If a company with intent to defraud renews a certificate or issues a duplicate thereof, the company shall be punishable with fine which may extend to one lakh rupees and every officer of the company who is in default shall be punishable with imprisonment for a term which may extend to six months, or with fine which may extend to one lakh rupees, or with both. [Section 84(3)]

Judicial Interpretations/Case Example	
Fresh certificates can be issued when the original certificates are surrendered to the company for cancellation. The company is required to issue share certificates for the same number of shares.	*Sharpe* v *Tophams Ltd.,* 1939, 1 All ER 373.
Where the directors of the company resolve to issue duplicate shares to the third respondent in lieu of original share certificates retained in the custody of the petitioner, the duplicate hare certificates so issued amount to dead security.	*Shailesh Rajnikant Parekh* v *Starline Travels (P) Ltd.,* 2004, 118 Comp Cas 145 (CLB).

■ *Procedure for Issue of Duplicate Share Certificate*

1. The shareholder is to submit to the office of the company secretary an indemnity bond, surety bond, copy of the FIR filed with the police and such other evidence as may be prescribed by the Board of directors for issue of duplicate certificate.

2. A general notice in a newspaper in the place of the registered office intimating the public of the loss of the share certificate and of the company's proposal to consider issue of a duplicate share certificate, in lieu of the one that is lost, is to be published. The cost of the publication of the general notice is normally borne by the shareholder. The Board may, at its discretion, dispense with the costly procedure of publication of general notice in the case of the smallness of value of the shares for which a duplicate share certificate is desired.

3. The proposal for issue of duplicate share certificate will be placed at a meeting of Board or Committee on receipt of compliance of the formalities, as required by the Board or Committee thereof, from the shareholder, and after expiry of the period specified in the general notice, and if the company does not receive any objection to its proposal.

4. Board will pass a resolution to issue duplicate copy of new share certificate.

5. The words 'duplicate issued in lieu of share certificate No...' shall be written on the face of the duplicate share certificate and the word 'Duplicate' will be stamped in bold letters across the face of the share certificate.

6. Particulars of duplicate share certificates issued will be entered in the register of renewed and duplicate share certificates indicating the name of the person to whom it is issued, the number and date of the new share certificate.

7. The issue of duplicate share certificate will also be entered in the register of members and the ledger folio of the concerned member.

8. Intimation shall also be given to all stock exchanges where the shares of the company are listed regarding issue of duplicate share certificate and cancellation of old share certificate.

Share Warrant

Issue and Effect of Share Warrants

□ A public company limited by shares, if so authorised by its articles, may, with the previous approval of the Central Government, with respect to any fully paid-up shares, issue under its common seal a warrant stating that the bearer of the warrant is entitled to the shares therein specified, and may provide, by coupons or otherwise, for the payment of the future dividends on the shares specified in the warrant. [Section 114 (1)]

□ A share warrant shall entitle the bearer thereof to the shares therein specified, and the shares may be transferred by delivery of the warrant. [Section 114 (3)]

Share Warrants and Entries in Register of Members

- ❑ As given in Section 115 (1), on the issue of a share warrant, the company shall strike out of its register of members the name of the member then entered therein as holding the shares specified in the warrant as if he had ceased to be a member, and shall enter in that register the following particulars, namely:

  - (a) The fact of the issue of the warrant;
  - (b) A statement of the shares specified in the warrant, distinguishing each share by its number; and
  - (c) The date of the issue of the warrant.

- ❑ The bearer of a share warrant shall, subject to the articles of the company, be entitled, on surrendering the warrant for cancellation and paying such fee to the company as the Board of Directors may from time to time determine, to have his name entered as a member in the register of members. [Section 115 (2)]

- ❑ The company shall be responsible for any loss incurred by any person by reason of the company entering in its register of members the name of a bearer of a share warrant in respect of the shares therein specified, without the warrant being surrendered and cancelled. [Section 115 (3)]

- ❑ Until the warrant is surrendered, the particulars specified in Section 115 (1) shall be deemed to be the particulars required by this Act to be entered in the register of members; and, on the surrender, the date of the surrender shall be entered in that register. [Section 115 (4)]

- ❑ Subject to the provisions of this Act, the bearer of a share warrant may, if the articles of the company so provide, be deemed to be a member of the company within the meaning of this Act, for any purposes defined in the articles. [Section 115 (5)]

- ❑ If default is made in complying with any of the requirements of this section, the company and every officer of the company who is in default shall be punishable with fine which may extend to five hundred rupees for every day during which the default continues. [Section 115 (6)]

■ *Share Certificate* v *Share Warrant*

S.N.	Share Certificate	Share Warrant
1	Both public and private company can issue.	Only a public company can issue.
2	Issue is a statutory obligation and therefore a provision in the articles may not be required.	A provision in the articles is mandatory.
3	For issue, approval of central government is not required.	For issue, approval of central government is required.

S.N.	Share Certificate	Share Warrant
4	Can be issued in respect of even partly paid shares.	Can be issued only in respect of fully paid shares.
5	Holder is a member.	Holder is not a member.
6	Transfer requires registration with company.	Transferred by mere delivery
7	Stamp duty is payable on transfer.	No Stamp duty is payable on transfer.
8	It is not a negotiable instrument.	It is a negotiable instrument.
9	It constitutes share qualification of a director.	It does not constitute share qualification of a director.
10	Holder can present a petition for the winding up.	Holder cannot present a petition for the winding up.

De-mat System

❑ Under the system of De-mat known as 'scripless trading system' the concept of issue of share certificate is replaced by the entries made in books by a 'depository' in respect of each member of the concerned company as beneficial owner of the shares held by him in such company.

❑ The 'depository' to be eligible to provide depository services must register with SEBI and shall maintain the account of the shares/securities of each such beneficial owner (*i.e.*, investor). The 'depository' is to maintain a register and an index of beneficial owners in the manner provided in Sections 150, 151 and 152 of the Companies Act, 1956.

❑ For the purpose of the operation of 'De-mat System', shares of a company are issued in the name of concerned 'depository' which is considered to be the registered holder of said shares/securities and is vested with certain limited rights like maintenance of account of each shareholder of every company which opt for the depository.

❑ The 'depository' considered to be the registered holder/owner of the said shares/securities, shall not have any voting or any other rights in respect of the securities held by it. It is only the beneficial owner, who is entitled to all the rights, benefits and is subjected to all the liabilities in respect of his shares/securities held by a 'depository'.

❑ Presently the National Securities Depository Limited (NSDL) and Central Depository Services (India) Limited (CDSL) are the two depository organizations working in India.

❑ A 'depository' interfaces with market participants *e.g.* brokers, clearing members, and investors, through its agents called 'depository participant (DP)'.

■ Depository Participant (DP)

- ❑ A 'depository participant (DP)' registered with SEBI, is an agent of the 'depository', which provides services to a 'depository', issuer and beneficial owner. The DP functions as the interacting medium between the 'depository' and the beneficial owner (*i.e.*, investor).
- ❑ Any body wishes to avail the services of 'depository' has to open an account with a 'DP'. The process of opening a depository account is similar to that of opening a bank account.
- ❑ A 'DP' possessing the requisite qualifications prescribed by the 'depository' is responsible for maintaining the investor's shares/securities account with the 'depository' and handles the account in accordance with the investor's written instructions.
- ❑ A 'DP' could be linked to a broker who deals on behalf of the investor.
- ❑ Financial institutions, banks, custodians, stock brokers, etc. can become DPs according to SEBI Regulations.
- ❑ The investor is at liberty to choose any 'DP' of his choice at any location to suit his convenience. He is also at liberty to deal with more than one 'DP' (similar to holding bank accounts with several banks).

■ Initial Offer of Securities to be in De-Materialised Form

Every listed public company, making initial public offer (IPO) of any security for a sum of rupees ten crores or more, shall issue the same only in de-materialised form by complying with the requisite provisions of the Depositories Act, 1996 and the regulations made there-under. [Section 68 B]. As per the SEBI (Disclosure and Investor Protection) Guidelines, 2000 (Clause 2.1.5.1), no company shall make public or right issue or an offer for sale of securities unless the company enters into an agreement with a 'depository' for de-materialisation of securities.

■ Investor's Option to hold Securities in Physical form or in De-Mat Mode

The investor subscribing to securities offered by an issuer company is at liberty to either receive the share certificate or hold those securities with a 'depository' in the electronic mode (De-mat). When the investor opts to hold a security with a 'depository', the issuer company shall intimate such 'depository' the details of allotment of the share/security. On receipt of such information the 'depository' shall enter in its records the name of the allottee as the beneficial owner of that security.

■ Procedure for Re-Materialisation

The investor will fill up a Re-mat Request Form (RRF) and submit it to the 'DP', which will forward the request to 'depository' after verifying that the investor has the necessary balances. The 'depository' in turn will intimate the company, which will print the share certificate and dispatch the same to the investor.

■ *Regulatory Framework for a Depository*

The De-mat operations of the 'depositories' are carried out in accordance with the SEBI (Depositories and Participants) Regulations, 1996, and the bye-laws framed by the 'depository' empowered under the Depositories Act, 1996. The regulatory frame-work for a depository system has been laid down in the following enactments:—

1. The Companies Act, 1956
2. Securities and Exchange Board of India Act, 1992
3. The Depositories Act, 1996
4. SEBI (Depositories and Participants) Regulations, 1996
5. Business rules and by-laws of depository

■ *Benefits De-mat System*

The De-mat system has following benefits that are not available in the physical system:

1. Reduction in paperwork involved in transfer of securities.
2. Reduction in transaction costs.
3. No stamp duty on transfer of securities.
4. Safe and convenient way to hold securities.
5. Elimination of risks associated with physical certificates such as forgery, fake securities, delays, thefts, etc.
6. Immediate transfer of securities.
7. Nomination facility available.
8. Even one share can be sold and therefore no odd lot problem.
9. Elimination of unnecessary correspondence with the companies in transmissions of securities.
10. Automatic credit of bonus, split/consolidation/merger, etc into Demat account.
11. Holding investments in equity and debt instruments in a single account.

Calls on Shares

❑ When shares are issued, the issue price may be collected either in one go or in installments. Installments other than the application and allotment money are generally referred to as calls.

❑ A call is a demand upon the shareholders to pay the whole or part of the balance still due on each class of shares allotted or held by them. The balance may be payable as and when called for in one or more calls. The prospectus and the articles of a company generally specify the amount payable at different times, as call (s).

❑ A company calls the money due on shares at intervals depending upon the requirements for funds, while the shareholders also like better to pay the amount on their shares in installments.

Essentials of a Valid Call

1. *Call may be Raised by a Resolution of Board*

The Board of directors of a company under Section 292 (1) (a) of the Companies Act exercises the power to make calls on shareholders in respect of money unpaid on their shares by means of resolutions passed at meetings of the Board. While making calls, the Board must observe the provisions of the articles, otherwise the call will be invalid, and the shareholder is not bound to pay. In making call, care must be taken that the directors making it are duly appointed and qualified, the meeting of the directors has been duly convened, proper quorum was present, and that the resolution making the call was duly passed and specifies the amount of the call, the time and place of payment. The Board of directors has the power to revoke or postpone a call after it is made.

2. *Calls may also be Raised by the Liquidator*

When the company is in the process of winding up, a call may also be made by the liquidator.

3. *Call is a Debt Due to the Company*

Under Section 36 (2) of the Companies Act, all money payable by any member to the company under the memorandum or articles shall be a debt due from him to the company. If a member fails to pay call money he is liable to pay interest not exceeding the rate specified in the articles or terms of issue, which the directors have power to waive. In the event of default in payment of a valid call, the company can even forfeit the shares if the call is not paid.

4. *A Proper Notice must be Given for Making a Call*

Notice for payment of calls must be in writing and must specify the amount called up, the date and place for payment and to whom it is to be paid. Notwithstanding provisions in the articles, for each call at least 14 days' notice must be given to members. An interval of thirty days is required between two successive calls and not more than twenty five per cent of the nominal value of shares can be called at one time.

Judicial Interpretations/Case Example	
The directors of the company decided to make call and passed two resolutions therefore. None of the resolutions specified the date and time of payment. The blanks were filled subsequently by the secretary who sent the notice. The call notice was held to be invalid.	*E and W Insurance Co. Ltd.* v *Kamala Mehta,* AIR 1956, Bom 537.
A call notice, which does not specify time of payment, is not valid but in case of directors who were present in meeting where resolution for call was adopted, plea of want of notice is not available.	*Major Teja Singh* v *Liquidator, Hindustan Petroleum Co. Ltd,* 1961, 31 Comp Cas 573 (Pun).

5. *Call must be Made for the Benefit of Company*

The power to make call must be exercised only for the benefit of the company, and not for the private ends of the directors. If the call is made for the personal benefit of the directors, the call will be invalid.

Judicial Interpretations/Case Example	
The directors of the company paid nothing on their shares but did not disclose this fact to the shareholders and called on them to pay certain amount partly as allotment money and partly as call money. The directors were held guilty of breach of trust and the call was held to be an abuse of power and the directors were bound to refund the remuneration drawn by them.	*Alexander* v *Automatic Telephone Co.,* 1900, 2 Ch. 56 (CA).

6. *Calls on Shares of Same Class to be made on Uniform Basis*

According to Section 91 of the Companies Act, any calls for further share capital are made on shares; such calls shall be made on a uniform basis on all shares falling under the same class. In other words, there cannot be any discrimination between shareholders of the same class as regards payment of call. For the purposes of this section, shares of the same nominal value on which different amounts have been paid-up shall not be deemed to fall under the same class.

7. *Power of Company to Accept Unpaid Share Capital, Although not Called-Up*

According to Section 92 (1) of the Companies Act, a company may, if so authorised by its articles accept from any member the whole or a part of the amount remaining unpaid on any shares held by him, although no part of that amount has been called-up. The member shall not however be entitled, where the company is one limited by shares, to any voting rights in respect of the moneys so paid by him until the same would, but for such payment, become presently payable.

Forfeiture of Shares

- ❑ A company's articles usually contains provisions for the forfeiture of shares of a member who fails to fails to pay any call, or installment of a call, on the day appointed for payment thereof. While making articles on forfeiture, companies normally adopts Regulations 29 to 35 of Table A. If the articles of a public company are silent on forfeiture, the Regulations given in TableA shall automatically apply. The provisions of Table 'A' regarding forfeiture of shares are as under:

    1. If a member fails to pay any call, or installment of a call, on the day appointed for payment thereof, the Board may, at any time thereafter during such time as any part of the call or installment remains unpaid,

serve a notice on him requiring payment of so much of the call or installment as is unpaid, together with any interest which may have accrued. [Regulation 29 of Table A]

2. The notice aforesaid shall name a further day (not being earlier than the expiry of fourteen days from the date of service of the notice) on or before which the payment required by the notice is to be made; and state that, in the event of non-payment on or before the day so named, the shares in respect of which the call was made will be liable to be forfeited. [Regulation 30 of Table A]

3. If the requirements of any such notice as aforesaid are not complied with, any share in respect of which the notice has been given may, at any time thereafter, before the payment required by the notice has been made, be forfeited by a resolution of the Board to that effect. [Regulation 31 of Table A]

4. A forfeited share may be sold or otherwise disposed of on such terms and in such manner as the Board thinks fit. At any time before a sale or disposal as aforesaid, the Board may cancel the forfeiture on such terms as it thinks fit. [Regulation 32(1) (2) of Table A]

5. A person whose shares have been forfeited shall cease to be a member in respect of the forfeited shares, but shall, notwithstanding the forfeiture, remain liable to pay to the company all moneys which, at the date of forfeiture, were presently payable by him to the company in respect of the shares. The liability of such person shall cease if and when the company shall have received payment in full of all such moneys in respect of the shares. [Regulation 33 (1) (2) of Table A]

6. A duly verified declaration in writing that the declarant is a director, the manager or the secretary, of the company, and that a share in the company has been duly forfeited on a date stated in the declaration, shall be conclusive evidence of the facts therein stated as against all persons claiming to be entitled to the share. The company may receive the consideration, if any, given for the share on any sale or disposal thereof and may execute a transfer of the share in favour of the person to whom the share is sold or disposed of. The transferee shall thereupon be registered as the holder of the share. The transferee shall not be bound to see to the application of the purchase money, if any, nor shall his title to the share be affected by any irregularity or invalidity in the proceedings in reference to the forfeiture, sale or disposal of the share. [Regulation 34 (1) (2) (3) and (4) of Table A]

7. The provisions of these regulations as to forfeiture shall apply in the case of non-payment of any sum which, by the terms of issue of a

share, becomes payable at a fixed time, whether on account of the nominal value of the share or by way of premium, as if the same had been payable by virtue of a call duly made and notified [Regn.35 of Table A]

The following rules may apply in connection with forfeiture of shares:

■ *Shares may be Forfeited if Call is not Paid*

If a member fails to pay a valid call within the stipulated time, the company may after waiting for a reasonable period, forfeit shares for non-payment provided clear power is given in the articles. Where power is given in the articles, it must be exercised strictly in accordance with the regulations; otherwise the forfeiture will be void. Regulations 29 to 35 of Table A on forfeiture shall apply if articles are silent.

Judicial Interpretations/Case Example	
The shares can be forfeited only of non-payment of calls and not for any other debt due from a member. Non-payment of calls is not the only reason for which shares can be forfeited; a company by its articles may provide for other grounds also.	*Naresh Chandra Sanyal* v *Calcutta Stock Exchange Association Ltd.,* 1971, SC 422, 41 Comp., Cas. 51 (SC)].
Shares of the shareholders, who were running business of the company, cannot be forfeited for losses suffered by company.	*Dilbhajan Singh* v *New Samundri Transport Co. (P) Ltd.,* 1985, 58 Comp., Cas. 247 (P&H).

■ *Proper Intimation for Forfeiture*

Before the shares have been forfeited, a proper notice to that effect must be served. After the shares have been forfeited, intimation is again sent to the shareholder concerned.

Judicial Interpretations/Case Example	
A proper notice is a condition precedent to forfeiture and even the slightest defect in the notice will invalidate the forfeiture.	*Public Passenger Services Ltd* v *M. A. Khader,* 1966, 1 Comp., Cas. LJ I.
There should be notice of forfeiture and power should be exercised following the procedure prescribed in the articles.	*Sulochana Nathany* v *Hindustan Malleables and Forgings Ltd.,* 2001, CLC 448 (CLB).

■ *Board Resolution for Forfeiture*

The forfeiture must be passed by a resolution at a meeting of the Board of directors at which proper quorum was present.

■ *Forfeiture must be Bona Fide and in the Interest of a Company*

The forfeiture must be exercised *bona fide* and in the interest of the company. It should not be collusive or fraudulent.

Judicial Interpretations/Case Example	
The forfeiture of shares was set aside, because it was found to have been carried out at the request of a shareholder to relieve him of liability. Such a forfeiture amounts to an abuse of power to forfeit and a fraud on other shareholders.	*Re: Esparto Trading Co.,* 1879, 12 Ch. D. 791.

■ *Forfeited Shares are Company Property*

Forfeited shares become the property of the company; till the shares are re-issued. Therefore, normally companies re-issue them.

■ *Cancellation of Forfeiture*

Board may cancel forfeiture of shares in case the defaulting shareholder approaches after forfeiture to cancel the forfeiture. The Board has been empowered to cancel such a forfeiture and claim due amount from the shareholder with interest.

Judicial Interpretations/Case Example	
Once forfeiture has been enforced, the contract between the company and the member comes to an end; there can be no subsequent recession of forfeiture without the shareholder's consent.	*Re: Exchange Trust Ltd.,* 1903, 1 Ch. 711.
If shares were forfeited for non-payment of a call which was invalid, the company could withdraw forfeiture and issue a fresh call.	*Bhagirath Spinning and Wvg. Co. Ltd.* v *Balaji Bhavani Power* AIR, 1930, Bom 267.

■ *Re-Issue of Forfeited Shares*

Shares forfeited by a company may either be cancelled or re-issued to another person at the discretion of the Board. Generally, forfeited shares are re-issued at a discount which cannot exceed the amount already paid on such shares. The total of the sum paid by the original owner of the shares together with the re-issue price should not be less than the par value. After the original holder has surrendered the share certificate, new allottee is issued a share certificate on the execution of a transfer deed by the company; otherwise, after a public notice in a newspaper, a new share certificate is issued.

Surrender of Shares

❑ Both the Companies Act, 1956 and Table A are silent on surrender of shares. Therefore, it depends on provisions in the articles of a company whether directors have power to accept surrender of shares or not.

Judicial Interpretations/Case Example	
Articles of some companies may allow surrender of shares as a short cut to the long procedure of forfeiture, where their forfeiture is otherwise justified.	*Trevor* v *Whitw,* 1887, 12 App. Cas. 409.
Mere handing over of share certificates cannot constitute surrender of shares and a surrender of shares can be made if the articles give the directors power to accept a surrender of shares.	*Re: Vasant Investment Corpn. Ltd.,* 1982, 52 Comp. Cas. 139 (Bom).

Transfer of Shares

❑ The word 'transfer' is an act of the parties by which title to property is transferred from one person to another, while the word 'transmission' is the result of operation of law, which takes place only on death or insolvency of a shareholder.

❑ According to Section 82 of the Companies Act, the share in a company is movable property, transferable in the manner provided by the articles of the company. As provided in Section 108 (1) of the Companies Act, a company shall not register a transfer of shares of the company, unless a proper instrument of transfer (share transfer form laid down in Regulation 20 of Table A) duly stamped and executed by or on behalf of the transferor and by or on behalf of the transferee and specifying the name, address and occupation, if any, of the transferee, has been delivered to the company along with the certificate relating to the shares or debentures, or if no such certificate is in existence, along with the letter of allotment of the shares or debentures: provided that where, on an application in writing made to the company by the transferee and bearing the stamp required for an instrument of transfer, it is proved to the satisfaction of the Board of directors that the instrument of transfer signed by or on behalf of the transferor and by or on behalf of the transferee has been lost, the company may register the transfer on such terms as to indemnity as the Board may think fit.

❑ Every instrument of transfer of shares shall be in the prescribed form and:

(*a*) Every such form shall, before it is signed by or on behalf of the transferor and before any entry is made therein, be presented to the prescribed authority, being a person already in the service of the Government, who shall stamp or otherwise endorse thereon the date on which it is so presented, and

(*b*) Every instrument of transfer in the prescribed form with the date of such presentation stamped or otherwise endorsed thereon shall, after it is executed by or on behalf of the transferor and the transferee and completed in all other respects, be delivered to the company, (*i*) In the case of shares dealt in or quoted on a recognised stock exchange, at any time before the date on which the register of members is closed, in accordance with law, for the first time after the date of the presentation of the prescribed form to the prescribed authority under clause (*a*) or within twelve months from the date of such presentation, whichever is later;

(*ii*) In any other case, within two months from the date of such presentation.

❑ Regulations 19 to 28 of Table A too provides rules concerning transfer (19 to 24 as regards transfer and 25 to 28 on transmission). According to Regulation 19 (1) (2), the instrument of transfer of any share in the company shall be executed by or on behalf of both the transferor and transferee. The transferor shall be deemed to remain a holder of the share until the name of the transferee is entered in the register of members in respect thereof. The Board may, subject to the right of appeal conferred by Section 111 of the Companies Act, under the Regulation 21, decline to register the transfer of a share, not being a fully paid share, to a person of whom they do not approve; or any transfer of shares on which the company has a lien. Further, according the Regulation 22, the Board may also decline to recognise any instrument of transfer unless (a) a fee of two rupees is paid to the company in respect thereof; (b) the instrument of transfer is accompanied by the certificate of the shares to which it relates, and such other evidence as the Board may reasonably require to show the right of the transferor to make the transfer; and (c) the instrument of transfer is in respect of only one class of shares.

Judicial Interpretations/Case Example	
Right of shareholder to transfer his shares is always subject to provisions in the articles.	*Mathrubhumi Printing and Publishing Co Ltd* v *Vardhaman Publishers Ltd.,* 1992, 73 Comp. Cas. 150.

Transfer Deed

The following rules may apply in connection with the transfer deed:

1. *Transfer Deed is Obligatory*

As per the requirement of Section 108, a proper transfer deed in Form 7B as provided in the Companies (Central Government's) General Rules and Forms, 1956, duly stamped and executed by or on behalf of the transferor and by or on behalf of the transferee, must be delivered to the company, or else a company shall not register a transfer of shares. Transfer deed specifying the name, address and occupation, if any, of the transferee, should be delivered to the company, along-with the share certificate, or if no such certificate is in existence, along-with the letter of allotment of the shares.

2. *Validity of Transfer Deed*

Under clause (*a*) of Section 108 (1A), every share transfer form shall, before it is signed by or on behalf of the transferor and before any entry is made therein, be presented to the prescribed authority, who shall stamp or otherwise endorse thereon the date on which it is so presented, and every instrument of transfer in the prescribed form with the date of such presentation stamped or otherwise endorsed thereon shall, after it is executed by or on behalf of the transferor and the transferee and completed in all other respects, be delivered to the company, in the case of shares dealt in or quoted on a recognised stock exchange, at any time before the date on which the register of members is closed, for the first time after the date of the presentation of the prescribed form to the prescribed authority or within twelve months from the date of such presentation, whichever is later; in any other case, within two months from the date of such presentation.

3. *Transfer Deed is Duly Stamped*

As required by Section 108, the stamp of adequate value should be affixed and cancelled on transfer deed. In case if the shares are listed on stock exchange, the value of the shares for the purpose of stamp will be determined on the basis of the quotations available on the stock exchange on the date of execution of transfer deed or the consideration paid which ever is higher. On the other hand, no transfer duty is applicable for transfer of shares in De-mat form. Value of share transfer stamps to be affixed on the transfer deed is 25 paise for every rupee 100 or part thereof of the value of shares as per the Notification issued by the Ministry of Finance, Department of Revenue dated 28-1-2004.

Judicial Interpretations/Case Example	
If the instrument is not properly executed or the stamp affixed to the instrument is not cancelled before execution or at-least at the time of execution, the said instrument must be deemed to be unstamped.	*Mathrubhumi Printing and Publishing Co Ltd* v *Vardhaman Publishers Ltd.,* 1992, 73 Comp., Cas. 80 (Ker HC).
All that Section 108(1A) (b) requires is that it is not necessary that stamps be affixed before transfer deed is executed, they are to be affixed before delivery. Further held, unless a particular mode of cancellation is prescribed in any State, crossing of stamps is sufficient.	*Prafulla Kumar Rout* v *Orient Engg. Works (P) Ltd.,* 1986, 60 Comp., Cas 65 (Ori).
In case shares are not quoted, the value of the shares for the purpose of stamp means the price that the shares would fetch at the time of transfer or consideration agreed, whichever is higher.	*Union of India* v *Kulu Valley Transport Ltd.,* 1958, 28 Comp. Cas 29 (Punj).

4. *Submission of Transfer deed to the Company*

A duly stamped and executed transfer deed may be submitted to the company either by the transferor or by the transferee together with the relevant share certificates.

Judicial Interpretations/Case Example	
Requirement that only transferor should execute instrument of transfer of shares is not absolute and such execution could be on behalf of transferor if it is authorised by transferor or by law. Therefore, when articles of association authorised execution of instrument of transfer by one of directors in contingencies contemplated therein, it would be incorrect to say that transfer of shares in question was in contravention of Section 108; however, such a compulsory transfer must be in interest of company but not for benefit of some of shareholders even if they are majority shareholders.	*Gothami Solvent Oils Ltd.* v *Mallina Bharathi Rao,* 2001, 105 Comp., Cas 710 (AP).

5. *When Transfer Deed is Lost*

If it is proved to the satisfaction of the Board that the transfer deed signed by or on behalf of the transferor and by or on behalf of the transferee has been lost, the company may register the transfer on such terms as to indemnify as the Board may think fit provided an application in writing has been made to the company by the transferee and bearing the stamp required for an instrument of transfer.

6. *Extension of Validity of Transfer Deed*

Where the validity period of a transfer form has expired, in the case of shares dealt in or quoted on a recognised stock exchange, the instrument is beyond 12 months from the date of presentation to the prescribed authority or from the date of book closure whichever is later in case of shares of a listed company and in other case 2 months from the date of presentation, the holder may make an application to the Registrar of Companies requesting for extension in the validity. The Registrar if satisfied shall extend the validity for a period of 30 days from the date of approval by it.

7. *Transfer in the Case of Partly Paid Shares*

Where the transferor has applied for the transfer of partly paid shares, it shall not be registered, unless the company gives notice of the application to the transferee who makes no objection to the transfer within two weeks from the receipt of the notice.

8. *Time Limit for Issue of Certificate on Transfer*

Every company, unless prohibited by any provision of law or any authority or an order of any Court/Company Law Board, shall, within 2 months after the application for the registration of the transfer, deliver the certificates of all shares transferred. The registration of transfers will be made within a period of 30 days in case of listed companies. The Central Government may, on an application in this behalf by the company, extend any of the periods within which the certificates of shares transferred shall be delivered, to a further period not exceeding nine months, if it is satisfied that it is not possible for the company to deliver such certificates within the said periods.

Judicial Interpretations/Case Example

Power of refusal to register transfer of shares is to be exercised by the company within two months from the date on which the instrument of transfer or the intimation of transfer, as the case may be is delivered to the company. Therefore, the company shall be required to give notice of the refusal to register transfer of shares to the transferor and transferee within a period of two months from the lodgment of transfer documents.	*Unit Trust of India* v *Jagdish Rai,* 2 2000, CPJ 106 Chd., SCmDRC
Action of returning transfer instruments more than once on one ground or other has to be construed as a deemed refusal to register transfer of shares without sufficient cause and in such a case only question to be examined is whether such return of documents is with sufficient cause.	*Premkumar (T.S.)* v *Tamilnadu Mercantile Bank Ltd.,* 2003. 117 Comp. Cas.734(CLB)(SRB)
If the transferee lost the share certificates, according to section 111A, still the transferee can be registered as a shareholder of company but he has to approach the CLB praying the issuance of duplicate share certificate and the register the same in his name. However, by executing indemnity bond, company Board can issue duplicate share certificate.	*Paltina Securities (P) Ltd. v Satyam Computers Services Ltd Comp.,* Cas. 2006, 118.
The refusal to register transfer of shares on the ground that the transferor has been indulging in acts which were against the interests of company shall not be tenable.	*Pawan Gupta* v *Hicks Thermometers (India) Ltd.,* 1999,21 SCL 90,CLB.
Merely because, with registration of transfer of shares, total holding of transferee would become dangerously close to 25%, company cannot refuse to register transfer.	*Bajaj Auto Ltd* v *CLB,* 1998, 17 SCL 223 (SC).

9. *Transfer Procedure not Applicable under the De-Mat System*

As per the requirement of Section 108, a duly stamped and executed transfer deed is required for transferring shares. But, the instrument of transfer and the associated formalities in Section 108 do not apply to the transfer of securities under the system of De-mat.

10. *Non-Compliance of Sections 108A to 108D*

- ❑ Any person who acquires any share in contravention of the provisions of Section 108A shall be punishable with imprisonment for a term which may extend to three years, or with fine which may extend to fifty thousand rupees, or with both. [Section 108-I (1)]

- Every body corporate which makes any transfer of shares without giving any intimation as required by Section 108B shall be punishable with fine which may extend to fifty thousand rupees. [Section 108-I (2 (a))]

- Where any contravention of the provisions of Section 108B has been made by a company, every officer of the company who is in default shall be punishable with imprisonment for a term which may extend to three years or with fine which may extend to fifty thousand rupees, or with both. [Section 108-I (2 (b))]

- Every body corporate which makes any transfer of shares in contravention of the provisions of Section 108 C shall be punishable with fine which may extend to fifty thousand rupees. [Section 108-I (3) (a)]

- Where any contravention of the provisions of Section 108C has been made by a company, every officer of the company who is in default shall be punishable with imprisonment for a term which may extend to three years, or with fine which may extend to fifty thousand rupees or with both. [Section 108-I (3) (b)]

- Every person who transfers any share in contravention of any order made by the Central Government under Section 108 B, or gives effect to any transfer of shares made in contravention of any direction made by the Central Government under Section 108 D, or who exercises any voting right in respect of any share in contravention of any direction made by the Central Government under Section 108 D, shall be punishable with imprisonment for a term which may extend to five years, and shall also be liable to fine. [Section 108-I (4) (a)]

- If any company gives effect to any voting or other right exercised in relation to any share acquired in contravention of the provisions of Section 108 B, or which gives effect to any voting right in contravention of any direction made by the Central Government under Section 108 D, the company shall be punishable with fine which may extend to fifty thousand rupees, and every officer of the company who is in default shall be punishable with imprisonment for a term which may extend to three years, or with fine which may extend to fifty thousand rupees, or with both. [Section 108-I (4) (b)]

Judicial Interpretations/Case Example	
Except sub-section (1) of Section 108, other provisions, namely sub-sections (1A) and (1C) are directory and not mandatory in nature.	*Dove Investments (P) Ltd.* v *Gujarat Industrial Investment Corpn. Ltd.,* 2005, 124 Comp Cas 399 (Mad).
It cannot be said that provisions contained in Section 108 are directory because non-compliance with section is not declared an offence.	*Chandran (P.V.)* v *Malbar and Pioneer Hosiery (P) Ltd.,* 1990, 69 Comp Cas 164 (Ker).

Forged Transfer

❑ Where a company in good faith registers a transfer on the request of the transferee and issues fresh share certificates to him but later it is found that the transfer was forged (signatures of transferor forged) and the company is compelled to restore the shares, the transferee is liable to indemnify the company against its liability. Thus, if a forged transfer is presented for registration and the company registers it, the company may be in severe problem, since the registration of the transfer does not defeat the title of the true owner of the shares, who has a right to require the company to restore his name. On discovering the forgery, the company may remove the name of the transferee from the registration. But, if the company has issued to the transferee a share certificate and a bona fide buyer has purchased the shares in good faith from the transferee (who had forged the transfer), not knowing that it is forged, the company may be liable to pay damages and compensate the subsequent buyer, because a certificate issued under the common seal of the company estoppes the company from denying the title of a person who has bought the shares in good faith and for value. A forged transfer of shares is, therefore, null and void and has no value in the eyes of law, and it cannot affect the title of the shareholder whose signature is forged.

Blank Transfer

❑ When a transferor shareholder signs a share transfer form without filling in the name and other details of the transferee and hands it over along-with the share certificate to the transferee, he is said to have made the transfer in blank, and it is called a blank transfer. Blank transfer which is considered valid facilitates the sale and purchase of shares by mere delivery, though in principle such a deed is not considered a negotiable instrument.

❑ The purpose of going transfer blank (columns of transferee in the transfer form blank) may include easy transferability, saving in the stamp duty, easy finance from banks, and speculation. Blank transfer is done by mere delivery *i.e.*, the moment it is handed over to another person, the ownership is transferred. Whosoever is holding it is considered the owner provided he has bought it for value and in good faith. Likewise, it results in saving of stamp duty as the duty is to be affixed by the last transferee who sends the transfer form/deed after filling his columns in the deed to the company for registration. Further, banks prefer blank transfer shares as security while giving loans. Additionally, blank transfer facilitates speculation as the transfer form/deed being valid in some cases for up-to 2 months, vast transactions are possible on just one transfer form during this period. When the final expiry date of validity comes ending, whosoever holding that form/deed fills transferee columns and sends to the company for registation.

❑ The title of transferee in blank transfer is subject to the title of the transferor. Thus, a person who buys shares in good faith and for value, from a person who has acquired a blank transfer form/deed by fraud, does not acquire better title to the shares included in the transfer form/deed.

❑ A blank transfer is valid in comparison to forged transfer.

Judicial Interpretations/Case Example	
A blank transfer, when accompanied by a share certificate, carries to the transferee both the legal and equitable rights to the shares and also the right to call upon the company to register the transfer.	*Colonial Bank* v *Cady,* 1980, 15 App. Cas. 267.
Right to get himself registered as a member is available to the transferee even after the death of the transferor.	*Re: Bengal Silk Mills Co Ltd.,* 1942, Comp. Cas. 206.

Transmission of Shares

❑ Transfer of shares is the voluntary and intentional act of the transferor, when by executing an instrument of transfer, the title of ownership is transferred from transferor to the transferee. Transmission, while, is the result of operation of law, whereby the shares are transmitted on the death, insolvency of a member or where the shareholder is a company, on its liquidation. No instrument of transfer is required for transmission.

❑ Regulations 25 to 28 of Table A provide rules concerning transmission. According to Regulation 25 (1), on the death of a member, the survivor or survivors where the member was a joint holder, and his legal representatives where he was a sole holder, shall be the only persons recognised by the company as having any title to his interest in the shares. Any person becoming entitled to a share in consequence of the death or insolvency of a member may, upon such evidence being produced as may from time to time properly be required by the Board, elect, either to be registered himself as holder of the share; or to make such transfer of the share as the deceased or insolvent member could have made. The Board shall, in either case, have the same right to decline or suspend registration as it would have had, if the deceased or insolvent member had transferred the share before his death or insolvency. If the person so becoming entitled shall elect to be registered as holder of the share himself, he shall deliver or send to the company a notice in writing signed by him stating that he so elects. If the person aforesaid shall elect to transfer the share, he shall testify his election by executing a transfer of the share. A person becoming entitled to a share by reason of the death or insolvency of the holder shall be entitled to the same dividends and other advantages to which he would be entitled if he were the registered holder of the share, except that he shall not, before being registered as a member in respect of the share, be entitled in respect of it to exercise any right conferred by membership in relation to meetings of the company: provided that the Board may, at any time, give notice requiring any such person to elect either to be registered himself or to transfer the share, and if the notice is not complied with within ninety days, the Board may thereafter withhold payment of all dividends, bonuses or other moneys payable in respect of the share, until the requirements of the notice have been complied with.

The following rules may apply in connection with the transmission:

■ When Shares are held in Joint Names

According to Regulation 25 (1), on the death of a member, the survivor or survivors where the member was a joint holder, and his legal representatives where he was a sole holder, shall be the only persons recognised by the company as having any title to his interest in the shares.

Judicial Interpretations/Case Example	
The deceased shareholder held shares jointly with the MD of the company. On his death, the question arose whether the shareholder's sister, with whom he stayed during his life time because of strained relations with his wife, could claim devolution of shares in her name on the production of some evidence in support of her claim. The CLB held that in the absence of any specific provisions relating to the status of the surviving joint shareholder in the Companies Act, the CLB shall be guided by the spirit of Regulation 25 of Table A according to which in the case of joint holdings it was only the surviving joint holders who would be entitled to the shares and not any legal heir or representative of the deceased joint holder.	*Jayalakshmi Acharya* v *Kal Electronics and Consultants (P) Ltd.,* 8th April 1997, CLB.

■ Execution of Transfer Deed not Required

It is not necessary to have any instrument of transfer executed for the purpose of transmission of shares.

Judicial Interpretations/Case Example	
The procedure provided under Sections 108 to 111 is not applicable to transmission of shares by order of a Court.	*Re: Hanuman Mills (P) Ltd.,* 1977, 47 Comp. Cas. 644 (All).
Where title to the shares comes to vest in another person by operation of law, it is not necessary to submit transfer deed/ form.	*Life Insurance Corpn. of India* v *Bokaro and Ramgur Ltd.* 1966, 36 Comp. Cas. 490 (Del).
The legal representatives of a deceased member can transfer the shares before getting themselves registered as members.	*Simpson* v *Molson's Bank* 1895, AC 270.

■ Evidences for Transmission of Shares

An application to the company by a legal representative supported by the following evidences is sufficient to apply for transmission:

1. Certified copy of death certificate;
2. Succession certificate;
3. Probate;
4. Specimen signature of the successor.

Judicial Interpretations/Case Example	
The executor or administrator of a deceased member does not become a member, unless he consents to be treated as such and to be entered on the register of members.	*Re: Bowling and Welby's Contract* 1895, 1 Ch 633.
Succession certificate covering shares held by a deceased member on the date of his death would cover subsequent issue of bonus shares and no fresh succession certificate would be required in respect of subsequently issued shares.	*Arun Kumar Israni* v *Cipla Ltd.,* 1999, 35, CLA 339 Mumbai, (CLB).
Where a succession certificate has been granted in respect of shares, the company cannot insist on the production of probate or letters of administration; the certificate affords full indemnity to company.	*Thenappa Chettiar* v *Indian Overseas Bank Ltd.,* 1943, 13 Comp. Cas. 202 (Mad).

■ Neither Consideration for Transfer nor Stamp Duty Required

Since the transmission is by operation of law, neither any consideration for transfer nor any stamp duty is required on instruments for transmission.

■ Shares Continue to be Subject to the Original Liabilities

In the case of a transmission of shares, shares continue to be subject to the original liabilities. If there was any lien on the shares for any sums due, the lien would exist, notwithstanding the transmission of the shares.

■ Right to Dividend, Rights Shares, and Bonus Shares to be held in Abeyance Pending Registration of Transfer of Shares

In the case transmission, the right to dividend, rights shares and bonus shares to legal representative shall be kept in abeyance. According to the Regulation 28 of Table A, a person becoming entitled to a share by reason of the death or insolvency of the holder shall be entitled to the same dividends and other advantages to which he would be entitled if he were the registered holder of the share, except that he shall not, before being registered as a member in respect of the share, be entitled in respect of it to exercise any right conferred by membership in relation to meetings of the company. Further, according to Section 206 A, where any instrument of transfer of shares has been delivered to any company for registration and the transfer of such shares has not been registered by the company, it shall, notwithstanding anything contained in any other provision of this Act, transfer the dividend in relation to such shares to the special account referred to in Section 205A unless the company is authorised by the registered holder of such share in writing to pay such dividend to the transferee specified in such instrument of transfer; and keep in abeyance in relation to such shares any offer of rights shares under clause (*a*) of sub-section (1) of Section 81 and any issue of fully paid-up bonus shares in pursuance of sub-section (3) of Section 205.

■ Legal Representatives Shall not be Entitled to Exercise Voting Rights

The legal representative of a deceased member shall not be entitled to exercise rights of membership *i.e.*, voting and other rights in general meetings of the company, unless he is registered as a member in respect of the shares.

Judicial Interpretations/Case Example	
Under Section 211 of the Indian Succession Act, the executors of a deceased person are the legal representatives for all purposes. But, the executors do not become members of the company unless their names are registered. Therefore, on the death of the shareholder his right to the shares or other interest as a member of the company devolved on the petitioners as executors.	*Hemendra Prasad Barooah* v *Bahadur Tea Co.* (*P*) *Ltd.*, 1991, 70 Comp. Cas. 792 (Gau).

Dividend

❑ Dividend means the portion of the profit of the company, which is legally available for distribution among the members. Dividend defined under Section 2 (14A) of the Companies Act, 1956, includes any interim dividend.

■ Interim Dividend

Dividend declared by the Board of directors between two annual general meetings of the company is called as interim dividend. However, with the insertion of sub-Section 14 A in Section 2 by the Companies (Amendment) Act, 2000, all the provisions relating to the payment of dividend shall be applicable on interim dividend also.

■ Final Dividend

Dividend declared at the annual general meeting of the company is said to be a final dividend. Final dividend once declared becomes a debt enforceable against the company.

■ Dividend v Interest

Dividend, which is an appropriation of profit, is paid on the company's paid up share capital including equity and preference shares whereas interest, which is considered charge against profit, is generally paid on debentures, loans and borrowings.

Payment of Dividend

Following Rules may apply for payment of dividend:

1. Authority in the Articles for Payment of Dividend

For the payment of dividend, there must be a specific provision given in the articles of association. Only then, the Board will be able to recommend interim final dividend for the approval of members. If the articles are silent on this matter, they should be suitably amended before taking any decision by the Board in this connection.

2. Compulsory Requirement for making Provisions for Depreciation

Unless exempted by the Central Government, no company can pay dividend in any year without charging depreciation in the profit and loss account for the current year and that there is no balance of un-provided depreciation of any earlier year or years.

3. Compulsory Transfer of Certain Percentage of Profit to Reserves

Before deciding to pay dividend, every company shall transfer a portion of its net profit of the year to general reserve. As per the Companies (Transfer of Profits to Reserves) Rules, 1975, the amount of net profit transferred to reserve shall vary with the rate of dividend proposed to be paid and

Judicial Interpretations/Case Example	
Profits carried to a reserve fund remain profits unless and until they are effectually capitalized and may be distributed as dividends.	*Re: Alsbury*, 1890, 45 Ch D 237.

4. Recommendation of the Board is Compulsory

It is the Board's discretion to recommend or not to recommend dividend for the year. The company in general meeting cannot consider payment of dividend if the Board has not recommended any dividend. Additionally, the member in general meeting cannot also increase the rate of dividend recommended by the Board, although, they can decrease the rate recommended by the Board. Since the Board's recommendation of dividend is only a proposal, it can be withdrawn by the Board before it is communicated to members in the notice of annual general meeting.

5. Closure of Member's Register

A company may close the register of members for the purpose of ascertaining who are eligible to receive dividend on the date of declaration of dividend. Listed companies are required to inform the Stock Exchange twenty one days in advance of closing the register of members for payment of dividend declared at the annual general meeting for determining the names of shareholders entitled to dividend. In the case of companies whose shares are in the compulsory de mat mode, the notice period for closure of register has been reduced to 15 days.

6. Final Dividend is Declared at an Annual General Meeting

One of the items for shareholders approval in the annual general meeting is declaration of dividend. However, a company, which could not declare a dividend at an annual general meeting, may declare the dividend at a subsequent general meeting.

Judicial Interpretations/Case Example	
A company, which could not declare a dividend at an annual general meeting, may do so at a subsequent general meeting. On the other hand, where a company has declared a dividend at a general meeting neither the company nor its directors can declare a further dividend for the same year.	*Biswa Nath Prasad Khaitan* v *New Central Jute Mills Ltd.,* 1961, 31 Comp. Cas. 125.

7. After Approval in the Annual General Meeting Dividend becomes Unsecured Debt

After the dividend has been approved by the shareholders at the annual general meeting, it becomes a debt against the company. Dividends once having been declared at the annual general meeting, the company cannot declare further dividend at an extraordinary general meeting.

Judicial Interpretations/Case Example	
Dividend is deemed to be receivable by the members only in the year at which the members declared the dividend and not at the time when the dividend was recommended by the Board.	*Upendra Kumar Joshi* v *Manik Lal Chatterjee,* 1982, 52 Comp. Cas. 177 (Pat).

8. Deposit of the Amount of Dividend into the a Separate Bank Account

According to Section 205A, the amount of declared dividend including interim dividend shall be deposited in a separate bank account within five days from the date of such declaration. This provision was inserted in the Companies (Amendment) Act, 2000. After this amendment, even the company cannot use the declared amount even up-to the period of actual payment (30 days), which the companies were earlier doing.

9. Dividend is Paid to Registered Shareholders and Beneficial Owners

According to Section 206 (1), no dividend shall be paid by a company in respect of any share therein, except to the registered holder of such share or to his order or to his bankers; or in case a share warrant has been issued in respect of the share in pursuance of Section 114, to the bearer of such warrant or to his bankers. In the case of joint holdings, the dividend shall be paid to the person whose name is registered first in the register. In case if the shares are held in De-Mat mode, the dividend will be credited to the beneficiary's account maintained in the DPs/depositories.

10. Dividend Warrant shall be Posted, within Thirty Days from the Date of Declaration

According to Section 207, where a dividend has been declared by a company but has not been paid, or the warrant in respect thereof has not been posted, within thirty days from the date of declaration, to any shareholder entitled to the payment of the dividend, every director of the company shall, if he is knowingly a party to the default, be punishable with simple imprisonment for a term which may extend to three years and shall also be liable to a fine of one thousand rupees for every day during which such default continues and the company shall be liable to pay simple interest at the rate of eighteen per cent per annum during the period for which such default continues: provided that no offence shall be deemed to have been committed within the meaning of the foregoing provisions in the following cases, namely:— (*a*) where the dividend could not be paid by reason of the operation of any law; (*b*) where a shareholder has given directions to the company regarding the payment of the dividend and those directions cannot be complied with; (*c*) where there is a dispute regarding the right to receive the dividend; (*d*) where the dividend has been lawfully adjusted by the company against any sum due to it from the shareholder; or (*e*) where, for any other reason, the failure to pay the dividend or to post the warrant within the period aforesaid was not due to any default on the part of the company. Once a dividend warrant is posted at the registered address of the member, it is deemed to have been paid within the meaning of Section 205A.

11. Declaration of Dividend should be Unconditional

Vide Circular No. 2/98/F. No. 2/12/98-CLVJ, dated 13th April, 1998, the Department of Company Affairs (now MCA) has advised that the declaration of dividends by the companies should be unconditional and that they should not declare dividends including interim dividend subject to any conditions.

12. Burden of Proof on Non-Receipt of Dividend

Wherever there is a complaint by the shareholder that, for a particular financial year, he did not receive the dividend pursuant to the declaration, the fact that he did not receive the payment cannot be established by the shareholder as it is a negative fact. The Company can simply free itself by establishing the fact that the unclaimed or unpaid dividend amount had in fact been transferred to a special account as required under Section 205.

Judicial Interpretations/Case Example	
Once the company establishes that it had in fact transferred the amount to the unpaid dividend account specially created as required under Section 205 the company discharges its responsibility and is no more liable for any punishment.	*Nutech Agros* v *Ch. Mohan Rao,* 2000, 26 SCL 447 (AP).

13. Unpaid Dividend to be Transferred to Special Dividend Account

According to Section 205 A (1), where, a dividend has been declared by a company but has not been paid, or claimed, within thirty days from the date of the declaration, to any shareholder entitled to the payment of the dividend, the company shall, within seven days from the date of expiry of the said period of thirty days, transfer the total amount of dividend which remains unpaid or unclaimed within the said period of thirty days, to a special account to be opened by the company in that behalf in any scheduled bank, to be called "Unpaid Dividend Account of .... Company Limited/ Company (Private) Limited".

14. Transfer of Unpaid/Un-Claimed Dividend to Investor Education and Protection Fund

Any money transferred to the unpaid dividend account of a company, which remains unpaid or unclaimed for a period of seven years from the date of such transfer shall be transferred by the company to the Investor Education and Protection Fund established under sub-section (1) of Section 205C. In terms of the provisions of Section 205C (2) (e) of the Companies Act, the interest accrued on the amount of unpaid dividend shall also be credited to the Investor Education and Protection Fund.

Investor's Education and Protection Fund

By amending the Companies Act in 1999, Investor's Education and Protection Fund was introduced. Under Section 205 C of the Companies Act, every Company is required to transfer certain sums to the Investor Education and Protection Fund constituted by the Central Government vide a notification on 1st October, 2001. The Companies which are required to credit amounts to this Fund, shall do so within 30 days from the due date and shall also file with the concerned ROC a copy of the challan evidencing deposit to the Fund along with a Statement in Form 1.The Fund may use the moneys so collected for the purposes of investor awareness programs and may release funds to such organizations, which are engaged in these activities. Following amounts are to be credited to the fund:

(*i*)   Amounts in the unpaid dividend accounts of companies;

(*ii*) The application money received by companies for allotment of any securities and due for refund;

(*iii*) Matured deposits with companies;

(*iv*) Matured debentures with companies;

(*v*)   The interest accrued on the amounts referred to in clauses (*i*) to (*iv*);

(*vi*) Grants and donations given to the Fund by the Central Government, State Governments, companies or any other institutions and

(*vii*) The interest or other income received out of the investments made from the Fund.

1. Define 'Share'. What are different types of shares that may be issued by a company?

2. When can a company issue redeemable preference shares? What are the restrictions on the power of a company to redeem such shares?

3. What is meant by 'sweat equity'? What are the conditions to be fulfilled by a company proposing to issue sweat equity under the Companies Act ,1956?

4. What are preference shares? Explain what is meant by:

   (a) Cumulative and non-cumulative preference shares.

   (b) Participating and non-participating preference shares.

   (c) Redeemable and irredeemable preference shares?

5. Differeciate between

   (a) Share and Stock.

   (b) Share and Share Certificate.

   (c) Equity Share and Share Capital

   (d) Equity Share and Equity Share with Differential Rights

   (e) Equity and Preference Share

6. What is the meaning of the term 'capital'? What are its different types?

7. Explain the concept of capital in relation to a limited company and state the various senses in which the term capital is used in company law.

8. What is meant by the term 'allotment'? What are the various rules as to allotment? What is the effect of irregular allotment of shares?

9. "If the minimum subscription is not received within 120 days after the opening of the issue, the money received shall be refunded." Comment.

10. What restrictions have been imposed by the Companies Act, 1956 on the allotment of shares? What are the effects of an irregular allotment?

11. Write a note on:

   (a) Initial Public Offer (IPO)

   (b) Only Public Limited Company can Issue Shares

   (c) Eligibility Norms for Companies Issuing Securities

   (d) Post-issue Guidelines

   (e) General Principles of Allotment

   (f) Statutory Conditions of Allotment

   (g) Cancellation of Allotment

   (h) Return of Allotment

   (i) Effect of Irregular Allotment

12. What is the law relating to issue of shares at a discount?

13. Discuss the provisions of the Companies Act, 1956, regarding issue of shares at a premium. State the purpose for which the premium on shares can be utilized.

14. Can a company issue shares at a premium and at a discount? Discuss the conditions which are to be complied with for issuing shares at discount.

15. Discuss the provisions of the Companies Act, 1956 relating to buy back of shares by a company.

16. "A company cannot buy back its own shares." Explain. Are there any exceptions to this rule?

17. Can a company buy its own shares? If so, under what circumstances, a company may buy its own shares?

18. Write a note on:

    (a) Sources of Buy-back

    (b) Conditions for Buy-back

19. "Section 81 is intended to prevent the directors from offering shares to outsiders before offer is made of further issue of capital as a right to the existing shareholder." Critically examine the statement.

20. State briefly the provisions of the Companies Act, 1956, relating to the further issue of equity capital by an existing public company. Also state the cases under which the said shares can be offered to outsiders.

21. "Issue of further shares should be made to the existing shareholders." Discuss. Explain the various aspects relating to Rights Issue of shares by an unlisted company.

22. What are SEBI guidelines regarding:

    (a) Minimum application value

    (b) Allotment of shares

    (c) Issue of bonus shares.

23. What are 'bonus shares'? What is the procedure for issue of bonus shares by a company?

24. Write a note on:

    (a) Regulations 96 and 97 of Table A in respect of issuance of bonus share

    (b) Guidelines for Bonus Issue

    (c) Procedure for issuance of Bonus Shares

    (d) Difference between Right Shares and Bonus Shares

25. Write a detailed note on Book Building.

26. Briefly explain the requirements of the Companies Act, 1956 relating to the issue of share certificates and share warrants. What is the object of a share certificate?

27. "A share certificate is a *prima facie* evidence of the title of a person whose name is entered on it." Examine the statement.

28. "A share certificate of a company is an official publication" Comment.

29. Give the statutory provisions with regard to share certificate and share warrant.

30. What are the circumstances under which and the conditions subject to which a duplicate share certificate can be issued?

31. Under what circumstances a share warrant may be issued by a public company?

32. What is meant by 'share warrant'? Explain the statutory provisions of the Companies Act,1956, relating to the issue of share warrant.In what respect does a share warrant differ from share certificate?

33. State the advantages of depository system.

34. How is transfer of share affected in the dematerialized form?

35. Write a detailed note on De-mat System.

36. What is meant by 'call on shares'? Explain in brief the rules for making a call.

37. Write a short note on:
    (a) Essentials of a Valid Call
    (b) Call may be Raised by a Resolution of Board
    (c) Call is a Debt due to the Company
    (d) A Proper Notice must be given for Making a Call
    (e) Call must be made for the Benefit of Company
    (f) Calls on Shares of Same Class to be made on Uniform Basis

38. Explain the law relating to forfeiture of shares.

39. Write a short note on:
    (a) Shares may be forfeited if call is not paid
    (b) Proper intimation for forfeiture
    (c) Board resolution for forfeiture
    (d) Forfeiture must be *bona fide* and in the interest of a company
    (e) Forfeited shares are company property
    (f) Cancellation of forfeiture
    (g) Re-issue of forfeited shares

40. When can a member validly surrender his shares? Under what circumstances surrender of shares is lawful?

41. "Surrender of shares is a shortcut to forfeiture of shares." Comment.

42. What do you understand by 'Certification of Transfer'? What is the period within which the company should register transfer deed?

43. State the procedure to be followed for transfer of shares.

44. Can the board of directors refuse to register a transfer of shares? What is the remedy open to the transferee in such cases?

45. Explain the legal position of transferor and transferee of shares pending registration by a company.

46. What does a company do in case of an incomplete transfer deed?

47. Write short notes on:

(*a*) Transfer Deed

(*b*) Transfer Deed is duly Stamped

(*c*) When Transfer Deed is Lost

(*d*) Extension of Validity of Transfer Deed

(*e*) Transfer in the case of Partly Paid Shares

(*f*) Time Limit for Issue of Certificate on Transfer

(*g*) Transfer Procedure not Applicable under the De-mat System

(*h*) Forged Transfer

(*i*) Blank Transfer

(*j*) Transmission of shares

(*k*) Evidences for transmission of shares

(*l*) Legal representatives shall not be entitled to exercise voting rights

48. "No dividend can be paid by a company except out of profits." Comment.

49. State the legal provisions relating to disposal of unpaid and unclaimed dividends?

50. Explain the circumstances, if any, under which a dividend, once declared, can be revoked.

51. The shareholder at the annual general meeting of a public limited company unanimously resolved for payment of dividend though the Broad of Directors did not recommend payment of any dividend. Discuss.

52. What do you understand by 'dividend'? Briefly state the legal provisions regarding payment of dividend.

53. Explain the rules for ascertaining the divisible profits for declaration of dividends.

54. Write a note on "Investor's Education and Protection Fund".

8

Company Directors

Why Directors?

- A company is an artificial person, invisible, intangible and exits only in the eyes of law. Therefore, somebody needs to act on its behalf in dealing with others. It needs natural persons who act as its eyes, ears, brain, nerves and essential limbs.

Judicial Interpretations/Case Example	
LJ Cairns said,"The company itself cannot act in its own person......; it can only act through directors".	*Ferguson* v *Wilson* (1866), *LR2 Ch.,* App 77 page 89 - 90.
Lord Wensleydate said, "The shareholders can only act through their directors and the act of individual shareholders has no effect on the company at large".	*Ernest* v *Nicholls,* (1857), 6HL Cas 401 page 419.

Meaning

- There is no statutory definition of a company director although section2 (13) of the Companies Act ,1956 does provide that the expression, 'Director' includes any person occupying the position of director, by whatever name called. Identical provisions exist in the English Company Law.
- Instead of name, designation or title, the definition of director is based purely on position occupied by him and functions he performs. Thus, as per the said provision, a person may be considered as a director if he or she is either formally appointed to the Board i.e., a 'de-jure director' or is a 'de-facto director', or is a 'shadow director'.

Classification of Directors

■ Deemed Director

- Explanation to Section 303 (1) provide that any person in accordance with whose directions or instructions, the Board of Directors of a company is accustomed to act shall be deemed to be a director of the company. Thus, as per this provision, a person who is not appointed formally as a director of a company but who gives directions to which the Board is accustomed to act is a director in the eyes of law.

❑ The interpretation of "person in accordance with whose directions or instructions directors are accustomed to act" according to Section 7 of the Act, is that professional advisors such as company secretaries, chartered accountants, auditors, solicitors, etc. are not deemed to be considered as directors. Thus, if the Board acts on the advice given by a person in professional capacity, that person will not be treated as deemed director.

❑ The word "accustomed to act" here implies repetitive behaviour or acting as a matter of regular practice over a period of time or acting in a series of transactions. Thus, acting of the Board once in a while on the directives of a person shall not make such person a director.

■ De-Facto Director

❑ Directors who have not been formally appointed yet openly act as or openly assume the position of director, despite a lack of authority and right to act, are *de-facto* directors.

■ Shadow Director

❑ Shadow director is not the same as a *de-facto* director.

❑ The phrase 'shadow director' is more suitable for someone who hides the fact that he is in control of the company whereas a *de-facto* director will be making it appear as if he is a director of the company in accordance with whose directions or instructions the Board is accustomed to act.

Judicial Interpretations/Case Example	
In order to establish that a person is a shadow director of a company: (*a*) It is not necessary to show that the person gives directions or instructions on every matter on which the directors act; but it must be shown that the person has a real influence in the company's corporate affairs. (*b*) Advice (excluding professional advice) may be a direction or instruction. (*c*) It is not necessary to show that the directors surrendered their discretion. (*d*) Despite the use of term 'shadow director' it is not necessary to characterize the person as to lurking in the 'shadows'. It is possible for a person to be as shadow director quite openly.	*Secretary of State for trading and industry (4F)* v *Deverell,* (2001) Ch 340.
Shadow director pre-supposes that there is a Board of Directors who acts in accordance with the instructions from someone else.	*Lo Line Electrics Motor Ltd.,* (1988) 2 (All) ER 692.

Contd...

Shadow director must be in-fact a puppet master controlling the actions of the Board, whilst the director must be "cats paw" of the shadow director. The directors on the Board must be persons who act on the directions or instructions of the shadow director as a matter of regular practice.	*Unisoft Group Ltd.,* No 2 (1994) per Harman J page 775.
It is possible for a parent company to be a shadow director of its subsidiary companies.	*Gramophone and Typewriter Fer Ltd.* v *Stanley,* (1908) 2KB 89.

■ First Director

- ❑ First directors are appointed by the promoters.
- ❑ Such directors are either named in the Articles of Association or appointed in the manner provided in the Articles.
- ❑ Where Articles are silent, then subscribers to the Memorandum of Association who are individuals are deemed to be the first directors in accordance with Section 254. The Ministry *vide* circular No. 195-1416194-CL-V dated 16.2.1995 has advised that at-least one of the promoters must be first directors. The subscribers to the Memorandum, who are deemed to be the directors, shall hold office until the first general meeting held after registration but prior to holding of first AGM.
- ❑ If all subscribers to the Memorandum are body corporate (promoters need not be individuals) and the first directors are not named in the Articles, the company in that case will have no directors till its Annual General Meeting.
- ❑ First directors hold office till directors are duly appointed in general meetings of the shareholders as per Section 255.

■ Additional Director [Section 260]

- ❑ This is a short cut to attract competent persons as directors on the Board.
- ❑ The Board has powers to appoint additional directors provided authorized by the Articles of Association.
- ❑ Number of the directors and additional directors together shall not exceed the maximum strength fixed for the Board by the Articles.
- ❑ Such director enjoys same powers as the other directors.
- ❑ Such director can be appointed either in Board meeting or through circulation.
- ❑ Such director can be appointed Managing Director or Whole-Time Director but in such a situation, his term may be only up-to the AGM.
- ❑ Such director should also purchase qualification shares as per the requirement of the Articles.
- ❑ Such director is to hold office till the next AGM.

■ Casual Director or Ad-Hoc Director [Section 262]

- ❑ Section 262 ensures timely filing of casual vacancy to facilitate smooth running of the company.
- ❑ In the case of a public company or a private company which is a subsidiary of a public company, if the office of any director appointed by the company in general meeting is vacated before his term of office will expire in the normal course, the resulting casual vacancy may, in default of and subject to any regulations in the articles of the company, be filled by the Board of directors at a meeting of the Board.
- ❑ Where the Articles are silent, the casual vacancy may be filled by the shareholders in a general meeting.
- ❑ Casual Director is appointed when there is a casual vacancy that may occur by death, resignation, disqualification, removal, insanity or insolvency; but not by retirement or expiration of time fixed for appointment. But, vacancy in the office of a non-rotational director cannot be regarded as casual vacancy.
- ❑ A casual vacancy if filled by the Board is again fallen vacant; the resulting vacancy cannot be filled by the Board as this vacancy strictly speaking is not casual. The Board in such a situation can appoint an additional director, if authorized by the Articles. The Department of Company Affairs (now MCA) has taken a different view and held that the Board in the interest of smooth functioning of the company may fill the casual vacancy as many times as may be necessary.
- ❑ Provisions of Section 262 shall not apply to a private company. It is not mandatory in that case to fill casual vacancy and the Board may decide to keep the vacancy unfilled.
- ❑ Tenure of casual director is not up-to the AGM but up-to the expiry of the term of the director in whose place; casual director is appointed.

■ Alternate Director [Section 313]

- ❑ Appointment of alternate director helps solving the problems of lack of quorum in Board meetings.
- ❑ Alternate director can be appointed by the Board by passing resolution in Board meeting or by circulation or in general meeting.
- ❑ The appointment should be authorized by the Articles or by a resolution passed by the company in general meeting.
- ❑ Such director is appointed to act for a director (called "the original director") during his absence for a period of not less than three months from the State in which meetings of the Board are ordinarily held.
- ❑ Such director shall not hold office as such for a period longer than that permissible to the original director in whose place he has been appointed

and shall vacate office if and when the original director returns to the State in which meetings of the Board are ordinarily held.

❑ Such director is not a representative proxy or an agent of the original director.

❑ Such director has the same rights, duties, obligations and liabilities like other directors.

❑ Provisions of Sections 268, 269, 270, 274, 283, 314 and provisions relating to managerial remunerations shall apply to an alternate director as they apply to an original director.

❑ Many provisions do not apply to alternate director *i.e.*, such director are not counted for maximum limit of directorship which a person can hold or such appointment is not considered as increase in strength of directors.

❑ The term of alternate director shall not exceed the term permissible to the original director. Thus if the original director ceases to be a director by reason of Section 283 (disqualifications, incapacity, insolvency, conviction, absence in consecutive three meetings of the Board, removal etc.), the alternate director shall immediately cease to held his office. The term of the alternate director comes to an end on the return of the original director to the state in which the Board meetings are ordinarily held.

❑ If the original director is non-rotational, then alternate director can continue indefinitely.

❑ Provisions about alternate directors in Section 313 apply to all companies including private.

■ Executive and Non-Executive Director

❑ The term 'executive director' is usually used to describe a person who is both a member of the Board and who also has day to day responsibilities in respect of the affairs of the company. Production director or finance director or managing director or whole time director is examples of executive director.

❑ Executive directors are in the employment of the company. They are in fact the inside directors. Non-executive directors on other hand are not in the employment of the company and are part time or outside directors. Such directors are not appointed under a contract of service and are not intimately connected with the company. Professional directors and nominee directors fall in this category. Non-executive directors are members of the Board, but normally take no part in the day to day implementation of Board policy within the company and are appointed to provide the company with the benefits of professional expertise and voice on the Board. They play very effective role in the governance of particularly listed companies.

❑ Only reference of these terms is in clause 49 of the Listing Agreement that has a provision for a 'Balanced Board' comprising both executive and non executive directors. At-least half of the Board as per clause 49, shall be non- executive directors.

Judicial Interpretations/Case Example	
Non-executive directors can be effective in ensuring that the Board acts in the interests of the company rather than a member or members of the Board. However, as held in this case, it is unrealistic to expect non-executive directors to control a determined and powerful managing director.	*Re: Polly Peck International PLC,* (no 2) (1994) 1 Be Le 574.

■ *Independent Director*

❑ Currently the Companies Act, 1956 is silent on the term 'independent director'. The Companies Bill, 2008 based on the recommendations of the JJ Irani Committee (2005) has some provisions on it.

❑ The term 'independent director' has been defined in the Clause 49 of the Listing Agreement that has provisions on independent director.

❑ As per clause 49, the company should have, a balanced Board, comprising executive, non-executive and independent directors. If the Chairman of the company is from executive side, at-least half of the Board should be independent and if the Chairman is from non-executive side, then at-least one third of the Board should be independent. The Companies Bill, 2008 has a provision that at-least one third of the Board should be independent.

Independent Director in Clause **49:** The expression 'independent director' in the Indian context shall mean a non-executive director of the company who:

(*a*) Apart from receiving director's remuneration, does not have any material pecuniary relationships or transactions with the company, its promoters, its directors, its senior management or its holding company, its subsidiaries and associates which may affect independence of the director.

(*b*) Is not related to promoters or persons occupying management positions at the board level or at one level below the board;

(*c*) Has not been an executive of the company in the immediately preceding three financial years;

(*d*) Is not a partner or an executive or was not partner or an executive during the preceding three years, of any of the following:

➢ The statutory audit firm or the internal audit firm that is associated with the company, and

➢ The legal firm (s) and consulting firm (s) that have a material association with the company.

(*e*) Is not a material supplier, service provider or customer or a lesser or lessee of the company, which may affect independence of the director; and

(*f*) Is not a substantial shareholder of the company (*i.e.*, owning two per cent or more of the block of voting shares)?

■ *Nominee Director*

- A director appointed by third party such as financial institutions or a bank which has provided financial assistance to the company is called a nominee director.
- Nominee directors act as a watchdog to safeguard the interest of the funding institutions. They ensure the compliance of the conditions or the loan agreement between the company and the funding institution.
- The appointment of the nominee director shall be authorized by the Articles of Association of the company.
- All the provisions of the Companies Act normally apply to nominee director. Therefore, a nominee director can also be prosecuted for default and non compliance of the provisions, if found guilty.
- But, the provisions of the Companies Act do not apply to a nominee director appointed under a Statutory Act. Therefore, the appointment of nominee director nominated by the IDBI, UTI, LIC, is governed by the relevant Act and not by the provisions of the Companies Act. Similarly, the directors nominated (appointed) by the consent of government under section 408 are also exempted by the provisions of the Companies Act. Such directors shall not retire by rotation, shall not be required to hold qualification shares, can be appointed even if the Articles do not have provisions, can be appointed even if the appointment results in increasing the strength of the Board, beyond the maximum limit specified in the Articles is not counted for the purpose of total strength of directors and can even be removed only by the appointing authority. However, the nominee directors appointed by the ICICI and IFCI are covered by the provisions of the Companies Act because ICICI and IFCI are incorporated under Companies Act and not by some Special Act.
- Clause 49 of the Listing Agreement treats nominee directors independent. JJ Irani Committee (2005) has recommended that nominee directors should not be treated as independent director.

■ *Small Shareholder's Director [Section 252A]*

- A public company having a paid up capital of Rs.5 crore or more and 1000 or more small shareholders may have a director elected by such small shareholders in the manner as may be prescribed in the Company (Appointment of Small Shareholder's Directors Rules, 2001). Small shareholder here means a shareholder holding shares of nominal value of Rs. 20,000 or less in a public company. Holding shares include both equity shares and preference shares.
- Small Shareholder's Director may be elected by the company *suo moto* or on the requisition of the small shareholders.

❑ It becomes obligatory for a company to appoint Small Shareholder's Director if there is a notice/demand from the required number of small shareholders.

❑ Requirements of the notice are:

➢ Notice is given at-least 14 days before the shareholder's meeting.

➢ Notice is given by at-least 1/10th of small shareholders.

➢ Notice is signed by at-least 100 small shareholders.

➢ Notice shall specify the name, address and number of shares held by the proposing small shareholder and the person whose name is proposed as Small Shareholder's Director.

❑ In the listed company Small Shareholder's Director shall be elected by the postal ballot method as prescribed under Section 192A. In the case of unlisted company, Small Shareholder's Director is elected if majority of small shareholders recommend his candidature in their meeting.

❑ Only a small shareholder can be appointed as a 'Small Shareholder's Director'.

❑ A consent in writing to act as a director is to be filed by the Small Shareholder's Director.

❑ A Small Shareholder's Director shall be appointed for a maximum period of 3 years. He may be re-elected for another 3 years.

❑ He shall not retire by rotation.

❑ He cannot be appointed in more than 2 companies.

❑ He cannot be appointed as a Whole Time Director or a Managing Director.

❑ Disqualifications provisions given in Section 274 (1) (4) inserted in the year 2000 shall not apply to such directors. The section provides that if a company fails to file annual accounts and annual returns for consecutive three financial years on and after 1st April, 1999 or has failed to repay deposits or interests, redeem debentures or repay dividends and such failure continues for one year, then the director of the company shall not be eligible for directorship in any company for 5 years.

❑ Small Shareholder's Director shall vacate his office if he ceases to be a small shareholder. But he shall not vacate office if he does not obtain qualification shares.

❑ Other grounds for vacation of office are same as applicable to any other director specified in Section 283.

■ Managing Director

❑ 'Managing Director' (MD) means a director who, by virtue of an agreement with the company or of a resolution passed by the company in general meeting or by its Board of directors or, by virtue of its memorandum or articles of association, is entrusted with substantial powers of management which would not otherwise be exercisable by him, and includes a director occupying the position of a managing director, by whatever name called.

■ *Whole Time Director (WTD)*

- ❑ The term Whole Time Director (WTD) is used simultaneously with MD in many sections.
- ❑ WTD has not been defined in the Act.
- ❑ WTD includes a director in whole time employment.

Board of Directors or Board

As per Section 252 (3), the directors of a company collectively are referred to as the 'Board' or 'Board of Directors', which is a group of individuals elected by the shareholders to manage the affairs of the company. Company being an artificial person acts only through human beings designated as directors who act as eyes, ears, brain, nerves and essential limbs of the company. The Board is the supreme authority that is entitled to exercise all such powers as the company is authorized to exercise except those powers which are exercised exclusively by the shareholders in their meetings. The success of the company depends upon the efficient functioning of its Board.

Appointment of Directors

■ *Who may be appointed as a Director? [Section 253]*

- ❑ Only individuals to be directors.
- ❑ No body corporate, association or firm shall be appointed director of a company and only individual shall be so appointed.
- ❑ Provided that no company shall appoint or re-appoint any individual as director of the company unless he has been allotted a Director Identification Number (DIN) under Section 266B.

Judicial Interpretations/Case Example	
Individuals are appointed as directors as it will be difficult to fix the responsibility of a body corporate, association or firm as a director.	*Oriental Metal Pressing Ltd.* v *B.K. Thakoor,* (1961) 31 Comp Cas 143.

Deemed Directors [Section 254]

- ❑ In default of and subject to any regulations in the articles of a company, subscribers to the Memorandum who are individuals shall be deemed to be directors until directors are duly appointed in accordance with Section 255.
- ❑ But, a deemed or shadow director need not be an individual.

■ *Minimum Number of Directors [Section 252]*

- ❑ Every public company (other than a public company which ' as become such by virtue of Section 43A) shall have at least three directors: Provided that a public company having a paid-up capital of five crore rupees or more; and one thousand or more small shareholders, may have a director elected by such small shareholders in the manner as may be prescribed. In this case, a public company shall have at-least 4 directors.

> *Explanation: For the purposes of this section 'small shareholders' means a shareholder holding shares of nominal value of twenty thousand rupees or less in a public company to which this section applies.*

- ❑ Every other company (*i.e.,* a private company) shall have at least two directors.
- ❑ Smaller number of directors not less than statutory minimum limit can validly act if Articles of Association provide so.
- ❑ Any business transacted after the number of directors fall below the minimum number of directors is void.
- ❑ Every company must have the minimum number of directors at all times during its life.

Judicial Interpretations/Case Example	
If the minimum number of directors provided is three and only 2 directors are appointed, allotment of shares by two directors is invalid, though 2 directors are required for forming a quorum.	*British Empire Match Co.,* (1988) 59 LT 291.

■ *Maximum Number of Directors*

- ❑ Companies Act does not provide any maximum number of directors. Thus, there is no limit on number of directors.
- ❑ All members may be appointed directors, since no maximum limit is mentioned in the Act.
- ❑ The Articles generally specify the minimum and maximum number of directors. For instance, the Articles may fix 5 as the minimum and 10 as the maximum number of directors on the Board. Directors appointed by the Central Government under Section 408 or the Company Law Board (now Tribunal) under Section 397 or 398 or special directors appointed pursuant to SICA or nominee directors appointed by public financial institutions are not to be counted for the purpose of maximum limit.

■ Appointment of Directors Retiring by Rotation [Section 255]

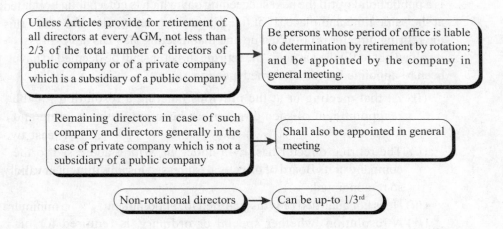

Unless Articles provide for retirement of all directors at every AGM, not less than 2/3 of the total number of directors of public company or of a private company which is a subsidiary of a public company → Be persons whose period of office is liable to determination by retirement by rotation; and be appointed by the company in general meeting.

Remaining directors in case of such company and directors generally in the case of private company which is not a subsidiary of a public company → Shall also be appointed in general meeting

Non-rotational directors → Can be up-to 1/3rd

■ Ascertainment of Number of Directors Retiring by Rotation [Section 256]

❑ At the first annual general meeting of a public company, or a private company which is a subsidiary of a public company, held next after the date of the general meeting at which the first directors are appointed in accordance with Section 255 and at every subsequent annual general meeting, one-third of such of the directors for the time being as are liable to retire by rotation, or if their number is not three or a multiple of three, then, the number nearest to one-third, shall retire from office. [Sec. 256(1)]

    (*a*) Not less than 2/3rd of total number of directors shall be the directors whose office is liable to determination by retirement by rotation. Any fraction contained in that 2/3rd shall be rounded off as one. These directors are referred to as rotational directors.

    (*b*) At every AGM, 1/3rd (or nearest to 1/3rd) of rotational directors (23rd of total) shall compulsorily retire from office.

    (*c*) Directors who are longest in the office since their last appointment shall retire first.

    (*d*) But, as between persons who became directors on the same day, those who are to retire shall, in default of and subject to any agreement among themselves, be determined by lot.

    (*e*) At the annual general meeting at which a director retires as aforesaid, the company may fill up the vacancy by appointing the retiring director or some other person thereto. [Sec. 256(3)]

❑ If the place of the retiring director is not so filled up and the meeting has not expressly resolved not to fill the vacancy, the meeting shall stand adjourned till the same day in the next week, at the same time and place, or if that day is a public holiday, till the next succeeding day which is not a public holiday, at the same time and place. If at the adjourned meeting also, the place of the retiring director is not filled up and that meeting also has not expressly resolved not to fill the vacancy, the retiring director shall be deemed to have been re-appointed at the adjourned meeting, unless:

(*i*) At that meeting or at the previous meeting a resolution for the reappointment of such director has been put to the meeting and lost;

(*ii*) The retiring director has, by a notice in writing addressed to the company or its Board of directors, expressed his unwillingness to be so re-appointed;

(*iii*) He is not qualified or is disqualified for appointment;

(*iv*) A resolution, whether special or ordinary, is required for his appointment or re-appointment in virtue of any provisions of this Act; or

(*v*) The proviso to sub-section (2) of Section 263 is applicable to the case.

Explanation: *In this section and in Section 257, the expression "Retiring Director" means a director retiring by rotation.*

Example: *ABC Company Ltd. has 5 directors. How many directors are liable to retire?*
Ans: *Number of rotational directors comes to 4 (2/3 of 5 is 3.33 rounded off and taken as 4). 1/3rd of 4 rotational directors to compulsorily retire comes to 1(1/3rd of 4 is 1.33 and nearest to 1.33 is 1). So, 1 director is to retire.*

If directors do not hold AGM in time, can they Continue till the General Meeting?

❑ As held in *BR Kundra* v *Motion Pictures Asson* 1976, 46 *Comp. Cas.* 339, *Delhi High Court,* the directors due to retire shall vacate office latest on the date on which AGM was to be held.

Deemed Reappointment of Retiring Director

❑ Vacancies caused by retirement be filled up at the same or adjourned meeting otherwise retiring director shall be deemed to have been appointed.

Private Company

❑ Rotation of directors is not compulsory.
❑ A private company can have perm nent directors unless they are removed under Section 284.

■ Right of Persons other than Retiring Directors to Stand for Directorship [Section 257]

- ❑ A person who is not a retiring director shall be eligible for appointment to the office of director at any general meeting, if he or some member intending to propose him, has given a notice to the company in writing under his hand signifying his candidature for the office of director or the intention of such member to propose him as a candidate for that office, as the case may be. [Sec. 257 (1)]
- ❑ Not less than 14 days notice is to be given to the company before the meeting.
- ❑ Company is required to give not less than 7 days notice to every member either by individual notice or through advertisement in at-least 2 newspapers circulating in the place where the registered office of the company is located, of which one is published in the English language and the other in the regional language of that place.
- ❑ Such a candidate is to deposit Rs. 500 which is refundable if the person succeeds in getting elected as a director.

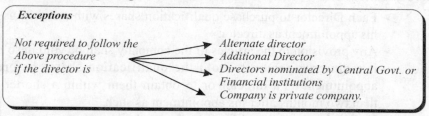

Exceptions

*Not required to follow the
Above procedure
if the director is* → *Alternate director
Additional Director
Directors nominated by Central Govt. or
Financial institutions
Company is private company.*

■ Increase or Reduction in the Number of Directors [Section 258]

- ❑ For increase or reduction in the number of directors within the limits fixed by the Articles, ordinary resolution in the shareholders meeting is required.
- ❑ No approval of Central Government required, if the increase is within the limits given in Articles.

Increase in Number of Directors to Require Government Sanction [Sec. 259]

- ❑ In the case of a public company or a private company which is a subsidiary of a public company, any increase in the number of its directors, except-

    (a) In the case of a company which was in existence on the 21st day of July, 1951, an increase which was within the permissible maximum under its articles as in force on that date, and

    (b) In the case of a company which came or may come into existence after that date, an increase which is within the permissible maximum under its articles as first registered, shall not have any effect unless approved by the Central Government, and shall become void if, and in so far as, it is disapproved by that Government.

Provided that where such permissible maximum is twelve or less than twelve, no approval of the Central Government shall be required if the increase in the number of its directors does not make the total number of its directors more than twelve.

> *Exemptions*
> - *Independent Private Company*
> - *Government Company*
> - *Company Registered under Section 25*

Qualifications of Director [Section 270]

❑ Act imposes no share qualifications for directorship. Article may contain provisions for the same; otherwise director need not be a shareholder unless he voluntarily wishes.

> *As per Regulation 66 of Table A, the qualification of a director shall be the holding of at least one share in the company.*

If share qualifications is fixed by the Articles:

➢ Each Director to purchase qualification shares within 2 months after his appointment as director.

➢ Any provision in the articles of the company shall be void in so far as it requires a person to hold the qualification shares before his appointment as a director or to obtain them within a shorter time than two months after his appointment as such.

➢ Nominal value of qualification shares shall not to exceed Rs. 5000 or the nominal value of one share where it exceeds five thousand rupees.

➢ Share warrant will not be counted for this purpose.

If Qualifications Shares are not Purchased within 2 Months [Section 272]

❑ The director is to vacate his office on the expiry of 2 months.

❑ If, after the expiry of the said period of two months, any person acts as a director of the company when he does not hold the qualification shares referred to in Section 270, he shall be punishable with fine which may extend to five hundred rupees for every day between such expiry and the last day on which he acted as a director. [Sec. 270]

❑ If a person functions as a director when he knows that the office of director held by him has become vacant on account of any of the disqualifications, he shall be punishable with fine which may extend to five thousand rupees for each day on which he so functions as a director. [Sec. 283 (2A)]

❑ Subscribers to Memorandum of Association who are deemed to be first directors need not hold qualification share unless the Articles provide.

Exemption: Independent Private Company.

Disqualifications [Section 274]

A person shall not be capable of being appointed director of a company, if he

(*a*) Has been found to be of unsound mind by a Court of competent jurisdiction and the finding is in force;

(*b*) Is an undischarged insolvent;

(*c*) Has applied to be adjudicated as an insolvent and his application is pending;

(*d*) Has been convicted by a Court of any offence involving moral turpitude and sentenced in respect thereof to imprisonment for not less than six months, and a period of five years has not elapsed from the date of expiry of the sentence;

(*e*) Has not paid any call in respect of shares of the company held by him, whether alone or jointly with others, and six months have elapsed from the last day fixed for the payment of the call; or

(*f*) An order disqualifying him for appointment as director has been passed by a Court in pursuance of Section 203 and is in force, unless the leave of the Court has been obtained for his appointment in pursuance of that section;

(*g*) Is already a director of a public company which:—

    (*i*) Has not filed the annual accounts and annual returns for any continuous three financial years commencing on and after the first day of April, 1999; or

    (*ii*) Has failed to repay its deposit or interest thereon on due date or redeem its debentures on due date or pay dividend and such failure continues for one year or more:

    Provided that such person shall not be eligible to be appointed as a director of any other public company for a period of five years from the date on which such public company in which he is a director failed to file annual accounts and annual returns or has failed to repay its deposit or interest or redeem its debentures on due date or pay dividend.

> ➤ The Central Government may, by notification in the Official Gazette, remove—
> (a) the disqualification incurred by any person in virtue of clause (d) of Section 274 (1), either generally or in relation to any company or companies specified in the notification; or (b) the disqualification incurred by any person in virtue of clause (e) of Section 274 (1).
>
> ➤ A private company which is not a subsidiary of a public company may, by its Articles, provide that a person shall be disqualified for appointment as a director on any grounds in addition to those specified in Section 274 (1).

Number of Directorship [Section 275]

◻ No person shall, save as otherwise provided in Section 276, hold office at the same time as director in more than fifteen companies.

Choice by Person becoming Director of more than 15 Companies [Section 277]

◻ Where a person already holding the office of director in fifteen companies is appointed, after the commencement of the Companies (Amendment) Act, 2000, as a director of any other company, the appointment—

(*a*) Shall not take effect unless such person has, within fifteen days thereof, effectively vacated his office as director in any of the companies in which he was already a director; and

(*b*) Shall become void immediately on the expiry of the fifteen days if he has not, before such expiry, effectively vacated his office as director in any of the other companies aforesaid.

◻ Where a person already holding the office of director in fourteen companies or less is appointed, after the commencement of the Companies (Amendment) Act, 2000, as a director of other companies, making the total number of his directorships more than fifteen, he shall choose the directorships which he wishes to continue to hold or to accept, so however that the total number of the directorships, old and new, held by him shall not exceed fifteen.

◻ None of the new appointments of director shall take effect until such choice is made; and all the new appointments shall become void if the choice is not made within fifteen days of the day on which the last of them was made.

Exclusion of Certain Directorships [Section 278]

◻ In calculating, for the purposes of Sections 275, 276 and 277, the number of companies of which a person may be a director, the following companies shall be excluded, namely:—

➢ Independent Private Company
➢ Unlimited Companies
➢ An as sociation not carrying on business for profit or which prohibits the payment of a dividend.
➢ Alternate directorship appointed during absence.

Penalty [Section 279]

◻ Any person who holds office, or acts, as a director of more than fifteen companies in contravention of the foregoing provisions shall be punishable with fine which may extend to fifty thousand rupees in respect of each of those companies after the first fifteen.

Who can Appoint Directors?

■ By Promoters

- ❑ First Director are either named in the Articles or appointed by the promoters in the manner provided in the Articles.
- ❑ When Articles are silent, then subscribers to the Memorandum of Association are deemed to be considered as the first directors. If all the subscribers to Memorandum are body corporate and first directors have not been named in the Articles, company will have no directors till the AGM.
- ❑ First directors are to hold office till directors are duly appointed in general meeting as per Section 255.

■ By Shareholders [Sections 253, 255, 256, 257]

- ❑ As explained earlier, directors of public company or of a private company which is a subsidiary of a public company are appointed by the shareholders in general meeting by the system of rotation as per the provisions of Sections 253, 255, 256 and 257.

■ By Board [Sections 260, 262, 313]

- ❑ As explained earlier, Board has powers to appoint additional directors, casual directors and alternate directors as per the provisions of Sections 260, 262, 313, provided authorized by the Articles of Association.

■ By Central Government [Section 408]

- ❑ The Central Government may appoint such number of persons as the CLB Tribunal may, by order in writing, specify as being necessary to effectively safeguard the interests of the company, or its shareholders or the public interests to hold office as directors thereof for such period, not exceeding three years on any one occasion, as it may think fit, if the Tribunal on a reference made to it by the Central Government or on an application of not less than one hundred members of the company or of the members of the company holding not less than one-tenth of the total voting power therein, is satisfied, after such inquiry as it deems fit to make, that it is necessary to make the appointment or appointments in order to prevent the affairs of the company being conducted either in a manner which is oppressive to any members of the company or in a manner which is prejudicial to the interests of the company or to public interest.

■ Appointment by Third Parties

- ❑ Financial institutions, foreign collaborations, holding companies, other lenders may also appoint directors.

Appointment by Proportionate Representation [Section 265]

❑ Ordinarily directors are appointed by majority:
  ➢ 51% or more may elect all the directors.
  ➢ 49% may not find representation on the Board.

❑ System of proportionate representation is to provide proportional representation to minority by way of single transferable vote or through the system of cumulative voting.

Single Transferable Vote:

$$\text{Quota} = \frac{\text{Votes Polled} + 1}{\text{No of Seats} + 1}$$

Cumulative Voting:

$$\text{Quota} = \frac{\text{Total Votes Polled (No. of shares (votes)} \times \text{No. of directors to be elected)}}{\text{No. of Seats}}$$

Removal of Directors

By Shareholders [Section 284]

❑ A company may, by ordinary resolution, remove a director (not being a director appointed by the Central Government in pursuance of Section 408) before the expiry of his period of office: provided that this sub-section shall not, in the case of a private company, authorise the removal of a director holding office for life on the 1st day of April, 1952, whether or not he is subject to retirement under an age limit by virtue of the articles or otherwise: provided further that nothing contained in this sub-section shall apply where the company has availed itself of the option given to it under Section 265 to appoint not less than two-thirds of the total number of directors according to the principle of proportional representation. [Sec. 284 (1)]

❑ Special notice shall be required of any resolution to remove a director under this section, or to appoint somebody instead of a director so removed at the meeting at which he is removed. [Sec. 284 (2)]

❑ On receipt of notice of a resolution to remove a director under this section, the company shall forthwith send a copy thereof to the director concerned, and the director (whether or not he is a member of the company) shall be entitled to be heard on the resolution at the meeting. [Sec. 284 (3)]

❑ A vacancy created by the removal of a director under this section may, if he had been appointed by the company in general meeting or by the Board in pursuance of Section 262, be filled by the appointment of another director in his stead by the meeting at which he is removed, provided special notice of the intended appointment has been given under sub-section (2). [Sec. 284 (5)]

❏ If the vacancy is not filled under sub-section (5), it may be filled as a casual vacancy in accordance with the provisions, so far as they may be applicable, of Section 262, and all the provisions of that section shall apply accordingly: provided that the director who was removed from office shall not be re-appointed as a director by the Board of directors. [Sec. 284 (6)]

❏ A director appointed in place shall hold office until the date up to which his predecessor would have held office if he had not been removed as aforesaid.

❏ Following cannot be removed:

   ➤ Appointed by Central Government under Section 408

   ➤ Of a private company for life as on April, 1952

   ➤ Elected by proportional representation under Section 265

   ➤ Appointed by Central Government under IDRA Act, 1951

   ➤ Special directors appointed under Sick Industrial Companies (Special Provisions) Act, 1985

   ➤ Appointed by financial institutions

   ➤ Nominee Directors

   ➤ Appointed by CLB/Tribunal under Section 402

By Central Government [Section 388 B]

❏ The Central Government can ask CLB/Tribunal to inquire into the case and order removal of the director/directors where in the opinion of the Central Government there are circumstances suggesting:

   (*a*) That any person concerned in the conduct and management of the affairs of a company is or has been in connection therewith guilty of fraud, misfeasance, persistent negligence or default in carrying out his obligations and functions under the law, or breach of trust; or

   (*b*) That the business of a company is not or has not been conducted and managed by such person in accordance with sound business principles or prudent commercial practices; or

   (*c*) That a company is or has been conducted and managed by such person in a manner which is likely to cause, or has caused, serious injury or damage to the interest of the trade, industry or business to which such company pertains; or

   (*d*) That the business of a company is or has been conducted and managed by such person with intent to defraud its creditors, members or any other persons or otherwise for a fraudulent or unlawful purpose or in a manner prejudicial to public interest,

By Company Law Board/Tribunal [Section 402]

❏ If, on any application, the Company Law Board (CLB)/Tribunal is of opinion that the company's affairs are being conducted in a manner prejudicial to public interest or in a manner oppressive to any member or members; or that by reason of any material change in the management or control of the company, it is likely that the affairs of the company will be conducted as aforesaid, and that to wind up the company would unfairly prejudice such member or members, but that otherwise the facts would justify the making of a winding up order on the ground that it was just and equitable that the company should be wound up; the CLB/Tribunal may, with a view to bringing to an end the matters complained of, make such order as it thinks fit. [Sections 397 and 398]

❑ Without prejudice to the generality of the powers of the CLB/Tribunal under Section 397 or 398, any order under either section may provide for the termination, setting aside or modification of any agreement, howsoever arrived at, between the company and any other director, upon such terms and conditions as may, in the opinion of the Tribunal be just and equitable in all the circumstances of the case. [Sec. 402]

Managing Director [Section 2 (26)]

❑ 'Managing Director' (MD) means a director who, by virtue of an agreement with the company or of a resolution passed by the company in general meeting or by its Board of directors or, by virtue of its memorandum or articles of association, is entrusted with substantial powers of management which would not otherwise be exercisable by him, and includes a director occupying the position of a managing director, by whatever name called.

❑ A director is entrusted with substantial powers of management

Powers may be entrusted	❑ By Board Resolution
	❑ Shareholder Resolution
	❑ By Memorandum
	❑ By Articles

❑ Not substantial powers, if he performs:

  ➢ Administrative acts (GM/ president),
  ➢ Acts of routine nature (affix common seal),
  ➢ Draws or endorses cheques,
  ➢ Signs any certificate of shares.

❑ 'Managing Director' is necessarily to be a director.
❑ 'Managing Director' is executive head of the company subject to control of Board.
❑ 'Managing Director' is entrusted with managerial functions even though he may be called technical advisor or technical director.
❑ 'Managing Director' can be treated as an employee as held by the Hon'ble Supreme Court in the *Employees State Insurance Corporation* (*ESIC*) v *Apex Engineering* (*P*) *Ltd.*, 1998.

Appointment of Managing Director [Section 2 (26)]

Ways:

> ➤ By an Agreement with Company
> ➤ By a Resolution of Shareholders
> ➤ By a Resolution of Directors
> ➤ By Virtue of Memorandum/Articles

❑ On and from the commencement of the Companies (Amendment) Act, 1988, no appointment of a person as a managing or whole-time director or a manager in a public company or a private company which is a subsidiary of a public company shall be made except with the approval of the Central Government unless such appointment is made in accordance with the conditions specified in Parts I and II of Schedule XIII (the said Parts being subject to the provisions of Part III of that Schedule) and a return in the prescribed form is filed within ninety days from the date of such appointment. [Sec. 269 (2)]

❑ If no approval is given by the Central Government, MD shall vacate office or pay fine Rs. 500 per day

Contravention of Schedule XIII

> ➤ Company liable to pay fine upto Rs. 50,000
> ➤ Every officer liable to pay fine upto Rs. 1,00,000
> ➤ MD /WTD/ Manager to refund amount of managerial remuneration received

Number of Companies in which a Person Appointed as Managing Director [Section 316 (1)]

❑ Public company or a private company that is subsidiary to public company, may appoint a person as MD if he is the MD or manager of not more than one company including a private company not subsidiary to public company, by passing unanimous resolution in the meeting of Board.

Ceiling [Section 316 (2)]

❑ MD or Manager is appointed in not more than 2 companies, in which atleast one a public company or private company subsidiary to public company.

> **Exception to Section 316 (2):** *The Central Government may, by order, permit any person to be appointed as a managing director of more than two companies if the Central Government is satisfied that it is necessary that the companies should, for their proper working function as a single unit and have a common managing director.* [Sec. 316 (4)]
>
> **Exception:** *Circular dated 16/7/85- wholly owned Government companies are exempted from Section 316.*

Private Company: A person can be appointed as MD of any number of private companies

- ❑ But a person cannot be appointed as Whole Time Director (WTD) in more than one company even with the Central Government approval.

Tenure [Section 317]

- ❑ Maximum term is 5 years each time, but eligible for reappointment.
- ❑ Section 317 does not apply to pure private companies or wholly owned Government companies.

Remuneration [Section 309]

- ❑ Maximum 5% of net profit for each and 10% for all.

Manager [Section 2 (24)]

'Manager' means an individual (not being the managing agent) who, subject to the superintendence, control and direction of the Board of Directors, has the management of the whole, or substantially the whole, of the affairs of a company, and includes a director or any other person occupying the position of a manager, by whatever name called, and whether under a contract of service or not;

- ➤ Only an individual can be appointed as a manager,
- ➤ Both a director or a non director can be appointed manager,
- ➤ Individual must be incharge of whole or substantially whole affairs of the company.

> A branch manager or a departmental manager is not called manager as he does not manage whole or substantially whole affairs of the company.

Simultaneous Appointment of Different Managerial Persons [Section 197A]

- ❑ Prohibition on simultaneous appointment of MD and manager, (either a manager or an MD)
- ❑ Only one manager can be appointed,
- ❑ No prohibition on company having more than one MD,
- ❑ No prohibition on simultaneous appointment of Whole Time Director and manager or MD and WTD

Tenure [Section 317]

- ❑ Not to be more than 5 years at a time, eligible for another term of 5 years or more.

Ceiling on Appointment [Section 386 (2)]

> If a person is a manger or MD, in one and not more than company
>
> ⟶
>
> Then his appointment in other company requires unanimous decision of all the directors

> **Exception [Section 386 (4)]:** *Central Government may permit any individual for appointment as manager in more than two companies.*

Distinction between Managing Director and Manager

Point of Distinction	Managing Director (MD)	Manager
Eligibility	Only a director can be appointed as MD.	An individual appointed as manager, may or may not be a director.
Appointment	MD is appointed under- ➤ An agreement ➤ By board resolution ➤ By general meeting resolution ➤ By provision in Memorandum ➤ By provision in Articles	Usually appointed under contract of service or by the BOD or Articles may also provide provision for the appointment.
Number	Company can have more than one MD.	Company cannot have more than one manager
Powers	Entrusted with substantial powers of management.	Management of whole or substantially whole of company.
Cease Office	MD on his ceasing to be a director automatically ceases to be MD as well.	MD on ceasing to be a director can continue as manager.
Disqualifications	Grounds remain effective for whole life and can not be waived by the Central Government.	Most grounds of disqualifications are only for 5 years and can also be waived by the Central Government.

Whole Time Director (WTD)
- ❑ The term Whole Time Director (WTD) is used simultaneously with MD in many sections.
- ❑ WTD has not been defined in the Act.
- ❑ WTD includes a director in whole time employment.

Appointment
- ❑ Similar provisions as are applicable to MD.

Remuneration

❑ Similar provisions as are applicable to MD.

Disqualifications

❑ Similar provisions as are applicable to MD.

Distinction between Managing Director and Whole Time Director

Point of Distinction	Managing Director	Whole Time Director
Appointment	May be appointed in 2 or more companies at the same time.	Cannot be appointed in more than one company.
Tenure	Cannot be appointed for more than 5 years at a time.	No such restriction.
Number	More than one MD can be appointed in a company.	Only one WTD can be appointed in a company.

Legal Position of Director

The position of directors in their relationship to the company is not only as the agent, but they act to some extent, trustee of the company and in the position of trustees, as an employee also. The directors have the following position in the company:

Directors as an Agent: The general position of the directors in the company is that they represent company in dealing with third party. A company, which is a legal entity, cannot act by itself and it can act only through natural persons who are known as the Board of directors. Therefore, as per the general principles of the law of agency, where the directors enter into contracts on behalf of a company in the ordinary course, the company will be liable as principal and not the directors. Directors are agents in transactions they enter into on behalf of the company, though they are not agents for individual shareholders or members.

Director as a Trustee: Directors are not trustees in the legal sense as the rules applicable to trustees under the Trustees Act do not apply to directors. But, for the assets and properties of the company, in addition to being agents of a company, the directors also act as trustee because they have to hold the company's properties with utmost trust and manage the affairs of the company for the benefit of the shareholders primarily. The duties attached to the directors are fiduciary in nature and they have to display good faith towards the company.

Director as an Employee: When a director is in the employment of the company as for example as managing director or whole-time director, he will be treated as an employee. Held in *S.M.S. Pharmaceuticals Ltd.* v *Neeta Bhalla,* (2005) 63 *SCL* 93 (*SC*). 'Managing Director' is treated as an employee as held by the Hon'ble Supreme Court in the *Employees State Insurance Corporation (ESIC)* v *Apex Engineering (P) Ltd.,* 1998.

Director is not Servant: Directors are not servants of the company but are to a certain extent act in the position of managers or managing partners.

Judicial Interpretations/Case Example	
Fiduciary capacity, within which directors have to act, enjoins upon them a duty to act on behalf of a company with utmost good faith, utmost care and skill and due diligence and in interest of company they represent.	*Dale and Carrington Investment (P) Ltd.* v *Prathapan (P.K.),* 2004, 54 SCL 601 (SC)
It is difficult to define the exact position of the directors. They are not servants of the company but are rather in the position of managers or managing partners.	*Re: Forest of Dean Coal Co.,* 1878, 10 Ch D 450.
A director may be deemed to be a servant or employee if he holds in addition a salaried employment or office in the company. *Held in Hutton* v *West Oak Ry ,*(1883) 23 Ch D 654; *Cyclists'Touring Club* v *Hopkinson ,*(1910) 1 Ch 179.	*Lee* v *Lee Air Farming Ltd.,* 1961, AC 12 .

Position of an Individual Director: No director of a company in his individual capacity has power to act on behalf of a company in any way unless the Board of directors has given him authority as provided in the Articles.

Judicial Interpretations/Case Example	
Any director acting individually has no power to act on behalf of the company in respect of any matter except to the extent to which any power or powers of the board have been delegated to him by the board within the limit permitted by the Companies Act or any other law. The position of the Chairman of the board of directors is not substantially different from an individual director.	*Shubh Shanti Services Ltd.* v *Manjula S. Agarwalla,*2005, 125 Comp Cas 477 (SC): 2005, 60 SCL 280 (SC) .
Individual directors are vested with only such powers as are available to them either under the memorandum or articles of the company or otherwise by the board of directors.	*Floating Services Ltd.* v *MV 'San Fransceco Dipalola'* 2004, 52 SCL 762 (Guj) .

Powers of the Board

- ❑ Powers of the Board can only be exercised by the Board of Directors in a collective manner and individual directors do not have any general powers referred in Section 291.
- ❑ Individual directors shall have only such powers, as are vested in them by the Memorandum and Articles.

Judicial Interpretations/Case Example	
Unless a power to file a suit is specifically conferred on a particular director, he has no authority to institute a suit on behalf of the company.	*Nibro Ltd.* v *National Insurance Co. Ltd.,* (1991) 70 Comp Cas 388 (DL).

General Powers of the Board [Section 291]

❑ The Board is entitled to exercise all such powers and to do all such acts and things as the company is authorized to exercise and do;

❑ But the Board cannot exercise any power or do any act or thing which is directed or required whether by this Act, or any other Act or by Memorandum or Articles or otherwise, to be exercised or done by the company in general meeting.

❑ No regulation made by the company in general meeting shall invalidate any prior act of the Board which would have been valid if that regulation had not been made.

Powers to be exercised at Board Meeting [Section 292]

(a) The power to make calls in respect of money unpaid on shares,

(b) The power to authorize the buy back,

(c) The power to issue debentures,

(d) The power to borrow moneys otherwise than on debentures,

(e) The power to invest the funds of the company, and

(f) The power to make loans.

> *Board by a resolution can delegate powers specified in clauses (c), (d) and (e) to any committee of the directors, the MD, the Manager or any other principal officer of the company or a branch officer on specified conditions.*

❑ Nothing in this section (Sec. 292) shall be deemed to affect the right of the company in general meeting to impose restrictions and conditions on the exercise by the Board of any of the specified powers.

Other Powers of Board exercised at Board Meeting

1. **Sec. 262 :** Power to fill up casual vacancy in the office of director.

2. **Sec. 293 :** A-Power to make political contributions.

3. **Sec. 293 :** B-Power of Board (or persons authorized) to contribute towards National Defense Fund.

4. **Sec. 297 :** Power to accord sanction for contracts in which directors or their relatives are interested.

5. **Sec. 299 :** Disclosure of interests at a Board meeting where director has interest.

6. **Sec. 316 (2):** Power to appoint a managing director if he is the MD or Manager of one and of not more than one other company (unanimous resolution required)

7. **Sec. 386 :** Power to appoint a Manager if he is the Manager or MD of one and not more than one company (unanimous resolution required)

8. Sec. 488 : Power to make declaration of solvency where it is proposed to wind up company voluntarily.

Power of Board Exercised in General Meetings [Section 93]

Following powers of Board, which are considered as restrictions on their powers, may be exercised only in general meetings:

(*a*) Sell, lease or otherwise dispose of the whole or substantially the whole of the undertaking of the company.

(*b*) Remit or give time for the repayment of any debt due by a director.

(*c*) Invest (otherwise than in trust securities) the amount of compensation received by the company in respect of the compulsory acquisition of any such undertaking referred above, without which it cannot be carried on or carried on only with difficulty or only after a considerable time.

(*d*) Borrow moneys if the money to be borrowed together with moneys already borrowed by the company, exceeds the aggregate of the paid up capital and free reserves of the company.

(*e*) Contribution to charitable and other funds, not directly relating to the business of the company or the welfare of its employees if the amount exceeds Rs.50, 000/- in any financial year, or 5% of average net profits during 3 immediately proceedings financial years.

Share Holders Power to Intervene

❑ Share holders by a amending the Articles of Association may restrict the Powers of the Board.

❑ If the shareholders are dissatisfied with the actions of the directors, the remedy available to them is to remove them in the manner provided in the Articles, or the Act.

❑ The general meeting of the share holders is competent to intervene and act in respect of matters delegated to the board in the following cases:

> ➤ Directors acting in complete disregard to the interest of the company. Held in the decided case, "*Marshall's Valve Gear Co.* v *Manning Wardle and Co. Ltd.,* (1909) 1*Ch* 267".

> ➤ Directors themselves are wrong doers and have acted malafide, the share holders in that case can steps to redress the wrong. Held in the decided case, "*Satya Charan Lal* v *R.P. Bajoria,* (1950) *SLR*394

> ➤ Where all the directors are interested in dealing or where none of the directors was validly appointed. In such a case, the share holders may exercise powers in general meeting. Held in the decided case, "*B.N.Vishwanathan* v *Tiffins BA and (P) Ltd.,* AIR 1953 Mad 510".

> ➤ Where there is deadlock in management so that directors cannot exercise their powers, the majority share holders may exercise the

powers in general meeting. In the instant case, Articles permitted the Board to appoint additional directors. But, for differences amongst the directors, the holding of the meeting of the Board was not possible. There was not provision in the Articles which permitted the share holders to increase the number of directors. Held, the company retained the power to appoint additional directors in general meeting. Held in the decided case, "*Barrom v Potter,* (1914) 1 *Ch.* 895".

Review Questions

1. Define a director. Who can be appointed as a director? Can a body corporate be appointed director of a company?
2. How are directors appointed in a company?
3. Distinguish between 'executive director' and 'Independent director'.
4. Distinguish between 'first director' and 'a director appointed in a casual vacancy'.
5. State in relation to a public company: When additional directors can be appointed and for what period? When alternate directors can be appointed and for what period?
6. How the office of a director is filled in case of casual vacancy and for what period?
7. Discuss the mode of appointment of non-rotational nominee directors on the board of an assisted company by a financial institution.
8. "Only members can be appointed as directors of a company." Comment
9. "Directors cannot appoint directors." Comment.
10. Briefly state the provisions of Companies Act regarding the mode of appointment of a director?
11. State the provisions of the Companies Act, 1956 relating to retirement of directors by rotation. In what manner does retirement of directors by rotation takes place and the vacancies filled up?
12. Is it possible for a retiring director to continue in his office beyond the date of the annual general meeting which had to be adjourned due to disturbances at the meeting? Explain.
13. Is it necessary that all the directors of a newly incorporated company must retire at the first annual general meeting?
14. State the provisions of the Companies Act, 1956 relating to the minimum and maximum number of directors that a company can have. How can the number of directors be increased or reduced?
15. A casual vacancy has occurred in a public company due to a director vacating his office before the expiry of his term. How the vacancy is to be filled?
16. Explain the legal provision and the suggested action in the following circumstances: The annual general meeting of a company was adjourned

sine die and a retiring director, who was otherwise eligible for reappointment could not be appointed before the adjournment.

17. How and when director be appointed by Central Government?

18. Can the directors be appointed by proportional representation?

19. How far the acts of the director will be valid, if his appointment is not valid?

20. State the disqualifications of a director. What will be the consequences if a person acts as a director without obtaining qualification shares?

21. Must a limited company under the Companies Act have directors? What are the qualifications of a director? When a person is disqualified for appointment as a director?

22. "The Companies Act, 1956 does not provide for any share qualifications for the directors." Comment.

23. State the ceiling on the maximum number of directorship that a person can hold. Which companies/directorships are not included for the purpose?

24. State the legal provisions on the directorships a person can hold. What steps are required to be taken when a person holds directorship in more than the required companies?

25. When the office of a director is deemed to be vacated? Can the directors of a company be removed during their term in the office?

26. Discuss the provisions of the Companies Act, 1956, relating to the removal of directors by the Central Government.

27. Distinguish between removal from office of the director and vacation of office by a director.

28. "Directors are not only agents, but are also in some sense trustees of the company." Discuss.

29. "The exact position of directors with regard to a company is hard to define; they are not the servants of the company but rather in the position of managing partners." Discuss the statement and bring out the exact position of directors of a company.

30. Explain the concept of managing director as used in the Companies Act, 1956. What are the restrictions imposed on the appointment and remuneration of a managing director?

31. Is it obligatory on the part of all companies to have a managing director or whole-time director or manager? When does the appointment of a manager or whole time director require the approval of the Central Government? What are the consequences, if such approval is not obtained?

32. What are the disqualifications for the appointment of a managing director?

33. Discuss briefly the provisions of Companies Act, 1956 as to the appointment of a manager.

34. Distinguish between

    (*a*)   Managing director and manager

    (*b*)   Managing director and whole-time director

35. Write short note on :

    (*a*)   Number of managing directorship

    (*b*)   Term of office of managing director

36. Sec.291 of the Companies Act, 1956, vests wide powers in the directors. Explain in detail.

37. State the powers of the board of directors of a company which it may exercise only by passing resolutions at the meeting of the board.

38. "Certain decision can only be taken by the board of directors by unanimous vote at the meeting." Discuss.

39. What are the powers which the board of directors may exercise only with the consent of the company in the general meeting?

40. "Decision taken by the board of directors cannot be altered or changed by the shareholders even if they want to approve it with unanimous majority." Comment.

41. "The board of directors of a company can do all such acts and things and exercise all such powers as the company itself may do and exercise." Discuss this statement.

9

Company Meetings

Why Meetings?

- ❑ Meetings are held to provide an opportunity to communicate information and opinions and to make decisions.
- ❑ In company form of organization decisions are always taken in a meeting. On certain matters the directors are authorized to decide, on certain other matters the shareholders are empowered to decide, and there are certain common grounds where both the bodies are involved in the decision making. For these reasons there are meetings of the director's and meetings of shareholder's.

Judicial Interpretations/Case Example	
The underlying reason for requiring a company to hold meetings is that members shall be able to attend in person so as to debate and vote on matters affecting the company.	*Bying* v *London Life Association Ltd.,*(1990) Ch. 170.
For the purpose of binding a company in its corporate capacity, individual assents given separately were not equivalent to the assent of a meeting. Held, an act which company is to do at a shareholders meeting cannot be done by obtaining separate consent of individual shareholders.	*Lee Behrens and Co.,* (1932) 2Comp Cas 588, (Ch.D).
It is not necessary for all the persons attending the meeting to be together at the same place (same room) provided there are adequate audio-visual links to enable everyone attending to see and hear what is giving on in all the rooms being used. At first, the Courts were unwilling to accept that a telephone conversation lacking a visual link could be a meeting. However, in *GIGA Investments Pty Ltd.,* (1995) 17 AC SR 472, it was held in the Federal Courts of Australia that two people can hold a meeting by ordinary telephone connection and more than two can meet using telephone conference facilities. Whether this position of the court is acceptable in UK or India remains to be seen.	*Re: Associated Color Laboratories Ltd.,* (1970) 12 DCR (3rd) 338, *Higgins* v *Nicol,* (1971) 18 FLR 343 page 357, *Magnacrete Ltd.* v *Dauglas Hill,* (1988) 148 SASR 567.

Meeting of Board

Board to Meet at Least Once in Every Three Calendar Months: In the case of every company, a meeting of its Board of directors shall be held at least once in every three months and at least four such meetings shall be held in every year: provided that the Central Government may, by notification in the Official Gazette, direct that the provisions of this section shall not apply in relation to any class of companies or shall apply in relation thereto subject to such exceptions, modifications or conditions as may be specified in the notification. [Section 285]

Notice: Notice of every meeting of the Board of directors of a company shall be given in writing to every director for the time being in India, and at his usual address in India to every other director. Every officer of the company whose duty it is to give notice as aforesaid and who fails to do so shall be punishable with fine which may extend to one thousand rupees. [Section 286 (1) (2)]

Quorum: The quorum for a meeting of the Board of directors of a company shall be one-third of its total strength (any fraction contained in that one-third being rounded off as one), or two directors, whichever is higher: provided that where at any time the number of interested directors exceeds or is equal to two-thirds of the total strength, the number of the remaining directors, that is to say, the number of the directors who are not interested present at the meeting being not less than two, shall be the quorum during such time. [Section 287 (2)]

In this section "total strength" means the total strength of the Board of directors of a company as determined in pursuance of this Act, after deducting there from the number of the directors, if any, whose places may be vacant at the time; and "interested director" means any director whose presence cannot, by reason of Section 300, count for the purpose of forming a quorum at a meeting of the Board, at the time of the discussion or vote on any matter.

Procedure where Meeting Adjourned for want of Quorum: If a meeting of the Board could not be held for want of quorum, then, unless the articles otherwise provide, the meeting shall automatically stand adjourned till the same day in the next week, at the same time and place, or if that day is a public holiday, till the next succeeding day which is not a public holiday, at the same time and place. The provisions of Section 285 shall not be deemed to have been contravened merely by reason of the fact that a meeting of the Board which had been called in compliance with the terms of that section could not be held for want of a quorum. [Section 288]

Passing of Resolutions by Circulation: No resolution shall be deemed to have been duly passed by the Board or by a committee thereof by circulation, unless the resolution has been circulated in draft, together with the necessary papers, if any, to all the directors, or to all the members of the committee, then in India (not being less in number than the quorum fixed for a meeting of the Board or committee, as the case may be, and to all other directors or members at their usual address in India, and has been approved by such of the directors as are then in India, or by a majority of such of them, as are entitled to vote on the resolution. [Section 289]

Validity of Acts of Directors: Acts done by a person as a director shall be valid, not with standing that it may afterwards be discovered that his appointment was invalid by reason of any defect or disqualification or had terminated by virtue of any provision contained in this Act or in the articles: provided that nothing in this section shall be deemed to give validity to acts done by a director after his appointment has been shown to the company to be invalid or to have terminated. [Section 290]

Vacation of Office by Director if he Absents from Three Consecutive Meetings: The office of a director shall become vacant if he absents himself from three consecutive meetings of the Board of directors, or from all meetings of the Board for a continuous period of three months, whichever is longer, without obtaining leave of absence from the Board. [Section 283 (1)]

Minutes of Proceedings: Every company shall cause minutes of all proceedings of every general meeting and of all proceedings of every meeting of its Board of directors or of every committee of the Board, to be kept by making within thirty days of the conclusion of every such meeting concerned, entries thereof in books kept for that purpose with their pages consecutively numbered. Each page of every such book shall be initialed or signed and the last page of the record of proceedings of each meeting in such books shall be dated and signed— in the case of minutes of proceedings of a meeting of the Board or of a committee thereof, by the chairman of the said meeting or the chairman of the next succeeding. In no case the minutes of proceedings of a meeting shall be attached to any such book as aforesaid by pasting or otherwise. The minutes of each meeting shall contain a fair and correct summary of the proceedings thereat. All appointments of officers made at any of the meetings aforesaid shall be included in the minutes of the meeting. In the case of a meeting of the Board of directors or of a committee of the Board, the minutes shall also contain— the names of the directors present at the meeting; and in the case of each resolution passed at the meeting, the names of the directors, if any, dissenting from, or not concurring in, the resolution. [Section 193]

Judicial Interpretations/Case Example	
The meeting of the Board could well be treated as a general meeting if all members of the company were also members of Board.	*P.V. Damodara Reddi* v *Indian National Agencies Ltd.*, (1945) 15 Comp. Cas 148 (Mad).
A Private Company had five directors who were the only share holders of the company. The Board passed a resolution approving the issue of debentures in which all of them were interested and were incompetent to vote. Held, the Board meeting may be considered as a general meeting of the company.	*Ref: Express Engg. Works,* (1920) 1 Ch. 466.

_Contd..

Although, it was referred to in minutes as a Board meeting, yet, if five persons present had said, "we will now constitute this a general meeting", it would have been within their power to do so. It was competent on their part to waive all formalities as regards notice of meeting, etc and to resolve themselves into a meeting of shareholder's and unanimously pass the resolution.

Meeting of Shareholders or General Meeting

A meeting that all members of a company are entitled to attend is called a "General Meeting" whereas a meeting which only one class of members may attend is called a "class meeting" that are important for decision making on class rights.

Judicial Interpretations/Case Example	
Meetings of the shareholders are called general meeting that includes the statutory meeting, the annual general meeting and the extra ordinary general meeting.	*Traco Enterprises (P) Ltd.* v *Alexandar Pala-thinkel*, AIR 1964 Ker 273.

Statutory Meeting [Sec. 165]

Purpose and Scope: Statutory meeting stands in a class by itself. Even though other general meetings like the AGM are also required to be held under the dictates of the Statute, yet they have not been termed as 'Statutory' (observed at page 269 by Head, Fasset and Wilson in their Manual of Secretarial Practice). One reason for naming this meeting as 'Statutory' may be that this meeting is held only once during the total life time of the company and that is why it is not considered as ordinary meeting like an AGM. Another reason may be that there are harsh consequences for not either convening this meeting or convening in an improper way. The company which has been very recently formed may be ordered to be wound up in the case of non-compliance of the provisions of this meeting. For these reasons, this meeting has been named distinctly.

Following may be the purpose of Statutory Meeting:

- As the statutory meeting is held immediately after formation of the company, it provides an opportunity of discussion on various matters arising out of the promotion and formation. Also, this meeting provides an opportunity to enable the members to know the financial position and future plans of the company.
- Members may discuss any matter relating to formation or arising out of statutory report, whether previous notice has been given or not. But no resolution can be passed for which prior notice has not been given.
- Right of discussion is available only to members present at the meeting. Members, who have not attended the meeting, cannot by way of written communication raise any issue in the meeting.

Which Company to hold Statutory Meeting?: Every company limited by shares, and every company limited by guarantee and having a share capital, shall hold general meetings of the members of the company, which shall be called "the statutory meeting". The following companies are not required to hold statutory meeting:

- Independent Private Company: As per the definition of a public company modified in the companies (Amendment) Act of 2000, a private company which is a subsidiary of a company which is not a private company will become a public company from the day on which it becomes such a subsidiary. Such a company shall comply all the provisions of the Companies Act, as are applicable to a public company including holding of a statutory meeting.
- Public Company not having Share Capital.
- Public Company limited by guarantee and not having Share Capital.
- Public Company having unlimited Liability.
- Government Company whether registered as a Private or Public Company

When to hold Statutory Meeting?: The statutory meeting shall be held within a period of not less than one month nor more than six months from the date at which the company is entitled to commence business,

Judicial Interpretations/Case Example	
The first general meeting of a company, which was incorporated on 3.1.1911, was held on 30.1.1911. The meeting was not held to be a Statutory Meeting as it was held before the expiry of one month.	*Garden* v *Iredale*, (1912) 1Ch. 700.

Requisites of a Statutory Meeting

- Generally Statutory Meeting is the first general meeting of the company.
- It is held only once and no such meeting is held during the life time of the company.
- Provisions of Section 165 regarding Statutory Meeting do not apply to a private company. But, if a private company converts itself into a public company within a period of six months from the date of its incorporation, it will have to hold a Statutory Meeting as per the requirements of Section 165.

Notice of Statutory Meeting

Length of notice for Calling Meeting: A general meeting of a company may be called by giving not less than twenty-one days' notice in writing. A general meeting may be called after giving shorter notice than that specified above if consent is accorded thereto— in the case of an annual general meeting, by all the members entitled to vote thereat; and in the case of any other meeting, by members of the company (*a*) holding, if the company has a share capital, not less than 95 per cent of such part of the paid-up share capital of the company as gives a right to vote at the meeting, or (*b*) having, if the company has no share capital, not less than 95 per cent of the total voting power exercisable at that meeting: provided that where any members of a company are entitled to vote only on some resolution or resolutions to be moved at a meeting and not on the others, those members shall be taken into account for the purposes of this sub-section in respect of the former resolution or resolutions and not in respect of the latter. [Section 171]

Contents and Manner of Service of Notice: Every notice of a meeting of a company shall specify the place and the day and hour of the meeting, and shall contain a statement of the business to be transacted thereat. [Section 172 (1)]

Persons on Whom Notice is to be Served: According to Section 172 (2), the notice of every meeting of the company shall be given:

(*i*) To every member of the company, in any manner authorised by sub-sections (1) to (4) of Section 53;

(*ii*) To the persons entitled to a share in consequence of the death or insolvency of a member, by sending it through the post in a prepaid letter addressed to them by name, or by the title of representatives of the deceased, or assignees of the insolvent, or by any like description, at the address, if any, in India supplied for the purpose by the persons claiming to be so entitled, or until such an address has been so supplied, by giving the notice in any manner in which it might have been given if the death or insolvency had not occurred; and

(*iii*) To the auditor or auditors for the time being of the company, in any manner authorised by Section 53 in the case of any member or members of the company:

Notice given by Advertising: Where the notice of a meeting is given by advertising the same in a newspaper circulating in the neighborhood of the registered office of the company under sub-section (3) of Section 53, the statement of material facts referred to in Section 173 need not be annexed to the notice as required by that section but it shall be mentioned in the advertisement that the statement has been forwarded to the members of the company.

Accidental Omission to give Notice: The accidental omission to give notice to, or the non-receipt of notice by, any member or other person to whom it should be given, shall not invalidate the proceedings at the meeting.

Judicial Interpretations/Case Example	
Meeting held on 14.2.1911, could not be described as a Statutory Meeting because the notice did not describe it as such.	*Garden* v *Iredate,* (1912) 1 Ch. 700 .

Contents of Notice

❑ Every notice of a meeting of a company shall specify the place and the day and hour of the meeting, and shall contain a statement of the business to be transacted thereat. [Section 172 (1)]

Day, Hour and Venue of Statutory Meeting

- ❑ Statutory Meeting may be convened even on a holiday, beyond business hours and at any convenient place in the country.
- ❑ The meeting may be adjourned from time to time and at any adjourned meeting any resolution of which proper notice has been given whether before or after the former meeting, may be passed.

Quorum for Meeting

- ❑ Unless the Articles of the company provide for a large number, as per Section 174 (1), five members personally present in the case of public company (other than a public company which has become such by virtue of Section 43A), and two members personally present in the case of any other company, shall be the quorum for a meeting of the company.

Adjournment of Statutory Meeting

- ❑ If within half an hour from the time appointed for holding a meeting of the company, quorum is not present, the meeting stands adjourned to the same day, at the same time and place in the next week or to such other day and at such other time and place as the Board may determine [Section 174 (3)(4)].
- ❑ If at the adjourned meeting also, quorum is not present within half an hour, the members present shall be a quorum [Section 174 (5)].

Agenda of a Statutory Meeting

- ❑ The agenda of the Statutory Meeting should be in the form of a report known as Statutory Report.
- ❑ A copy of Statutory Report should be send to each member along with the notice, at least 21 clear days before the day of meeting. The Statutory Report sent later, shall be considered forwarded if it is so agreed upon by all the members entitled to attend and vote at the meeting.
- ❑ A copy of the Statutory Report shall be sent to the Registrar for registration after copies of it have been sent to members.
- ❑ The Statutory Report shall be certified as correct by not less than 2 directors of the company, one of whom shall be a Managing Director, if there is one.
- ❑ The Auditors of the company will certify the matters in the report as relate to the shares allotted by the company, the cash received and the receipts and payments as appeared in the report.
- ❑ List of members showing the names, address, occupation, and number of shares held by them, respectively is to be produced at the commencement of the Statutory Meeting. The list should remain open and accessible to the members during the continuance of the meeting.

Contents of the Statutory Report: The Statutory Report shall set out:

1. The total number of shares allotted, distinguishing share allotted as fully or partly paid up, otherwise than in cash and the extent to which they are so paid up, and in either case, the consideration for which they have been allotted.

2. The total amount of cash received in respect of the entire share allotted distinguished as aforesaid.

3. The abstract of the receipts of the company and of the payments made there upon; up to a date within 7 days of the date of Statutory Report, exhibiting under distinctive headings and particulars concerning the balance remaining in hand. An account or estimate of the preliminary expenses of the company showing separately any commission or discount paid or to be paid on the issue or sale of shares or debentures; shall also be given in the Report.

4. The names, addresses and occupations of the company's directors, auditors, manager (if any) and secretary and the changes, if any, which have occurred in such details since the date of incorporation.

5. The particulars of any contract which or the modifications or the proposed modifications of which, is to be submitted to the meeting for its approval together with the particulars of the modification or proposed modification,

6. The extent, if any, to which each underwriting contract, if any, has not been carried out and the reasons thereof,

7. The arrears, if any, due on calls from every director and from the manager.

8. The particulars of any commission or brokerage paid or to be paid in connection with the issue or sale of shares or debentures to any director or the manager.

Default in Compliance

☐ A company may be wound up by the CLB (Tribunal), if default is made in delivering the statutory report to the Registrar or in holding the statutory meeting. Every director or other officer in default shall be punishable with fine which may extend to Rs.5000/-.[Section 433(b)]

Judicial Interpretation/Case Example	
According to Section 433 (b), if a default is made in delivering the Statutory Report to the Registrar or in holding the Statutory Meeting, the CLB (Tribunal) may order for the winding up of the company. As the provisions of Section 165 apply to a public company, the mandate prescribed in Section 433 (b) thus applies to	*S.R. Subramaniam v Drivers and Conductors Bus Service (P) Ltd.,* (Mad) 1978 (48) Comp Cas 672.

Contd..

a public company and not a private company. The ground on which the winding up is sought by the petitioner that a default was made by the company in non-delivering the Statutory Report to the Registrar or to the petitioner, as the case may be, is not available to him for providing the court to exercise the discretionary jurisdiction to wind up a running concern.

Annual General Meeting (AGM) [Section 166]

❑ From the earliest days of chartered and joint stock companies, it has been considered important to hold meetings of members usually once every 3 or 6 months. Such meetings were known as 'Ordinary General Meetings'.

❑ But, in the mid 19th Century, it became a usual feature to hold a general meeting of the members once a year under the title 'Annual General Meeting'.

❑ The current position in Companies Act, 1956 (Sec. 166) or the Companies Act of UK is that every kind of company must hold annual general meeting each year.

❑ The option to dispense with annual general meeting is available under the Companies Act of UK if the decision is taken by the unanimous resolution or if it is the case of a private company. If a private company has resolved to dispense with annual general meeting, any single member by giving notice in writing to the company or using electronic communication to the company not later than 3 months before the end of the year may require the company to hold an AGM for a particular year. Such dispensation is not available in India.

Purpose of AGM

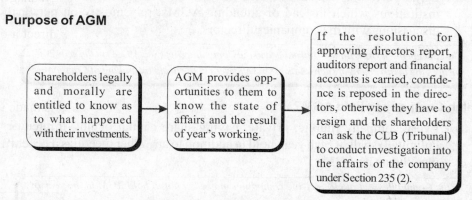

Shareholders legally and morally are entitled to know as to what happened with their investments. → AGM provides opportunities to them to know the state of affairs and the result of year's working. → If the resolution for approving directors report, auditors report and financial accounts is carried, confidence is reposed in the directors, otherwise they have to resign and the shareholders can ask the CLB (Tribunal) to conduct investigation into the affairs of the company under Section 235 (2).

❑ AGM enables share holders to exercise control over the working of the company.

AGM when Least Successful?

Although annual general meetings are compulsory for companies (public companies in UK) these meetings are in practice least successful in terms of providing an opportunity to the shareholders (members) to discuss company performance. Their may be several reasons for this including the following:

(a) The shareholders range from individuals shareholders with a few hundred shares in their hand to institutional share holders with millions of shares. Few family controlled shareholders may own substantial numbers of share. As per a study, 80% of the company's shareholders are individuals holding about 20% of the shares while 20% of the shareholders may be institutions holding 80% of the shares and the votes. The effectiveness of the shareholders control through general meeting will to a large extent be determined therefore by the willingness of the institutional investors to exercise their voting power. (*Source: Brenda Hannigan* (2003) *"Company Law", Lexis Nexis Butterworths, Page* 476.)

(b) The members of most public listed companies are widely scattered not only in India but in any part of the world. For this reason, members find it impracticable to attend the AGM as it involves traveling long distances and incurring expenses on their travel and stay.

(c) Another reason for the meager participation of large number of shareholders may be that AGM's in India held only at the registered office of the company or the city in which the registered office is situated. Thus, only members who live in or around the city where the registered office is situated, normally attend the AGM. Those at far off places have little interest.

(d) Most of the agenda items are decided before hand by members who control substantial number of proxies.

(e) Large portion of shares of listed companies are controlled by financial institutions which instead of attending AGMs, rely mostly on personal discussions with the companies directors.

> *The concept of "Postal Ballot" introduced in the Companies Act (Sec. 192 A) in the year 2000 ensures the involvement of such kinds of shareholders in the decision making of Companies.*

Which Company to hold AGM?

- Every company (public, private, having share capital or not, limited or unlimited) shall in each year, hold in addition to any other meetings a general meeting as its AGM.

> *In the Companies Act of UK, private companies may elect not to hold AGM in the year of formation and future years.*

- The company shall specify the annual general meeting as such in the notices calling it.
- As the Companies Act is silent on the definition of "year", the word "year" is to be interpreted under the General Clauses Act and there it means calendar year.

Judicial Interpretations/Case Example	
Year means calendar year from Ist January to 31ˢᵗ December, both days included and not 12 months from the date of registration.	*Gibson* v *Barton,* (1875) 10 QBD 329.

When to hold AGM (Section 166 read with Section 210)?

First AGM

- ❏ First AGM may be held within 18 months from the date of its registration (Section 166). Similar provisions exist in the Companies Act of UK.
- ❏ First AGM must be held not later than 9 months from the date of the closing of its financial year [Section 210(3) (a)].

> *The first AGM is held within a period of 18 months from the date of incorporation, it shall not be necessary for the company to hold any AGM in the year of its incorporation or in the following year. For example, if a company is registered in the month of December, 1995, it may hold its first AGM by May ,1997, and such a meeting will be deemed to be the AGM for 1995, 1996 and 1997.*

Subsequent AGM

- ❏ There must be one AGM in each calendar year.
- ❏ The gap between two AGM's must not exceed 15 months. This period of 15 months may be extended for some special reasons to 18 months by the permission of Registrar of Companies, as clarified by the Department of Company Affairs vide its letter dated 13.1.1972. The court has no power to extend the period [Section 210 (3) (b)].

> *Delay in completion of audit of annual accounts does not ordinarily constitute "special reason" justifying extension. In case the annual accounts are not ready for placement before the annual general meeting, the better course for the company is to hold the AGM to approve item other than approval of accounts and adjourn it to a suitable date for considering accounts. The adjourned meeting must however, be held within the maximum permissible period. [Clarification given by the Department of Company Affairs dated 02.02.1974.]*

- ❏ The AGM must be held not later than 6 months from the close of financial year or in cases where an extension of time has been granted by the Registrar, in a maximum period of 9 months. [Section 210 (3) (b)].

> *AGM should be held at the earliest of the three dates prescribed under Sections 166 and 210 i.e., last day of the next calendar year, 15 months from the previous AGM and 6 months after close of financial year.*

Two AGMs on the Same Day

- ❏ Since the Companies Act does not prohibit a company to hold two AGM's on the same day, a company can hold AGM for the current year and also for the previous year on the same day provided there is no provision to the contrary in the Articles of the company.

- ❏ But, the two meetings should be held at separate timings after giving separate notices for each meeting.

Judicial Interpretations/Case Example	
The provisions contemplate two separate and distinct requirements: 1. Holding meeting within 15 months and, 2. Holding it in the year.	*Smedley* v *ROC.*, (1919) 1 KB 97.
The period allowed for holding of AGM is 15 months from the date of last AGM. Extension of this period is permissible by the order of the Registrar for any special reason by a period not exceeding 3 months. Thus, there cannot be a gap of more than 18 months between an AGM and another.	*B.R.Kundra* v *Motion Picture Asson.*, 1978 (48) Comp. Cas. 564 (Del).
The extension of 3 months can be sanctioned only by the Registrar and courts have no power to grant extension under Section 166.	*Nungambakkam Dhanarakshaka Saswatha Nidhi Ltd.* v *ROC.*, (1972) 42 Comp. Cas. 632 (Mad).
Meeting held beyond the time cannot be held to be void or illegal. If the Company Law Board or Central Government or the Tribunal does not extend the date of holding of AGM under Section 167, the directors shall be subjected to increasing penalty up to Rs.50,000/- and additional fine up to Rs.2500/- per day for default, but the meeting shall be a valid meeting. Otherwise, the position in law would become impossible.	*Hungerford Investment Trust Ltd.* v *Turner Morrison Co. Ltd.*, ILR (1972) Cal.

Notice of AGM

- ❏ If members who do not attend a meeting are to be bound by the meetings decision, all members must be given a reasonable opportunity of attending the meeting that is, they must be given proper notice, the meeting itself must be property conducted; their must be a quorum and proper voting.

Length of Notice for Calling AGM: A general meeting of a company may be called by giving not less than twenty-one days' notice in writing. Meeting may be called after giving shorter notice than that specified above, if consent is accorded thereto— in the case of an annual general meeting, by all the members entitled to vote thereat. [Section 171 (1) (2)]

In the UK company law, the notice calling the AGM must specify that it is the AGM.

Judicial Interpretations/Case Example	
A notice of a meeting issued by a person who does not have authority to issue such notice is void and even if the meeting takes place, its decisions will be void.	*Re: Hycraft Gold Reduction and Mining Co.,* (1900) 2Ch. 230 Re: State of Wyoming Syndicate (1901) 2 Ch. 431.

Contents of Notice

❑ Every notice of a meeting of a company shall specify the place and the day and hour of the meeting, and shall contain a statement of the business to be transacted thereat. [Section 172 (1)]

Day, Hour and Venue of AGM

❑ Every AGM shall be called at a time during business hours, on a day that is not a public holiday and shall be held either at the registered office of the company or at some other place within the city, town or village in which the registered office of the company is situated. [Section 166 (2)]

> *AGM can be held at any place within the postal limits and local municipal limits (wider of the two if the two do not coincide) of city, town or village in which the registered office of the company is situated as clarified vide circular no.1/1/80-CL-V dated 16.2.1981.*

❑ The central government may exempt any class of companies from the provisions of Section 166 (2) subject to such conditions as it may impose.

❑ A public company or a private company which is a subsidiary of a public company, may by its Articles fix the time for its AGM's and may also by a resolution passed in one AGM fix the time for its subsequent AGM's and a private company (which is not a subsidiary of a public company) may in like manner and also by a resolution agreed to by all the members thereof fix the time as well as the place for its AGM.

Interpretation of Public Holiday

❑ The Department of Company Affairs (now Ministry of Corporate Affairs) has clarified that "not convening AGM on public holidays" is a mandatory provision.

❑ "Public holiday" means a public holiday within the meaning of the Negotiable Instruments Act, 1881 [(Section 2 (38) of Companies Act)].

❑ 'Sunday' is deemed to be a public holiday as per explanation given to Section 25 of the Negotiable Instruments Act.

- ❑ Bank holidays for the purpose of bank closing shall not be treated as public holidays though they are declared as public holidays under the Negotiable Instruments Act, but for the limited purpose of half yearly closing. (Clarified by the Department of Company Affairs (now MCA) in the year 1981)

Exceptions: In the following cases, the AGM may be held on a public holiday:

(*i*) If the day of the meeting is declared by the Central Government to be a public holiday after the issue of notice convening such a meeting, it shall not be considered as a public holiday [Section 2 (38) of Companies Act, 1956].

(*ii*) Where the AGM is adjourned for lack of quorum, it is to be held normally on the same day, same time and place in the next week. If that day happens to be public holiday, the holding of AGM on that day shall not amount to contravention of Section 166 (2) as has been clarified by the Department of Company Affairs (now MCA).

(*iii*) Where a public company or its subsidiary has by its Articles or by a resolution passed in any AGM, fixed the date of its AGM and the day turns out to be a public holiday [Section 166 (2) (a)].

(*iv*) Like a public company or its subsidiary, if a private company (which is not a subsidiary of a public company) by a resolution agreed to by all the members thereof fix the time as well as the place of its AGM and if that day happens to be a public holiday [Section 166 (2) (b)].

(*v*) Companies formed under Section 25 of the Companies Act have been exempted by an order issued by the Central Government dated 1.7.1961.

Judicial Interpretations/Case Example	
An outsider other than the members of the company cannot raise objections to the irregularity in holding the meeting at place other than registered office.	*Bharat Commerce and Industries Ltd.,* 1973 (43) Comp.Cas 162 (Cal).
On a petition under Section 397/398, praying for holding of election to the Board, the Court held, the appointment of directors has to be done at an AGM and not otherwise. As the AGM had to be held in the city where the registered office is situated *i.e.,* Delhi, the direction issued by the Company Judge to hold AGM at Delhi, Kanpur and Allahabad to conduct election to the Board at these places was set aside.	*Dineker Rai Desai* v *R.P.Bhasin,* (1986) 60 Comp Cas. 14 (Delhi).

Quorum for Meeting

- ❑ Unless the Articles of the company provide for a large number, as per Section 174 (1), five members personally present in the case of public company (other than a public company which has become such by virtue of

Section 43A), and two members personally present in the case of any other company, shall be the quorum for a meeting of the company.

Adjournment of AGM

- If within half an hour from the time appointed for holding a meeting of the company, quorum is not present, the meeting stands adjourned to the same day, at the same time and place in the next week or to such other day and at such other time and place as the Board may determine [Section 174 (3)(4)].
- If at the adjourned meeting also, quorum is not present within half an hour, the members present shall be a quorum [Section 174 (5)].

Judicial Interpretations/Case Example

Section 174 (4) deals with two situations. In the first situation, the adjournment is not to any specific date. In that case, it is an automatic adjournment to the same day in the next week. The second situation is when the Board decides to hold the adjourned meeting on some specific time and place on the day of the meeting itself or any date before the commencement of the same day in the next week. If no such date is fixed by the Board before the time limit, the first part of sub-section 4 operates automatically and the holding of the meeting on the same day in the next week at the same time and place is nothing but legal and proper.	*Ashok Mathew Zacharia* v *Majestic Kuries and Loans* (P) *Ltd.,* (1987) (62) Comp Cas. 865 (Ker) 1988 (1) Comp. LJ 54
Held, it does not permit to indefinitely postpone the meeting on account of chaos and confusion. Suppose the AGM of a company is called on the last day of the 15th month from the date of its earlier AGM and is adjourned by an appropriate resolution to some future date, such adjournment may go ad-infinitum and in such contingency the provisions of Sections 166, 168 and 210 of the Act, would be rendered worthless, leading to chaos and confusion in the matter of enforcement of the relevant provisions of the Act by the Registrar of Companies. It would render the statutory provisions of the Act meaningless and ineffective, while the intention of the legislature is not like that.	*Bejoy Kumar Karnani* v *Asstt ROC,* 1985 (1) Comp. LJ 21,Cal (DB) 1985 (58) Comp Cas. 293.
If accounts are not ready, the better course is to hold the AGM on the schedule date, transact all business except the approval of accounts and adjourn the AGM for some future date when accounts will be ready. But suitable resolution is to be passed for the adjournment. The adjourned meeting is only the continuation of original meeting.	*M.D. Mundra* v *Asstt.,* ROC (1980) 50 Comp. Cas. 346 (Cal).
In case the annual accounts are not ready and AGM is adjourned, it must be held within the maximum time limit allowed under Section66.	*Subha Dutta and Sons* (P) *Ltd.* v *Asstt.,* ROC WB (1986)3Comp.LJ73.

Contd..

Even adjourned AGM must be held within 15 months of the previous meeting. If a Statute enjoins that a meeting is to be held within a specified period, it follows by necessary implication that it must be completed within the said period. If the otherwise position is accepted, the AGM of a company may be deferred with impunity at the pleasure of the shareholders for years together and so also the laying of balance sheet and profit and loss account rendering the statutory provisions of the Act meaningless and ineffective.	*Bejoy Kumar Karnani* v *Asstt.,* ROC (1985) 58 Comp. Cas. 293 (Cal).
An annual general meeting adjourned to next calendar year does not become meeting of that year. If it were correct, a general meeting held in 1934 could be adjourned to 1935 and again adjourned to 1936 and so on without limit but that would obviously not satisfy Section76 of the Companies Act of 1913. The adjourned meeting held on 31.3.1935, was not a different meeting from the one which began on 30.12.1934, it was the same meeting. Section 76 required that in 1935, a separate and distinct meeting should have been held.	*Sree Meenakshi Mills Co. Ltd.* v *Asstt. Registrar of Joint Stock Companies.,* (1938) 8 Comp Cas. 175 (Mad).

Business Transacted in the AGM

❑   In the case of an annual general meeting, all business to be transacted at the meeting shall be deemed special, with the exemption of business relating to (*i*) the consideration of the accounts, balance sheet and the reports of the Board of directors and auditors, (*ii*) the declaration of a dividend, (*iii*) the appointment of directors in the place of those retiring, and (*iv*) the appointment of, and the fixing of the remuneration of the auditors. Both ordinary business and special business may be transacted in the AGM.

Ordinary Business: The following matters termed as ordinary business constitutes the usual business of an AGM:

(*i*) Consideration of accounts, balance sheet, and reports of the Board of directors and auditors,

(*ii*) Declaration of dividend,

(*iii*) Appointment of directors in the place of those retiring, and

(*iv*) Appointment of and the fixing of remuneration of the auditors.

> *The English Company Law does not dictate the business to be conducted at an AGM, but the typical business of such a meeting includes; (i) approval of accounts, director's report, the director's remuneration report, auditors report (ii) election or re-election of directors (iii) appointment of auditors and fixing their remuneration (often delegated to Board), and (iv) dividend declaration.*

Special Business: Business other than ordinary business is called as special business

❑   Business other than mentioned above and termed as special business may also be transacted in the AGM.

❑   For transacting special business there shall be annexed to the notice of the meeting an explanatory statement as per Section 173 (2).

Judicial Interpretations/Case Example	
The declaration of dividend could take place only at an ordinary general meeting (*i.e.*, AGM) at which the accounts were laid before the company.	*Nicholson* v *Rhodesia Trading Co.*, (1897) 1 Ch. 434.
The provisions of the Companies Act insist on supply of information to members and others. But that does not mean that every question asked at the general meeting should be forthwith answered without even considering whether they relate to the affairs of the company as understood in law and whether it would be possible to answer such questions without due notice. A business organization like a company cannot function like a legislative assembly.	*Kumaranunni* v *Mathrubhumi Printing and Publishing Co. Ltd.*, 1983 (54) Comp Cas. 370 (Ker).
Company is to call an AGM and it is no excuse that books of accounts were in the possession of custodian due to nationalization.	*Hindustan Coop. Insurance Society Ltd.*, 1961 (31) Comp Cas. 193.
A clear duty is cast on the directors to call the AGM whether or not the accounts, the consideration of which is one of the matters to be dealt with at an AGM, are ready or not.	*ROC* v *Radhika Prasad Nanda*, 1977 Tax LR 1610 (*Ori*) *Dalmia Cement (Bharat) Ltd* v *Registar Joint Stock Companies.*, AIR 1954 Mad 276.
A shareholder has an undoubted interest in the company that is represented by his share holdings. The rights of the shareholders include: (*i*) the right to elect directors, (*ii*) to vote on resolutions at the meetings of the company, (*iii*) to receive dividends, (*iv*) to apply to the concerned authorities for relief in the case of oppression and mis-management, (*v*) to apply the Court (Tribunal) for winding up of the company and (*vi*) to share in the surplus on winding up. Held, the shareholders cannot be restrained from calling a general meeting to remove existing directors and elect new directors.	*LIC* v *Escorts Ltd.*, (1986) 59 Comp. Cas. 548 (SC).

Default in Holding AGM

❑ If default is made in holding an AGM in accordance with Section 166, the Central Government may, notwithstanding anything contained in this Act or in the Articles of the company, on the application of any member of the company, call or direct the calling of a general meeting to be deemed to an AGM of the company, and give such ancillary or consequential directions as the Central Government thinks expedient in relation to the calling, holding and conducting of the meeting [Section 167 (1)].

❑ The direction given under this section may include a direction that one member of the company present in person or by proxy shall be deemed to constitute a meeting [explanations to Section 167 (1)].

❑ According to Section 168, if default is made in holding a meeting of the company in accordance with Section 166, or in complying with any directions of the CLB/Tribunal or the Central Government, as the case may be under sub-section (1) of Section 167, the company, and every officer of the company who is in default, shall be punishable with fine which may extend to fifty thousand rupees and in the case of a continuing default, with a further fine which may extend to two thousand fivehundred rupees for every day after the first during which such default continues.

> Under the UK Company Law, if a company has defaulted to hold AGM, the Secretary of State for Trade and Industry (DTI) acting on the application of any member, may direct the company to hold AGM.

Judicial Interpretations/Case Example

The responsibility for calling of AGM is that of directors taken together. They cannot be allowed to take advantage in the form of prolonging the tenure of some of them who may be due to retire at AGM. Such directors are deemed to have retired on the due date of AGM and must vacate office. Retiring directors are, however, eligible for re-election.	*B.R. Kundra* v *Motion Picture Association,*(1976) 46 Comp. Cas. 339 (Delhi HC).
The default in not holding an AGM and preparing statement of returns and filing them before the Registrar of Companies or in not laying of the balance sheet and profit and loss account before the AGM required under Sections 159 and 160 (Annual Return to be filed with the ROC) or 161 (Annual Return and certificate to be annexed thereto), 166 (AGM) and 210 (Board shall lay before the AGM its balance sheet and profit and loss account) cannot be pleaded in defense of a prosecution that no AGM was held for the non filing of the copies of the balance sheet or profit and loss account or the non attachment of the statement------. The directors of the company are liable for prosecution and the failure to hold AGM is no defense to such prosecution------------. While it is open to the Registrar to prosecute the persons who have committed default of Sections 166, 159 to 162 and 210 willfully not holding a meeting and not fulfilling the requirements of these provisions for which no period of limitation is prescribed under the Act, any prosecution under section 220 (three copies of balance sheet to be filed with the Registrar) would be pre-mature without such a meeting in fact held.	*Andhra Provincial Potteries Ltd* v *ROC,* (AP FB) 1969 (39) Comp. Cas 1000; 1970 (1) Comp LJ 172. *State of Bihar* v *Linkers (P) Ltd.,* 1970 (40) Comp. Cas 17 (Pat).1969 (1) Comp. LJ 240.
The failure to place the balance sheet and profit and loss account before AGM and consequent failure in filing their requisite copies	

Contd..

with the Registrar of Companies, held, the defense of not holding of AGM not available. Held, the directors were knowingly and willfully guilty of the default in not filing the balance sheet and profit and loss account and in not calling the AGM. As per the facts of the case, the balance sheet and the profit and loss account could not be placed before the AGM as it were not received from the Auditors. But, nothing is evidenced from the records that the directors took any pains to get the audit report expedited by the auditor so that the AGM could be called in time. In the circumstances, it can be safely held that they were knowingly and willfully guilty of the default in not filing the balance sheet and profit and loss account and not calling the AGM. The three directors could have got the advantage of Section 210(5) first proviso provided they had brought on the record some evidence to show that the managing director was charged with the duty of calling AGM and laying before it the balance sheet and profit and loss account. A mere statement on their part will not exonerate them from the liability.	
Section 167 provides as to what should be done when default is there in the holding of the AGM within the stipulated time. Only the Central Government (earlier CLB) has the power to order the convening of a meeting after the statutory time is elapsed.	*Nungambakkm Dhanarakshaka Saswatha Nidhi v Ltd.,* v ROC (1972) 42 Comp.Cas 632 (Mad).
AGM called in December, 1934 was adjourned and held in March, 1935. Subsequent AGM was held in Feb., 1936. Prosecution was for not holding the AGM in 1935.	*Shri Meenakshi Mills Ltd.* v *Asstt.,* ROC AIR 1938 Mad 640.
If accounts books were seized by the police, thereby rendering directors unable to call AGM. *Held,* the offence is not punishable.	*Ref: Asia Udyog (P) Ltd.,* (1961) 31 Comp Case. 269.
Held, confusion and pandemonium at the venue of AGM preventing the commencement of meeting cannot be deemed to be valid. In the instant case, the Board and the President who were present in the AGM found that the pandemonium that prevailed at that time in the Hall, made it impossible for them to commence and thereafter hold the meeting. By the mere distribution of the agenda and the balance sheet, it cannot by any stretch of imagination be interpreted that the AGM has commenced. The pandemonium and the confusion that were admittedly created by the shareholders made it practically impossible for the directors to commence, conduct and hold the AGM. After recording such a fact, they announced that the meeting could not be held. Shareholders, who subsequently purport to have met and passed certain resolution, cannot be said to have been passed by the body of share holders. This is not a case covered by	*V.Selvaraj* v *Mylapore Hindu Permanent Fund by its Secretary,* 1968 (1) Comp. LJ 92 (Mad).

Contd..

Section 167, because there was no default on the part of the Board to hold the meeting. Powers of the Central Government cannot be invoked as there was no initial default.	
If at the time when AGM is due to be held there is only one member present (the other having died), no offence is committed when the AGM is not held.	*State of Keralav West Coast Planners Agencies (P) Ltd.,* (1958) 28 Comp Cas 13.
Where in a company two brothers were the sole shareholders, default of not holding the AGM due to brother's illness could not be called willful.	*Kastoor Mal Banthiya* v *State,* AIR 1951, Ajmer 39.

Extra Ordinary General Meeting (EGM)

❑   All general meetings other than annual general meetings shall be named extra ordinary general meeting (EGM) [Clause 47 of Table A].

❑   Usually Articles of company contains provisions regarding calling of such meetings. But, if the Articles are silent, then in the case of a public company, provisions given in Table A shall automatically apply.

> *UK Companies Act: Under UK Companies Act if for any reason, it is 'impracticable' to call or conduct meeting of a company in any manner in which meetings of that company may be called, the Court may order a meeting to be called, held and conducted in any manner the Court thinks fit. The Court may direct that one person of the company present in person or by proxy be deemed to constitute a meeting. The Court may make such an order of its own motion or on the application of any director of the company or any member entitled to vote at the meeting. This power only arises where it is 'impracticable' to call a meeting. Held, the word 'impracticable' is not synonymous with the word 'impossible'. Ref: E.I Sombrero Ltd. 1958 Ch. 900.*

Purpose of EGM

❑   EGM is convened to discuss some urgent or special business that cannot be postponed till the next AGM. Thus, such meetings are held between two AGMs.

Judicial Interpretations/Case Example	
All general meetings except the AGMs are EGMs. The meeting to consider the resolution for alteration of memorandum need not have been held only at the registered office of the company.	*Bharat Commerce and Industries Ltd.* v *ROC,* (1973) 43 Comp Cas. 275 (Cal).

Who may call EGM?

Board at its Own

❑   The Board may, whenever it thinks fit, call an EGM [Clause 48 (1) of Table A]

> *If at any time, there are not within India directors capable of acting who are sufficient in number to form a quorum, any director or any two members of the company may call an EGM [clause 48 (2) of Table A]*

- ❑ The Board may call a general meeting at any time by giving not less than 21 days notice [Section 171(1)]. A Shorter notice may, however, be given if consent is accorded thereto by members of the company holding 95% or more of the voting rights [Section 171(2) (ii)].
- ❑ Resolutions to call EGM must be passed at a properly held Board's meeting. Where the EGM is irregularly convened, Board has the power to ratify it before the time fixed for EGM.
- ❑ If allowed by the Articles, Board may also call EGM by circulation.

Judicial Interpretations/Case Example	
No individual director or a Manager has the powers to call EGM.	*Gibson* v *Borton,* 1875, LRQB 329.
Chairman or and Managing Director cannot prevent the Board from convening and holding an EGM.	*K.G.Khosla* v *Rahul Kirloskar,* 2002 (35) SCL 546 (Delhi HC).
The director's power to call EGM is a fiduciary power which must be exercised by the directors bonafide in what they consider is the interest of the company and not for any collateral purpose.	*Pergamon Press Ltd.* v *Maxwell,* (1970) 1 WLR 1167.

Board on Requisition (Section 169)

Board must convene a general meeting upon demand or requisition if following conditions have been satisfied:

1. The number of members entitled to requisition a meeting in regard to any matter shall be—(*a*) in the case of a company having a share capital, such number of them as hold at the date of the deposit of the requisition, not less than one-tenth of such of the paid-up capital of the company as at that date carries the right of voting in regard to that matter; (*b*) in the case of a company not having a share capital, such number of them as have at the date of deposit of the requisition not less than one-tenth of the total voting power of all the members having at the said date a right to vote in regard to that matter. [Section 169 (4)]

2. The Board of directors of a company shall, on the requisition of required number of members of the company, forthwith proceed duly to call an extraordinary general meeting of the company. [Section 169 (1)]

3. The requisition shall set out the matters for the consideration of which the meeting is to be called, shall be signed by the requisitionists, and shall be deposited at the registered office of the company. [Section 169 (2)]

4. The requisition may consist of several documents in like form, each signed by one or more requisitionists. [Section 169 (3)]

5. Where two or more distinct matters are specified in the requisition, the provisions shall apply separately in regard to each such matter; and the requisition shall accordingly be valid only in respect of those matters in regard to which the condition specified in that sub-section is fulfilled. [Section 169 (5)]

By Requisitionists Themselves

❑   If the Board does not, within twenty-one days from the date of the deposit of a valid requisition in regard to any matters, proceed duly to call a meeting for the consideration of those matters on a day not later than forty-five days from the date of the deposit of the requisition, the meeting may be called by the requisitionists themselves as per the provisions of Section 169 (6) as follows:

(a) In the case of a company having a share capital by such of the requisitionists as represent either a majority in value of the paid-up share capital held by all of them or not less than one-tenth of such of the paid-up share capital of the company as is referred to in clause (a) of sub-section (4), whichever is less; or

(b) In the case of a company not having a share capital, by such of the requisitionists as represent not less than one-tenth of the total voting power of all the members of the company referred to in clause (b) of sub-section (4).

❑   A meeting called by the requisitionists or any of them as per Section 169(6):

(a) Shall be called in the same manner, as nearly as possible, as that in which meetings are to be called by the Board; but

(b) Shall not be held after the expiration of three months from the date of the deposit of the requisition.

Explanation: Nothing in clause (b) shall be deemed to prevent a meeting duly commenced before the expiry of the period of three months aforesaid, from adjourning to some day after the expiry of that period.

❑   Where two or more persons hold any shares or interest in a company jointly, a requisition, or a notice calling a meeting, signed by one or some only of them shall, for the purposes of this section, have the same force and effect as if it had been signed by all of them. [Section 169 (8)]

❑   Any reasonable expenses incurred by the requisitionists by reason of the failure of the Board duly to call a meeting shall be repaid to the requisitionists by the company; and any sum so repaid shall be retained by the company out of any sums due or to become due from the company by way of fees or other remuneration for their services to such of the directors as were in default. [Section 169 (9)]

Judicial Interpretations/Case Example	
Held, shareholders who have not paid a call made on them are not entitled to requisition an EGM. From the reading of Section 169 (4) it is clear that only those shareholders who have a right to vote, can requisition a meeting.	*Col. Kuldip Singh Dhillon* v *Paragon Utility Financiers (P) Ltd.,* (1986) 60 Comp. Cas. 1075 (P and H).
Members other than requisitionists have no right to have business put on the agenda for a requisitioned extraordinary general meeting. But the directors who convene the meeting may put their own business on the agenda	*Ball* v *Metal Industries Ltd.,* 1957 SC 315.
If the objects for which a meeting is requisitioned cannot be legally carried into effect in any manner, the directors are justified in refusing to act on the requisition. Cases referred include *National Roads and Motorists Association* v *Parker* ,(1986) 6 NS WLR 517	*Isle of Wight Railway Co.* v *Tahourdin,* (1883) 25 Ch D. 320 page 344.
The request for requisition not having been acted upon, the requisitionists called their meeting at the registered office of the company. The item of the agenda was the removal of the managing director. The managing director, on the day of meeting, locked the company premises and the members moved to a place a few yards of the registered office and held the meeting there. *Held,* there was no violation of law and the meeting was a valid meeting. The contention being that a meeting at another place would be held only after it was adjourned by the Chairman, which was not there in the instant case, was rejected. It was observed that the petitioner, who had himself prevented the meeting from taking place at the registered office, could not question the validity of the meeting because of its change venue. No man can take advantage of his own wrongs.	*Mrs. Rathnavelusami Chettiar* v *Mrs. Manickavelu Chettiar,* (1951) 21 Comp Cas. 93 (Mad).

Company Law Board (CLB)/Tribunal to Order EGM to be Called

❑ If for any reason it is impracticable to call a meeting of a company, other than an annual general meeting, in any manner in which meetings of the company may be called, or to hold or conduct the meeting of the company in the manner prescribed by this Act or the Articles, the CLB/Tribunal may, as per Section 186 (1), either of its own motion or on the application of any director of the company, or of any member of the company who would be entitled to vote at the meeting,— (*a*) order a meeting of the company to be called, held and conducted in such manner as the CLB/Tribunal thinks fit; and (*b*) give such ancillary or consequential directions as the CLB/Tribunal thinks expedient, including directions modifying or supplementing in relation to the calling, holding and conducting of the meeting, the operation of the provisions of this Act and of the company's articles.

> **Explanation:** *The directions that may be given under this sub-section may include a direction that one member of the company present in person or by proxy shall be deemed to constitute a meeting.*

❑ Any meeting called, held and conducted in accordance with any such order shall, for all purposes, be deemed to be a meeting of the company duly called, held and conducted. [Section 186(2)]

Business Transacted in the EGM

❑ EGM is called to transact some urgent or special business, the decision of which cannot be postponed till the AGM. So all business discussed in such a meeting is called as special business. The ordinary business can only be discussed in the AGM.

❑ Any item of agenda of the EGM must be accompanied by an explanatory statement setting out all material fact concerning each such item of business. Such statement shall be annexed to the notice of the meeting. [Section 173(2)]

Contents of Notice

❑ Every notice of a meeting of a company shall specify the place and the day and hour of the meeting, and shall contain a statement of the business to be transacted thereat. [Section 172 (1)]

Day, Hour and Venue of EGM

❑ EGM may be convened even on a holiday, beyond business hours and at any convenient place in the country.

❑ The meeting may be adjourned from time to time and at any adjourned meeting any resolution of which proper notice has been given whether before or after the former meeting, may be passed. The EGM called on requisition is not adjourned but dissolved.

Quorum for Meeting

❑ Unless the Articles of the company provide for a large number, as per Section 174 (1), five members personally present in the case of public company (other than a public company which has become such by virtue of Section 43 A), and two members personally present in the case of any other company, shall be the quorum for a meeting of the company.

Adjournment of EGM

☐ If within half an hour from the time appointed for holding a meeting of the company, quorum is not present, the meeting stands adjourned to the same day, at the same time and place in the next week or to such other day and at such other time and place as the Board may determine. [Section 174 (3), (4)]

☐ If at the adjourned meeting also, quorum is not present within half an hour, the members present shall be a quorum. [Section 174 (5)]

☐ If within half an hour from the time appointed for holding a meeting of the company, a quorum is not present, the meeting, if called upon the requisition of members, shall stand dissolved. [Section 174 (3)]

Requisites of a Valid General Meeting

Golden Rule about a general meeting is that it should be properly convened, properly constituted, and the decision must be taken and recoded in a proper way. A valid meeting has the following requisites:

1. **Should be Properly Convened**

   ➤ Convened by Proper Authority
   ➤ Proper and Adequate Notice

      ● Contents-Day, Time, Venue

   ➤ Proper Agenda

      ● Contents-Ordinary Business, Special Business with Explanatory Statement and Proxy Form

2. **Should be Properly Constituted**

   ➤ Proper Chairman
   ➤ Proper Quorum
   ➤ Proper Proxy in the case of General Meeting

3. **Decisions should be Taken in a Proper Way**

   ➤ Voting (Voice Vote, Raising of Hands, Polls, Postal Ballot, etc)
   ➤ Resolutions (Ordinary, Special and Resolutions Requiring Special Notice)

4. **Decisions Taken should be Properly Recoded**

   ➤ Minutes

■ *Convening Authority*

A general meeting may be convened by any of the following authority:

Board of Directors: Under the Common Law, the proper authority to convene general meetings is the Board of Directors whether expressly given in the Articles of Association or not. Board empowers the Company Secretary to give notice for the general meetings. The sanction may be given if so facto.

Shareholders (Members): The members in certain circumstances may requisition extraordinary general meeting.

Central Government under Section **167**: If default is made in holding an AGM in accordance with Section 166, the Central Government may notwithstanding anything contained in the Act or in the Articles, on the application of any member, under Section 167 call or direct the calling of a general meeting of the company with directions as the Central Government thinks expedient. The directions may include a direction that one member present in person or by proxy shall be deemed to constitute a meeting and that a general meeting held in pursuance to Section 167(1) shall be deemed to be an AGM of the company.

Company Law Board (CLB)/Tribunal under Section **186**: If for any reason, it is impracticable to call a meeting of the company other than an AGM, in the manner prescribed by the Act or the Articles, the CLB/Tribunal may either of its own motion or on the application of any director or member who would be entitled to vote at the meeting

- ❑ Order that a meeting of the company to be called, held and conducted in such manner as the CLB/Tribunal thinks fit, and
- ❑ Give such directions as it deems fit including a direction that one member present in person or by proxy shall be deemed to be constitute a meeting.

■ *Proper and Adequate Notice*

- ❑ The decision taken by members in meeting is binding on members who did not attend in person or by proxy, provided everyone entitled to attend it was given adequate notice with sufficient details of business to be transacted at the meeting, to enable each member to decide whether to attend meeting or not.
- ❑ A valid notice must comply with certain rules
    - ➤ General rules,
    - ➤ Rules laid down in the Articles, and
    - ➤ Rules under the Companies Act.

Who may give Notice?

- ❑ Notice of a meeting must be issued by a person who has the authority to issue such notice. The proper authority is normally the Board that empowers the Company Secretary to give notice for the general meetings.

Judicial Interpretations/Case Example	
Notice of a meeting issued by a person who does not have authority to issue such notice is void and the decisions of the meeting shall also be void. *Re: State of Wyoming Syndicate* (1901) 2 *Ch* 431.	*Re: Haycraft Gold Reduction and Mining Co.,* (1900) 2 Ch 230.

Who should be given Notice?

The notice of general meetings must be given as per [Section 172(2)] to

- ➢ Every member,
- ➢ Legal representative of a deceased member,
- ➢ Receiver or official assignee of an insolvent member, and
- ➢ Auditor or auditors

Judicial Interpretations/Case Example	
A preference shareholder who is only entitled to vote on certain matters concerning his interest is disentitled to receive notice of a meeting at which none of these matters will be discussed. This view was taken by Justice Astbury in *Machenzie and Co. Ltd.* (1916) 2 *Ch* 450.	*John Shaw and Sons* (*Salford*) *Ltd* V *Shaw,* (1935) 2 KB 113.

Contents of Notice

- ❑ Every notice of a meeting of a company shall specify the place and the day and hour of the meeting, and shall contain a statement of the business to be transacted thereat. [Section 172 (1)]
- ❑ Where any items of business to be transacted at the meeting are deemed to be special, there shall be annexed to the notice of the meeting a statement setting out all material facts concerning each such item of business, including in particular the nature of the concern or interest, if any, therein, of every director and the manager, if any: provided that where any item of special business as aforesaid to be transacted at a meeting of the company relates to, or affects, any other company, the extent of share-holding interest in that other company of every director and the manager, if any, of the first mentioned company shall also be set out in the statement if the extent of such shareholding interest is not less than twenty per cent of the paid-up share capital of that other company. [Section 173 (2)]
- ❑ Where any item of business consists of the according of approval to any document by the meeting, the time and place where the document can be inspected shall be specified in the statement aforesaid. [Section 173 (3)]

How Much Days before Notice be Given?

- ❑ A general meeting may be called by giving not less than 21 day's (clear days) notice in writing.
- ❑ Shorter notice as per Section 171(2) may be given if consent in Form 22A in accorded thereto:
    - ➢ In the case of AGM, by all the members entitled to vote thereat, and
    - ➢ In the case of any other meeting (Statutory or EGM), by members
        - • Holding not less than 95% of paid up capital if the company has a share capital or

- Not less than 95% of the total voting power exercisable at that meeting if the company has no share capital.

Shorter Notice *vis-à-vis* Private Company

- ❏ A private company which is not a subsidiary of a public company can provide in its Articles that meeting may be held at shorter notice than 21 days. (Section 170)
- ❏ The provisions of Sections 171 to 186 regarding convening, chairman, quorum, proxy, polls, etc shall, unless otherwise specified or unless the Articles of the company otherwise provide, apply with respect to general meetings of a private company which is not a subsidiary of a public company.

> *Clear days means the day of the service of the notice and the day of holding of the meeting are excluded. Where notice is given by post, it means excluding the day on which the notice is posted, the day of the meeting and 48 hours are given for postal transit (section 53). Therefore, notice of a general meeting must be send atleast 25 days before the date of meeting.*

Judicial Interpretations/Case Example

Failure to give timely notice will invalidate the meeting and nullify the proceedings.	
Where majority of members holding more than 95% of paid of share capital had agreed subsequent to the meeting, to a shorter notice and had ratified and accepted the special resolutions passed at the meeting and not a single objection received from any other members, held the resolutions must be deemed to be valid in view of the subsequent consent obtained. In this case, out of 277 members holding 1,90,000/- equity shares, 226 members holding 1,82,250 shares have given post consent to the resolution and waived the requirement of the notice. The consenting members represent more than 95% of the total equity share. If such members had accorded their consent and waived the requirement of 21 days notice prior to the meeting, the meeting could have been valid and legal in view of Section 171 (2). The waiver made after the meeting and the consent given subsequently could be taken in the same spirit as not a single objection was received from any of the other members. Therefore, even a consent given subsequently validates a resolution passed at a meeting on shorter notice.	*Smyth v Darley,* (1849) 2 HLC 789. *Re: Parikh Engineering and Body Building Co. Ltd.,* (1975) 45 Comp Cas. 157 (Pat).
Post consent validates a special resolution passed without proper notice.	*Re: Self Help Private Industrial Estate (P) Ltd.,* (1972) 42 Camp. Cas 6, (Mad).

Contd...

Each of the 21 days must be full calendar days so as to constitute notice of not less than 21 clear days. Any part of the day after the hour at which notice was served must be excluded .Similarly, any part of the day before the time of meeting should be excluded. *Ref: Pioneer Motors (P) Ltd.v Municipal Counsel, Nagar Coil,* AIR 1967 SC 684.	*Bharat Kumar Dilwali* v *Bharat Carbon and Ribbon Manufacturing Co. Ltd.,* 1972 (1) 1 LR (Del) 837 (DB) 1973 (43) Comp Cas 197 (Del) (DB).

Notice by Post

- ❏ A document may be served by a company on any member thereof either personally or by sending it by post to him to his registered address or if he has no registered address in India, to the address, if any, within in India supplied by him to the company for giving of notice to him. [Section 53 (1)]
- ❏ Where a document is sent by post, service there of shall be deemed to be effected by properly addressing, prepaying and posting a letter, containing the document, provided that where a member has intimated to the company in advance that document should be sent to him under a certificate of posting or by registered post with or without acknowledgement due and has deposited with the company a sum sufficient to defray the expenses of doing so, service of the document shall not be deemed to be effected unless it is sent in the manner intimated by the members [Section 53 (2) (a)].
- ❏ Such service shall be deemed to have been effected in the case of a notice of a meeting, at the expiration of 48 hours, after the letter containing the same is posted and in other case at the time of which the letter would be delivered in the ordinary course of post (Section 53 (2) (b) (i & ii).
- ❏ Where notice of a meeting is served by post, the day of the posting of notice, 48 hours for posted transit and the day at meeting shall be excluded. In that case, a notice of a general meeting must be sent at least 25 days before the date of the meeting

Use of Electronic Communication

- ❏ Electronic communication is defined as a communication transmitted (whether from one person to another, from one device to another or from a person to a device or *vice versa*) by means of a tele-communication system or in an electronic form. For example, notice may be given by fax or email or accessed on website.

> *Under the company law of UK, instead of notice in writing, a company may give notice of meetings by electronic communication to a member where the member has agreed to that method of communication.*

Notice through Newspaper

- ❏ Section 53 permits advertisement of notice in a newspaper circulating in the neighborhood of the registered office of the company.
- ❏ The notice published in the newspaper shall be deemed to have been duly served on the day on which the advertisement appears. Period of 21 days in that case begins from the day on which advertisement appears.
- ❏ Such notice shall be deemed to have been served on every member who has no registered address in India, and has not supplied to the company an address within India, for the giving of notice to him. Thus, publication of notice in newspaper shall not serve as a substitute for sending a notice to every member by hand or by post.
- ❏ Where the notice of a meeting is given by advertising the same in a newspaper circulating in the neighborhood of the registered office of the company under sub-section (3) of Section 53, the statement of material facts referred to in Section 173 need not be annexed to the notice as required by that section but it shall be mentioned in the advertisement that the statement has been forwarded to the members of the company.

Failure to give Notice

- ❏ There is a long established law of meetings that failure to give notice of a meeting to a member entitled to notice invalidates the proceedings of the meeting.
- ❏ However, a person who does not received adequate notice but who attends the meeting may waive the entitlement to the notice.

Judicial Interpretations/Case Example	
Subject to Articles and any restrictions imposed on any shares, notice of general meetings must be given to all members, all persons entitled to a share in consequence of death or bankruptcy of a member and the directors and auditors. An omission to give notice to any person entitled to it invalidates the meeting.	*Smyth* v *Darley,* (1849) 2 HLC 789.
In Australia a gathering of members without proper notice cannot be treated as a meeting if a person who was entitled to notice of meeting but has no voting rights (such as an auditor) did not attend and waive the entitlement to notice.	*Re: Compaction Systems Pvt. Ltd.,* (1976) 2 NSWLR 477.
Gathering without proper notice cannot be a valid meeting unless all persons entitled to attend meeting are present including those who are not entitled to notice.	*Re: Stanley W. Johnson Pty Ltd.,* (1936) V LR 59, cf.

Accidental Omission of Notice

- ❏ The accidental omission to give notice to or the non receipt of notice by any member or other person to whom it should be given shall not invalidate the proceedings at the meeting [Section 172 (3)].

Judicial Interpretations/Case Example	
A few members did not receive a notice because their address plates were inadvertently not put in an addressing machine. The non receipt of notice in this case will not invalidate the proceedings.	*Re: West Canadian Collieries Ltd.,* (1962) Ch. 370.
The company deliberately failed to give notice of its AGM to the claimants, in the mistaken belief that the claimants were not entitled to attend the meeting because they had sold their shares in the company even though the purchaser had not yet been entered in the register of members. Held, the claimants as registered holders of shares were entitled to attend the meeting and that accordingly, the AGM was invalid for want of notice to the claimants.	*Mussel White* v *CH. Mussel White and Sons Ltd.,* (1962) Ch. 964.

Exemptions: Section 25 companies have been exempted from the provisions of Section 171 requiring 21 days notice. In their case, a general meeting may be called by giving 14 days notice in writing.

■ *Proper Agenda*

❑ Every notice of a meeting of a company shall contain a statement of the business to be transacted thereat, which is called agenda. The agenda may be ordinary business and special business. The agenda of the statutory meeting is the statutory report, of AGM is the audited financial statements and reports and the EGM is special business with an explanatory statement.

Ordinary Business: Both ordinary business and special business may be transacted in the AGM. The following matters termed as ordinary business constitutes the usual business of an AGM:

(*i*) Consideration of accounts, balance sheet, and reports of the Board of directors and auditors,

(*ii*) Declaration of dividend,

(*iii*) Appointment of directors in the place of those retiring, and

(*iv*) Appointment of and the fixing of remuneration of the auditors.

Special Business: Business other than ordinary business is called as special business. Special business may be transacted both in the AGM and EGM. The business of EGM is always special. For special business, there shall be annexed to the notice of the meeting an explanatory statement as perSsection 173 (2) and proxy form.

■ *Chairman*

❑ Unless the articles of the company otherwise provide, the members personally present at the meeting shall elect one of themselves to be the chairman thereof on a show of hands. [Section 175 (1)]

❑ If a poll is demanded on the election of the chairman, it shall be taken forthwith in accordance with the provisions of this Act, the chairman elected on a show of hands exercising all the powers of the chairman under the said provisions. [Section 175 (2)]

- If some other person is elected chairman as a result of the poll, he shall be chairman for the rest of the meeting. [Section 175 (3)]
- The chairman, if any, of the Board shall preside as chairman at every general meeting of the company. [Table A-50]
- If there is no such chairman, or if he is not present within fifteen minutes after the time appointed for holding the meeting, or is unwilling to act as chairman of the meeting, the directors present shall elect one of their number to be chairman of the meeting. [Table A-51]
- If at any meeting no director is willing to act as chairman or if no director is present within fifteen minutes after the time appointed for holding the meeting, the members present shall choose one of their number to be chairman of the meeting. [Table A-52]

■ Quorum

Quorum for General Meeting

- Unless the Articles of the company provide for a large number, as per Section 174 (1), five members personally present in the case of public company (other than a public company which has become such by virtue of Section 43A), and two members personally present in the case of any other company, shall be the quorum for a meeting of the company.
- Quorum at the General Meeting is ensured only at the beginning and not throughout.
- If within half an hour from the time appointed for holding a meeting of the company, a quorum is not present, the meeting, if called upon the requisition of members, shall stand dissolved. [Section 174 (3)] In any other case, the meeting shall stand adjourned to the same day in the next week, at the same time and place, or to such other day and at such other time and place as the Board may determine. If at the adjourned meeting also, a quorum is not present within half an hour from the time appointed for holding the meeting, the members present shall be a quorum. [Section 174 (5)]

Quorum for Board Meeting

- The quorum for a meeting of the Board of directors of a company shall be one-third of its total strength (any fraction contained in that one-third being rounded off as one), or two directors, whichever is higher: provided that where at any time the number of interested directors exceeds or is equal to two-thirds of the total strength, the number of the remaining directors, that is to say, the number of the directors who are not interested present at the meeting being not less than two, shall be the quorum during such time. [Section 287 (2)]

- In this section "total strength" means the total strength of the Board of directors of a company as determined in pursuance of this Act, after deducting there from the number of the directors, if any, whose places may be vacant at the time; and "interested director" means any director whose presence cannot, by reason of Section 300, count for the purpose of forming a quorum at a meeting of the Board, at the time of the discussion or vote on any matter.
- Quorum at the Board Meeting is ensured not only at the beginning but throughout the meeting.
- If a meeting of the Board could not be held for want of quorum, then, unless the articles otherwise provide, the meeting shall automatically stand adjourned till the same day in the next week, at the same time and place, or if that day is a public holiday, till the next succeeding day which is not a public holiday, at the same time and place. The provisions of Section 285 shall not be deemed to have been contravened merely by reason of the fact that a meeting of the Board which had been called in compliance with the terms of that section could not be held for want of a quorum. [Section 288]

One Man Meeting

Normally, one person cannot constitute a valid meeting even if he holds proxies for all the members in a meeting. But, there are some exceptions to this rule when even a single member present in the meeting may constitute a valid meeting.

Exceptions

- If default is made in holding an AGM in accordance with section 166, the Central Government may, notwithstanding anything contained in this Act or in the Articles of the company, on the application of any member of the company, call or direct the calling of a general meeting to be deemed to an AGM of the company, and give such ancillary or consequential directions as the Central Government thinks expedient in relation to the calling, holding and conducting of the meeting [Section 167 (1)]. The direction given under this section may include a direction that one member of the company present in person or by proxy shall be deemed to constitute a meeting [explanations to Section 167 (1)].
- If for any reason it is impracticable to call a meeting of a company, other than an annual general meeting, in any manner in which meetings of the company may be called, or to hold or conduct the meeting of the company in the manner prescribed by this Act or the Articles, the CLB/Tribunal may, as per Section 186 (1), either of its own motion or on the application of any director of the company, or of any member of the company who would be entitled to vote at the meeting,— (*a*) order a meeting of the company to be called, held and conducted in such manner as the CLB/Tribunal thinks fit; and (*b*) give such ancillary or consequential directions as the CLB/Tribunal

thinks expedient, including directions modifying or supplementing in relation to the calling, holding and conducting of the meeting, the operation of the provisions of this Act and of the company's articles.

■ Proxy

❑ Any member of a company entitled to attend and vote at a meeting of the company shall be entitled as per Section 176 to appoint another person (whether a member or not) as his proxy to attend and vote instead of himself; but a proxy so appointed shall not have any right to speak at the meeting: provided that, unless the articles otherwise provide—(a) this sub-section shall not apply in the case of a company not having a share capital; (b) a member of a private company shall not be entitled to appoint more than one proxy to attend on the same occasion; and (c) a proxy shall not be entitled to vote except on a poll. [Section 176(1)]

❑ The instrument appointing a proxy shall—

    (a) Be in writing; and

    (b) Be signed by the appointer or his attorney duly authorised in writing or, if the appointer is a body corporate, be under its seal or be signed by an officer or an attorney duly authorised by it.

❑ In every notice calling a meeting of a company which has a share capital, or the articles of which provide for voting by proxy at the meeting, there shall appear with reasonable prominence a statement that a member entitled to attend and vote is entitled to appoint a proxy, or, where that is allowed, one or more proxies, to attend and vote instead of himself, and that a proxy need not be a member. If default is made in complying with this sub-section as respects any meeting, every officer of the company who is in default shall be punishable with fine which may extend to five thousand rupees. [Section 176(2)]

❑ Any provision contained in the articles of a public company or of a private company which is a subsidiary of a public company which specifies or requires a longer period than forty-eight hours before a meeting of the company, for depositing with the company or any other person any instrument appointing a proxy or any other document necessary to show the validity or otherwise relating to the appointment of a proxy in order that the appointment may be effective at such meeting, shall have effect as if a period of forty eight hours had been specified in or required by such provision for such deposit. [Section 176(3)]

❑ If for the purpose of any meeting of a company, invitations to appoint as proxy a person or one of a number of persons specified in the invitations are issued at the company's expense to any member entitled to have a notice of the meeting sent to him and to vote thereat by proxy, every officer of the company who knowingly issues the invitations as aforesaid or willfully authorises or permits their issue shall be punishable with fine which may extend to ten thousand rupees: provided that an officer shall not be punishable under this sub-section by reason only of the issue to a member at his request in writing of a form of appointment naming the proxy, or of a list of persons willing to act as proxies, if the form or list is available on request in writing to every member entitled to vote at the meeting by proxy. [Section 176 (4)]

❑ An instrument appointing a proxy, if in any of the forms set out in Schedule IX, shall not be questioned on the ground that it fails to comply with any special requirements specified for such instrument by the articles. [Section 176 (6)]

❑ Every member entitled to vote at a meeting of the company, or on any resolution to be moved thereat, shall be entitled during the period beginning twenty-four hours before the time fixed for the commencement of the meeting and ending with the conclusion of the meeting, to inspect the proxies lodged, at any time during the business hours of the company, provided not less than three days' notice in writing of the intention so to inspect is given to the company. [Section 176 (7)]

■ Resolutions

Ordinary Resolution: A resolution shall be an ordinary resolution when at a general meeting of which the notice required under this Act has been duly given, the votes cast (whether on a show of hands, or on a poll, as the case may be,) in favour of the resolution (including the casting vote, if any, of the chairman) by members who, being entitled so to do, vote in person, or where proxies are allowed, by proxy, exceed the votes, if any, cast against the resolution by members so entitled and voting. [Section 189 (1)]

Special Resolution: A resolution shall be a special resolution when:

(*a*) The intention to propose the resolution as a special resolution has been duly specified in the notice calling the general meeting or other intimation given to the members of the resolution;

(*b*) The notice required under this Act has been duly given of the general meeting; and

(*c*) The votes cast in favour of the resolution (whether on a show of hands, or on a poll, as the case may be), by members who, being entitled so to do, vote in person, or where proxies are allowed, by proxy, are not less than three times the number of the votes, if any, cast against the resolution by members so entitled and voting. [Section 189(2)]

Resolutions Requiring Special Notice: Where, by any provision contained in this Act or in the articles, special notice is required of any resolution, notice of the intention to move the resolution shall be given to the company not less then fourteen days before the meeting at which it is to be moved, exclusive of the day on which the notice is served or deemed to be served and the day of the meeting.

[Section 190 (1)] The company shall, immediately after the notice of the intention to move any such resolution has been received by it, give its members notice of the resolution in the same manner as it gives notice of the meeting, or if that is not practicable, shall give them notice thereof, either by advertisement in a newspaper having an appropriate circulation or in any other mode allowed by the articles, not less than seven days before the meeting. [Section 190 (2)]

Special notice is required in the following cases:

1. Special notice shall be required for a resolution at an annual general meeting appointing as auditor a person other than a retiring auditor, or providing expressly that a retiring auditor shall not be re-appointed. [Section 225]

2. A company may, by ordinary resolution, remove a director (not being a director appointed by the Central Government in pursuance of section 408) before the expiry of his period of office. Special notice shall be required of any resolution to remove a director under this section, or to appoint somebody instead of a director so removed at the meeting at which he is removed. [Section 284 (1) (2)]

Resolutions Passed at Adjourned Meeting: Where a resolution is passed at an adjourned meeting of—(*a*) a company; (*b*) the holders of any class of shares in a company; or (*c*) the Board of directors of a company; the resolution shall, for all purposes, be treated as having been passed on the date on which it was in fact passed, and shall not be deemed to have been passed on any earlier date. [Section 191]

Passing of Resolution by Postal Ballot [New Sec. 192A]

❑ A listed company may, and in the case of notified matters, shall get resolution passed by means of a postal ballot, instead of transacting the business in general meeting.

❑ The notice shall be sent by registered post acknowledgement due, or by any other method as may be prescribed by the Central Government in this behalf, and shall include with the notice, a postage pre-paid envelope for facilitating the communication of the assent or dissent of the shareholder to the resolution within the said period.

❑ Notice is given to all shareholders along with draft of resolution explaining reasons and a request to send back assent or dissent on a postal ballot in prepaid envelop by registered post within 30 days.

❑ In this way participation of almost each shareholder in the decision-making on vital issues that concerns the whole organisation, is ensured.

Following matters have been notified by the Central Government to be passed by postal ballot:

➢ Matters relating to alteration in memorandum.
➢ Sale of whole or substantially whole of the undertaking.

> Corporate restructuring.
> Entering a new business area.
> Sale of investments in the company where shareholders or voting rights of company exceeds 25%.
> Making a further issue of shares through preferential allotment or private placement.
> Variation in rights attached to class of securities.
> Matters relating to change in management.

Non-compliance:- Fine up to Rs.50000

■ Voting

Voting to be by Show of Hands in First Instance: A resolution put to the vote at any general meeting, shall unless a poll is demanded under Section 179, be decided on a show of hands. [Section 177]

Chairman's Declaration of Result of Voting by Show of Hands to be Conclusive: A declaration by the chairman in pursuance of Section 177 that on a show of hands, a resolution has or has not been carried, or has or has not been carried either unanimously or by a particular majority, and an entry to that effect in the books containing the minutes of the proceedings of the company, shall be conclusive evidence of the fact, without proof of the number or proportion of the votes cast in favour of or against such resolution. [Section 178]

Demand for Poll: Before or on the declaration of the result of the voting on any resolution on a show of hands, a poll may be ordered to be taken by the chairman of the meeting of his own motion, and shall be ordered to be taken by him on a demand made in that behalf by the persons or person specified below, that is to say:

(a) In the case of a public company having a share capital by, any member or members present in person or by proxy and holding shares in the company

    (i) Which confer a power to vote on the resolution not being less than one-tenth of the total voting power in respect of the resolution, or

    (ii) On which an aggregate sum of not less than fifty thousand rupees has been paid-up,

(b) In the case of a private company having a share capital, by one member having the right to vote on the resolution and present in person or by proxy if not more than seven such members are personally present, and by two such members present in person or by proxy, if more than seven such members are personally present,

(c) In the case of any other company, by any member or members present in person or by proxy and having not less than one-tenth of the total voting power in respect of the resolution. [Section 179 (1)]

The demand for a poll may be withdrawn at any time by the person or persons who made the demand. [Section 179 (2)]

Time of taking Poll: A poll demanded on a question of adjournment shall be taken forthwith. A poll demanded on any other question (not being a question relating to the election of a chairman which is provided for in Section 175) shall be taken at such time not being later than forty-eight hours from the time when the demand was made, as the chairman may direct. [Section 180 (1) (2)]

■ *Minutes*

- ❏ Every company shall cause minutes of all proceedings of every general meeting and of all proceedings of every meeting of its Board of directors or of every committee of the Board, to be kept by making within thirty days of the conclusion of every such meeting concerned, entries thereof in books kept for that purpose with their pages consecutively numbered. [Section 193 (1)]
- ❏ Each page of every such book shall be initialed or signed and the last page of the record of proceedings of each meeting in such books shall be dated and signed:
    - (*a*) In the case of minutes of proceedings of a meeting of the Board or of a committee thereof, by the chairman of the said meeting or the chairman of the next succeeding meeting;
    - (*b*) In the case of minutes of proceedings of a general meeting, by the chairman of the same meeting within the aforesaid period of thirty days or in the event of the death or inability of that chairman within that period, by a director duly authorised by the Board for the purpose.
- ❏ In no case the minutes of proceedings of a meeting shall be attached to any such book as aforesaid by pasting or otherwise. [Section 193 (1B)]
- ❏ The minutes of each meeting shall contain a fair and correct summary of the proceedings thereat.
- ❏ All appointments of officers made at any of the meetings aforesaid shall be included in the minutes of the meeting.
- ❏ In the case of a meeting of the Board of directors or of a committee of the Board, the minutes shall also contain— the names of the directors present at the meeting; and in the case of each resolution passed at the meeting, the names of the directors, if any, dissenting from, or not concurring in, the resolution.
- ❏ Nothing contained in these provisions shall be deemed to require the inclusion in any such minutes of any matter which, in the opinion of the chairman of the meeting— is, or could reasonably be regarded as, defamatory of any

person; is irrelevant or immaterial to the proceedings; or is detrimental to the interests of the company.

> *Explanation:* The chairman shall exercise an absolute discretion in regard to the inclusion or non-inclusion of any matter in the minutes on the grounds specified in this sub-section.

- ❏ If default is made in complying with the foregoing provisions of this section in respect of any meeting, the company, and every officer of the company who is in default, shall be punishable with fine which may extend to five hundred rupees. [Section 193 (6)]

Minutes to be Evidence

- ❏ Minutes of meetings kept in accordance with the provisions of section 193 shall be evidence of the proceedings recorded therein. [Section 194]

Inspection of Minute Books of General Meetings

- ❏ The books containing the minutes of the proceedings of any general meeting of a company held on or after the 15th day of January, 1937, shall— be kept at the registered office of the company, and be open, during business hours, to the inspection of any member without charge, subject to such reasonable restrictions as the company may, by its articles or in general meeting impose, so however that not less than two hours in each day are allowed for inspection. [Section 196 (1)]
- ❏ Any member shall be entitled to be furnished, within seven days after he has made a request in that behalf to the company, with a copy of any minutes referred to in sub-section (1), on payment of such sum as may be prescribed for every one hundred words or fractional part thereof required to be copied. [Section 196 (2)]
- ❏ If any inspection required under sub-section (1) is refused, or if any copy required under sub-section (2) is not furnished within the time specified therein, the company, and every officer of the company who is in default, shall be punishable with fine which may extend to five thousand rupees in respect of each offence. [Section 196 (3)]
- ❏ In the case of any such refusal or default, the Central Government may, by order, compel an immediate inspection of the minute books or direct that the copy required shall forthwith be sent to the person requiring it. [Section 196(4)]

Review Questions

1. What is meant by meeting? Describe briefly the different kinds of company meetings.
2. Comment on 'one –man meeting'.
3. Write a note on class meetings.

4. What are the requirements of a valid board meeting? When is a board meeting said to be duly convened and properly constituted?

5. How is the chairman of a board meeting appointed? Can a board meeting be held if the designated chairman is absent?

6. Write a detailed note on 'agenda of a board meeting'.

7. Write a note on quorum at board meeting.

8. State the provisions of the Companies Act, 1956 regarding the recording and signing of minutes of the proceedings of board meeting.

9. Write a short note on 'resolution by circulation'.

10. "The general meeting alone is the company's primary organ and the directors are merely the company's agent or servants at all time subservient to the general meeting." Comment.

11. What are different kinds of meetings of the shareholder of a company? When and how are these meetings held?

12. What is a statutory meeting? When and how it is held? State the contents of the statutory report.

13. What are the statutory provisions regarding the holding of annual general meeting? What business is transacted at such a meeting? What are the consequences of default in holding an annual general meeting?

14. Can the directors of a company postpone the holding of its annual general meeting beyond the statutory time limit on the grounds that the annual accounts are not ready?

15. Explain the statutory provisions with regard the following points in the context of an annual general meeting:

   (*i*) Length and contents of notice
   (*ii*) Persons entitled to receive notice
   (*iii*) Time and place of meeting

16. Can annual general meeting (AGM) of a public company be held on a public holiday?

17. What is an 'extraordinary general meeting'? When and by whom can an extraordinary general meeting be called?

18. Distinguish between 'extra-ordinary general meeting' and 'annual general meeting'.

19. State the requisites of a valid general meeting.

20. Who are the persons entitled to receive the notices of the general meeting?

21. "Directors and auditors must attend every general meeting". Comment.

22. Can a director who is not a member of the company demand a notice of a general meeting?

23. What are the provisions of the Companies Act, 1956 as to the length of notice required for calling general meetings of the company? In what

circumstances a general meeting may be validly held when the notice is given is shorter than that normally required by the Act?

24. "A faulty notice of meeting can be fatal to the validity of a meeting." Comment.

25. What are the requisites of a valid notice of a company meeting? What do you mean by clear days in connection with issue of notices?

26. Explain 'ordinary business' and 'special business' which may be transacted at general meetings of a company. State also the meetings in which such businesses are transacted?

27. When is an explanatory statement required to be annexed to the notice calling the general meeting of the company?

28. Who is a chairman of a meeting? How is the chairman appointed? Describe his powers and duties in the conduct of company meetings.

29. Is it compulsory to publish chairman's speech in newspapers?

30. Define quorum. What is the quorum for a general body meeting and a board meeting?

31. What do you understand by quorum? Must a quorum be present throughout the meeting? What is the procedure if quorum is never formed?

32. What is the status of joint share-holders for the purpose of the quorum at the general body meeting?

33. What do you understand by proxy? What are the statutory provisions regarding proxies? When should a proxy be lodged with a company?

34. Explain the different kinds of resolutions which may be passed at the meeting of shareholders of a company. Under what circumstances do special resolution becomes necessary?

35. Explain the provisions of the Companies Act, 1956 with regard to the 'resolutions requiring special notice'. When such a notice is required?

36. State the provisions of the Companies Act, 1956, regarding the registration of resolution.

37. What is motion? Distinguish between motion and resolution.

38. What is an ordinary resolution? Give four such matters that require ordinary resolution.

39. Write a short note on Special Resolution.

40. Explain the various modes of ascertaining the sense of general meetings of a company.

41. What are the methods of voting at a meeting of a company? Is voting by show of hands is a satisfactory method of voting?

42. When 'poll' can be demanded in the general meeting of a company? Who can demand such a poll?

43. What are the legal requirements to be complied with regard to recording of minutes and maintenance of minute's book?

44. How is minute's book maintained? Is it compulsory to maintain minutes book? If so, why?

45. Can a member inspect book of minutes of the board meeting? Does it make any difference if the member wishes to inspect of general meeting?

46. Write a short note on 'minutes in loose leaf'.

47. Point out the difference between the following :

   (*a*) Adjournment, postponement and dissolution of a meeting.

   (*b*) Special resolution and resolution requiring special notice.

48. Distinguish between :

   (*a*) Ordinary resolution and special resolution.

   (*b*) Ordinary business and special business.

□□□

10

Winding Up of A Company

History of Winding up Laws

- Law of company winding up India is the cherished child of English parents born and brought up in England. Such laws passed in India from time to time have been following the English provisions with, minor changes here and there. Therefore, a brief resume of the origin and growth of winding up laws in England is essential for logical understanding of winding up laws in India.

- Four phases are noticeable in the course of this development *viz.*, the first covers the period up to 1844; the second phase throws light that between 1844 and 1856; the third which may be regarded as the period modeled on English Provisions, commences with the passing of the Joint Stock Companies Act, 1856, and extends to 1956 and the final phase that starts from 1956 and extends to the present day is known as the era of modern Company Law. The phase-wise discussion follows in the succeeding paragraphs:

Prior to 1844 : In England, prior to 1844, there was no distinct body of legal principles that could be regarded as the law of company liquidation. All companies, except those that enjoyed the rate privilege of incorporation by statute, or charter, were of the deed settlement type, and so far as the law was concerned, were treated as enlarged partnerships. To their winding up, therefore, the law of partnership applied. The liability of the members of a company, like partners, was unlimited. Secondly, no satisfactory procedure existed for compulsory winding up at the instance of contributories. Thus, need was felt for a simple form of procedure for making company's assets available for the payment of debts, as well as some means by which the members could bring an unsuccessful venture to an end, and so fix a limit to the amount of their liabilities. To achieve these objects, various Acts were passed from 1844 to 1856, which were known as winding up Acts.

1844 to 1856 : Winding up Acts passed from 1844 to 1856 had some defects, such as no provision was made to limit the liability of shareholders. While corporate assets constituted the primary fund out of which liabilities were to be satisfied, any deficiency could be made good by resorting to the members' private property. Secondly no attempt was made to limit the remedies of creditors as to levy execution on the personal property of the shareholders. The Companies Act of 1856 removed these defects.

1856 - 1956 : With the passing of Joint Stock Companies Act, 1856, a single system of winding up, which could be set in motion by any contributory, creditor, or by the company itself, was introduced. The Act also provided for the limited liabilities of shareholders as to the nominal value of their respective shares. A procedure for enabling voluntary winding up subject to court's supervision was introduced by the Act of 1857, and extended in the following year. These Acts were repealed by the Companies Act of 1862 providing for three modes of winding up. - winding up by the court; voluntary winding up; and voluntary winding up subject to supervision of the court, The Act of 1890 and the rules there under introduced a procedure for winding up. These provisions subsequently were reproduced by the English Companies Act of 1948, which now constitutes the existing legislation, and also governs the company liquidation in England today. In India, following the English Act of 1844, an Act was passed in 1850 containing similar provisions of company liquidation. Another Act was passed in 1860 on the lines of the English Act of 1856 and 1857. After enacting various amending Acts between 1882 and 1913, the Act of 1913 came into force that modified the winding up provisions to a great extent. Gradually, the Companies Act, 1956, amending the law and procedure relating to compulsory winding up, came into oper .ion and is operational till date.

After 1956 : The final phase that starts from 1956 and extends to the present day is known as the era of Modern Company Law.

Meaning of Winding up

A company comes into existence by a legal process and when it is desired to end its existence it must again go through the legal process of winding up its affairs. Winding up of company is the process whereby its life is ended and its property is administered for the benefit of its creditors and members. An administrator is appointed and he takes control of the company, collects its assets, pays its debts and finally distributes any surplus among the members in accordance with their rights. Thus, winding up is the last stage in the life of the company.

Winding up v Dissolution

The terms 'winding up' and 'dissolution' are sometimes mistakenly used to mean the same thing, whereas they are in-fact quite different in their meanings. A company does not become dissolved at the commencement of either a compulsory or voluntary winding up. Winding up of company is the process whereby all assets of the company are realized and used to pay off the debts and equity. In the winding up, the property of the company is administered for the benefit of its creditors and members. Dissolution of the company on the other hand takes place after the entire process of winding up is over. Dissolution puts an end to the life of the company. A dissolution order passed by the Court is treated as issuing 'Death Certificate' to the company.

Modes of Winding up [Section 425]

Companies Act provides a mechanism for ending the life of the company. There are three modes of winding up of a company under the Act. A company may be wound up by an order of the Court that is called 'compulsory winding up' or 'winding up by the Court'. Winding up by the creditors or members without any intervention of the Court is called 'voluntary winding up'. In voluntary winding up, the company and its creditors are left free to settle their affairs without going to the Court. In case of voluntary winding up, the creditors or members may apply to the Court for directions or orders. Such a winding up is known as 'winding up subject to the supervision of the Court'.

Winding up by the Court/Tribunal [Section 433]

Section 433 provides that a company may be wound up by the High Court/Tribunal, if:

(a) Company has by special resolution resolved that the company be wound up by the Court/Tribunal;

(b) Default is made in delivering the statutory report to the Registrar or in holding the statutory meeting;

(c) Company does not commence its business within a year from its incorporation, or suspends its business for a whole year;

(d) Number of members is reduced, in the case of a public company, below seven, and in the case of a private company, below two;

(e) Company is unable to pay its debts;

(f) The Court/Tribunal is of the opinion that it is just and equitable that the company should be wound up;

(g) Company has made a default in filing with the Registrar, its balance sheet and profit and loss account or annual return for any five consecutive financial years;

(h) Company has acted against the interests of the sovereignty and integrity of India, the security of the State, friendly relations with foreign States, public order, decency or morality;

(i) Court/Tribunal is of the opinion that the company should be wound up under the circumstances specified in Section 424G .

Provided that the Court/Tribunal shall make an order for winding up of a company under clause (h) on an application made by the Central Government or State Government.

A company may be wound up in terms of the provisions of Section 433 in the following circumstances:

By Passing a Special Resolution: A company may be wound up by the order of Court/Tribunal if it resolves so by passing a special resolution. It may in that case present an application to the Court/Tribunal for winding up.

Failure to hold Statutory Meeting or File Statutory Report: Every public company limited by shares or a public company limited by guarantee and having a share capital is required by Section 165, to prepare a statutory report and hold statutory meeting within a period of not less than one month and not more than six months from the date at which the company is entitled to commence business. It is required to send the statutory report to the members and the Registrar of Companies duly certified at least 21 clear days before the holding of the statutory meeting. If default is made in delivering the statutory report to the Registrar or in holding the statutory meeting, a company may be wound up by the High Court/Tribunal.

Failure to Commence Business: Where a company does not commence business within a year from its incorporation or where a company suspends its business for a whole year, it becomes a ground for compulsory winding up.

Reduction in Number of Members below Statutory Minimum: Where the number of members in a public company is reduced to less than seven or in a private company to less than two, it becomes a ground for compulsory winding up.

Inability to Pay its Debts: If it is proved to the satisfaction of the Court/Tribunal that the company owes a sum exceeding rupees one lakh to a creditor and when the creditor has served on the company at its registered office a demand to pay the sum so due and the company has for three weeks thereafter neglected to pay the sum, or to secure the debt to the satisfaction of the creditor, a company is considered unable to pay its debts. A large amount of discretion is available to the Court/Tribunal under this clause. The Court/Tribunal may, however, refuse to wind up the company if it is just and equitable to do so.

Arrears of unpaid salary and the dues of an employee, is not a debt within the meaning of this section.

Judicial Interpretations/Case Example	
The machinery for winding up is not allowed to be used for realization of the debts.	*Amalgamated Commercial Traders (P) Ltd. v A. C. K. Krishnaswami,* 1965, 35 Comp Cas 456 (SC).

Contd...

Held, a winding up petition is not a legitimate means of seeking enforcement of a debt which is bona fide disputed. A petition presented ostensibly for a winding up order, but really to exercise pressure should be dismissed; otherwise the said provision can be misutilised.	*Ambala Bus Syndicate (P) Ltd.* v *Bala Financiers (P) Ltd.,* 1984, 2 Comp LJ 372 (P and H): 1986, 59 Comp Cas 838 (P and H)].
It is well settled that the mere fact that certain liabilities will accrue in future or have accrued by itself is not a ground to wind up a company. Where debt is *bona fide* disputed, it cannot be said that the company is to be wound up. What is a *bona fide* dispute had to be decided on the facts of each case. In other words, if the defense is real and substantial, the order for winding up will not be passed.	*Praneet Enviroquips Pvt. Ltd., Chandigarh* v *Vishal Papertech (India) Ltd.,* (1999) 4 CLJ 280 (P and H).

Just and Equitable: Under this clause the Court/Tribunal is gifted with very large discretion to arrive at a judgment that it is just and equitable to wound up the company. The Court/Tribunal may use this discretion under several circumstances, some of them, discussed below:

(a) When there is a deadlock in the management (members of Board are not on talking terms).

(b) Purpose for which the company was formed has been either lost or the company has abandoned it.

(c) If any of the company's objects is illegal or fraudulent or against the public policy.

(d) When the company is a bubble (like a 'fly- by- night' company).

(e) When it is a case of oppression of minority shareholders.

Default in filing with the Registrar the Balance Sheet or Annual Return: If a company commits default in filing of the balance sheet or annual return with the Registrar of Companies (required under Sections 159 and 220 of the Companies Act), for any five consecutive financial years, it becomes a ground for compulsory winding up.

Acting against the Interest of the Country: If a company has acted against the interests of the sovereignty and integrity of India, the security of the State, friendly relations with foreign States, public order, decency or morality, it becomes a ground for compulsory winding up.

If the Company is a Sick Industrial Company and is not Likely to Become Workable in Future: After inquiring into all the relevant facts and circumstances, and after hearing all the concerned parties, if the Court/Tribunal is of the opinion that the sick industrial company is not likely to become viable in future, it may record its findings and order winding up of the company.

Who can file Petition for Winding up? [Section 439]

An application to the Court/Tribunal for the winding up of a company can be made by:

- (*a*) The company;
- (*b*) Any creditor or creditors, including any contingent or prospective creditor or creditors;
- (*c*) Any contributory or contributories;
- (*d*) By all or any of the parties at (*a*), (*b*) and (*c*), whether together or separately;
- (*e*) The Registrar of Companies;
- (*f*) Any person authorised by the Central Government as a result of investigation carried out on the affairs of a company pursuant to Section 237;
- (*g*) The Central Government or a State Government, in a case falling under clause (*h*) of Section 433.

Appointment of Official Liquidator [Section 448]

- ☐ For the purposes of this Act, so far as it relates to the winding up of a company by the Tribunal, there shall be an Official Liquidator who may be appointed from a panel of professional firms of chartered accountants, advocates, company secretaries, costs and works accountants or firms having a combination of these professions, which the Central Government shall constitute for the Court/Tribunal; or may be a body corporate consisting of such professionals as may be approved by the Central Government from time to time; or may be a whole-time or a part-time officer appointed by the Central Government, provided that, before appointing the Official Liquidator, the Court/Tribunal may give due regard to the views or opinion of the secured creditors and workmen. [Section 448 (1)]

- ☐ The terms and conditions for the appointment of the Official Liquidator and the remuneration payable to him shall be approved by the Court/Tribunal, subject to a maximum remuneration of five per cent of the value of debt recovered and realisation of sale of assets; approved by the Central Government. [Section 448 (2)]

- ☐ Where the Official Liquidator is an officer appointed by the Central Government, the Central Government may also appoint, if considered necessary, one or more Deputy Official Liquidators or Assistant Official Liquidators to assist the Official Liquidator in the discharge of his functions, and the terms and conditions for the appointment of such Official Liquidators and the remuneration payable to them shall also be in accordance with the rules made by the Central Government. [Section 448 (3)]

- ☐ The amount of the remuneration payable shall form part of the winding up order made by the Court/Tribunal; be treated as first charge on the realisation of the assets and be paid to the Official Liquidator or to the Central Government, as the case may be. [Section 448 (5)]

❑ The Official Liquidator shall conduct proceedings in the winding up of a company and perform such duties in reference thereto as the Court/Tribunal may specify in this behalf: provided that the Court/Tribunal may transfer the work assigned from one Official Liquidator to another Official Liquidator for the reasons to be recorded in writing; remove the Official Liquidator on sufficient cause being shown; proceed against the Official Liquidator for professional misconduct. [Section 448 (6)]

■ Official Liquidator to be Liquidator [Section 449]

❑ On a winding up order being made in respect of a company, the Official Liquidator shall, by virtue of his office, become the liquidator of the company.

■ Audit of Liquidator's Accounts

❑ The liquidator shall at least twice each year, present to the Court/Tribunal an account of his receipts and payments as liquidator and the said account shall be audited. One copy of the audited accounts shall be filed with the Court/Tribunal and another copy with the Registrar, which shall be open to the inspection of the creditors, contributories or other interested persons. [Section 462]

■ Committee of Inspection

❑ At the time of making the winding up order, the Court/Tribunal may give direction to the official liquidator to appoint a committee of inspection to act with liquidator. The committee may consist of not more than 12 members, being creditors and contributories. Within two months of the direction of the Court/Tribunal, the official liquidator shall, convene a meeting of creditors for the purpose of constitution of the committee. The approval of the contributories on the formation of the committee shall also taken. In the case of difference of opinion between the creditors and the contributories, the official liquidator shall apply to the Court/Tribunal for direction. [Sec. 464]

■ Statement of Affairs to be made to the Official Liquidator

❑ It shall be the duty of the directors of the company to prepare a statement as to the affairs of the company in the prescribed form and submit it to the official liquidator duly verified within 21 days of the winding up order or within 12 days of the appointment of a provisional liquidator. Any creditor or contributory shall be entitled, by payment of necessary fees, to inspect the statement or ask for a copy thereof. [Section 454]

■ *Contents of Statement of Affairs*

❑ Where the Court/Tribunal has made a winding up order or appointed the Official Liquidator as provisional liquidator, unless the Court/Tribunal in its discretion otherwise orders, there shall be made out and submitted to the Official Liquidator a statement as to the affairs of the company in the prescribed form, verified by an affidavit, and containing the following particulars, namely:

(*a*) The assets of the company, stating separately the cash balance in hand and at the bank, if any, and the negotiable securities, if any, held by the company;

(*b*) Its debts and liabilities;

(*c*) The names, residences and occupations of its creditors, stating separately the amount of secured and unsecured debts; and in the case of secured debts, particulars of the securities given, whether by the company or an officer thereof, their value and the dates on which they were given;

(*d*) The debts due to the company and the names, residences and occupations of the persons from whom they are due and the amount likely to be realised on account thereof;

(*e*) Such further or other information as may be prescribed, or as the Official Liquidator may require.

❑ The statement shall be submitted and verified by one or more of the persons who are at the relevant date the directors and by the person who is at that date the manager, secretary or other chief officer of the company, or by such of the persons mentioned, as the Official Liquidator, subject to the direction of the Court/Tribunal, may require to submit and verify the statement, that is to say, persons—

(*a*) Who are or have been officers of the company;

(*b*) Who have taken part in the formation of the company at any time within one year before the relevant date;

(*c*) Who are in the employment of the company, or have been in the employment of the company within the said year, and are, in the opinion of the Official Liquidator, capable of giving the information required;

(*d*) Who are or have been within the said year officers of, or in the employment of, a company which is, or within the said year was, an officer of the company to which the statement relates.

Contributories

❑ According to Section 428 of the Companies Act, the term 'contributory' means every person liable to contribute to the assets of a company in the event of its being wound up, and includes the holder of any shares which are fully paid-up; and for the purposes of all proceedings for determining, and all proceedings prior to the final determination of, the persons who are to be deemed contributories, includes any person alleged to be a contributory.

Liability as Contributories of Present and Past Members: According to Section426 (1), in the event of a company being wound up, every present and past member shall be liable to contribute to the assets of the company to an amount sufficient for payment of its debts and liabilities and the costs, charges and expenses of the winding up, and for the adjustment of the rights of the contributories among themselves, subject to the provisions of Section 427 and subject also to the following qualifications, namely:

(*a*) A past member shall not be liable to contribute if he has ceased to be a member for one year or upwards before the commencement of the winding up;

(*b*) A past member shall not be liable to contribute in respect of any debt or liability of the company contracted after he ceased to be a member;

(*c*) No past member shall be liable to contribute unless it appears to the Tribunal that the present members are unable to satisfy the contributions required to be made by them in pursuance of this Act;

(*d*) In the case of a company limited by shares, no contribution shall be required from any past or present member exceeding the amount, if any, unpaid on the shares in respect of which he is liable as such member;

(*e*) In the case of a company limited by guarantee, no contribution shall, subject to the provisions of sub-section (2), be required from any past or present member exceeding the amount undertaken to be contributed by him to the assets of the company in the event of its being wound up;

(*f*) Nothing in this Act shall invalidate any provision contained in any policy of insurance or other contract whereby the liability of individual members on the policy or contract is restricted, or whereby the funds of the company are alone made liable in respect of the policy or contract;

(*g*) A sum due to any past or present member of the company in his character as such, by way of dividends, profits or otherwise, shall not be deemed to be a debt of the company payable to that member, in a case of competition between himself and any creditor claiming otherwise than in the character of a past or present member of the company; but any such sum shall be taken into account for the purpose of the final adjustment of the rights of the contributories among themselves.

❑ In the winding up of a company limited by guarantee which has a share capital, every member of the company shall be liable, in addition to the amount undertaken to be contributed by him to the assets of the company in the event of its being wound up, to contribute to the extent of any sums unpaid on any shares held by him as if the company were a company limited by shares. [Sec. 426 (2)]

Nature of Liability of Contributory: The liability of a contributory shall create a debt accruing due from him at the time when his liability commenced, but payable at the times specified in calls made on him for enforcing the liability. No claim founded on the liability of a contributory shall be cognizable by any Court of Small Causes sitting outside the presidency-towns. [Sec. 429 (1) (2)]

Dissolution of a Company

❏ When the affairs of a company have been completely wound-up or when the Court/Tribunal is of the opinion that the liquidator cannot proceed with the winding up of a company for want of funds and assets or for any other reason whatsoever and it is just and reasonable in the circumstances of the case that an order of dissolution of the company should be made, the Court Tribunal shall make an order that the company be dissolved from the date of the order, and the company shall be dissolved accordingly. [Sec. 481 (1)]

❏ A copy of the order shall; within thirty days from the date thereof, be forwarded by the liquidator to the Registrar who shall make in his books minute of the dissolution of the company. [Sec. 481 (2)]

❏ If the liquidator makes default in forwarding a copy as aforesaid, he shall be punishable with fine which may extend to five hundred rupees for every day during which the default continues. [Sec. 481 (3)]

Review Questions

1. What do you understand by the winding up of a company? What are the different modes of winding up?
2. When a company be wound up by the Court/Tribunal? Who are the persons entitled to present a petition for the winding up of a company by the Court Tribunal and under what circumstances the Court/Tribunal order a compulsory winding up of a company?
3. On what grounds may a petition for compulsory winding up be filed and who may file such a petition? Discuss.
4. "It is in just and equitable that a company should be wound up when its substratum is shown to have gone." Discuss the test to be applied in this regard before winding up order is passed under 'just and equitable' clause.
5. There are only two members of a company and both of them are not on speaking terms. Can the company be wound up on this ground?
6. Who is a contributory? Who are the persons liable as contributories?
7. What do you understand by 'List A' and 'List B' contributories?

8. Distinguish between 'winding up' and 'dissolution of a company.' State the circumstances under which a company can be wound up by the Court Tribunal.

9. Which Court/Tribunal has jurisdiction to wind-up a company? Discuss.

10. Distinguish between winding up and dissolution.

11. Write a short note on :

    (*i*)   Official liquidator

    (*ii*) Committee of inspection

    (*iii*) Dissolution of company

    (*iv*) Just and equitable

    (*v*) Contributories

Emerging Issues in Company Law

Introduction

❑ In the midst of grave balance of payment, the government of India in 1991 redrafted its economic policy to lead new era of deregulation, decontrol, liberalization and global integration. Since then significant policy initiatives have been taken to provide stimulus to accelerated growth, industrial efficiency, and global competitiveness. As a part of reform process, government of India has initiated number of legislative reforms and radical changes in the area of company laws. New issues, concepts and practices keep on emerging in respect of the working and administration of corporate sector. Many new and unheard concepts have been introduced in the Companies Act and many are in the pipeline. Shelf Prospectus, Postal Ballot, Audit Committee, Corporate Identity Number (CIN), Director Identity Number (DIN), Electronic Filing of documents and Online Registration of Companies has been made a part of the Companies Act. Concept of One Person Company (OPC), Small Company, Associate Company, Independent Director, Insider Trading, National Company Law Tribunal, are in the pipeline. The enactment of the Limited Liability Partnership Act, 2008 is also a major development. The process of reforming the company laws is still on and the central government has introduced in the Parliament new Company Bill, 2009 to totally revamp the Company Law. An attempt in this chapter has been made to throw some light on all such issues.

Producer Company

The Companies (Amendment) Act, 2002 has brought manufacturing types of cooperative societies in the country under the purview of Companies Act. The amendment is based on the recommendations of Dr.Y.K.Alagh Committee, which was constituted in 1999 to frame legislation to enable incorporation of cooperatives as companies and converting the existing cooperatives into companies. Accordingly, Part IX A with 12 chapters has been inserted in the Companies Act, 1956 (sections

581A to 581 2T) that contains provisions on the formation, management, decision making, conversion of existing industrial cooperatives into producer companies and matters connected therewith. An option has been given to the existing multi-state cooperative societies to transform into Producer Company. The Irani Committee (2005) recommended a separate legislation for Producers Companies, which are at present part of the Companies Act.

Important Features:

Incorporation

Producer Company can be formed by

> 1. Any 10 or more individual producers or
> 2. Two or more producer institutions or
> 3. A combination of (*i*) and (*ii*)

Conditions Contained in the Memorandum of Association

(*i*) Memorandum will consist of name clause, situation clause, objects clause, capital clause, liability clause and subscription clause.

(*ii*) The name of the Producer Company should end with the words "Producer Company Limited".

(*iii*) The Producer Company can have only equity capital.

(*iv*) It is not possible to form a Producer Company with unlimited liability.

(*v*) The alteration procedure for various clauses of Memorandum is mostly similar to other types of Companies formed under the Companies Act, 1956.

Articles of Association

(*i*) Articles can be altered on the proposal (demand) of not less than 2/3 of the elected directors or by not less than 1/3 of the members of the Producer Company.

(*ii*) The members of the Company should adopt the amendment by special resolution.

(*iii*) The altered Articles together with the copy of special resolution duly certified by two directors should be filed with the Registrar within 30 days.

Effect of incorporation

> ➤ *After incorporation, every shareholder of erstwhile inter-state cooperative society shall become the shareholder of the Producer Company to the extent of face value of shares held by him.*
> ➤ *All directors of erstwhile inter-state cooperative society shall continue their office in the Producer Company for one year.*
> ➤ *All employees shall continue/become employees of the Producer Company.*

Management of Producer Company

❑ Producer Companies can have at least 5 and maximum 15 directors.

Retirement of Directors

❑ The Producer Company can state in its Articles that its directors are not required to retire by rotation. All provisions that are not applicable to private companies are not applicable to the Producer Companies.

❑ The tenure of directorship of a Producer Company cannot be less than one year and not exceed five years. Even the Articles cannot provide a tenure, which exceeds the prescribed five years.

Whole Time Company Secretary

❑ The appointment of a whole-time company secretary for a Producer Company having exceeding 5 crore annual turnover in 3 consecutive years, is compulsory.

General Meetings

❑ First AGM should be held within 90 days of incorporation.

❑ The gap between two AGM should not exceed 15 months.

Quorum for Shareholders Meetings: The quorum for the general meeting including the AGM is 1/4th of the total number of members of the Producer Company.

Quorum for Board Meeting: The quorum for board meeting is 1/3 subject to a minimum of three.

One Person Company (OPC)

❑ To facilitate formation of 'One Person Company (OPC)' in the country, based on the recommendations of JJ Irani Committee, Companies Bill, 2009 has proposed the incorporation of a single person economic entity in the form of 'One Person Company (OPC)' in the country. Such an entity may be provided with a simpler regime through exemptions so that the single entrepreneur is not compelled to fritter away his time, energy and resources on procedural matters. The Bill defines One Person Company as a company which has only one person as a member who by subscribing their names or his name to a memorandum in the manner prescribed and complying with the requirements in respect of registration can form One Person Company, provided that the memorandum of a One Person Company shall indicate the name of the person who shall, in the event of the subscriber's death, disability or otherwise, become the member of the company. It shall be the duty of the member of a One Person Company to intimate the Registrar the change, if any, in the name of the person referred to in the preceding proviso and indicated in the memorandum within such time and in such form as may be prescribed, and any such change shall not be deemed to be an alteration of the memorandum. The One Person Company may have one director. Letters 'OPC' to be suffixed with the name of the One Person Company to distinguish it from other companies.

❑ The One Person Company proposed by the Irani Committee and also recommended by the 2nd Naresh Chandra Committee, is modeled on English provisions. It is nothing but a copy-book of the Single Member Private Company (SMPC) of UK with minor changes here and there.

❑ The SMPC of UK has the following distinct features:

(a) A private company limited by shares or guarantee may be formed with only one member or one director though more can be appointed if required.

(b) There are no restrictions on the right to transfer the shares or on the number of its members unless the articles provide otherwise.

(c) The documents, which are sent to Companies House, are the same, as those required for multi-member private companies.

(d) If a sole member/director dies, there is no board to approve the transfer of his or her shares. The company is then in effect paralyzed, being without shareholders or a board. The proper course in that case is the alteration of articles so as to allow the company secretary to authorize a transfer or allow the representatives of the deceased member to appoint a nominee director if the company has none. The director could then approve the transfer and the business of the company could proceed.

(e) Notwithstanding any provision to the contrary in the articles, one member present in person or by proxy shall form a quorum. If the sole-member takes a decision, which could have been taken in the general meeting, he shall provide the company with a written record of it and there is no requirement of signatures.

(f) All the formalities of calling and holding a meeting will have to be complied with.

Small Company

❑ The Companies Bill, 2009 has proposed the incorporation of a 'Small Company' in the country. The Bill defines 'Small Company' as a company other than a public company, (i) Whose paid-up share capital does not exceed such amount as may be prescribed and the prescribed amount shall not be more than five crore rupees; or (ii) Whose turnover as per its last profit and loss account does not exceed such amount as may be prescribed and the prescribed amount shall not be more than twenty crore rupees: provided that nothing in this clause shall apply to —(*a*) A holding company or a subsidiary company; (*b*) A company registered under Section 4; or (*c*) A company or body corporate governed by any special Act.

❑ The Irani Committee (2005) while recommending very strongly the introduction of small companies in the country, observed, "Company law should enable simplified decision making procedures by relieving small companies from select statutory internal administrative procedures. Such companies should also be subjected to reduced financial reporting and audit requirements and simplified capital maintenance regimes. Essentially the regime for small companies should enable them to achieve transparency at a low cost through simplified requirement. Such a framework may be applied to small companies through exemptions, consolidated in the form of a Schedule to the Act." The Irani committee proposal of small company draws its strength from the recommendations of the 2nd Naresh Chandra Committee (2003), which while giving recommendations for such companies stated that most of small companies do not even file annual returns and are either defunct and exist only on papers. The recommendations aim at removing the bottlenecks being presently faced by such private companies. According to the 2nd Naresh Chandra Committee, a new sub-classification within the category of private companies named Small Private Company (SPC) should be introduced in the Act with the following features: (*a*) Paid up capital reserves up to Rs.50 lakhs; (*b*) Aggregate receipts annual from sales/service up to Rs.5 crores; and (*c*) Registered as a SSI.

❑ Small and Medium Sized Private Companies are prevalent in UK. A small company in UK is one, which has been within the limits of two of the following thresholds since incorporation or if not within the limits at incorporation, then for the current financial year, and the one before:

(*a*) Turnover of £ 2.8 million or less.

(*b*) Balance Sheet total (*i.e.*, total assets) £ 1.4 million or less.

(*c*) Employees 50 (average) or less.

❑ A medium company in UK is one, which has been within the limits of two of the following thresholds since incorporation or if not within the limits at incorporation, then for the current financial year, and the one before:

(*a*) Turnover of £ 11.2 million or less.

(*b*) Balance Sheet total (*i.e.*, total assets) £ 5.6 million or less.

(*c*) Employees 250 (average) or less.

❑ Provisions under UK Companies Act provide accounting exemptions to small and medium private companies. These provisions give benefit of confidentiality of information and draw a distinction between the reporting requirements in regard to the accounts which smaller medium companies prepare for the members and those, which they file with the Registrar of Companies. They are allowed to file with the Registrar what the Act refers to as 'abbreviated' and 'modified' accounts. The Companies Act of UK permits (but does not require) a small company to dispense with the filing of its director's report and profit and loss account and allows the filing of the abbreviated balance sheet only. The result of all this is that the members of the public examining these abbreviated accounts at company's registered office will have no trading information and will know nothing about the director's emoluments or the company's dividend. The Accounting Standards Board has freed small companies from the burden of complying with many accounting standards.

Associate Company

❑ The Companies Bill, 2009 has proposed the incorporation of an 'Associate Company' in the country. The Bill defines 'Associate Company' in relation to another company, as a company in which that other company has a significant influence, but which is not a subsidiary company of the company having such influence or of any other company. For the purposes of this clause, "significant influence" means control of at-least twenty six percent of total voting power, or of business decisions under an agreement.

Shelf Prospectus

❑ The Companies Act, 2000 introduced the concept of 'Shelf Prospectus' by inserting Section 60 A. As per the provisions of Section 60 A prospectus filed by the financial institutions is valid for one year. In the case of financial institutions and banks that require frequent raising of capital from the market, the prospectus prepared by them called shelf prospectus is valid for one year. This shall not only save their huge cost incurred on printing of prospectus each time but also save them from the cumbersome process of registration and issue of prospectus. The Companies Bill, 2008 defines 'Shelf Prospectus' as a prospectus in respect of which the securities or class of securities included therein are issued for subscription in one or more issues over a certain period without the issue of a further prospectus.

Postal Ballot

❑ The Companies Act, 2000 introduced the concept of 'Postal Ballot' by inserting Section 192 A. As per the provisions, a listed company may, and in the case of notified matters, shall get resolution passed by means of a postal ballot, instead of transacting the business in general meeting. The Companies (passing of the Resolution by Postal Ballot) Rules,2001 in this connection have been notified. Notice is given to all shareholders along with draft of resolution explaining reasons and a request to send back assent or dissent on a postal ballot in prepaid envelop by registered post within 30 days. In this way participation of almost each shareholder in the decision-making on vital issues that concerns the whole organisation, is ensured. The non compliance of the requirements means fine up to Rs.50,000. Following matters have been notified by the Central Government to be passed by postal ballot:

(*i*)   Matters relating to alteration in memorandum.

(*ii*)   Sale of whole or substantially whole of the undertaking.

(*iii*)   Corporate restructuring.

(*iv*)   Entering a new business area.

(*v*)   Sale of investments in the company where shareholders or voting rights of company exceeds 25%.

(*vi*)   Making a further issue of shares through preferential allotment or private placement.

(*vii*)   Variation in rights attached to class of securities.

(*viii*) Matters relating to change in management.

Audit Committee

❑   The concept of 'Audit Committee' was introduced by inserting Section 292A in the Companies Act in the year 2000 and by inserting in the same year clause 49 in the listing agreement. As per the provisions of Companies Act, every public company, (listed and unlisted-private companies exempted), having paid up capital (equity and preference) of Rs.5 crores or more should constitute an Audit Committee. The Audit Committee of Board shall consist of not less than 3 directors, two third of which should be directors other than Managing Director or Whole Time Director. Committee is to elect chairman who shall attend the AGM. Auditors, director finance, internal auditor shall be invited to the meeting. The Committee would ensure transparency and that the financial disclosures/financial statements are correct and creditable. It will also ensure that, frauds, irregularities, failure of internal control system within the organization, are minimized. The non-compliance of the requirements of the Companies Act means fine up to Rs.50,000 or one year imprisonment or both. In the provisions of clause 49, all members shall be financially literate and at-least one member shall have accounting or related financial management expertise. The penalty for non-compliance of the requirements of clause 49 on 'Audit Committee' would attract the penal provisions contained in Sections 23 (2), and 23E of the Securities Contracts (Regulation) Act, 1956. The penalty that was a meager amount of 1000 rupees until the provisions of Sections 23 (2) and 23E were amended with effect from 12th October 2004, was raised to an unimaginable fine extendable to 25 crore rupees by also including imprisonment for a term, which may extent to 10 years (earlier imprisonment was up-to one year).

Independent Director

❑ The clause 49 of the listing agreement lays down certain requirements for independent director. As per the requirements, atleast 1/2 of the Board must be non executive directors. If chairman is from the executive director's category, than at least 1/2 of the Board must be independent directors and if chairman is from the non-executive director's category, than at-least 1/3 must be independent directors. (1/2 if the non-executive chairman is promoter or relative of promoter or of some senior management.) The Companies Act is currently silent on independent director. The new Company Law that has been introduced in the Lok Sabha on 3rd August, 2009 has defined independent director differently from the way it has been defined in the clause 49. As per the requirements of the Bill, every listed public company having such amount of paid-up share capital as may be prescribed shall have at the least one-third of the total number of directors as independent directors. The Central Government may prescribe the minimum number of independent directors in case of other public companies and subsidiaries of any public company.

❑ The expression 'independent director' as per clause 49 shall mean a non executive director of the company who apart from receiving director's remuneration:

(*a*) Does not have any material pecuniary relationships or transactions with the company, its promoters, its directors, its senior management or its holding company, its subsidiaries and associates which may affect independence of the director;

(*b*) Is not related to promoters or persons occupying management positions at the board level or at one level below the board;

(*c*) Has not been an executive of the company in the immediately preceding three financial years;

(*d*) Is not a partner or an executive or was not partner or an executive during the preceding three years, of any of the following:

    (*i*) The statutory audit firm or the internal audit firm that is associated with the company, and

    (*ii*) The legal firm (s) and consulting firm (s) that have a material association with the company.

(*e*) Is not a material supplier, service provider or customer or a lesser or lessee of the company, which may affect independence of the director; and (*f*) Does not a substantial shareholder of the company *i.e.* owns two percent or more of the block of voting shares?

Small Shareholder's Director on Board

❑ The Companies Act, 2000 introduced the concept of 'Small Shareholders on Board' by inserting Section 252A. As per the provisions, a public company, having paid up capital of Rs.5 crore or more and 1000 or smaller shareholders (holding shares up to Rs.20,000), may elect small investors representative on the Board. Even though, the appointment of such a director is optional but as a measure of good corporate governance, listed companies have been directed by stock exchanges for implementing this concept. It becomes obligatory for the company to elect representation of small shareholders on Board if there is a demand/notice from the small shareholders.

Director Identity Number (DIN)

❑ Amending the Section 253 of the Companies Act, 1956 in May 2006 and inserting new Sections 266 A to G to the Act have made DIN possible. The Amendment Act provides for the allotment of mandatory Director Identification Number (DIN) for all existing and future directors on company boards. Only a single DIN is required for an individual irrespective of number of directorships held by him. DIN is also mandatory for directors of Indian companies who are not citizens of India (foreigner). But, DIN is not mandatory for directors of foreign company having branch offices in India. Every director is to intimate his/her DIN in form DIN-2 to all companies where he/she is a director and all companies are required to inform the DIN's of its directors to the Registrar of Companies (ROC).

Purpose

❑ With the introduction of the concept of DIN offences committed by the directors will be immediately detected as all the 20 offices of the Registrars of Companies (ROC) have been networked.

❑ Investors will also get the chance to take more informed decision by knowing the top management of the company.

❑ Issuing electronic identification number after verifying the credentials of directors will help the government to keep track of the people who run the companies. It shall help prevent a defaulting director from hiding his past deeds and joining another board. This would also facilitate effective legal action against the directors of such companies under the law, keeping in view the possibility of fraud by companies and the phenomenon of companies that raise funds from t..e public and vanish thereafter.

Procedure to Apply for DIN

❑ The procedure to apply for DIN is to visit MCA Portal and fill DIN application online, a simple form available on the link 'Apply For DIN' (apply for DIN on www.mca.gov.in).

❑ On submission of this form, a 'Provisional DIN' is generated by the system and is displayed on the screen.

❑ A print out of the filled form should be taken and is to be affixed with applicant's photograph and sent along with photocopies of identity and residence proof duly attested by Notary/Gazetted Officer/Certified Professionals (CA/CS/ICWA) to the address: MCA DIN Cell, P.O. Box No. 03, Noida, Uttar Pradesh.

❑ The MCA DIN Cell will process the form.

❑ Once approved, DIN confirmation and activation letter will be sent to the applicant. An email in this regard will also be sent to the applicant at the email id provided in the DIN application.

❑ No charges (only Rs 100 charged) are payable for applying for DIN.

❑ The Central Government has notified the Companies (Director Identification Number Rules), 2006. The provisions of these Rules have come into force with effect from 1st November, 2006. From 1st July, 2007, the DIN is mandatory for all directors. The following forms have been notified for the purpose:

DIN Form 1 : Application for allotment of DIN.

DIN Form 2 : Director is to intimate his DIN to the company or all companies.

DIN Form 3 : Company is to intimate DIN to Registrar within one week of receipt from the Director.

DIN Form 4 : Changes in the particulars of a Director are to be filed within 30 days of change.

DIN Cell based at NOIDA issued around 5 lakhs DIN by May,2007 and in March, 2009, the figure has crossed 9.5 lakhs.

Corporate Identity Number (CIN)

❑ Beginning with about 30,000 companies in 1956 when the Companies Act was enacted, India now (March, 2009) has the largest corporate base with over 9 lakh companies at work, which are spread through out the country, and larger numbers of new companies are being incorporated every year. But, the administrative mechanism to administer company law has not been developed at such a fast speed. Resultantly, limited numbers of 20 Registrars of Companies (ROC) in the country with little infrastructure feel handicapped administering such number of companies. In order to provide prompt and efficient service to companies, the Ministry has networked electronically all the offices of ROCs under its MCA 21 Programme. Keeping in view the administrative aspect of company law, the MCA 21 has made it mandatory for all companies including private companies to obtain a Corporate Identity Number (CIN). This CIN can be located from the MCA 21 portal (web site) through search based on registration number issued by the Registrar of Companies, present or the old name of the company, or through inactive CIN. Based on the recommendations of E-Corporate Business Working Group to synergic the provisions of Companies Act with the Information Technology Act of 2000, Corporate Identity Number were introduced in the country with effect from November 1ˢᵗ, 2000. The purpose of introducing CIN is to make Corporate Governance investors friendly, corporate friendly and compatible with the provisions of Information Technology Act, 2000.

MCA-21

- ❑ The Ministry of Company Affairs on the recommendations of Department of Information Technology has implemented a comprehensive E-governance system and programme through a project named as "MCA-21". On the 18ᵗʰ February 2006, the country entered into a new era of E-governance when the Ministry of Corporate Affairs launched its new web site www.mca.gov.in at Coimbatore in Tamil Nadu and after exactly one month on 18ᵗʰ March, the Prime Minister at New Delhi formally put into action the Project MCA 21. It is one of the largest E-governance project costing 345 crore rupees. It is being planned and monitored under the National E-Governance Plan (NEGP) by the National Institute of Smart Governance (NISG). Being a public-private-partnership model, it is being executed by private sector software solution provider Tata Consultancy Service (TCS) in a BOOT (Built, Open, Operate and Transfer) mode. The first phase of this project was to be completed by 24rth April, 2006. As per the agreement, the TCS will run the portal for six years and then hand it over to the MCA.

- ❑ The MCA-21 is aimed at total digital, paperless functioning of the offices of the four Regional Directors, 20 Registrars and 53 facilitation Centers named Physical Front Offices in the country. The project will provide the public, corporate entities and others an easy and secure online access to the corporate information, including filing of documents and public access to the information required to be in the public domain under the Statute, at any time and from anywhere. This would also result in efficiency in statutory supervision of corporate processes and efficient professional services under the Companies Act, 1956.

Online Filing of Documents

❑ The newly inserted Sections 610 B to E in the Companies Act have made the filing of applications and documents through electronic form, mandatory. The Amended provisions of 2006 have made possible the filing of company returns by a simple click on www.mca.gov.in and to make payment of fees by using credit card and internet banking. However, conventional payment methods such as by cash, demand draft or cheque are allowed at authorized bank branches. The electronic filing of corporate documents in the country has been made mandatory with effect from September 16, 2006. The Ministry of Corporate Affairs vide GSR NO 557 (E) dated 14th September 2006, has notified the Company (Electronic Filing and Authentication of Documents) Rules, 2006. The Central Government (Ministry of Corporate Affairs) has framed the following rules in this connection:

➢ Every e-form or application or document or declaration required to filed or delivered under the Companies Act and rules made there under, shall be filed in computer readable electronic form, in portable document format (pdf) and authenticated by a managing director, director, or company secretary or person specified in the Act for such purpose by the use of a valid digital signatures.

➢ Every such MD, director or secretary or specified person shall obtain a digital signature certificate from the Certifying Authority for the purpose of such authentication.

➢ Such certificate should be of class II or class III specification under the Information Technology Act, 2000.

➢ Central government has set up and maintain a website or portal to provide access to the electronic registry and as many registrar's front offices as may be necessary, for filing of e-forms, documents, applications, viewing and inspection of documents in the electronic registry.

➢ The central government has set up and maintains a secure electronic registry in which all the documents filed electronically shall be stored.

➢ Every document, application or certificate or notice, etc, required to be signed by the registrar (ROC) or an officer of the central government, shall be authenticated through a valid digital signature of such person or a system generated digital signature.

➢ The ROC or the central government, as the case may be, may send any communication either to the company or its authorized representatives, directors or both in the electronic manner for which the company shall create and maintain at all times a valid electronic address e.g., e-mail, user identification etc. capable of receiving and acknowledging the receipt of such communication, automated or otherwise.

> The ROC or the central government shall issue certificate, license, receipt, approval or communicate endorsement or acknowledgement in the electronic form. Provided that if it is not able to issue in electronic manner, it may issue in physical form under manual signature affixing seal of the office. But the reasons are to be recorded in writing.

Following are the key steps for e-filing:

1. Go to portal (www.mca.gov.in) and register as a user.
2. Visit e-filing corner on the portal for guidance notes on e-filing.
3. Annual filing corner on the portal contains details on filing of annual returns, balance sheet, profit & loss accounts. Balance sheet and profit and loss accounts must be filed as separate attachments.
4. In case of any help, the offices of the Registrar's Front Offices; the Certified Filing Offices; the MCA help line 64506000 or the mail address at appl.helpdesk@mca.gov.in can be approached.

Over 3 lakh fillings were made (B/S and Annual Returns) electronically by December, 2006 (within a span of 3 months) after the launch of e-governance project (MCA21) in September, 2006. The number of filings through electronic mode has been 1.83 crore by May, 2007 and by March, 2009, the figure crossed 5.45 crores.

Online Registration of Company

□ The MCA 21 has made the online registration of companies in the country, which was once considered as a dream, possible. The first such company registered online was in south India (Coimbatore) in the summer of 2006, when the Minister of Corporate Affairs launched its new web site www.mca.gov.in. Around 18,000 companies were incorporated on line up to November, 2006. By the May, 2007, 44,000 companies were registered online. The number of such online registered companies increased to 67,744 by August, 2007 and by March, 2009, the figure crossed 2.5 lakhs (out of total companies in India numbering over 9 lakhs).

□ As the registration of a company at the first stage requires name approval from the ROC, the prospective promoters shall now require filling up of DIN to be able to submit the Form 1A for the availability of the proposed name in the records of the ROC. All the other persons who are proposed to be appointed as the directors in the yet to be formed company are to submit their DIN as well. As the form is now required to be signed digitally, the applicants shall require Digital Certificate of the requisite class before the submission. The promoters are required to file Memorandum of Association and Articles of Association duly signed by the subscribers, in terms of Secs. 15 and 30 of the Companies Act, 1956 for the formation of a company. As the MCA 21 has arranged the online payment of fees, the filing of Memorandum and Articles in the electronic form has been made operative. These documents have to be digitalized by scanning so that the same can be digitally attached to e-Form 1. The attachment, consisting of the MOA and the AOA are scanned images. The e-Form is digitally signed and the complete set of documents is filled in a secure environment whereby the interests of the promoters are fully secured. Similar digital process shall be followed for filling up of Forms 18 and 32 required in the process of incorporation.

National Company Law Tribunal (NCLT)

❑ Companies (Second Amendment) Act, 2002 was enacted to dissolve the Company Law Board (CLB) and w.e.f 13th January, 2003, powers under various provisions of the Companies Act, 1956 were proposed to be transferred from the Company Law Board (CLB), the Board for Industrial and Financial Reconstruction (BIFR) and the High Courts to the proposed National Company Law Tribunal (NCLT). As the NCLT has not yet been constituted by the Central Government, the CLB, BIFR and the High Courts would continue to discharge their functions as before.

❑ Justice V. Bala Krishna Eradi (retired Supreme Court Judge) Committee constituted by the Central Government recommended setting up of the National Company Law Tribunal (NCLT). The need for setting up of the NCLT was felt for the following reasons:

(a) The powers and jurisdiction presently being exercised by various judicial bodies like CLB, BIFR or High Courts needs to be consolidated and entrusted to a single body, which shall serve as a single window settlement of cases, related to the corporate affairs.

(b) Since powers of Court are delegated to the NCLT and no appeals are preferred in High Court, the setting up of NCLT will save time of the High Courts as well.

(c) The appearance of chartered accountants, company secretaries, cost accountants and lawyers before the Company Law Tribunal and Appellate Tribunal declines the time and cost to the clients.

(d) The Tribunal is also entrusted with powers of Contempt of Court. This provides a built-in-seriousness in the entire proceedings before the NCLT.

(e) The NCLT and the Appellate Tribunal have the power to regulate their own proceedings within the framework of the Companies Act and the Code of Civil Procedure does not bind them.

Features

Sec. 10FB : *Constitution*

❑ Central Government is to constitute the National Company Law Tribunal.

Sec. 10FC : *Composition*

❑ The National Company Law Tribunal shall comprise of the President and not more than 62 judicial/technical members who are appointed by the Central Government.

Sec. 10FD : *Qualifications*

President: Has been or is qualified to be a Judge of a High Court.

Judicial Member: Held for at-least 15 years a judicial office or has been for at-least 10 years an advocate of a High Court or has partly held judicial office and has been partly in practice as an advocate for a total period of 15 years or has held for at-least 15 years a group A post or an equivalent

Technical Member

(*a*) Has held for at-least 15 years a group A post or equivalent post under the Central or State Government, or

(*b*) Is or has been a Joint Secretary to the Government of India for at-least 5years and has adequate knowledge of company laws, or

(*c*) Is or has been for at-least 15 years in practice on a chartered accountant or cost accountant or company secretary, or

(*d*) Is a person of ability, integrity and knowledge and professional experience of not less than 20 years in Science, Technology, Economics, Law, Industry, Accountancy, Management, etc, or

(*e*) Is or has been a Presiding Officer of a Labour Court, Tribunal or National Tribunal constituted under the Industrial Disputes Act, 1947

(*f*) Is a person having special knowledge and experience of not less than 15 years in the matters relating to labour.

Sec. 10FE : *Term of Office*

❑ 3 years for both President and Members

❑ But, shall not be eligible for re-appointment

> ***Retirement Age:*** President - 67 years
>
> Members - 65 years

Sec. 10FL : *Benches*

❑ The Central Govt. may decide the number of Benches to be constituted.

❑ The President constitutes benches.

❑ The President may constitute one or more Special Bench.

❏ The Principal Bench shall be at New Delhi that is to be presided over by the President of the Tribunal.

❏ The Principal Bench shall have powers of transfer of proceedings from any Bench to another Bench.

National Company Law Appellate Tribunal

Sec. 10FQ : *Appeal*

❏ Every appeal shall be filed within 45 days of the receipt of a copy of the judgment of the Tribunal.

❏ The Appellate Tribunal may entertain an appeal after 45 days if satisfactory reason is given.

❏ The Appellate Tribunal may pass such orders as it thinks fit.

Sec. 10FR : *Constitution*

❏ The Central Government is to constitute the Appellate Tribunal consisting of a chairman and not more than two members to be appointed by the Government.

❏ The Chairman shall be a person who has been a Judge of the Supreme Court or the Chief Justice of a High Court.

❏ A member of the Appellate Tribunal shall be a person who shall have special knowledge and professional experience of not less than 25 years in Science, Technology, Economics, Law, Industry, Labour, Management, etc.

Sec. 10FT : *Term of Office*

❏ 3 years for both chairman and members

❏ Who shall be eligible for reappointment?

        Retirement Age: Chairman - 70 years

                                    Member   - 67 years

Sec. 10GF : *Appeal before Supreme Court*

❏ Any person aggrieved by the decision of or order of the Appellate Tribunal may file an appeal to the Supreme Court within 60 days from the date of receipt of the order.

❏ The Supreme Court for satisfactory reasons may grant the Appellant further period not seconding 60 days.

Limited Liability Partnership (LLP)

❏ With the growth of the Indian economy, the role played by its entrepreneurs as well as its technical and professional manpower has been acknowledged internationally. It is felt opportune that entrepreneurship, knowledge and risk capital combine to provide a further impetus to India's economic growth. In this background, a need has been felt for a new corporate form that would provide an alternative to the traditional partnership, with unlimited personal liability on the one hand, and, the statute-based governance structure of the limited liability company on the other, in order to enable professional expertise and entrepreneurial initiative to combine, organise and operate in flexible, innovative and efficient manner. The Limited Liability Partnership (LLP) introduced in the Country by enacting the LLP Act of 2008, is viewed as an alternative corporate business vehicle that provides the benefits of limited liability but allows its partners the flexibility of organising their internal structure as a partnership based on a mutually arrived agreement. The LLP form would enable entrepreneurs, professionals and enterprises providing services of any kind or engaged in scientific and technical disciplines, to form commercially efficient vehicles suited to their requirements. Owing to flexibility in its structure and operation, the LLP would also be a suitable vehicle for small enterprises and for investment by venture capital. Detail Rules on LLP, conversion of Companies and firms into LLP, winding up of LLPs, have also been announed by the Ministry of Corporate Affairs in 2009, separately. The first LLP in the Country was registered on 2nd April, 2009.

Salient Features

Status: The LLP is a body corporate and a legal entity separate from its partners. It is an artificial person being invisible, intangible having no body, no mind and no soul and exists only in the eyes of law. Any two or more persons, associated for carrying on a lawful business with a view to profit, may by subscribing their names to an incorporation document and filing the same with the Registrar, form an LLP. The LLP that has perpetual succession, any change in the partners of an LLP shall not affect the existence of the LLP. Thus, status-wise an LLP is more akin to a company.

Separate Legal Entity: LLP is a body corporate created by law having a distinct name and perpetual succession. It has a legal entity separate from its partners, its own rights and liabilities are distinct from those of its partners and any change in the partners of such partnership shall not affect its liabilities. Having the same capacity to enter into contracts as a private individual, the LLP will be able to own all and any of the assets of the business which it is carrying on, ranging from intellectual property rights to freehold and leasehold land; and it will be able not only to hold shares in a company, but also itself to be a partner of another LLP, or to be a partner in a partnership under the Partnership Act, 1932, whatever business that other LLP, or those partnerships, may be carrying on. There will also be no limitation on its legal capacity to borrow.

Number of Partners: Every LLP has at least two partners and also has at least two individuals as Designated Partners, of whom at least one shall be resident in India.

There is no maximum limit for the number of partners for the LLP. If at any time the number of partners of a LLP is reduced below two and the LLP carries on business for more than six months while the number is so reduced, the person, who is the only partner of the LLP during the time that it so carries on business after those six months and has the knowledge of the fact that it is carrying on business with him alone, shall be liable personally for the obligations of the LLP incurred during that period.

Designated Partners: Every LLP has at least two Designated Partners who are individuals and at least one of them shall be a resident in India, provided that in case of an LLP in which all the partners are bodies corporate or in which one or more partners are individuals and bodies corporate, at least two individuals who are partners of such LLP or nominees of such bodies corporate shall act as Designated Partners.

Mandatory Electronic Identification Number for Designated Partners: On the lines of DIN (electronic identification number) for company directors, Designated Partner Identification Number (DPIN) has been made mandatory for Designated Partners of LLPs. The allotment of DPIN for all existing and future Designated Partners of an LLP is mandatory. Only a single DPIN is required for an individual irrespective of number of partnership held by him. Issuing DPIN in LLPs after verifying the credentials of Designated Partners will help the government to keep track of the people who run the LLPs. It shall help prevent a defaulting Designated Partner from hiding his past deeds and joining another LLP. This would also facilitate effective legal action against the Designated Partners of such LLPs under the law, keeping in view the possibility of fraud by LLPs.

Limited Liability: Every partner of an LLP is, for the purpose of the business of the LLP, the agent of the LLP, but not of other partners. A partner is not personally liable, directly or indirectly for an obligation solely by reason of being a partner of the LLP. The provisions shall not affect the personal liability of a partner for his own wrongful act or omission, but a partner shall not be personally liable for the wrongful act or omission of any other partner of the LLP. The liabilities of the LLP and partners who are found to have acted with intent to defraud creditors or for any fraudulent purpose is unlimited for all or any of the debts or other liabilities of the LLP.

Incorporation: For an LLP to be incorporated, two or more persons associated for carrying on a lawful business with a view to profit subscribe their names to an incorporation document. The incorporation document is filed in such manner and with such fees, as may be prescribed with the Registrar of the State in which the registered office of the LLP is to be situated. There is filed along with the incorporation document, a statement in the prescribed form, made by either an advocate, or a company secretary or a chartered accountant or a cost accountant, who is engaged in the formation of the LLP and by any one who subscribed his name to the incorporation document, that all the requirements of this Act and the rules made there-under have been complied with, in respect of incorporation and matters precedent and incidental thereto. When the incorporation document and the compliance statement have been duly filed with the Registrar, he registers the incorporation document within a period of fourteen days and gives a certificate signed by him and authenticated by his official seal that the LLP is incorporated by the name specified in the incorporation document. When given, the certificate is conclusive evidence that the LLP is incorporated by the name specified in the incorporation document. It is, therefore, the issue of the incorporation certificate which determines the status of LLP that it has taken birth and is a body corporate, having separate legal personality and perpetual succession.

LLP Agreement: LLP agreement means any written agreement between the partners of the LLP or between the LLP and its partners which determines the mutual rights and duties of the partners and their rights and duties in relation to that limited liability partnership. The 'LLP agreement' in broader terms is equivalent of the articles of association for a company. There is, however, a basic difference between an LLP agreement and a traditional partnership agreement. A traditional partnership is considered exclusively with the legal relations between the individual partners whereas the LLP agreement covers not only the relationship between the individual partners, but also the relationship between the partners and LLP (a body corporate having separate legal entity).

Form of Contribution: A contribution of a partner may consist of tangible, movable or immovable or intangible property or other benefit to the LLP, including money, promissory notes, other agreements to contribute cash or property, and contracts for services performed or to be performed. The monetary value of contribution of each partner is accounted for and disclosed in the accounts of the limited liability partnership in the manner as may be prescribed.

Annual Accounts and Annual Return: The LLP shall be under an obligation to maintain annual accounts reflecting true and fair view of its state of affairs. A statement of accounts and solvency is filed by every LLP with the Registrar every year. The accounts of LLPs are audited, subject to any class of LLPs being exempted from this requirement by the Central Government. Similarly, every LLP files an annual return duly authenticated with the Registrar within sixty days of closure of its financial year in such form and manner and accompanied by such fee as may be prescribed. Any LLP which fails to comply with the provisions of this section is punishable with fine which shall not be less than twenty-five thousand rupees but which may extend to five lakh rupees. If the LLP contravenes the provisions, the designated partner of such an LLP are punishable with fine which shall not be less than ten thousand rupees but which may extend to one lakh rupees.

Electronic Filing of Document: Any document required to be filed, recorded or registered under the LLP Act may be filed, recorded or registered in such manner and subject to such conditions as may be prescribed by rules by the Central Government. A copy of or an extract from any document electronically filed with or submitted to the Registrar which is supplied or issued by the Registrar and certified through affixing digital signature as per the Information Technology Act, 2000 to be a true copy of or extract from such document shall, in any proceedings, be admissible in evidence as of equal validity with the original document.

Investigation: The Central Government has powers to investigate the affairs of an LLP, if required, by appointment of competent Inspector for the purpose.

Compromise or Arrangement: The compromise or arrangement including merger and amalgamation of LLPs shall be in accordance with the provisions of Sections 60 to 62 of the LLP Act.

Decision Making: Any matter or issue relating to the LLP shall be decided by a resolution passed by majority in number of the partners, and for this purpose, each partner shall have one vote. The decisions by designated partner are to be made as a body by majority vote, with necessary quorum and chairman's casting vote. The LLP agreement may provide procedural provisions in this regard. As per the Schedule 1st, every LLP shall ensure that decisions taken by it are re-corded in the minutes within thirty days of taking such decisions and are kept and maintained at the registered office of the LLP.

Conversion to LLP: A firm, private company or an unlisted public company may be allowed to be converted into LLP in accordance with the provisions of Sections 55 to 58 of the LLP Act. Upon such conversion, on and from the date of certificate of registration issued by the Registrar in this regard, the effects of the conversion shall be such as are specified in the LLP Act. On and from the date of registration specified in the certificate of registration, all tangible (movable or immovable) and intangible property vested in the firm or the company, all assets, interests, rights, privileges, liabilities, obligations relating to the firm or the company, and the whole of the undertaking of the firm or the company, shall be transferred to and shall vest in the LLP without further assurance, act or deed and the firm or the company, shall be deemed to be dissolved and removed from the records of the Registrar of Firms or Registrar of Companies, as the case may be. The Ministry of Corporate Affairs has announced the Rules on conversion of Companies and firms effective from 22nd May ,2009.

Winding Up and Dissolution: The winding up of an LLP may be either voluntary or by Tribunal to be established under the Companies Act, 1956 and LLP, so wound up may be dissolved. Till the Tribunal is established, the powers in this regard have been given to the High Court. The Ministry of Corporate Affairs has announced Rules on winding up of LLPs.

Whistle Blower: The LLP Act has given adequate protection to a whistle blower. The Court or Tribunal may reduce or waive any penalty leviable against any partner or employee of a LLP in case such partner or employee has provided useful information during investigation of such LLP for finding out the offence. No such partner or employee shall be discharged, demoted, suspended, threatened, harassed or in any other manner discriminated merely because of his providing information to the Court or Tribunal. A whistle blower who helps in the conviction of the guilty will thus be protected. These measures have been taken as a safeguard to ensure that the benefits of an LLP are not abused.

Doctrine of Ultra Vires: The doctrine of ultra vires that is considered important in relation to the transactions entered into by companies has no place in relation to LLPs.

Non-applicability of the Indian Partnership Act, 1932: The provisions of Indian Partnership Act, 1932 do not apply to an LLP. It is also not the position that, in default of any other governing provision, partnership law applies to an LLP. The reason is understandable since the concept of separate legal entity and perpetual succession are strange to partnerships.

Need Based Application of the Companies Act: The provisions of Companies Act on National Company Law Tribunal, DIN, and Registrar of Companies have been made applicable straight to LLPs. Clause 67 of the LLP Act confers powers on the Central Government to direct that any of the provisions of the Companies Act, 1956 specified in the notification shall apply to any LLP; or shall apply to any LLP with such exception modification and adaptation, as may be specified, in the notification.

Foreign LLPs: The Ministry of Corporate Affairs has announced rules in relation to establishment of place of business by foreign LLPs within India and carrying on their business therein.

Taxation: The LLP Act, 2008 had skipped the question of taxation of LLPs. The issue of whether LLPs would be taxed like companies or like partnerships or in some other way was left for the Finance Ministry to decide separately. The Ministry of Corporate Affairs wanted the profit making activities of an LLP and its assets to be treated as the activities and assets of the partners and not that of the LLP- a right not available to a company or to a partnership firm. In that case, the partners would be taxed for capital gains as the assets are treated as their investments. The advantage of giving the ownership of assets to the partners is that a partner can use his assets any time and if he exits the LLP, he can take his money out easily without the LLP being dissolved. (*News published in the Economic Times, New Delhi of 8th December, 2006 p. 11*). Ministry of Corporate Affairs (MCA) wanted to let the foreign investors to set up LLPs in India to choose a tax structure of their liking depending on the way they organize their business under LLP. This would give investors from countries that have double taxation avoidance pacts with India the choice of a taxation model that suits them best. The idea is to reduce tax burden and compliance hassles for professionals and investors to do business together. Ministry of Corporate Affairs (MCA) has in a Cabinet Note recommended to the Finance Ministry that it is international practice to let LLPs choose the mode of taxation based on how they are structured. If an LLP's operations are decentralized and the partners act autonomously, their income could be taxed in the hands of the partners. If the LLP has centralized operations and assets, then the LLP itself could be taxed. Outside investors who form cross-borders LLPs with Indian professionals would prefer taxation at the partner level since that would mean taxation at only one level. If the LLP is taxed, a foreign partner in a cross-border partnership (LLP) may end up paying in his country for his income from the partnership registered in India even if the entire income has been taxed already in India. If the LLP generated income here as well as abroad, the entity will have to pay tax here even for the income generated abroad. Taxing individual partners would ensure these disadvantages are eliminated. Taxing at the partner level means paying taxes in the respective countries by the partners for whatever income they get from the LLP. The partner in one country need not bear the tax burden in another. (*News published in the Economic Times, New Delhi of 11th Feb., 2008, front page*).

Corporate Governance

□ Till about two decades ago, corporate governance was relatively an unknown subject. The subject came into prominence in late 80's and early 90's when the corporate sector in a number of countries was surrounded with problems of questionable corporate policies or unethical practices. Junk Bond fiasco of USA and failure of Maxwell (Maxwell Communication Corporation and Mirror Group Newspapers, UK, 1991) BCCI (Bank of Credit and Commerce International, 1991) and Polypeck in UK resulted in the setting up of the Treadway Committee in USA in the year 1987 and the Cadbury Committee in UK in 1991. Scandals in number of countries specially the United States triggered reforms in corporate governance, accounting practices and disclosures the world over. Enron debacle in 2001 and number of other scandals involving large US companies (table of such companies follows) such as the Tyco, Quest, Global Crossings, Adelphia Communications, the World.Com and the exposure of auditing lacunae, which led to the collapse of the Andersen, set in motion the reform process and resulted in the passing of the Public Accounting Reform and Investor Protection Act of 2002 known as Sarbanes-Oxley (SOX) Act, 2002 in USA. (Sponsors Paul Sarbanes, a former US Senate and Michael Oxley, the vice president NASDAQ). The main objective of the Oxley Act is to repose investor's confidence by preventing corporate frauds and ensuring transparency and disclosures. The Oxley (SOX) Act established new standards for public company Boards, management and accounting firms in USA and its major provisions include (*i*) Creation of the Public Company Accounting Oversight Board (PCAOB) to Monitor Auditors, (*ii*) Independence of Auditor and (*iii*) Corporate Governance.

Defining Corporate Governance

❑ There is no single, accepted definition of corporate governance. Different persons, at different times, under different situations and circumstances have defined the word corporate governance in their own different ways. The term 'Governance' is derived from the Latin word *'Gubernare'* which means 'to steer' usually applying to the steering of a ship (steer means to direct or control the course of a ship, boat, car, etc). Thus, 'Governance' implies direction or control that is one of the prominent functions of management. Based on this meaning, the father of Corporate Governance Sir Adrian Cadbury (1992) defined the concept as the way in which companies are directed and controlled.

Theories of Corporate Governance: Agency Theory *v* Stakeholders Theory

❑ There are many ways of defining Corporate Governance, ranging from narrow view that focuses on relationship between the company and its shareholders called traditional finance paradigm, expressed in 'agency theory', to broader view that focuses on relationships, not only between a company and its shareholders but also between a company and broad range of other 'stakeholders' like employees, customers, suppliers, bondholders, to name but a few. Such a view tends to expressed in 'stakeholders theory'. It is based on the satisfaction of all kinds of stakeholders, CSR and business ethics.

Models of Corporate Governance

Single Tier System (Single Board): In the Single Tier System, there is only one Board like we have in India. This single Board may be small Board or Large Board depending upon the country.

> *Smallest Board* : USA, UK, Canada with 10 to 15 members of Board
> *Large Boards* : India, Japan, Korea with members of Board even exceeding 30.

Two Tier System (Two Boards or Dual Boards): Two Boards in Germany are called as Supervisory Board and Management Board. Supervisory Board also represented by the employees is equivalent to the Board of Directors under the Single Tier System. A certain percentage of members on this Board must be labor representatives elected by employees. The Supervisory Board, acting as agent of the shareholders, is responsible for appointing, supervising and advising members of the Management Board, and developing fundamental corporate strategy. Management

Board of a dual board system (that is, the German vorstand, French directoire or conseil d'administration or the Indonesian board of directors) is equivalent to the Executive Management Team (Executive Board) in companies following the single board model. This Board, which typically includes 5 to 15 senior executives appointed by the Supervisory Board, is headed by a chairperson (corresponding to the CEO in the single board model) and is responsible for daily management of individual businesses/divisions or control functions; the chairperson serves as coordinator of their work.

> **Dual Boards in Europe:** *Dual Boards are mandatory in Austria, Germany, Switzerland, Netherlands, Denmark, Luxembourg, Sweden, Norway, and Finland and optional in France and Italy.*
>
> **Dual Boards in Asia:** *China, Indonesia and Taiwan and various other emerging nations.*

Which Board Structure is more Effective or Efficient?: There is no apparent consensus or empirical evidence on which board structure is more effective or efficient. Some believe that the single board system provides for better information flow, stronger relationships, and greater cooperation between directors and executives; others feel that the dual board system permits greater independence as a result of separation of duties.

What constitutes Good Corporate Governance?

Corporate governance is about how an organization is managed?
It is about
- Commitment to Values,
- Ethical Business Conduct, and
- Exercise of Powers in a Responsible Way.

Corporate Governance *v* Corporate Excellence
- Both are Closely Connected
- It is Difficult to achieve Excellence without good Governance in long term

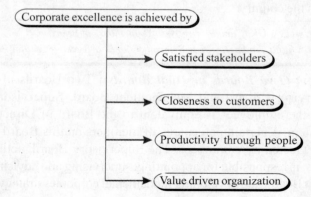

Benefits of Good Corporate Governance (Measures of Excellence)
- Increase in profitability
- Increase in revenue/profit growth
- Building brand image (a case of Infosys)
- Increase in growth in market shares, and
- Satisfied stakeholders:
  - Shareholders
  - Employees
  - Suppliers
  - Creditors
  - Government

Ills of Corporate Governance Reforms: But, not all praise reforms in corporate governance. The big question is do the reforms in corporate governance really improve the effectiveness of corporations and their accountability? There are certainly those who are opposed to the ongoing process of corporate governance reform. They give the following reasons:

- The presence of non-executive and independent directors on the boards results in loss of individual decision-making power,
- It slows down decision making,
- It adds an unnecessary level of bureaucracy and red tape as happened in the case of Richard Branson's Experiment with the stock market,
- Makes running a company unnecessarily difficult, hindering innovation and creativity.
- *Nil Secrecy:* There is the growing pressure to communicate their strategies and policies to their primary institutional investors.
- Human nature cannot be altered through regulation, checks and balances.

Codes and Standards on Corporate Governance

Every stakeholder connected with the company wants it to be well managed or atleast manage for their benefits. Of all the stakeholders, the only group actually in a position to ensure that the company is managed for the benefits of directors is Board and the only group who is in a position to control the directors are the shareholders. But in reality, the situation is totally different. The three major players-stakeholders in the area of Corporate Governance in reality are:

(*i*) Boards : Family managed with unchallenged control.

(*ii*) Shareholders : Generally scattered, ill organized and have little say.

(*iii*) Employees : Financially poor to act or react.

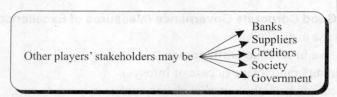

Management should act in the best interest of all these stakeholders. But does it act? - No, it does not. Therefore, need is felt for Code and Standards on Corporate Governance.

Key Codes and Standards on Corporate Governance

- ❑ Sir Adrian Cadbury Committee (UK), 1992
- ❑ Greenbery Committee (UK), 1995
- ❑ Bosch Report (Australia), 1995
- ❑ Vienot Report (France), 1995
- ❑ Calpers Global Corporate Governance Principles (USA), 1996
- ❑ Hampel Committee on Corporate Governance (UK), 1997
- ❑ Combined Code of Best Practices (London Stock Exchange), 1999
- ❑ Blue Ribbon Committee (USA), 1999
- ❑ OECD Principles of Corporate Governance, 1999
- ❑ CACG Guidelines/Principles for Corporate Governance in Commonwealth, 1999
- ❑ Euroshareholders Corporate Governance Guidelines, 2000
- ❑ Principles of Good Governance and Code of Best Practice (UK), 2000
- ❑ Joint Committee on Corporate Governance (Canada), 2001

Clause 49 on Corporate Governance

- ❑ Securities Exchange Board of India (SEBI) on May 7, 1999, appointed an 18 member committee under the chairmanship of Mr. Kumar Mangalam Birla (a chartered accountant himself) and a member of SEBI Board, to promote and raise the concept of corporate governance in India. The committee submitted its report containing 25 recommendations in January, 2000, and since then, it has been accepted by SEBI and put to implementation. The committee came out with two sets of recommendations-the mandatory recommendations and the non-mandatory recommendations. The mandatory recommendations focus on strengthening the responsibilities of audit committees, improving the quality of financial disclosures, including those pertaining to related party transactions and proceeds from initial public offerings, requiring corporate executive boards to assess and disclose business risks in the annual reports of companies, calling upon the Board to adopt a formal code of conduct, the position of nominee directors and improved disclosures relating to compensation to non-executive directors and shareholders' approval of the same.

❑ With a view to promote and raise standard of corporate governance in respect of listed companies, SEBI concluded that the easiest and quickest way of enforcing the recommendations of the Kumarmanglam Birla Committee was to make the recommendations a part of the listing agreements. Accordingly clause 49 on Corporate Governance was inserted in the listing agreement in 2000. *Vide* Circular No CFD/ DIL/CG/1/2006/1/1dated 13th January, 2006, SEBI issued revised clause 49 of the listing agreement that has come into effect from January 1, 2006.

Schedule of Implementation

The amendments to the listing agreement have to be implemented as per schedule of implementation given below:

❑ For entities seeking listing for the first time, at the time of seeking in-principle approval for such listing.

❑ For existing listed entities which were required to comply with Clause 49 which is being revised *i.e.,* those having a paid-up share capital of Rs.3 cores and above or net worth of Rs.25 crores or more at any time in the history of the company, by December 31, 2005.

Penalty for Non-Compliance

❑ Any non-compliance of Clause 49 would attract the penal provisions contained in section 23(2), 23E and 24 of the Securities Contracts (Regulation) Act, 1956.

❑ The penalty was a meager amount of 1000 rupees until the provisions of Sections 23 (2) and 23E were amended with effect from 12th October 2004, and it was raised to an unimaginable fine extendable to 25 crore rupees by also including imprisonment for a term, which may extent to 10 years (earlier imprisonment was up-to one year).

❑ As per Section 24 of the SCR Act, where a company has committed offence, every person who at the time when the offence was committed, was in charge of, and was responsible to the company for the conduct of the business, shall be guilty of the offence.

❑ It may also lead to the de-listing of the securities of the company under Section 21A of the SCR Act. But, that may result punishing the shareholders (give more harm than benefit), as they may not be able to trade the same in the stock exchange. The shares will also lose their liquidity in the market that may ultimately punish the shareholders.

Clause 49 has the following codes on Corporate Governance:

1. Composition of Balanced Board
2. Qualified and Independent Audit Committee

3. Relationship with the Subsidiary Companies
4. Disclosures and Transparency
5. CEO/CFO Certification
6. Report on Corporate Governance
7. Compliance Certificate

Corporate Social Responsibility (CSR)

Different people at different times, under different situations and circumstances have taken a different meaning of the word CSR.

- ❑ Is it philanthropy and charity?
- ❑ Is it social, community or humanitarian work?
- ❑ Is it protecting the environment?
- ❑ Is it undertaking public service tasks or doing something for the betterment of public at large, which normally government should be doing? or
- ❑ Is it all of these?

The real meaning of CSR of a company should be undertaking all actions as would maximize the probability of its long term survival and sustained growth.

CSR is no Longer Restricted to Philanthropy: CSR is not just philanthropy activity that means the giving of grants and donation. The corporate donate huge amounts of money towards the cause which is not part of the main business of the company, for example, donating computers to schools, staff volunteering to work with local community groups, etc. Nowadays the CSR is no longer restricted to philanthropy

Some Definitions

According to the World Business Council for Sustainable Development (WBCSD), 1999 "Corporate Social Responsibility is the continuing commitment by business to behave ethically and contribute to economic development while improving the quality of life of the workforce and their families as well as of the local community and society at large".

According to CSR Asia, a social enterprise, "CSR is a company's commitment to operate in an economically, socially and environmentally sustainable manner whilst balancing the interests of diverse stakeholders."

According to UK Government, "CSR means the voluntary actions that business can take, over and above compliance with minimum legal requirements, to address both its own competitive interests and the interests of wider society."

Increased Demand for CSR: The corporate scams and failures worldwide increased the demand for CSR on a global scale. The abuses at Enron, Tyco, Global Crossing, Adelphia and World.Com in the US and more recently, collapse of Satyam in India, have severely impacted investor and other stakeholder confidence in the integrity of those charged with the supervision and management of large companies. The widespread corruption and lack of transparency and accountability also led to the emergence of CSR.

Business Ethics

❑ Business ethics means equal, fair and honest treatment to all the stakeholders besides shareholders. The company which treats its stakeholders ethically and meets its responsibilities towards them is awarded with a high degree of loyalty, honesty, quality and productivity. Business ethics provides a solid foundation for the business to operate. An organization has to inculcate ethics in its culture for actual CSR implementation because CSR on paper and not in spirit is of no use.

Insider Trading

❑ As per the concept of "Insider Trading", a director or an employee of the company for making or giving advice on investment decisions on securities shall not use or spread information, which is not available to the investing public (available through website, statements, memorandum/articles, prospectus). The insider information may include financial results, issue and buyback of shares, declaration of dividend, stock splits, bonus issue, acquisition and divestiture of business, joint ventures, launch of new and innovative products, merger, amalgamation or takeover, selling of whole or substantial part of undertaking, major expansion plan, execution of new projects or significant changes in policies, plans or operations of the company, significant legal disputes.

Three sets of people are likely to possess privileged information about the company:

Classic Insiders: Like employees and directors and large shareholders.

Constructive Insiders: Like company's auditors, lawyers etc who become insiders by virtue of their fiduciary relationship with the company, and

Family Members: Who receive tips from the earlier two?

Insider Trading Rules, **2002:** Insider Trading Rules in India intends to prevent the directors or employees from taking advantage of possessing the price sensitive information that may have material affect on the price of securities of the company in securities market. SEBI in January, 2008 banned former MD of Tata Finance Dilip S Pendse, his wife Anuradha Pendse and Nalini Properties, Anjali Beke from accessing the securities market and also prohibited them from buying, selling or otherwise associating with the securities market in any manner for a period of 5 years in an insider trading case. SEBI found them guilty of trading in shares of Tata Finance on the basis of unpublished information. (News published in the Times of India, New Delhi of 12th January, 2008, page 25). SEBI is investigating into allegations of insider trading in shares of Mukesh Ambani's Reliance Petroleum

(RPL). As per the written reply to a question in the Rajya Sabha, Reliance Industries had raised Rs 4023 crore by divesting 4.01% of its stake in RPL. (News published in the Economic Times "SEBI Probing RPL Insider Trading Allegation", 19th March 2008, page 17).

Companies Bill, 2009 on Insider Trading: Companies Bill, 2009 introduced in the Lok Sabha on 3rd August, 2009, has provision for penalizing directors and key managerial personnel of a company found to be using non-public price sensitive information for own benefit or to benefit another person. The Bill has proposed punishment which could extend to 5 years imprisonment or fine of Rs 5 lakhs to 1 crore or both. SEBI's existing regulation prescribes up-to 10 years of imprisonment.

Rating Agencies

Role of Rating Agencies in Corporate Governance: Rating agencies rate the creditworthiness, or financial strength, of individual companies to determine their capacity to repay obligations. Since credit ratings are an assessment of a company's ability to repay obligations, they relate to debt and hybrid securities, rather than equity securities. Agencies thus focus primarily on the repayment ability and financial condition of companies:

> Liquidity,
> Leverage,
> Cash Flows,
> Earnings,
> Market Shares and Competition,
> Litigation and Contingencies, and so forth.

Functioning of Rating Agencies

There are various aspects related to the functioning of rating agencies such as the rating process and methodology followed to assign the rating, symbols to indicate rating etc that have been discussed in the succeeding paragraphs:

Rating Process

There are various stages which an instrument has to pass through before it gets rated. The rating process is thus divided in the stages as (http://icra.in):

Initiating Rating Action: Rating process in India is initiated on the receipt of a formal request (or mandate) from the prospective issuer, however, the rating agencies abroad, undertake assessment even if the company does not approach them *i.e.,* Unsolicited rating is issued. This is the only difference between the rating process of Indian rating agencies and the rating agencies abroad. Thereafter the process of assigning rating is same for all the rating agencies worldwide.

Analytical Team: The credit rating agency assigns the task to a Rating Team, which usually consists of two analysts with the expertise and skills required to evaluate the business of the issuer. An issuer is provided a list of information requirements and the broad framework for discussions. These requirements are worked out on the basis of understanding of the issuer's business, and broadly cover all aspects that may have a bearing on the rating.

Meeting with the Issuer: The rating involves assessment of a number of qualitative factors with a view to estimating the future earnings of the issuer. This requires extensive interactions with the issuer's management, specifically on subjects relating to plans, outlook, competitive position, and funding policies. The team of specialists thus obtains and analyse the information received from the detailed schedules and interactions with client. This enables to incorporate non-public information in the rating decision and it is the duty of the agency to maintain the complete confidentiality of the information provided by the company. In the case of manufacturing companies, plant visits are made to gain a better understanding of the issuer's production process. These visits also help in assessing the progress of projects under implementation.

Rating Committee: After completing the analysis, a Rating Report is prepared, which is then presented to the Rating Committee composed of senior analysts with expertise in relevant fields. A presentation on the issuer's business and management is also made by the Rating Team. The Rating Committee is the final authority for assigning ratings. It minutely goes through the data; the analysis prepared by the team and assigns a rating after detailed scrutiny. The assigned rating, along with the key issues, is communicated to the issuer's top management for acceptance.

Surveillance: If the issuer does not find the rating acceptable, it has a right to appeal for a review by providing certain fresh inputs. The Rating Committee would revise the initial rating decision, if the inputs and fresh clarifications so warrant. It is mandatory to monitors all assigned ratings over the tenure of the rated instruments. They are generally reviewed yearly or when circumstances have altered and there are greater doubts about the creditworthiness of the issuer. Regular surveillance helps upgrading or downgrading the given ratings. Before downgrading the issue, the agency put it on "credit watch" *i.e.* the rating is under review and might get lower in the near future. When a debt issue is on credit watch, the rating agency will advise investors to use the rating with caution.

Rating Symbols

The rating agency reduces complex risk factors into simplistic outcomes by assigning simple to understand symbols like A, B or C, the symbols are used to covey the safety grade to the investor. Some agencies use alphabets, others use numbers, and many use a combination of the two for ranking the risk of default. Sometimes, the suffix "+", "-" are used along with the main symbol to indicate the comparative position of the instrument within the group *i.e.*, if the position is better than most of the companies' instruments in the same group then the suffix '+' are added. Suffix (P) is also quite common; it shows that the money raised shall be put into a new project. The default risk varies from extremely safe to highly speculative. Separate symbols are used for long, medium and short term debt instruments. Long term instruments include debentures and bonds of companies, medium term includes public deposits and short term includes the commercial paper issued by corporate *e.g.*, CRISIL uses AAA to B for long term instruments, FAAA to FD for medium term instruments and P1 to P5 for short term instruments to convey their risk from highest safety to default expected. The ratings are classified into two grades depending on the risk characteristics of the instrument rated: (*a*) Investment grade denotes highest safety in terms of timely payment of interest and principal. The issuer is fundamentally strong *e.g.*, securities rated AAA and (*b*) Speculative grade denotes inadequate safety in terms of timely payment of principal and interest, *e.g.*, the securities rated below BBB.

Rating Fees

The credit rating agencies earn their revenue by charging fees from the issuers they rate. Initially, ratings were published and the rating agencies financed their operations through sale of publications and related materials to the users of rating services, such as investors, financial intermediaries. But due to the fear that too many investors would obtain their information through cheap photocopies (say, from friends or libraries) rather than by buying the rating companies' manuals themselves, they began to charge issuers for ratings.

Coverage

According to A ora, Mamta (2003), "Credit Rating in India-Institutions, Methods and Evaluation", New Century Publications, p. 22, the credit rating agencies cover various areas in the market, for *e.g.*,:

- ❑ In manufacturing companies, debt instruments are rated.
- ❑ In finance companies, structured obligations are rated.
- ❑ In banks, fixed deposit programs and commercial papers are rated.
- ❑ For financial institutions, project reports are prepared.
- ❑ For insurance companies, rating on their financial strength is provided.
- ❑ Builder's rating, infrastructure companies rating, mutual funds rating, rating for marketers of LPG and many more are other areas covered by rating agencies.

But, according to Shahani, Rakesh (2008), "Financial Markets in India", Anamika Publishers and Distributors (P.) Ltd, nowadays credit rating is not just confined to debt instruments but any activity where risk is involved is going in for rating. Some of these include:

(*a*) Country/Sovereign Ratings
(*b*) Rating of Indian States
(*c*) Rating of Real Estate builders and developers:

(*d*) Insurance Firms' Financial Strength Ratings
(*e*) Rating of Indian Banks
(*f*) Rating of Asset Management Companies (AMCs)
(*g*) Rating of Equity
(*h*) Corporate Governance Rating

Rating agencies are also diversifying their activities in other fields such as hospitals, schools, etc. where schools must be rated if they want to participate in certain financial assistance programs, and where a highway project might need a rating to be able to get government funds.

Spreading out of Rating Agencies

With the growing importance of credit rating agencies and the resultant need arise to obtain rating before entering the market, regulators in many countries have started referring to the ratings to judge an instrument. As the complexity in the financial market grow over time and regulators increased their reliance on the opinions of the credit rating agencies such that regulations turned into rating dependent regulation, the number of rating agencies operating in the United States and other countries have risen sharply. Although there are around 100 rating agencies located around the world, the number of "globally recognized" agencies is very small that includes Standard and Poor's, Moody's, and Fitch. The following table gives an overview of the leading credit rating agencies worldwide:

Leading Credit Rating Agencies Worldwide

CRA	Nation	Type	Rating		Year of
			High	Low	Set up
A.M. Best Company, Inc.	USA	NRSRO	A+++	S	1899
Standard and Poors (S and P)	USA	NRSRO	AAA	D	1941
Moody's Investors Service	USA	NRSRO	Aaa	C	1909
Fitch Ratings, Ltd.	USA	NRSRO	AAA	D	1913
Veribanc Inc.	USA	Independent	Colors and Stars 1982		
Dominion Bond Rating Service (DBRS)	Canada	NRSRO	R1 (high)	D	1976
Mikuni and Co., Ltd.	Japan	Independent	AAA	DDD	1983
Taiwan Ratings, Corp. (TCR)	Taiwan	S and P Affiliate	AAA	D	1997
Türk KrediRating (TCRating)	Turkey	Independent	TCR	TCR D	2007
Global Credit Rating Co.	S.Africa	Independent	A1+- C	1996	
Rus Ratings	Russia	Independent	AAA+-	D +-	2001

CRA	Nation	Type	Rating		Year of
			High	Low	Set up
Investment Information and Credit Rating Agency (ICRA)	India	Independent	AAA	D	1991
CRISIL, Ltd.	India	S&P Affiliate	AAA	D	1987
ONICRA Credit Rating Agency of India, Ltd.	India	Independent	SEIA	SE5C	1993
Dagong Global Credit Rating Co., Ltd.	China	Independent	AAA	C	1994
Shanghai Far East Credit Rating Co., Ltd.	China	Independent	AAA (pi)	C (pi)	1999
Lanka Rating Agency, Ltd. (LRA)	Sri Lanka	Subsidiary of RAM	AAA	D	2005
Malaysian Rating Corporation Berhad (MARC)	Malaysia	Fitch Affiliate	AAA	D	1995
RAM Rating Services Berhad (RAM)	Malaysia	S adn P Affiliate	AAA	D	1990
P.T. PEFINDO Credit Rating Indonesia	Indonesia	Independent	AAA	CCC	1993
Philippine Rating Services, Corp. (PhilRatings)	Philippines	Independent	AAA	C	
Capital Intelligence, Ltd.	Cyprus	Independent	AAA	D	1985
Credit Rating Agency of Bangladesh, Ltd. (CRAB)	Bangla-desh	Independent	AAA	D	2004
Pakistan Credit Rating Agency, Ltd. (PACRA)	Pakistan	Fitch former affiliate	AAA	C	1994
Agusto & Co. Ltd.	Nigeria	Independent	Aaa	D	1992
Caribbean Information and Credit Rating Services Ltd. (CariCRIS)	Carib-bean	Independent	AAA	D	2004
Sociedad Calificadora de Riesgo Centroamericana, S.A. (SCRiesgo)	Costa Rica	Independent	Scr AAA	Scr E	1997

Source: Compiled from websites of Credit Rating Agencies

Dubious Role of Credit Rating Agencies

Credit rating agencies have been time and again accused of their lax attitude in assessing issuers and giving misleading ratings without thorough analysis. They have been heavily criticized regarding their role and for the accuracy of their ratings. In the ongoing financial crisis leading to the fall of large investment banks in US *e.g.*, Lehman Brothers due to the flimsy ratings assigned by rating agencies to subprime mortgages raised questions on the performance of credit rating agencies. The whole corporate India has been shocked with the debacle of corporate governance norms in a company of a magnitude and status like Satyam that suddenly collapsed despite the positive assessment given by the company's socalled renowned watchdogs including its raters. The rating agencies based their analysis on fraudulently prepared and audited financial statements and thereby failed to warn investors about Satyam's deteriorating condition. The ratings given by the major ratings agencies were equally dismal in numerous other instances, including Enron and World.Com. Close supervision of rating agencies and the enforcement of IOSCO Code are some of the suggestions made to enable credit rating industry operate efficiently.

Review Questions

1. During the most recent years, some new concepts have emerged in the company law in India. Explain briefly any ten such issues.
2. Distinguish between any three:
   - (*i*)   Company and Producer Company
   - (*ii*) Company and One Person Company
   - (*iii*) Company and Small Company
   - (*iv*) Company and Associate Company
   - (*v*)   Company and Limited Liability Partnership (LLP)
   - (*vi*) Prospectus and Shelf Prospectus
   - (*vii*) Company Law Board and National Company Law Tribunal (NCLT)
3. Write short note on any five of the following:
   - (*i*)   Postal Ballot
   - (*ii*)   Audit Committee
   - (*iii*)   Independent Director
   - (*iv*)   Small Shareholders on Board
   - (*v*)   Director Identity Number (DIN)
   - (*vi*)   Corporate Identity Number (CIN)
   - (*vii*)   MCA-21
   - (*viii*) Online Filing of Documents
   - (*ix*)   Online Registration of Company
   - (*x*)   Corporate Governance
   - (*xi*)   Clause 49
   - (*xii*)   CSR
   - (*xiii*) Business Ethics
   - (*xiv*)   Insider Trading
   - (*xv*)   Rating Agencies

□□□

Part-II Compensation Laws

1

Employees' State Insurance Act, 1948

Historical Background

It was strongly felt after World War I that universal peace based on social justice was essential. In order to achieve this, the International Labour Organisation (ILO) was formed in 1919. In the first session of ILO held at Washington in 1919, India also participated as an original member.

The role of ILO since its inception in creating international standards of social insurance and in promotion of social security has been very significant. It was on the initiative and influence of the ILO that the first legislation of its kind towards social security in the country namely, 'Workmen's Compensation Act, 1923' was enacted. But the Employees' State Insurance Act, 1948 is much wider than the Workmen's Compensation Act, 1923 when it comes to question of providing compensation and other social security benefits to the employees.

Recommendations of Royal Commission on Labour

Royal Commission on Labour in India was appointed in 1929. This Commission deliberated upon the issue of social security provisions including certain benefits to employees in case of sickness and employment injury. The important recommendations of the commission are:—

(*i*)   The aid during sickness should be split into two parts (*a*) medical benefits (*b*) financial benefits.

(*ii*) The medical benefit should be the responsibility of the State (Government) on a non-contributory basis.

(*iii*) The financial benefits should be effected through the employers on contributory basis by the employers and workers, and

(*iv*) The Government should encourage private employers to inaugurate old age pension and provident fund.

But the Government during that period failed to do anything effective on those recommendations.

Recommendations of Labour Enquiry Committees

During World War II, the Cawnpore Labour Enquiry Committee 1938, the Bihar Labour Enquiry Committee 1940, the Bombay Textile Labour Enquiry Committee 1940 recommended the introduction of sickness insurance. The question of sickness insurance was also considered by the Conference of Labour Ministers in 1940. Their second Conference in 1941 decided to study its financial implications in certain big industries, and third Conference in 1942 ultimately decided that sickness insurance scheme be applied to workers in cotton, jute and heavy engineering industries and the financial burden be shared by the Government workers and employers. The task to formulate the health scheme was given by the Government to Prof. B.P. Adarkar, whose report in 1944 was implemented by introducing a Bill in this connection. The Bill was introduced as Workmen's State Insurance Bill, 1946 and the Select Committee replaced the word 'employees' in place of 'workmen' and the Employee's State Insurance Act was enacted in 1948.

The Scheme thereafter was first implemented in the industrial towns of Kanpur and Delhi on 24th February, 1952, which was gradually followed in other States too.

Important Amendments

1966 : Amendment Act, 1966

The objective of the Amendment was to remove difficulties which were being faced in the administration of the Act. The major amendments are:

(*i*) The definition of the term 'employee' was amended to include administrative staff engaged in sale, distribution and other connected functions.

(*ii*) The definition of the term 'family' was amended to cover dependent parents of female insured persons.

(*iii*) The wage limit for coverage of 'employees' was raised from Rs. 400 to Rs. 500 per month to ensure benefits to larger number of employees.

(*iv*) The number of representatives of Parliament on the ESIC were raised from 2 to 3.

(*v*) Provision for granting funeral benefit upto Rs. 100 was introduced in the case of insured death.

(*vi*) The scheme of maternity benefit was enlarged.

(*vii*) Provision was made to allow ESIC to take over from the State Government, the administration of the medical benefit.

(*viii*)The rate of disablement benefit was increased.

1984 : Amendment Act, 1984

(*i*) The wage limit which was raised from Rs. 500 to Rs. 1,000 per month in 1975, was again raised to Rs. 1,600 per month.

(*ii*) Employers contribution was delinked from employees' contribution. The amendment also provided for recovery of employers' as well as employees contribution at a fixed percentage of wages.

(*iii*) The levels of average daily wages was raised from below Rs. 2 to below Rs. 6 for the purpose of exemption from payment of employee's contribution. The purpose was to give relief to low-paid employees.

(*iv*) The unit of contribution was changed from a 'a week' to a 'wage period'.

(*v*) The existing list of occupational diseases in the 3rd Schedule was substituted by a revised list.

1989 : *Amendment Act,* **1989**

The amendments based on the reports of two Committees submitted in 1978 and 1982, are as follows:

(*i*) The Act which was applicable only to factories and extended establishments after giving 6 months notice was made applicable simultaneously to factories and other establishments.

(*ii*) Children upto the age of 21 years and infirm children without any age restriction were also included in the definition of family, so as to make them also eligible for medical benefit.

(*iii*) The number of representatives of employees and employers on the ESIC was raised from 5 to 10 each.

(*iv*) ESI Corporation was given power to frame regulations in respect of methods of recruitments, salaries, conditions of service, etc. of officers and staff of ESIC.

(*v*) To put a curb on unnecessary litigation by the employers, it was made obligatory on the part of the employer to deposit 50% of the amount claimed, before disputing the claim of ESI Corporation for payment of contribution or other dues.

(*vi*) The penal provisions were made more stringent.

2008 : *Employees' State Insurance (Amendment) Ordinance,* **2008**

The ordinance is effective from 3-7-2008.

Notwithstanding anything contained in this Act, the Central Government may by notification in the Official Gazette, frame Scheme for other beneficiaries and the members of their families providing medical facility in any hospital established by the Corporation in any area which is underutilized hospital on payment of user charges. The user charges collected from the other beneficiaries shall be deemed to be contribution and shall form part of the Employee's State Insurance Fund.

The Scheme may provide for all or any of the following matters, namely:

(*i*) The other beneficiaries who may be covered under this Scheme;

(*ii*) The time and manner in which the medical facilities may be availed by the other beneficiaries;

(*iii*) The form in which the other beneficiary shall furnish particulars about himself and his family whenever required as may be specified by the Corporation;

(*iv*) Any other matter which is to be provided for in the scheme or which may be necessary or proper for the purpose of implementing the Scheme.

The Government's much-hyped plan to extend heath care facilities by Employees State Insurance Corporation hospitals to BPL families covered under the Rashtriya Swashya Bima Yojana has gone sour. An ordinance by the labour ministry amending the Employees State Insurance Act to extend the health care facilities to BPL families has lapsed and is no longer in effect. The ordinance issued in July, 2008 has expired as it could not be ratified by Parliament. The government can make changes to law through ordinance when Parliament is not in session. However, it has to be validated by Parliament within six months, or when Parliament comes into session before six months. In this case, six months have already passed since the ordinance was issued in July. The amendment could not be passed by Parliament as it was sent to a Parliamentary Standing Committee.

The Employees' State Insurance Act is a social security legislation that provides medical care in case of sickness, maternity, disablement and death due to employment injury to employees drawing wages upto Rs. 10,000 per month. Rashtriya Swashya Bima Yojana is a scheme that provides health insurance cover upto Rs. 30,000, tapped in a smart card given to the below povery line (BPL) families. So far, nine lakh smart cards have been issued. The labour ministry had amended the ESI Act after it realized that facilities at the hospital under ESIC were under-utilised. It issued the Employees' State Insurance (Amendment) Ordinance, 2008 on July 3, 2008, hoping to extend facilities provided by the vast network of hospitals under ESIC to the unorganized sector workers under the Rashtriya Swasthya Bima Yojana Scheme, and providing medical care on user charges, wherever the same are under-utilised. ESIC operates 144 hospitals and 1,397 dispensaries in the country. (Source: Economic Times, dated 2nd January, 2009, page 10)

Objectives, Scope and Applicability of the Act

The Employee's State Insurance Act, 1948 is a beneficial piece of legislation to provide certain benefits to employees in case of sickness, maternity and employment injury. It also provides for medical benefit in kind to employees and their families. It is a self financing social security scheme in which every contributory is a beneficiary.

The promulgation of Employees' State Insurance Act, 1948 envisaged an integrated need based social insurance scheme that would protect the interest of workers in contingencies The Act also guarantees reasonably good medical care to workers and their immediate dependants. The Act further absolved the employers of their obligations under the Maternity Benefit Act, 1961 and Workmen's Compensation Act, 1923. The benefits provided to the employees under the Act are also in conformity with ILO conventions. Following the promulgation of the ESI Act, the Central Government set up the ESI Corporation to administer the Scheme.

Mission Statement

To provide for certain benefits to employees in case of sickness, maternity and employment injury and to make provisions for related matters.

Coverage under the Act

The Act was originally applicable to non-seasonal factories using power and employing 20 or more persons; but it is now applicable to non-seasonal power using factories employing 10 or more persons and non-power using factories employing 20 or more persons. Under Section 1 (5) of the Act, the Scheme has been extended to shops, hotels, restaurants, cinemas including preview theatre, road motor transport undertakings and newspaper establishment employing 20 or more persons.

Applicability of the Scheme

- ❑ The Act extends to the whole of India.
- ❑ The Act applies to all factories including government factories.
- ❑ Appropriate government, in consultation with ESIC, can extend any of provisions of the Act to any establishment including industrial, commercial, agricultural or otherwise. The Act has been extended by many States to shops, hotels, restaurants, cinemas, newspapers establishments, road transport undertakings, etc. employing 20 or more persons
- ❑ The establishment shall continue to be governed by this Act even if the number of persons employed therein at any time falls below the specified limit or manufacturing process has ceased to be carried on with the aid of power.
- ❑ The Scheme does not apply to seasonal factories.

Wage Limit under the Act

- ❑ In 1975, the wage limit under the scheme was raised from Rs. 500 to Rs. 1,000 p.m.
- ❑ In 1984, it was increased from Rs. 1,000 to Rs. 1,600 p.m.
- ❑ In 1992, it was raised from Rs. 1,600 to 3,000.
- ❑ In 1996, it was enhanced from Rs. 3,000 to Rs. 6,500.
- ❑ In 2004, it was raised to Rs. 7,500 (w.e.f. April 2004)
- ❑ In 2006, it was raised to Rs 10,000 (w.e.f. 1st Oct, 2006)

Judicial Interpretations/Case Example	
The Act is a beneficial piece of social legislation in the interest of labour in factories or to any other establishments.	*Kumbakonam Milk Supply Cooperative Society* v *ESIC*, 2003 LLR 844.
Once a notification is issued by a State Government under Section 1(5) of the ESI Act covering a particular establishment of the State, automatically the said notification would cover all branches of such an establishment situated even outside such State, having complete functional integrity with the main activity of the establishment.	*Transport Corporation of India* v *ESIC*, 2000 LLR 1 (SC).

Educational Institutions

The notification has been issued under Section 1(5) of E.S.I, Act, 1948, which is as follows: "The appropriate Government may, in consultation with the Corporation and where the appropriate Government is a State Government, with the approval of the Central Government after giving six months' notice of its intention of so doing by notification in the official Gazette, extend the provisions of this Act or any of them, to any other establishment or class of establishments, industrial, commercial, agricultural or otherwise, provided that where the provisions of this Act have been brought into force in any part of a State, the said provisions shall stand extended to any such establishment or class of establishments within that part if the provisions have already been extended to similar establishment or class of establishments in another part of that State". The petitioner has challenged the coverage notice dated 22.8.2008 and notification dated 30.6.2008. Through the impugned notification, educational institutions have been brought under the Act. Held, the word "otherwise" is of wide amplitude. ESI Act can be extended upon educational institutions and minority educational institutions could be brought under the Act.	*Maharishi Shiksha Sansthan and Another* v *State of U.P. and Another,* 2009 LLR 98 (Allahabad HC).

Coverage of Cooperative Societies

Held, the co-operative societies rendering services to the members are domestic in nature like operating lifts, water supply, electricity, cleaning, sweeping and security that are essential for existence and security of members and premises. Rendering such services to members is not economic activity. The co-operative societies cannot be treated as establishments even though twenty or more employees employed or were employed for wages on any day of the preceding twelve months, as contemplated under the ESI Act. Hence unless extended and made applicable specifically by notification and/or by any other mode, the society and/or such companies cannot be treated as an establishment as defined under the ESI Act.	*Regional Director, Employees' State Indurance Corporation* v *Tulsiani Chanbers Premises Cooperative Society,* 2008 LLR 362, (Bombay High Court).

Coverage of Shops

When an establishment is registered as a 'Shop', the ESI Act shall apply.	*Duvent Fans (P) Ltd.* v *ESIC,* 2001 LLR 783 (Karn HC).
Held, though a shop is not defined under ESI Act for coverage there under, a liberal meaning is to be given since a shop will not be a place where only goods are sold but also a company registered under the Companies Act as engaged in activities of rendering financial services to its members in the form of loan and accepting deposits.	*Employees' State Insurance Corporation* v *Manipal Sowbhagya Nidhi, Ltd.,* 2007 LLR 1109 (Maharashtra High Court).

Contd..

The word 'Shop' has not been defined either in this Act or in the Notification. The ESI Act being social welfare legislation intended to benefit as far as possible workers belonging to all categories. One has to be liberal in interpreting the words in such social welfare legislation. Held. there should not be much emphasis on the on the words. What is important is that the interpretation must be consistent with the object the general purpose and policy of the statute.	*Brook Bond India Ltd.* v *ESIC,* 1980 2 LLJ 27 (Kerala).

Hotels and Restaurants

Under the amended provisions of ESI Act applicable with effect from 20th October' 1989, hotels and restaurants employing 10 or more persons (if using power) or 20 or more persons (if not using power) are covered.	*GL Hotels Ltd.* v *TC Sarin,* 1993 LLR 945 (SC).

Cinemas/Theatres

While counting 20 or more persons, those employed in the canteen or restaurants or cycle stand run by the cinema/theatre house are also counted.	*Royal Talkies,* 1978 Lab IC 1245 (SC): AIR 1978 SC 1478.

Petrol Pumps

Petrol pumps are covered and pumping of oil, washing and servicing of vehicles at petrol pumps has been held as manufacturing process.	*Kanchamba Service Station* v *Union of India,* LLR 450 (Karn HC).

Hospital/Dispensaries

Hospitals and Dispensaries are covered.	*Christian Medical College* v *ESIC,* 2001 LLR 60 (SC).

Club

A club is covered as the manufacturing process with the aid of power is carried on in the kitchen of a club.	*ESIC* v *Jalandhar Gymkhana Club,* 1992 LLR 733: (P&H HC).

Employees Engaged for Building Repairs

This is a case which relates to the liability of the respondent to pay contribution for the employees engaged in building repairs. The respondent engaged services of contractor for this purpose. Repair of building, by its very nature is casual and occasional. Still if such work is attended by employees directly, appointed by the employer or engaged by him through any other agency, his liability to make	*ESIC Hyderabad and Another* v *AP Electrical Equipment Corp (a unit of ECE Industries Ltd),* Vishakha- *Contd..*

the contributions gets attracted, subjected however, to other conditions. The High Court, in appeal, is not convinced to disturb the findings recorded by the Trial Courts in holding that the respondent establishment though covered under the Act, is not under the obligation to pay contributions for the employees engaged for the building repairs.	Patnam 2005 LLR 466 (APHC).

Finance and Investment Companies

Where a company is engaged in the business of finance and investment and earns profits by such investments, such business will amount to sale of services for remuneration and covered by this Act.	*ESIC v Peerless General Financial and Investment Co. Ltd.*, 1997 1 LLJ 82 (Cal)

Employees Working Far Away from the Place where Manufacturing Process is Carried on

The appellant is a partnership firm engaged in the manufacture of orid flour. An inspection was conducted by the Insurance Inspector on 18-4-2000 at the appellant's factory premises. Nine persons were seen employed in the factory and its premises. It has come out in evidence that usually the number of employees engaged in the factory and its premises is seven, but, during two months the appellant had on some days engaged two more casual employees. It was found out from records that the appellant had a sales depot at Kozhlkode. Two persons were employed in the sales depot. Therefore, demands were issued for covering the establishment under the Employees' State Insurance Scheme including those two persons also as employees of the factory. It is the contention of the appellant that his establishment is not a factory covered under the Employees' State Insurance Scheme as it is employing less than 10 persons in the factory and its premises and since it is not a covered establishment, it is not liable to pay any contribution to the employees employed in the factory or elsewhere. An appeal was filed before the Court and the matter was referred to the Division Bench for deciding the question whether employees working far away from the place where manufacturing process is carried on can be counted as workers in the factory 'for the purpose of coverage under the Employees' Insurance Scheme.? Held, when at no point of time 10 or more persons worked in factory premises including precincts thereof where manufacturing process is carried on, it is not a coverable establishment under the Act. Therefore, the question of demanding E.S.I. contributions in view of wider definition of term "employee" did not arise. The demand as made by ESIC and the judgment of Employees' Insurance Court are set aside.	*Managing Partner, M/S Shanthi Flour Mills* v *Regional Director, Employees' State Insurance Corp, Thrissur* 2008 LLR 1192 (Kerala High Court).

Employees Working in Sales Depots/Franchise

ESI Act will be applicable to the employees working in sales depots and officers of Bata India since its factory is covered under the Act.	*Bata India Ltd.* v *ESIC*, 2003 LLR 1018 (Cal HC).

Unit Operating within the Premises of Railways

Through a letter, dated 21-11-1988, the respondents (ESIC) informed the appellant stating that the unit need not be registered, since it is operating within the premises of Railways. The unit of the appellant was once again inspected on 2-11-1990 and the Inspector recommended that the establishment must be brought under coverage, since more than 250 employees were working and the power was being utilized in the manufacturing process. In pursuance thereof, necessary steps were taken for the registration of the unit under the Act and contribution was being paid regularly. In the year 1992, another Inspector examined the registers once again and took the view that the appellant is liable to pay the contribution for the period from 15-12-1985 to 31-10-1990 also. Interest was also levied. Feeling aggrieved by the same, the appellant filed E.I. Case before the Industrial Tribunal-I. Through its order, dated 5-4-1999, the Tribunal upheld the contention of the respondents and directed that the appellant is liable to pay the contribution with effect from 15-12-1985. Hence, this appeal under Section 82 of the Act. The Court observed "What emerges from the record is that a conscious and well-informed decision taken by the respondents as regards the coverage of the unit and the same could not have been unsettled by an employee of inferior category. The whole episode discloses that the decisions rendered by the superior authorities in the organization were virtually set aside, if not reviewed by an Inspector. Even the Deputy Regional Director could not have reviewed his own decision." Held, the demand made against the appellant cannot be sustained in law. Hence, the respondents are directed to refund the amount recovered from the appellant towards the demand in question, within a period of two months from the date of receipt of a copy of this order.	*Rayalseema Concrete Sleepers Pvt. Ltd.* v *Employees' State Insurance Corporation and Others*, 2008 LLR 316 (Andhra Pradesh HC).

Newspaper Establishments

All the persons working in newspaper establishments are covered.

Road Transports Establishments

Road transports establishments are covered and all employees including those working outside the premises such as drivers, cleaners, booking clerks, mechanics etc. are covered.

Apprentices

Apprentices are not covered under the ESI scheme. But, if they are not engaged under the Apprentice Act, 1961 or under the standing orders of the establishment, then they are covered.

Trainee

The students' trainees who are being paid stipend will be considered as apprentices. If they have been appointed under the Apprentice Act, 1961 or under the standing orders of the establishment, they will not be covered under the ESI Act.

Daily Wage Earner

Employees engaged on daily wages for few days, are covered by the ESI provisions if the establishment employ's 20 or more persons on any day in the previous year if no power is used and 10 or more persons if power is used. In the instant case, the daily wage employees are covered, provided the number of employees employed are 20 (10 in the case of use of power) or more.

Clubbing of Units

The appellant is a partnership firm known as Tops Food Products' situated at village Kanwali, Dehradun and there are two partners in the firm namely Meena Marwah and Anil Marwah. The said firm is registered under Shop and Establishment Act and is also registered with the Sales-Tax Department and Income-Tax Department etc. It has been stated that the applicant has another firm known as 'M/s. Tops Food Product (Bakery Division)' which is proprietor firm of Anil Marwah. Both the aforesaid firms *i.e.*, M/s. Tops Food Product and M/s. Tops Food Product (Bakery Division) are separate firms and have separate sales-tax number. Both the firms have separate licenses under Shop and Establishment Act. Separate documents and records are being maintained separately in case of both the firms. As will appear from the aforesaid finding that both the firms of applicant are separate and it is unjust to compel the provisions of E.S.I. Act after clubbing both the firms as the 18 employees who have been shown to be employed in single firm are the employees of two different firms. Besides this, the sales-tax registration and electricity connections of both the firms are separate and, therefore, the E.S.I contributions which have been demanded are invalid. While deciding the issue as to whether the recovery of the defendant is null and void, E.S.I. Tribunal has recorded the finding that both the firms in question are separate and none of the firm carries more than 10 employees have been found working and, as such, no contribution can be recovered from the applicant and recovery against the applicant is null and void.	*Employees' State Insurance Corporation, Kanpur* v *Tops Food Products,* 2008 LLR 42 (Uttarakhand High Court).

Contd..

Aruna Textile in the whole sale section and Aruna Stores in the retail section are really an integrated single unit. The building and electricity connections are common for both the establishments; cash counter and packing section are common and there is common security and common path and common supervision for both. The proprietor of Aruna Stores is the mother of the proprietor of Aruna Textiles. Ostensibly they are two units but there is functional integrity between the two. Hence for the purpose of industrial laws, they have to be treated really as one unit, even though, for the purpose of sales tax or for some other purposes they may be treated separately. Held, M/s Aruna Stores and Aruna Textiles are one unit for the purpose of the ESI Act. There is functional integrity between the two units and it seems they were shown two different units probably to reduce the tax liability.	*Regional Director ESIC Madras and Anr. v Aruna Stores, Proprietor J Shanta and Anr.,* 2005 LLR 501 (Madras HC).
Three concerns will be clubbed together for ESI purposes when there is geographical unity and functional integrity.	*Madona Textiles* v *ESIC* 2000 LLR 1036 (Ker HC).

Distinction between ESI Act, 1948 and Workmen's Compensation Act, 1923

The Workmen's Compensation Act, 1923, is the first legislation of its kind towards social security in the country. Before this Act came into force, social security legislation was unknown in the country. The Employees' State Insurance Act, 1948 which replaces the Workmen's Compensation Act, 1923 in the areas where the Employee's State Insurance Act has been made applicable, is far wider than the Workmen's Compensation Act and enlarges the scope of compensation.

Point of Distinction	*ESI Act, 1948*	*Workmen's Compensation Act, 1923*
Objectives	Objective of ESI Act is to provide benefits to employees in case of sickness, maternity and employment injury by accidents or occupational diseases.	Objective of Workmen's Compensation Act is to provide compensation to workmen for injury by accidents or occupational diseases.
Wage limit	The wage limit under the ESI scheme is at present Rs. 10,000 p.m. (w.e.f. 1st Oct, 2006)	There is no such wage limit at present. The wage limit was abolished in 1984.
Workman	The term 'employee' is of wide connotation and includes within its scope clerical, labourer, part time worker, apprentices and even casual employees but does not include members of armed forces.	Workman means any person who is a railway servant, a master or other member of the crew of a ship or an aircraft, a person recruited in connection with motor vehicle but does not include members of armed forces.

Point of Distinction	ESI Act, 1948	Workmen's Compensation Act, 1923
Authorities	ESI Act is administered through ESI Corporation, Standing Committee, Medical Benefit Council and Employees Insurance Court.	Workman Compensation Act is administered through Commissioners.
Suit barred	Section 53 of the ESI Act bars an insured person or his dependents to claim compensation or damages under Workmen's Compensation Act, 1923 or any other Law for the time being in force.	No compensation is payable under this Act if workman has instituted a suit either in a Civil Court or if claims have been filed under ESI Act, 1948.

Definitions [Section 2]

■ Employment Injury [Section 2 (8)] Means

A personal injury to an employee caused by	accident or an occupational disease	arising out of and in the course of his employment being an insurable employment	whether the accident occurs or the occupaional disease is contracted within or outside the territorial limits of India

Judicial Interpretations/Case Example	
The word 'injury' does not mean only visible injury in the form of some wound. Such a narrow interpretation would be inconsistent with the purposes of the Act which provides certain benefits in cases of sickness, maternity and employment injury	Shyam Devi v ESIC, AIR 1964 All 427 (HC): 1961 (1) LLJ 725 (All).
The words 'in the course of employment' and 'arising out of employment' imply a nexus or casual relationship between the accident and the employment.	Machinnon Mckenzie v Ibrahim M. Issak 1969 2 SCC 607: 1970 Lab IC 1413 SCC.
The moment it is proved that the accident arose in the course of employment, it is to be presumed that the accident has arisen out of that employment.	Smt. Harjinder Kaur v ESIC, (1987) 71 FJR 149 (P&H).
A person employed to load and unload the products of a manufacturing company while accompanying their trucks, tried to cross over the railway line to buy bidis for him from a shop on the other side and received serious injury from an ongoing train. He suffered employment injury.	ESIC v Gulab bux Mulla, (1986) 2 LLN 503 (Bom): 1987 Lab IC 141.
In this case, deceased Purshothaman was milk vender for the distribution of milk by riding cycle. He sustained chest pain and fell down from his cycle on which he was carrying milk. While in	Chandra Matti v ESIC, 2003 (4) LLN 1143 (Ker HC).

Contd...

hospital for treatment, he died of heart attack. He being servant of the milk society was an insured person under ESI Schemes. The High Court held that the deceased died on account of employment injury on the plea that the ESI Act should be interpreted liberally in favour of the person for whose benefit the legislation has been enacted.	
Accident which is found to have arisen in the course of employment of the insured person shall be presumed, in the absence of any evidence to the contrary, to have arisen out of employment.	*Saraswati Bai* v *ESIC,* 2003 (4) LLN 730 (Karn DB).
In this case, the employee was assaulted at the bus stop while he was waiting for the bus to his house. The injury caused to the employee in this case, cannot be said to have arisen out of employment, unless it can be shown that the employee was doing something incidental to his employment. Out of this employment here indicates that the injury must be caused by an accident which had its origin in the employment. The injury which the employee in this case sustained due to the assault of strangers on his way to his house cannot be said to have its origin in the employment in the factory. There is no connection between the accident and the employment.	*ESIC* v *C.M. Sasi,* 2002 Lab IC 1071 (Ker-HC).
When the employee had died in the course of his employment (during period of his employment in the factory) it must be presumed that accident leading to his death had arisen out of his employment when there is no evidence to the contrary. Deceased met accidental death while returning from Katkona Colliery after handing over an application for permission to join duty. It was not established that accidental death occurred within the precinct of Katkona Colliery. Held, it would not be treated as an accident arising out of and during the course of employment for payment of compensation since the deceased has not been accepted on duty. Hence, findings of the Commissioner under the workmen's Compensation Act are liable to be set aside.	*Sarawati Bai and Others* v *ESIC Banglore ,*2004 LLR 35 (Karn HC); *South Eastern Coal Fields Ltd. And others* v *Smt. Shyama Nagvanshi and other,* 2008 LLR 783 (Chattisgarh HC).

Notional Extension of Employment

An employment injury need not necessarily be confined to any injury sustained by a person within the premises or the establishment where a person works. Whether in a particular case, the theory of notional extension of employment would take in the time and place of accident so as to bring it within an employment injury, will have to depend on the assessment of several factors. There should be a nexus between the circumstances of the accident and the employment. ... Each case is to be decided on its own facts ... It is sufficient if it is proved that the injury to the employee was caused by an accident arising out of and in the course of employment, no matter when and where it occurred.

Judicial Interpretations/Case Example	
There is not even a geographical limitation. The accident may occur within or outside the territorial limits of India. However, there should be a nexus or casual connection between the accident and employment. Mere road accident on a public road while employee was on his way to place of employment cannot be said to have its origin in his employment in the factory.	*Regional Director ESIC* v *Francis de Costa,* (1996) 6 SCC 1: 1996 SCC (L&S) 1361 (SC).
An employee deputed by the management to participate in a football match, met with an accident resulting in his death on his way to the playground. Held, his death occurred due to employment injury within the meaning of Section 2 (8).	*ESIC* v *Parmes-waran Pillai,* (1976) 49 FJR 440 Kerala.
Injury caused to a workman by a motor vehicle while he was returning to the factory from his residence where he had gone from the factory for taking lunch during lunch break, was held to be an employment injury.	*Regional Director ESIC* v *Mary Cutinho,* (1994) Lab IC 2420: (1994) 69 FLR 633 (Bom).
The injury received by an employee while returning home from the factory, at the hands of his enemies on account of personal ill will arising out of a land dispute, is not an employment injury.	*T Rajappa* v *ESIC,* (1992) 2 LLJ 714: (1992) Lab IC 1490: (1992) 1 LLN 805 (Kar) (DB).
Deceased workman was staying in the quarters in the factory premises. Residents of the quarters used to carry water from the bore well which is also situated within the factory premises. In the early hours while taking bath at the bore well, deceased died due to electrocution at the bore well which is situated near his quarter. He had not commenced work on that day and he was not attending to any duty connected with his employment. Held, the doctrine of notional extension of employment cannot be applied in the instant case because there is no connection between the cause of his death and his employment as mechanic in the factory.	*Mummi Dipalli Syamala Devi* v *ESIC,* 2003 LIC 2845 (AP-HC).

■ Factory [Section 2 (12)]

> *It is similar to the definition of factory given under the Factories Act, 1948.*

Factory means any premises including the precincts thereof

(*a*) Whereon 10 more persons are or were employed on any day of the preceding 12 months and in any part of which a manufacturing process is being carried on with the aid of power or is ordinarily so carried on, or

(*b*) Whereon 20 or more persons are or were employed and in any part of which manufacturing is being carried on without the aid of power or is ordinarily so carried on but does not include a mine subject to the operation of Mines Act, 1952 or a railway running shed.

Judicial Interpretations/Case Example

The petitioner is a partnership firm and has been doing cloth business. At any point of time, under petitioner more than 18 employees have not been served. Therefore, petitioner has not come within the purview of ESI Act, 1948. The inspector of the respondent has inspected the petitioner on several occasions. The ESI inspector found that 21 employees were working with respondent, hence liable to be covered under the ESI Act and subsequently a notice has been issued, wherein it was stated that from 1.4.1987 to 30.6.1990 the petitioner has to pay Rs. 7488.75 towards premium notice dated 19.12.1990. The persons namely Periyannan, Somasundaram & Shanmugam have served as partners of the petitioner and therefore, the petitioner is not liable to pay the amount demanded by the respondent. Further it is stated in the petition that as per notice dated 27.7.1990 the petitioner is not liable to pay the amount of Rs. 26,085.70 to the respondent. Under the said circumstances, with regard to the amount of Rs.7488.75 ESIOP No 12 of 2001 has been filed and likewise, with regard to the amount of Rs. 26,085.70 ESIOP No 20 of 2001 has been filed. The Employee Insurance Court, after considering all contentions raised on either side, has rightly allowed the petitions in holding that the coverage of the establishment under ESI Act was not proper hence in view of factual and legal aspects, High Court has not found illegality or infirmity in the common order passed by the court and, therefore, the present civil miscellaneous appeals as filed by ESIC are dismissed.	*Regional Director, Employees State Insurance Corporation* v *Anandha Silks Paradise*, 2008 LLR 1243(Madras High Court).
Separate buildings even though located at some distance apart when used for one continuous manufacturing process will constitute a single factory.	*Agents and Manufacturers Delhi* v *ESIC,* (1973) 2LLJ 447.
The activity in the kitchen of a cricket club has a direct connection with the activities carried on in the rest of the club premises. Hence, such a club employing the statutory number of employees, is a factory and the applicability of the Act extends to all of its employees and is not confined to the employees working in the kitchen and pantry.	*Cricket Club of India* v *ESIC* ,1994 Lab IC 1213: (1994) 69 FLR 19: (1994) 1 LLN 644 (Bom).
From the date an establishment becomes a "factory" within the meaning of Section 2(12) of this Act, it becomes liable to pay contribution.	*Southern Road-ways (P) Ltd* v *ESIC*, 1973 Lab IC 1555 (AP).
As long as the number of persons working on the premises is 20 or more, the premises is a factory whether they are paid wages or not.	*ESIC* v *Siddiqui*, M.1. 1905 (1) LLJ 37.

Contd..

Ready made garments are made on a premise without the aid of power, but ironing of those garments is done with the aid of power. Thus, the premise is a factory.	*Kalphana Dress* v *ESIC*, 1977 (50) FJR 219 (Bom HC).
All persons employed in a factory need not be employed in the manufacturing process.	*T.W. Cooperative Production and Sale Society Ltd.* v *ESIC*, 1977 Lab IC 1514.
The definition of factory also includes a seasonal factory which works for a period not exceeding seven months in a year in manufacturing processes as have been specified by central government by notification. The seasonal factory must be exclusively engaged in processes like cotton ginning, cotton or jute processes, decortications of ground nuts, manufacture of coffee, indigo, lac, rubber, sugar (including gur,, and tea. It is immaterial whether the manufacturing process is carried on by the factory continuously or only intermittently due to non availability of raw material or other reason.	*Suresh Gokuldas* v *ESIC*, AIR 1965 Mad 287.
Satish Motors is an establishment employing number of workman at Akola. ESIC issuing notices under Section 2(12) and subsequently under Section 1(5) contends that provisions of the Act were applicable to the firm in question from previous date and hence demanding arrears from the firm. Corporation also contends unavailability of relevant documents during inspections hence determining arrears under Section 45A, but without giving opportunity to firm to be heard. Held, the corporation was not able to point out as to why the establishment c .me to be covered under Section 1(5) with effect from backdate. If the corporation itself sure of the premises on which it has charged, the date of applicability of the provisions of the Act, it would be improper to expect the employer to comply with the demand and therefore demand of arrears is liable to be set aside.	*Joint Regional Director ESIC* v *Srared Chaure and Anr.*, 2006 Lab IC 937 (Bom HC).

■ *Manufacturing Process* [*Section* 2 (14AA)]

> *It is similar to the definition of manufacturing process given in the Factories Act, 1948.*

Judicial Interpretations/Case Example

The definition of manufacturing process in the Factories Act, 1948 does not depend upon and is not co-related with any end product being manufactured out of a manufacturing process. It includes even repair, finishing, oiling or cleaning process with a view to its use; sale, transport, deliver or disposal. The activity of pumping petroleum products with the aid of power employing more than 10 persons is sufficient to bring petrol pump within the definition of "manufacturing process"	*Qazi Noorul Hassan Hamid Hussain Petrol Pump* v *ESIC*, 2003 II LLJ 341 (All HC).

Contd..

Preserving or storing, article in cold storage is deemed to be manufacturing process.	*Kumbakonam Milk Supply Cooperative Society* v *ESIC,* 2003 (II) CLR 738 (Mad HC).
A cooperative society was purchasing milk from cattle owners and after selling the same, used to store the excess milk in the cold storage so that it could be sold later on. The Court held the activity is manufacturing process covered by the ESI Act.	*Velli Palayam Cooperative Supply Society* v *ESIC,* 2004 LLR 887: 2004(II) LLJ 885 (Mad HC).
In this case, the appellants were tapping the blood for the purpose of diagnosis, storing it and conducting the tests by way of cross matching and giving their reports. Held, the process would not amount to any "manufacturing process" as defined under Section 2(k) of the Factories Act so as to cover the appellant's establishments under the ESI Act. Similar such decisions have been taken by *Calcutta High Court in the case of ESIC* ,2005 Lab IC 2118.	*Vijaya Diagnostic Centre and etc.* v *ESIC,* Hyderabad 2006 Lab IC 1 (AP HC).

■ *Wages [Section 2 (22)] Means*

All remuneration paid or payable in cash to an employee and includes any payment in respect of any period of authorised leave, lock-out, legal strike or lay-off and other additional remuneration, if any, paid at intervals not exceeding 2 months but does not include:

- (*a*) Employer's contribution to any pension fund or PF or under this Act
- (*b*) Any traveling allowance or traveling concession
- (*c*) Any sum paid to the person employed to defray special expenses entailed on him by the nature of his employment or
- (*d*) Any gratuity payable on discharge.

Judicial Interpretations/Case Example

The question raised in this case is whether payment made to independent contractor for material costs; machinery and other expenditure comes under the purview of wages under Section 2 (22) of the Act. Held, it does not amount to 'wages' as defined under Section 2 (22) of ESI Act, 1948 to attract ESI contribution. Another question raised in this case is whether Insurance/Labour Court is empowered to pass a relief of refund of amount wrongly obtained under compulsion coercion. Held, when Insurance Court is empowered to entertain appeal under Section 75 of the Act and it comes to a definite conclusion that ESI contribution has been wrongly obtained, it is competent to order refund and no separate proceedings seeking refund are required.	*Regional Director, ESI Corporation, Bangalore and others* v *Management of Shagil Precision India,* 2009 LLR 72 (Karnataka High Court).

Contd..

Wages includes 'HRA' 'night shift allowance' 'incentive allowance' and heat, gas and dust allowance'	*Harihar Poly fibres* v *Regional Director ESIC,* (1984) 4 SCC 324: 1984 SCC (L&S) 747 SCC.
Wages includes 'incentive bonus', though made at the end of each quarter.	*Modella Woollens Ltd.* v *ESIC* ,(1994) Supp (3) SCC 580: 1995 SCC (L&S) 164 (SC).
Special allowance and mid-day meal allowance payable in terms of a settlement are wages.	*Hind Art Press* v *ESIC* (1989) 2 LLN 394: 59 FLR 778 (Kant).
Wages covers the subsidy given for LIC (life insurance) premium.	*ESIC* v *Shri Ram Chemicals Industries,* (1987) 2 LLN 227 (Raj): (1987) Lab IC 1747 (Raj).
Remuneration received by a Managing Director for discharging certain functions is wages.	*ESIC* v *M&R Oil Co. (P) Ltd.,* (1984) Lab IC 844 (Kant): (1983) 2 LLN 918 (Kant).
Payment made to respondent workman under the nomenclature of "good work wages" for an extra work done have been held not wages.	*Modern Threads (India) Ltd.* v *ESIC,* 2003 III CLR 250 (Raj HC).
Amount paid as interim relief as directed by the Government, would not come within the purview of wages under Section 2 (22) of the ESI Act and the ESIC is not entitled to demand contribution.	*ESIC* v *Narsimha Mills Ltd., Coimbatore* 2003 (2) LLN 65 (Mad DB).
Incentive paid every 3 months as a part of settlement is a part of wages and the periodicity of payment in this case is irrelevant.	*United Breweries Ltd.* v *ESIC* ,2003 (1) LLN 694 (Ker DB).
The question in this case raised is whether overtime wages, loading and unloading charges and canteen allowance can be treated as wages? Held, overtime wages would be wages to attract contribution thereon. But fixed amount paid to an employee when there is no canteen facility in the establishment is not an allowances but only a distribution of subsidy which will not attract contribution. As regards loading and unloading charges paid to casual employees from outside for work done inside the establishment has been held incidental to the main work and contribution is payable.	*ESIC Aluminium Industries Ltd.,* 2003 (1) LLN 189: 2003 (96) FLR 512 (Ker HC).
Conveyance allowance forms part and parcel of wages and the same cannot be excluded while calculating contribution	2002 LabIC 3138 (Kant) 2002 AIR Kant HCR 2515.

Not wages

Bonus by way of *ex-gratia* payment as a gesture of goodwill by branch factories of the company to their workmen.	*Regional Director ESIC* v *Bata Shoe Co.*, (1985) 4 SCC 460: 1986 SCC (L&S) 129 SCC
The *ex-gratia* payment in the form of coffee allowance and washing allowance, not being the payment under contract of employment, would not be wages to attract ESI contributions.	*Regional Director (Tamil Nadu), Employees' State*
Subsistence allowance paid during suspension.	*ESIC* v *Kirlosker Systems Ltd.* (1984) 2 LLN 780 (Kant) (DB) 1985 Lab IC 275 (Kant)
'Tea Allowance' and 'Milk Allowance'.	*ESIC* v *Gedore Tools India (P) Ltd.*, (1987) 1 LLN 653 (P&H): 1987 Lab IC 570 (P&H).
'Inam' ir incentive given to contractual labour by the principal employer.	*Eagle Flask Industries Ltd* v *ESIC*, (1997) 2 LLJ 1141 (1997): 1 LLN 599: 1997 Lab IC 655 (Bom)
Reward for good work paid for exceeding the production target is not wages.	*Malabar Fruits Co.* v *ESIC*,(1992) 2 LLJ 786: (1992) 1 LLN 198: (1992) 64 FLR 149 (Ker)
Stipend paid to apprentices and trainees has been held to be not falling within the definition of wages.	*ESIC* v *Andhra Prabha (P) Ltd.* (2000) 2 Lab LJ 709 (AP)

■ *Temporary Disablement [Section 21]*

It is a condition resulting from an employment injury which requires medical treatment and renders an employee, as a result of such injury, temporarily incapable of doing the work which he was doing prior to or at the time of injury.

■ *Permanent Partial Disablement* [**Section 15A**]

Disablement of a permanent nature, as reduces earning capacity of an employee	In every employment which he was capable of undertaking at the time of accident resulting in the disablement
Every injury specified in Part II of 2nd Schedule to the Act shall be deemed to result in permanent partial disablement.	

■ *Permanent Total Disablement* [**Section 15B**]

Disablement of a permanent nature, as incapacitates an employee	For all work which he was capable of performing at the time of the accident resulting in such disablement
Every injury specified in Part I of 2nd Schedule to the Act or from any combination of injuries specified in Part II, where aggregate % of loss of earning capacity amounts to 100% or more.	

Employee's State Insurance Corporation

The administration of the ESI Scheme under the Act is entrusted to an autonomous body called the ESI Corporation. The Union Minister for Labour is the Chairman and the Secretary to Government of India Ministry of Labour is the Vice-Chairman of this corporation. It consists of members representing Central and State Governments, employers and employees' organizations, medical profession and Parliament. There is a Standing Committee, constituted from the members of the Corporation, which acts as an executive body for the administration of the Scheme. The chief executive officer of the Corporation is the Director General who is assisted by the following four Principal Officers:

(*i*) Insurance Commissioner
(*ii*) Medical Commissioner
(*iii*) Financial Commissioner
(*iv*) Actuary

There is a Medical Benefit Council, which is headed by the Director General of Health Services, Government of India, which is assisted by the Medical Commissioner in all matters relating to medical relief. Medical Benefit Council advises the ESI Corporation on matters connected with the provision of medical benefit. Besides the Hqrs.Office in New Delhi, the ESI Corporation has for the day-to-day administration, 23 Regional Offices and 12 sub-Regional Offices at Vijayawada, Vadodara, Surat, Hubli, Pune, Nagpur, Coimbatore, Madurai, Tirunelveli, Noida, Varanasi and Barrackpore and 844 Local Offices and Cash offices all over the country for the administration of the Scheme. There are Inspection Officers throughout the country to inspect factories and for checking insurability of employees and correct payment of contributions.

■ *Establishment of ESI Corporation [Section 3]*

❑ *Central Government* by Notification establishes ESIC for the purpose of administering the ESI Scheme

❑ It is a body corporate with ⟵ Perpetual succession / Common seal, and / Can sue and be sued

Constitution of ESI Corporation [Section 4]

(*i*)	A chairman	To be <u>appointed</u> by the Central Government (nominated before 1989)
(*ii*)	A vice-chairman	
(*ii*)	Not more than 5 persons appointed by Central Government	
(*iii*)	One person to represent the Union Territories	
(*iv*)	10 persons representing employers	
(*v*)	10 persons representing employees	
(*vi*)	2 persons representing medical profession	
(*vii*)	3 Member of Parliament (2 from Lok Sabha, 1 from Rajya Sabha)	
(*viii*)	Director General of the ESIC – *ex officio*	
One person each, representing each of State in which this Act is in force		To be appointed by State Government

Term of Office of Members [Section 5]

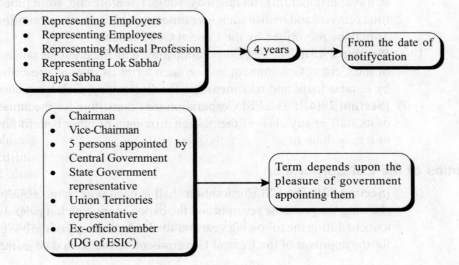

- Representing Employers
- Representing Employees
- Representing Medical Profession
- Representing Lok Sabha/ Rajya Sabha

→ 4 years → From the date of notifycation

- Chairman
- Vice-Chairman
- 5 persons appointed by Central Government
- State Government representative
- Union Territories representative
- Ex-officio member (DG of ESIC)

→ Term depends upon the pleasure of government appointing them

Powers of the ESI Corporation

(*i*) **[Section 17]:** The ESI Corporation may employ such other staff of officers and servants as may be necessary for the efficient transaction of its business provided that the sanction of the Central Government shall be obtained for the creation of any post the maximum monthly salary of which exceeds such salary as may be prescribed by the Central Government.

(*ii*) **[Section 19]:** The ESI Corporation may, in addition to the Scheme of benefits specified in this Act, promote measures for the improvement of the health and welfare of insured persons and for the rehabilitation and re-employment of insured persons who have been disabled or injured and may incur in respect of such measures expenditure from the funds of the Corporation within such limits as may be prescribed by the Central Government.

(*iii*) **[Section 25]:** The ESI Corporation may appoint Regional Boards, Local Committees and Regional and Local Medical Benefits Councils in such areas and in such manner, and delegate to them such powers and functions, as may be provided by the regulations.

(*iv*) **[Section 29(1)]:** The ESI Corporation may, subject to such conditions, as may be prescribed by the Central Government, acquire and hold property both movable and immovable, sell or otherwise transfer any movable or immovable property which may have become vested in or have been acquired by it and do all things necessary for the purposes for which the Corporation is established.

(*v*) **[Section 29(2)]:** The ESI Corporation may from time to time, invest any moneys which are not immediately required for expenses properly defrayable under this Act and may, subject as aforesaid, from time to time reinvest and realise such investments, subject to such conditions as may be prescribed by the Central Government.

(*vi*) **[Section 29(3)]:** The ESI Corporation may, with the previous sanction of the Central Government and on such terms as may be prescribed by it, raise loans and take measures for discharging such loans.

(*vii*) **[Section 29(4)]:** The ESI Corporation may constitute for the benefit of its staff or any class of them, such provident or other benefit fund as it may think fit.

Duties of the ESI Corporation

(*i*) **[Section 32]:** The ESI Corporation shall in each year frame a budget showing the probable receipts and the expenditure which it proposes to incur during the following year and shall submit a copy of the budget for the approval of the Central Government before such date as may be fixed by it in that behalf. The budget shall contain provisions adequate in the opinion of the Central Government for the discharge of the liabilities incurred by the Corporation and for the maintenance of a working balance.

(*ii*) **[Section 33]:** The ESI Corporation shall maintain correct account of its income and expenditure in such form and in such manner as may be prescribed by the Central Government.

(*iii*) **[Section 34]:** The accounts of the ESI Corporation shall be audited annually by the Comptroller and Auditor General of India and any expenditure incurred by him in connection with such audit shall be payable by the Corporation to the Comptroller and Auditor General of India.

(*iv*) **[Section 35]:** The ESI Corporation shall submit to the Central Government Annual Report of its work and activities.

(*v*) **[Section 36]:** The Annual Report, the audited accounts of the Corporation, together with the report of the Comptroller and Auditor General of India thereon and the comments of the Corporation on such report under Section 34 and the budget as finally adopted by the Corporation shall be placed before the Parliament.

(*vi*) **[Section 37]:** The Corporation shall, at intervals of five years, have a valuation of its assets and liabilities made by a valuer appointed with the approval of the Central Government.

Wings of ESI Corporation

■ *Standing Committee*

Constitution [*Section 8*]

➤ Standing Committee is constituted from amongst members of ESI Corporation.

➤ It acts as an Executive Body of ESI Corporation.

➤ It administers the affairs of ESI Corporation subject to general superintendence and control of ESIC.

Composition

(*i*) A chairman – appointed by Central Government

(*ii*) 3 members of ESI Corporation appointed by Central Government

(*iii*) 3 members of ESI Corporation representing such 3 State Governments as specified by Central Government

(*iv*) 8 members elected by ESI Corporation:
    — 3 members of ESIC representing employers
    — 3 members of ESIC representing employees

Appointed

Elected

— 1 member of ESIC representing Medical profession
— 1 member of ESIC elected by Parliament
(v)   The Director-General of ESIC

 Ex-Officio

Term of Office of Members [Section 9]

➢ Representing employers ➢ Representing employees ➢ Representing medical profession ➢ Representing Parliament ➢ Director General of ESIC	2 years of Notification

Chairman/representing Central Government/ representing State Government	Term depends upon the pleasure of Government

Powers and Functions of Standing Committee

The powers of the Standing Committee given in Section 18 are:

(a) Subject to the general superintendence and control of the ESI Corporation, the Standing Committee shall administer the affairs of the ESI Corporation and may exercise any of the powers and perform any of the functions of the Corporation.

(b) The Standing Committee shall submit for the consideration and decision of the ESI Corporation all such cases and maters as may be specified in the regulations made in this behalf.

(c) The Standing Committee may, in its discretion, submit any other case or matter for the decision of the Corporation.

■ Medical Benefit Council (MBC)

Constitution [Section 10]

Central Government is to constitute MBC	To advise ESIC and Standing Committee on matters relating to administration of medical benefits

Composition

Appointed by Central Government	(i) Chairman – Director General Health Services (ex-officio) (ii) A Dy. Director General Health Services (iii) Medical Commissioner of ESI Corp–(ex-officio) (iv) 3 Members representing employers (v) 3 Members representing employees (vi) 3 members (not less than one woman) representing medical profession
Appointed by State Government	One member each representing each of States in which the Act is in force

Term of Office

• Employers representative • Employees representative • Medical profession	4 years

• Director/Dy. Director General Health Services • State Government representative	Term depends upon the pleasure of the Government appointing them

Powers and Duties of Medical Benefit Council

Powers of the Medical Benefit Council as given in Section 22 are:

(*a*) To advise the ESI Corporation and the standing committee on matters relating to the administration of medical benefit, the certification for purposes of the grant of benefits and other connected matters;

(*b*) To have such powers and duties of investigation as may be prescribed in relation to complaints against medical practitioners in connection with medical treatment and attendance; and

(*c*) To perform such other duties in connection with medical treatment and attendance as may be specified in the regulations.

Additional Powers of MBC

The Employees State Insurance Rules, 1950 provides for the following additional powers and duties of MBC

1. To advice the ESI Corporation, in regard to the constitution, setting up duties and powers of the Regional and Local Medical Benefit Councils.

2. To make recommendations to the ESI Corporation in regard to:—

   (*i*) The scale and nature of medical benefit provided at hospitals, dispensaries, clinics etc. and the nature and the extent of medicines, staff and equipments which shall be maintained at such institutions.

   (*ii*) Medical certification including the procedures and the forms for such certification, statistical returns, registers and other medical records.

   (*iii*) Measures undertaken for the improvement of the health and welfare of insured persons and the rehabilitation and re-employment of insured persons, disabled or injured.

3. To advise the ESI Corporation on any matter relating to the professional conduct of any medical practitioner employed for the purpose of providing medical benefit under the Act.

Miscellaneous Provisions

Miscellaneous provisions related to Employee's State Insurance Corporation, Standing Committee and Medical Benefit Council are:

Eligibility for Re-nomination or Re-election

According to Section 6, an outgoing member of the ESI Corporation, the Standing Committee, or the Medical Benefit Council shall be eligible for reappointment or re-election as the case may be.

1. *Resignation of Membership*

As per Section 11, a member of the ESI Corporation, the Standing Committee or the Medical Benefit Council may resign his office by notice in writing to the Central Government and his seat shall fall vacant on the acceptance of the resignation by that Government.

2. *Cessation of Membership*

As per Section 12, a member of the ESI Corporation, the Standing Committee or the Medical benefit Council shall cease to be a member of that body if he fails to attend three consecutive meetings thereof. However, the ESI Corporation, the Standing Committee or the Medical Benefit Council, as the case may be, may subject to rules made by the Central Government in this behalf, restore him to membership.

Where in the opinion of the Central Government any person appointed or elected to represent employers, employees or the medical profession on the ESI Corporation, the Standing Committee or the Medical Benefit Council, as the case may be, has ceased to represent such employers, employees or medical profession, the Central Government may, by notification in the Official Gazette, declare that with effect from such date as may be specified therein, such person shall cease to be a member of the ESI Corporation, the Standing Committee or the Medical Benefit Council, as the case may be.

A Member of Parliament nominated as member or the ESI Corporation, shall cease to be member, when he ceases to be a Member of Parliament.

3. *Disqualification*

As per Section 13, a person shall be disqualified from becoming a member of the ESI Corporation, the Standing Committee or the Medical Benefit Council:—

(*a*) If he is declared to be of unsound mind by a competent Court; or

(*b*) If he is an un-discharged insolvent; or

(*c*) If he has directly or indirectly by himself or by his partner had interest in a subsisting contract with, or any work being done for the Corporation except as a medical practitioner or as a shareholder (not being a Director) of a Company; or

(*d*) If before or after the commencement of this Act, he has been convicted of an offence involving moral turpitude.

4. *Filling of Vacancies*

As per Section 14, the vacancies in the office of appointed or elected members of the ESI Corporation, the Standing Committee and the Medical Benefit Council shall be filled by appointment or election, as the case may be.

A member of the ESI Corporation, the Standing Committee or the Medical Benefit Council appointed or elected to fill a casual vacancy shall hold office only as long as the member in whose place he is appointed or elected, would have been entitled to hold office if the vacancy had not occurred.

5. *Fees and Allowances*

As per Section 15, members of the ESI Corporation, the Standing Committee and the Medical Benefit Council shall receive such fees and allowances as may from time to time be prescribed by the Central Government.

6. *Principal Officers/CEO*

As per Section 16, the Central Government may, in consultation with the ESI Corporation appoint a Director General who shall be the Chief Executive Officer of the ESI Corporation and also appoint a Financial Commissioner.

Terms of Office of Principal Officers: The Director General or the Financial Commissioner shall hold office for such period, not exceeding five years, as may be specified in the order appointing him. An outgoing Director General or Financial Commissioner shall be eligible for re-appointment if he is otherwise qualified.

Salary and Allowances: The Director General or the Financial Commissioner shall receive such salary and allowances as may be prescribed by the central Government.

Disqualifications: A person shall be disqualified from being appointed as or for being the Director General or the Financial Commissioner if he is subject to any of the disqualifications specified in Section 13.

Removal: The Central Government may at any time remove from the office the Director General or the Financial Commissioner and shall do so if such removal is recommended by a resolution of the ESI Corporation passed at a special meeting called for the purpose and supported by the votes of not less than two-thirds of the total strength of the corporation.

Functions and Duties: As per Section 16 (3), the Director General and the Financial Commissioner shall be whole-time officer of the ESI Corporation and shall not undertake any work unconnected with their office without the sanction of the Central Government and of the Corporation.

As per Section 23, the Director General and the Finance Commissioner shall exercise such powers and discharge such duties as may be prescribed. They shall also perform such other function as may be specified in the regulations.

7. *Recruitment of Staff* [*Section* 17]

The ESI Corporation may employ such other staff of officers and servants as may be necessary for the efficient transaction of its business, provided that the sanction of the Central Government shall be obtained for the creation of any post the maximum monthly salary of which exceeds such salary as may be prescribed by the Central Government. Their recruitment provisions are as follows:

(a) As per Section 17 (2), the method of recruitment, salary and allowances, discipline and other conditions of service of the members of the staff of the of the ESI Corporation shall be such as may be specified in the Regulations made by the ESI Corporation in accordance with the rules and orders applicable to the officers and employees of the Central Government drawing corresponding scales of pay.

Where the ESI Corporation is of the opinion that it is necessary to make a departure from the said rules or orders in respect of any of the matters aforesaid, it shall obtain the prior approval of the Central Government.

(b) In determining the corresponding scales of pay of the members of the above staff, the ESI Corporation shall have regard to the educational qualifications, mode of recruitment, duties and responsibilities of such officers and employees under the Central Government and in case of any doubt, the Corporation shall refer the matter to the Central Government whose decision thereon shall be final.

(c) Every appointment to posts, other than medical post, corresponding to Group A and Group B post under the Central Government shall be made in consultation with the Union Public Service Commission.

However, the above shall not apply to an officiating or temporary appointment for a period not exceeding one year. Further, any such officiating or temporary appointment shall not confer any claim for regular appointment and services rendered in that capacity shall not count towards seniority or minimum qualifying service specified in the regulation for promotion to next higher grade.

(d) If any question arises whether a post corresponds to Group A and Group B post under the Central Government, the question shall be referred to that Government whose decision thereon shall be final.

8. *Meetings of ESI Corporation, Standing Committee and Medical Benefit Council* [*Section 20*]

The ESI Corporation, the Standing Committees and Medical Benefit Council shall meet at such time and places and shall observe such rules or procedure in regard to transaction of business at their meetings as may be specified in the regulations made in this behalf.

In exercise of the powers conferred by Section 95 of ESI Act, 1948, the Central Government has made rules under Employees State Insurance (Central) Rules, 1950 on the convening, conduct and decision making, in the meetings of ESI Corporation, Standing Committee and Medical Benefit Council. The rules are:

Members Register

The ESI Corporation shall maintain a Roll of members separately for the ESI Corporation, Standing Committee and the Medical Benefit Council.

Minimum Number of Meetings

1. The ESI Corporation and the Medical benefit Council shall meet at least twice each year.
2. The Standing Committee shall meet at-least four times each year.
3. On a requisition of not less than one half members, the chairman shall within 15 days of the receipt of requisition, call a meeting thereof.

Notice of Meetings and List of Business

Not less than 21 days notice and agenda shall be given to every member

Chairman of the Meeting

Chairman or in his absence Vice-Chairman of the ESI Corporation, the Standing Committee or the Medical Benefit Council, as the case may be, shall preside at the meetings. In the event of Chairman's absence, the members present may elect any of them to preside.

Quorum

Quorum for the meetings shall be 15 members in the case of ESI Corporation, 5 members in the case Standing Committee and 7 members in the case of Medical Benefit Council.

Minutes

1. Minutes of a meeting of ESI Corporation, Standing Committee and the Medical Benefit Council shall be kept in separate registers.
2. A copy of the confirmed minutes shall be forwarded to the Central Government within 15 days of confirmation of minutes.

Supersession of ESIC and Standing Committee [Section 21]

- ❑ Central Government may supersede by notification if—
  - ➢ Default in performing duties imposed on it, or
  - ➢ Abuses its powers
- ❑ After giving reasonable opportunity to ESIC/Standing Committee.
- ❑ After supersession of ESIC, all members shall be deemed to have vacated office.

- ❏ After supersession of Standing Committee, new Standing Committee be immediately constituted as per Section 8.
- ❏ When ESIC is superseded?
  - — Central Government may immediately appoint new members of ESIC and Standing Committee
  - — Central Government may appoint some agency to perform the functioning of ESIC
  - — Central Government to send full report to be laid before Parliament not later than 3 months from the supersession.

Acts of ESIC/Standing Committee/MBC [Section 24]

The acts of ESIC, Standing Committee or MBC are not invalid by reason of defect in their constitution

Appointment of Regional Boards, Local Committees, Regional and Local Medical Councils [Section 25]

ESIC may appoint in such areas and in such manner and delegate those such powers as may be provided by regulations.

Contributions

All Employees to be Insured [Section 38]

All employees in factories or establishments to which this Act applies shall be insured in the manner provided by the Act.

Judicial Interpretations/Case Example	
This appeal is filed by the Employees State Insurance Corporation, which insisted that the respondent should insure its employees under the E.S.I. Act and issued notice demanding contribution. The respondent-applicant approached the E.I. Court contending that it is not a covered establishment and only 8 persons are employed in the establishment. Two persons supplying parts of machinery manufactured by company, are not employed for wages, and are not working in the factory. They are free to make articles for others and thus are not coverable under the Act. The finding of Employees' Insurance Court is confirmed. When it was proved that the employer is employing only 8 persons, it is for the ESI Corporation to prove that two persons as alleged to be employees of the company even though they are not working in the premises of the establishment as such no interference by the High Court is called for in the order of Employees' Insurance Court holding that the establishment was not to be covered by ESI Act. Burden of proof to prove strength of employees lies upon the E.S.I. Corporation when employer contends that only 8 persons were employed.	*Employees' State Insurance Corporation* v *Baby Francis,* 2008 LLR 462 (Kerela High Court).

Rate of Contributions [Section 39]

The contribution payable under this Act, in respect of an employee shall comprise of employer's contribution and employees contribution. The contribution shall be paid to ESI Corporation at the following rates:

> Rates prescribed by the Central Government w.e.f. 1.10.2005 are: ⟶ Employer's contribution – 4.75% of employee's wages
> Employee's contribution – 1.75% of employee's wages

- ❑ Contributions payable in respect of each wage period shall ordinarily fall due on the last day of the wage period and where the employee is employed for part of wage period, the contributions shall fall due on days specified in the regulations.
- ❑ The principal employer is liable to pay simple interest @ 12% p. a. or higher rate specified in regulations if the payable contribution is not paid on the date provided the higher shall not exceed the lending rate of interest charged by the scheduled bank.
- ❑ Any interest recoverable may be recovered as an arrear of land revenue.

Judicial Interpretations/Case Example	
Held, the provisions of ESI Act cannot be made applicable retrospectively and the ESI Corporation cannot demand contribution for period prior to date of application of Act. Also, the ESI Corporation is not entitled to scrutinize record of establishment or to call for record from establishment for previous years of notification.	*Employees' State Insurance Corporation* v *Park Fishnet Pvt. Ltd.,* 2009 LLR 221 (Gujarat High Court).
Respondent is a factory covered under the ESI Act. The wage ceiling for coverage under the Employees' State Insurance Act was extended from Rs. 3000 to Rs. 6500 with effect from January 1, 1997. Unions challenged the above notification before this Court and this Court granted a stay. In view of the above stay order, respondent was not able to collect the contribution from the employees who were drawing salary between Rs. 3000 and Rs. 6500, but, later, stay was vacated and coverage was accepted by the Court. When the stay was vacated, the entire employees' contribution and employers' contribution were paid by the respondent. Then, appellant ESI Corporation demanded interest for the delayed payment. Contention of the respondent was that they were willing to pay the amount even at the first instance, but, they were unable to pay the amount because of the stay and, therefore, they are unable to pay the interest. It is not the respondent employer who obtained the stay, but, employees got the stay. After vacation of the stay, Corporation got the entire contribution without paying any benefit, that is, employers' and employees' contribution.	*E.S.I. Corporation* v *Appollo Tyres Ltd.* ,2008 LLR 660 (Kerala HC).

Contd..

Therefore, actually, it is the Corporation who gained because of the stay. In any event, after paying all the benefits and paying retrospective contribution, whether they are liable to pay interest also for no fault on their part is the question. On identical facts, this Court in *Regional Director, ESI Corporation* v *Cannanore Spinning and Weaving Mills,* 2001-II LLJ 1973 (Kerala) held that interest is not liable. On the facts of this case, the Court see no ground to interfere in the order of the E.I. Court.	
Held, relationship of employer and employee for coverage of employees under ESI Act arises when a new factory or an establishment commences the work and not prior to that. Hence the demand for contributions by ESI Authorities on the construction and operational work prior to commencement of business was not justified since the contracts were awarded to the contractors to complete the work of construction.	*E.S.I.C.* v *Hotel Corporation of Delhi,* 2008 LLR 640 (Delhi HC).
Held once the contribution is directed to be payable from a particular date and if there is delay, the interest is payable from that date as it is a statutory obligation.	*E.S.I. Corporation* v *Bharat Hotel,* (Kerala HC, 2008 LLR 1001).
The employer under Section 39 is statutorily bound to contribute, whether he has sufficient resources or not	*S. India Viscoss Coop Stores Ltd* v *Reg. Dir ESIC,* 1986 (2) LLJ 149: (1986) 2 LLN 598 (Mad).
Even if the employees had not availed the benefit of insurance, contributions for the past period are recoverable	*ESIC* v *Hotel Kalpaka International,* (1993) 2 SCC 9: 1993 SCC (L&S) 305: 1993 LLR 177 (SC).

Manner and Time Period for Making Payment of Contribution

❏ The total amount of contribution (both employer and employee share) is to be deposited in cash or by cheque or DD with the designated branches of State Bank of India or other schedule bank authorised by the ESIC on or before 21st of the month following the calendar month in which the wages fall due. If the day is a holiday, the contribution may be deposited on the following day. The contribution is deposited through a challan in quadruplicate.

Contribution Period and Benefit Period

In a year, there are two contribution periods of six months each. The corresponding benefit period of six months is as follows:

Contribution Period	Corresponding Benefit Period
1. 1st April to 30th September	1st January of the year following 30th June
2. 1st October to 31st March of the year	Following 1st July to 31st December of the calendar year

Damages for Late Payment of Contributions or Other Amount Due but not Paid in Time

The ESIC is empowered to recover damages from an employer as per the Regulation 31C of ESI (General) Regulations, 1950 and Section 85B (1) of ESI Act, which are as follows:

Period of delay	Rate of Damages on Amount Due
(*i*) Less than 2 months	5% p. a.
(*ii*) 2 months and above but less than 4 months	10% p. a.
(*iii*) 4 months and above but less than 6 months	15% p. a.
(*iv*) 6 months and above	25% p. a.

Provided that the ESIC in relation to any factory or establishment which is declared sick and in respect of which a rehabilitation scheme has been sanctioned by BIFR may completely wave up to 50% or wave either totally or partly the damages levied or leviable.

Judicial Interpretations/Case Example

The employer has contended before the Insurance court that he could not pay the insurance contribution in time, due to financial stringency and loss of business. Held, financial stringency and loss of business cannot be ground for non payment of contribution. When an employer who received contributions from the employees and had used it for his own purposes, he cannot escape from the payment of damages claimed by the corporation. Similar position was taken by the Supreme Court in the case of *Hindustan Times Ltd* v *Union of India,* 1998 SCC (L&S) 481: 1998 Lab IC 483, wherein the court held that power – cut, financial problems, disputes between partners were not relevant explanations and the same cannot be accepted for interfering with the imposition of damages by the corporation.

Regional Director, ESIC Thrissur v *MD, Transmatic SystemLtd, Trivandrum,*2006 Lab IC 1043 (Ker HC).

Principal Employer to Pay Contribution in the First Instance [Section 40]

❑ The principal employer shall pay in respect of each employee whether directly employed by him or through immediate employer both the employer's and the employee's contribution.

- ❑ However, he can recover the employee's contribution by deductions from wages.
- ❑ If principal employer defaults in payment on due date he shall be liable to pay simple interest @ 12% p.a.

Judicial Interpretations/Case Example	
Any interest recoverable under this clause may be recovered as an arrear of land revenue.	*Regional Director ESIC* v *Cannanore Spinning and Weaving Mills,* 2001 2 Lab LJ 1573 (Ker).
The principal employer shall bear the expenses of remitting the contributions to the ESIC.	*ESIC* v *Dharwal Co-op. Milk Producers Societies Union Ltd.,* (2001) 1 Lab LJ 355.

Recovery of Contribution from Immediate Employer [Section 41]

The principal employer who has paid contribution in respect of an employee employed by or through an immediate employer, shall be entitled to recover the amount of contribution so paid from the immediate employer, either by deduction from any amount payable to him (immediate employer) by the principal employer under any contract or as a debt payable by the immediate employer.

Judicial Interpretations/Case Example	
The employer company cannot escape the liability by taking the plea that it has been sick. Payment of contribution under Sections 39 to 41, is the responsibility of the principal employer after it becomes due.	*ESIC* v *APS Star Industries CLR,* 122 (2003) (3) LLN 534 (Karn HC).

General Provisions as to Payment of Contributions [Section 42]

No employee's contribution shall be payable by or on behalf of an employee whose average daily wages are below such wages as may be prescribed by the central government.

Method of Payment of Contribution [Section 43]

ESI Corporation may make regulations in this connection to provide for	(*i*)	The manner and time of payment of contribution
	(*ii*)	Payment of contributions by means of adhesive or other stamps affixed to
	(*iii*)	The entry in books or records of particulars of contributions paid

Employers to Furnish Returns and Maintain Registers in Certain Cases [Section 44]

Every principal and immediate employer shall submit to the ESI Corporation such returns in such form and containing such particulars relating to persons employed as may be specified in the regulations made in this behalf.

Every principal and immediate employer shall maintain such registers or records in respect of his factory or establishment as may be required by regulations made in this behalf.

Judicial Interpretations/Case Example	
There is no definite statutory law or rule regarding the preservation of account books and other documents in the factory from its inception.	*ESIC* v *K.L. Malhotra* ,(1962) 4 FLR 1870: (1962) 2 LLJ 535 (Cal).
If any register is maintained by the employer in which the additional parti-culars required are also shown, it will be deemed to be a sufficient compliance.	ESIC (Gen) Regulations R. 32 (*i*).
Non-production of documents demanded by the Inspector of ESI Corporation for scrutiny is not a continuing offence.	*ESIC* v *Krishna Das*, (1992) 81 FJR 581 (Kant).

Appointment of Inspectors and Their Functions [Section 45]

❑ The ESI Corporation may appoint such persons as inspectors, as it thinks fit, within such local limits as it may assign to them.

Functions and Duties of the Inspectors

(*a*) May require any principal/immediate employer to furnish to him such information as is considered necessary, or

(*b*) May enter any office, factory, establishment or other premises of the principal or immediate employer and ask them to produce such accounts, books and other documents or information, as he may consider necessary, or

(*c*) May examine the principal or immediate employer or his agent or servant or any other person found in the factory/office/establishment/ premises, or

(*d*) Make copies of or take extracts from any register, book or other document maintained in such factory, establishment, office or premises, or

(*e*) May exercise such other powers as may be prescribed.

Determination of Contribution by the ESIC in Certain Cases [Section 45A]

The ESI Corporation may on the basis of information available to it, determine the amount of contribution payable where	No returns, registers, books, records are submitted or maintained, or Any inspector/officer of ESIC is prevented in any manner in exercising his functions

Judicial Interpretations/Case Example

The respondent-factory has been engaged in the business of manufacturing garments for export and the factory is covered under the ESI Act. The respondent has been complying with the provisions of the Act. The appellant issued C18 notice dated March 7, 1989, for Rs. 20,909.35 towards contribution for the period from November, 1987 to August, 1988 relating to salaries and wages account, ironing charges, labour charges and conveyance account. Due to unavoidable circumstances, the respondent had not sent reply to the said notice. Therefore the appellant passed an order under Section 45A of the Act against the respondent for Rs. 20,909.35 towards contribution for the period November, 1987 to August, 1988 with interest and also directed the respondent to pay the amount within 15 days. The appellant also issued another CIS notice on August 25, 1988 for Rs. 24,137.10 in respect of seven items, *viz.* (*i*) Machinery maintenance account, (*ii*) Freight and cooly account, (*iii*) Salary, wages, (*iv*) Ironing charges, (*v*) Labour charges, and (*vi*) Conveyance account. The Employees' Insurance Court held that respondent is liable to pay contributions in respect of salaries and wages paid to temporary packers and machinery maintenance account but not liable to pay in respect of freight, cooly, ironing labour charges and conveyance account. Such factual finding given by Employees' Insurance Court is based on valid materials and evidence. No error is committed in the order of the Employees' Insurance Court so as to warrant interference by High Court under Article 226 of Constitution of India. The questions as challenged by the ESIC have been decided in favour of respondent (employer).	*Regional Director, Employees' State Insurance Corporation* v *Madhavi Enterprises,* Madras 2009 LLR 17, (Madras High Court).
The purpose of the provisions of Section 45A (1) is to clothe the ESI Corporation with the authority to determine on a best judgment or ad hoc basis the contribution to be paid by the principal employer or immediate employer in case where returns, particulars, registers or records are not made available to the ESI Corporation or access to them is obstructed by the principal employer or the immediate employer.	*Hindustan Insecticides Ltd* v *T.M. Jaleel,* (1985) 1 LLJ 176 (Ker).

Contd..

An order made by the ESIC under Section 45A, is a sufficient proof of the claim of the Corporation under Section 75 or for recovery of the amount determined by such order as an arrear of land revenue under Section 45B or the recovery under Sections 45C to 45-I.	*Dream Bar and Restaurant* v *Deputy Regional Director, ESIC,* (2001) 2 Lab LJ 1461 (Kant).
No such order shall be passed by the ESIC unless the principal or immediate employer or person incharge, has been given a reasonable opportunity of being heard.	*ESIC* v *Trichy Distt. Coop. Milk Products Union Ltd.,* (1996) 72 FLR 449 (Mad).
Section 45A does not confer any arbitrary power on the ESI Corporation.	*BMK Industries* v *ESIC,* 39 FLR 258: 1979 Lab IC 942.
An assessment made under Section 45A is within the scope of judicial review by the Insurance Court.	*Prajatantra Prachar Samiti* v *Regional Director ESIC,* (1986) 62 Cut LT 434.

Recovery of Contribution [Section 45B]

❑   Any contribution payable under this Act may be recovered as an arrear of land revenue

Judicial Interpretations/Case Example	
ESIC can initiate recovery proceedings either under the Central Act or under the State Act.	*ESIC* v *Overseas Metal Industries,* 1994 SCC (L&S) 1129: 1994 Suppl (2) SCC 510.
Section 45B is purely procedural in nature and can have retrospective effect.	*ESIC* v *Dwarka Nath Bhargava,* (1997) 7 SCC 131: 1997 SCC (L&S) 1680.
Proceedings for recovery of employer's contribution due from a company can be taken against the company alone and not against the directors of the company personally.	*Mansingh L. Bhakta* v *State of Maharashtra,* (1991) 63 FLR 740: (1991) Lab IC 1361 (Bom).
A final assessment of contribution made under Section 75 (2) (*a*) cannot be executed under Section 45B.	*R. S. Ganesh Das Dhomi Mal* v *ESIC,* (1988) 56 FLR 111 (Del).
While making recovery of dues, the ESI authorities are under obligation to serve a notice before proceeding with recovery.	*Parmeshwar Singh* v *State of Jharkhand,* 2004 LLR 456 (Jhar HC).

Contd..

Amended provisions for recovery of ESI contributions will have retrospective effect.	*Vishaka and others* v *State of Rajasthan,* 1997 LLR 991 (SC).
On transfer of establishment the transferee will not be liable for arrears of ESI's contributions.	*ESIC* v *Balaraman,* 2001 LLR 249 (Ker HC).
Limitation Act will not be applicable for recovery of ESI contribution.	*Jayant Vitamins Ltd. Ratlam* v *ESIC,* 2001 LLR 271 (MP HC).

Benefits

Following benefits under Section 46 are provided under the ESI Act:

❑ The ESI Corporation may, at the request of appropriate government, and subject to such conditions as may be laid down in the regulations, extend the medical benefits to the family of an insured person.

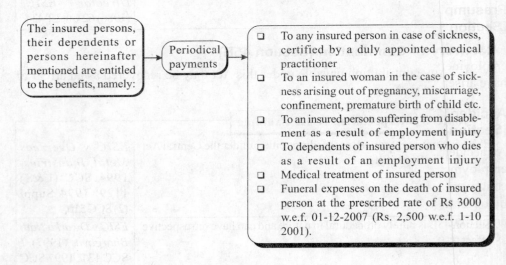

The insured persons, their dependents or persons hereinafter mentioned are entitled to the benefits, namely: → Periodical payments →

❑ To any insured person in case of sickness, certified by a duly appointed medical practitioner

❑ To an insured woman in the case of sickness arising out of pregnancy, miscarriage, confinement, premature birth of child etc.

❑ To an insured person suffering from disablement as a result of employment injury

❑ To dependents of insured person who dies as a result of an employment injury

❑ Medical treatment of insured person

❑ Funeral expenses on the death of insured person at the prescribed rate of Rs 3000 w.e.f. 01-12-2007 (Rs. 2,500 w.e.f. 1-10 2001).

Sickness Benefit [Section 49]

The qualification of a person to claim sickness benefit, the conditions subject to which such benefit may be given, the rates and period thereof shall be such as may be prescribed by the Central Government.(Daily rate of sickness benefit has been enhanced from about 50% of average daily wage to about 60% of average daily wage w.e.f 01-12-2007)

Maternity Benefit [Section 50]

The qualification of an insured woman to claim maternity benefit, the conditions subject to which such benefit may be given, the rates and period thereof shall be such as may be prescribed by the Central Government.

Disablement Benefit [Section 51]

Subject to the provisions of this Act,—

(a) A person, who sustains temporary disablement for not less than three days (excluding the day of accident) shall be entitled to periodical payment at such rates and for such period and subject to such conditions as may be prescribed by the Central Government (the daily rate of disablement and dependant benefit was enhanced from about 70% to about 75% of wage w.e.f 1-12-2007).

(b) A person, who sustains permanent disablement, whether total or partial, shall be entitled to periodical payment at such rates and for such period and subject to such conditions as may be prescribed by the Central Government. (Basic rate of permanent disablement benefit and dependant benefit have been enhanced ranging from 1% to 46% in February, 2008).

Presumption as to Accident arising in Course of Employment [Section 51A]

For the purposes of this Act, an accident arising in the course of an insured person's employment shall be presumed, in the absence of evidence to the contrary, also to have arisen out of that employment.

Accidents Happening while Acting in Breach of Regulations, etc. [Section 51B]

An accident shall be deemed to arise out of and in the course of an insured person's employment notwithstanding that he is at the time of the accident acting in contravention of the provisions of any law applicable to him, or of any orders given by or on behalf of his employer or that he is acting without instructions from his employer, if—

(a) The accident would have been deemed so to have arisen had the act not been done in contravention as aforesaid or on without instructions from his employer, as the case may be; and

(b) The act is done for the purpose of and in connection with the employer's trade or business.

Accidents Happening while Traveling in Employer's Transport [Section 51C]

An accident happening while an insured person is, with the express or implied permission of his employer, traveling as a passenger by any vehicle to or from his place of work shall, notwithstanding that he is under no obligation to his employer to travel by that vehicle, be deemed to arise out of an in the course of his employment, if—

(*a*) The accident would have been deemed so to have arisen had he been under such obligation; and

(*b*) At the time of the accident, the vehicle—

    (*i*) Is being operated by or on behalf of his employer or some other person by whom it is provided in pursuance of arrangements made with his employer, and

    (*ii*) Is not being operated in the ordinary course of public transport service. In this section "vehicle" includes vessel and an aircraft.

Accidents Happening while Meeting Emergency [Section 51D]

An accident happening to an insured person in or about any premises at which he is for the time being employed for the purpose of his employer's trade or business shall be deemed to arise out of and in the course of his employment, if it happens while he is taking steps, on an actual or supposed emergency at those premises, to rescue, succor or protect persons who are, or are thought to be or possibly to be, injured or imperiled, or to avert or minimize serious damage to property.

Dependent's Benefit [Section 52]

If an insured person dies as a result of an employment injury sustained as an employee under this Act (whether or not he was in receipt of any periodical payment for temporary disablement in respect of the injury) dependents' benefit shall be payable at such rates and for such period and subject to such conditions as may be prescribed by the Central Government to this dependents specified in sub-clause (*i*), sub-clause (*ia*) and sub-clause (*ii*) of clause (6A) of Section 2.

In case the insured person dies without leaving behind him the dependents as aforesaid, the dependents' benefit shall be paid to the other dependents of the deceased at such rates and for such period and subject to such conditions as may be prescribed by the Central Government.

Occupational Disease [Section 52A]

(*a*) If an employee employed in any employment specified in Part A or Part B or Part C of the 3rd Schedule contracts any disease therein as an occupational disease peculiar to that employment, the contracting of the disease shall be deemed to be "an employment injury" arising out of and in the course of employment.

(*b*) ESI Corporation after giving, by notification, not less than 3 months notice, may add any description of employment to the employment specified in the 3rd Schedule and shall specify in the case of employment so added, the disease which shall be deemed for the purpose of this section to be occupational diseases peculiar to those employment respectively.

Judicial Interpretations/Case Example	
The loss of required vision to act as a driver is not an occupational disease nor is it covered by any other provisions of the Act.	*Anand Bihari* v *Rajasthan SRTC,* (1991) 1 SCC 731: 1991 SCC (L&S) 393.

Bar Against Receiving Compensation or Damages under any other Law [Section 53]

Insured person or his dependents shall not be entitled to receive any compensation or damages under the Workmen's Compensation Act, 1923 or any other law for the time being in force or otherwise, in respect of an employment injury sustained by the insured person as an employee under this Act.

Judicial Interpretations/Case Example	
An employee receiving compensation under ESI Act will not be entitled to claim damages under any other law or torts.	*Western India Plywood Ltd.* v *P.A. Shokan,* (1997) 7 SCC 638: 1998 SCC (L&S) 376.
For the application of Section 53, two conditions are necessary *viz.,* (*i*) that the person must have sustained employment injury and (*ii*) that he must have been insured under the ESI Act.	*Dy. GM Karnataka State Road Transport Corporation* v *Gopal Mudaliar,* (1983) 1 LLJ 340 (Kar).
Having exercised their option by filing application under ESI Act, dependents were not entitled to file application under Motor Vehicles Act because of the bar created by Section 53 of ESI Act.	*United India Insurance Co. Ltd* v *Saraswathi,* (1997) 2 Cur LR 684: (1997) 77 FLR 273 (Mad).
Workman covered under ESI Act cannot claim compensation under the Workmen's Compensation Act, 1923.	*A. Trehan* v *Associated Electrical Agencies,* (1996) 4 SCC 255: 1996 SCC (L&S) 928.
Where the employer defaulted in making his contributions under the ESI Act in respect of his employees, including the deceased employee, it was held that an award of compensation under the Workmen's Compensation Act was not barred.	*Management of Bharanji Mills* v *Deputy Commissioner of Labour,* (2000) 2 Lab LJ 568 (Mad).

Determination of Question of Disablement [Section 54]

Any question—

(*a*) Whether the relevant accident has resulted in permanent disablement; or

(*b*) Whether the extent of loss of earning capacity can be assessed provisionally or finally; or (*c*) Whether the assessment of the proportion of the loss of earning capacity is provisional or final; or

(*d*) In the case of provisional assessment, as to the period for which such assessment shall hold good,

shall be determined by a medical board constituted in accordance with the provisions of the regulations and any such question shall hereafter be referred to as the "disablement question".

References to Medical Boards and appeals to Medical Appeal Tribunals and Employees' Insurance Courts [Section 54A]

The case of any insured person for permanent disablement benefit shall be referred by the Corporation to a Medical Board for determination of the disablement question and if, on that or any subsequent reference, the extent of loss of earning capacity of the insured person is provisionally assessed, it shall again be so referred to the Medical Board not later than the end of the period taken into account by the provisional assessment.

If the insured person or the Corporation is not satisfied with the decision of the medical board, the insured person or the Corporation may appeal in the prescribed manner and within the prescribed time to—

(*i*) The medical appeal tribunal constituted in accordance with the provisions of the regulations with a further right of appeal in the prescribed manner and within the prescribed time to the Employees' Insurance Court, or

(*ii*) The Employees' Insurance Court directly:

Provided that no appeal by an insured person shall lie under this sub-section if such person has applied for commutation of disablement benefit on the basis of the decision of the medical board and received the commuted value of such benefit. No appeal by the Corporation shall lie under this sub-section if the Corporation paid the commuted value of the disablement benefit on the basis of the decision of the medical board.

Review of Decisions by Medical Board or Medical Appeal Tribunal [Section 55]

Any decision under this Act of a medical board or a medical appeal tribunal may be reviewed at any time by the medical board or the medical appeal tribunal, as the case may be, if it is satisfied by fresh evidence that the decision was given in consequence of the non-disclosure or misrepresentation by the employee or any other person of a material fact (whether the non-disclosure or misrepresentation was or was not fraudulent).

Any assessment of the extent of the disablement resulting from the relevant employment injury may also be reviewed by a medical board, if it is satisfied that since the making of the assessment there has been a substantial and unforeseen aggravation of the results of the relevant injury:

Provided that an assessment shall not be reviewed under this sub-section unless the medical board is of opinion that having regard to the period taken into account by the assessment and the probable duration of the aggravation aforesaid, substantial injustice will be done by not reviewing it.

Except with the leave of a medical appeal tribunal, an assessment shall not be reviewed under sub-section (2) on any application made less than five years, or in the case of a provisional assessment, six months, from the date thereof and on such a review the period to be taken into account by any revised assessment shall not include any period before the date of the application.

Subject to the foregoing provisions of this section, a medical board may deal with a case of review in any manner in which it could deal with it on an original reference to it, and in particular may make a provisional assessment notwithstanding that the assessment under review was final; and the provisions of Section 54A shall apply to an application for review under this section and to a decision of a medical board in connection with such application as they apply to a case for disablement benefit under that section and to a decision of the medical board in connection with such case.

Review of Dependents' Benefit [Section 55A]

Any decision awarding dependents' benefit under this Act may be reviewed at any time by the Corporation if it is satisfied by fresh evidence that the decision was given in consequence of non-disclosure or misrepresentation by the claimant or any other person of a material fact (whether the non-disclosures or misrepresentation was or was not fraudulent) or that the decision is no longer in accordance with this Act due to any birth or death or due to the marriage, re-marriage or cesser of infirmity of, or attainment of the age of eighteen years by, a claimant.

Subject to the provisions of this Act, the Corporation may on such review as aforesaid, direct that the dependents' benefit be continued, increased, reduced or discontinued.

Medical Benefit [Section 56]

An insured person or (where such medical benefit is extended to his family) a member of his family whose condition requires medical treatment and attendance shall be entitled to receive medical benefit.

Such medical benefit may be given either in the form of out patient treatment and attendance in a hospital or dispensary, clinic or other institution or by visits to the home of the insured person or treatment as in-patient in a hospital or other institution.

A person shall be entitled to medical benefit during any period for which contributions are payable in respect of him or in which he is qualified to claim sickness benefit maternity benefit or is in receipt of such disablement benefit as does not disentitle him to medical benefit under the regulations:

Provided that a person in respect of whom contribution ceases to be payable under this Act may be allowed medical benefit for such period and of such nature as may be provided under the regulations. An insured person who ceases to be in insurable employment on account of permanent disablement shall continue, subject to payment of contribution and such other conditions as may be prescribed by the Central Government, to receive medical benefit till the date on which he would have vacated the employment on attaining the age of superannuation had he not sustained such permanent disablement. An insured person, who has attained the age of superannuation, and his spouse shall be eligible to receive medical benefit subject to payment of contribution and such other conditions as may be prescribed by the Central Government.

In this section, "superannuation", in relation to an insured person, means the attainment by that person of such age as is fixed in the contract or conditions of service as the age on the attainment of which he shall vacate the insurable employment or the age of sixty years where no such age is fixed and the person is no more in the insurable employment.

Scale of Medical Benefit [Section 57]

An insured person and (where such medical benefit is extended to his family) his family shall be entitled to receive medical benefit only of such kind and on such scale as may be provided by the State Government or by the Corporation, and an insured person or, where such medical benefit is extended to his family, his family shall not have a right to claim any medical treatment except such as is provided by the dispensary, hospital, clinic or other institution to which he or his family is allotted, or as may be provided by the regulations.

Nothing in this Act shall entitle an insured person and (where such medical benefit is extended to his family) his family to claim reimbursement from the Corporation of any expenses incurred in respect of any medical treatment, except as may be provided by the regulations.

Provisions of Medical Treatment by State Government [Section 58]

The State Government shall provide for insured persons and (where such benefit is extended to their families) their families in the State reasonable medical, surgical and obstetric treatment. The State Government may, with the approval of the Corporation, arrange for medical treatment at clinics of medical practitioners on such scale and subject to such terms and conditions as may be agreed upon.

Where the incidence of sickness benefit payment to insured persons in any State is found to exceed the all-India average, the amount of such excess shall be shared between the corporation and the State Government in such proportion as may be fixed by agreement between them. The Corporation may in any case waive the recovery of the whole or any part of the share which is to be borne by the State Government.

The corporation may enter into an agreement with a State Government in regard to the nature and scale of the medical treatment that should be provided to insured persons and (where such medical benefit is extended to the families) their families (including provisions of buildings, equipment, medicines and staff) and for the sharing of the cost thereof and of any excess in the incidence of sickness benefit to insured persons between the Corporation and the State Government.

In default of agreement between the Corporation and any State Government as aforesaid the nature and extent of the medical treatment to be provided by the State Government and the proportion in which the cost thereof and of the excess in the incidence of sickness benefit shall be shared between the Corporation and that Government, shall be determined by an arbitrator (who shall be or shall have been a Judge of the High Court of a State) appointed by the Chief Justice of India and the award of that arbitrator shall be binding on the Corporation and the State Government.

Establishment and Maintenance of Hospitals, etc. by Corporation [Section 59]

The Corporation may, with the approval of the State Government establish and maintain in a State such hospitals, dispensaries and other medical and surgical services as it may think fit for the benefit of insured persons and (where such medical benefit is extended to their families) their families.

The Corporation may enter into agreement with any local authority, private body of individual in regard to the provisions of medical treatment and attendance for insured persons and (where such medical benefit extended to their families) their families, in any area and sharing the cost thereof.

Provision of Medical Benefit by the Corporation in lieu of State Government [Section 59A]

Notwithstanding anything contained in any other provisions of this Act, the Corporation may, in consultation with the State Government, undertake the responsibility for providing medical benefit to insured persons and where such medical benefit is extended to their families, to the families of such insured persons in the State subject to the condition that the State Government shall share the cost of such medical benefit in such proportion as may be agreed upon between the State Government and the Corporation.

In the event of the Corporation exercising its power under sub-section (1), the provisions relating to medical benefit under this Act shall apply, so far as may be, as if a reference therein to the State Government were a reference to the Corporation.

General Provisions [Sections 60 to 73]

General provisions with regards to benefits are as follows:

(*i*) *Benefits are not Assignable or Attachable* [*Section* 60]

The right to receive any payment of any benefit under this Act shall not be assignable or attachable. No cash benefit payable under this Act shall be liable to attachment or sale in execution of any decree or order of any court.

(*ii*) *Bar of Benefits under other Enactments* [*Section* 61]

When a person is entitled to any of the benefits provided by this Act, he shall be barred from receiving any similar benefit admissible under the provisions of any other enactment.

(*iii*) *Persons not to Commute Cash Benefits* [*Section* 62]

This section provides that no person shall be entitled to commute for a lump sum any disablement benefit admissible under this Act.

(*iv*) *Persons are not Entitled to Receive Benefit in Certain Cases* [*Section* 63]

Section 63 provides that no person shall be entitled to sickness benefit or disablement benefit for temporary disablement on any day on which he works or remains on leave or on a holiday in respect of which he receives wages or on any day on which he remains on strike.

(*v*) *Recipient of Sickness or Disablement Benefit to Observe Certain Conditions* [*Section* 64]

A person who is in receipt of sickness benefit or disablement benefit (other than benefit granted on permanent disablement)—

- (*a*) Shall remain under medical treatment at a dispensary, hospital, clinic or other institution provided under this Act and shall carry out the instructtions given by the medical officer or medical attendant in charge thereof;
- (*b*) Shall not while under treatment do anything which might retard or prejudice his chances of recovery;
- (*c*) Shall not leave the area in which medical treatment provided by this Act is being given, without the permission of the medical officer, medical attendant or such other authority as may be specified in this behalf by the regulations; and
- (*d*) Shall allow himself to be examined by any duly appointed medical officer or other person authorised by the ESI Corporation, in this behalf.

(*vi*) *Benefits not to be Combined* [*Section* 65]

Any insured person shall not be entitled to receive for the same period—

- (*a*) Both sickness benefit and maternity benefit; or
- (*b*) Both sickness benefit and disablement benefit for temporary disablement; or
- (*c*) Both maternity benefit and disablement benefit for temporary disablement.

Where a person is entitled to more than one of the benefit mentioned above, he shall be entitled to choose the benefit he shall receive.

(vii) ESI Corporation's Rights, where a Principal Employer fails or Neglects to Pay any Contribution [Section 68]

If any principal employer fails or neglects to pay any contribution which under this Act he is liable to pay in respect of any employee and by reason thereof such person becomes disentitled to any benefit or entitled to a benefit on a lower scale, the ESI Corporation may, on being satisfied that the contribution should have been paid by the principal employer, pay to the person the benefit at the rate to which he would have been entitled if the failure or neglect had not occurred and the ESI Corporation shall be entitled to recover from the principal employer either—

(a) The difference between the amount of benefit which is paid by the ESI Corporation to the said person and the amount of the benefit which would have been payable on the basis of the contributions were in fact paid by the employer; or

(b) Twice the amount of the contribution which the employer failed or neglected to pay, Whichever is greater?

(viii) Liability of Owner or Occupier of Factories for Excessive Sickness Benefit [Section 69]

Where the ESI Corporation considers that the incidence of sickness among insured persons is excessive by reason of—

(a) Insanitary working conditions in a factory or establishment or the neglect of the owner or occupier of the factory or establishment to observe any health regulations enjoined on him by or under any enactment;

(b) Insanitary conditions of any tenements or lodgings occupied by insured persons and such insanitary conditions are attributable to the neglect of the owner of the tenements or lodgings to observe any health regulations enjoined on him by or under any enactment, the ESI Corporation may send a claim for the payment of the amount of the extra expenditure incurred by the Corporation as sickness benefit to the owner or occupier of the factory or establishment or to the owner of tenements or lodgings as the case may be. If the claim is not settled by agreement, the Corporation may refer the matter, with a statement in support of its claim, to the appropriate Government.

If the appropriate Government is of the opinion that a prima facie case for inquiry is disclosed, it may appoint a competent person or persons to hold an inquiry into the matter. If upon such inquiry it is proved to the satisfaction of the person or persons holding the inquiry that the excess in incidence of sickness among the insured persons is due to the default or neglect of the owner or occupier of the factory or establishment or the owner of the tenements or lodgings, as the case may be, the said person or persons shall determine the amount of the extra expenditure incurred as sickness benefit, and the person or persons by whom the whole or any part of such amount shall be paid to the Corporation.

(ix) *Repayment of Benefit Improperly Received [Section 70]*

(a) Where any person has received any benefit or payment under this Act when he is not lawfully entitled thereto, he shall be liable to repay to the ESI Corporation, the value of the benefit or the amount of such payment, or in the case of his death, his representative shall be liable to repay the same from the assets of the deceased, if any, in his hands.

(b) The value of any benefits received other than cash payments shall be determined by such authority as may be specified in the regulations made in this behalf and the decision of such authority shall be final.

(c) The amount recoverable under this section may be recovered as if it were an arrear of land revenue or under Sections 45C to 45-I.

(x) *Benefit Payable up to and Including Day of Death [Section 71]*

Where a person dies during any period for which he is entitled to a cash benefit under this Act, the amount of such benefit upto and including the day of his death shall be paid to any person nominated by the deceased person in writing in such form as may be specified in the regulations or, if there is no such nomination, to the heir or legal representative of the deceased person.

(xi) *Employer not to Reduce Wages or Discontinue or Reduce Benefits [Section 72]*

No employer by reason only of his liability for any contributions payable under this Act shall, directly or indirectly, reduce the wages of any employee, or except as provided by the regulations, discontinue or reduce benefits payable to him under the conditions of his service which are similar to the benefits conferred by this Act.

(xii) *Bar on Discharge, Dismissal, Reduction or Punishment of Employees [Section 73]*

(a) No employer shall dismiss, discharge, or reduce or otherwise punish an employee during the period the employee is in receipt of sickness benefit or maternity benefit, or shall he, except as provided under the regulations, dismiss, discharge or reduce or otherwise punish an employee during the period he is in respect of disablement benefit for temporary disablement or is under medical treatment for sickness or is absent from work as a result of illness duly certified in accordance with the regulations to arise out of the pregnancy or confinement rendering the employee unfit for work.

(b) No notice of dismissal or discharge or reduction given to an employee during the period specified above shall be valid or operative.

Judicial Interpretations/Case Example	
Section 73 places an embargo upon the powers of an employer to dismiss, discharge or otherwise punish an employee in the circumstances mentioned therein.	*Municipal Corporation Greater Bombay* v *B.E.S.T. Worker's Union,* (1973) 3 SCC 546: 1973 SCC (L&S) 177 SCC.
The burden is on the workmen to claim protection under Section 73.	*Mysore Steel Works* v *Jitendra Chandra,* (1971) 1 LLJ 543.
Termination of service following automatically either from a contract or from a standing order by virtue of unauthorised absence for the specified period does not attract Section 73 (1).	*Buckingham and Carnatic Co. Ltd.* v *Venkatiah,* (1963) 2 LLJ 638: (1963) 7 FLR 343 (SC).
A notice of discharge or dismissal given in contravention of sub-section (1) of Section 73 will not be valid or operative.	*Management of Ghest Keen Williams Ltd.* v *Presiding Officer IInd Addn Labour Court* ,(1992) 1 LLJ 846 (Kar).

Transitory Provisions:—Transitory provisions with regards to benefits are as follows:

1. Employer's Special Contribution [Section 73A]

(*a*) Every principal employer shall pay to the ESI Corporation a special contribution at the specified rates.

(*b*) The employer's special contribution shall consist of such percentage not exceeding five per cent of the total wage bill of the employer, as the Central Government may, by notification in the Official Gazette, specify from time to time.

(*c*) The employer's special contribution shall fall due as soon as the liability of the employer to pay wages accrues, but may be paid to the ESI Corporation at such intervals, within such time and in such manner as the Central Government may, by notification in the Official Gazette, specify and any such notification may provide for the grant of a rebate for prompt payment of such contribution.

2. Special Tribunal for decisions where there is no Employee's Insurance Court [Section 73B]

(*a*) If any question or disputes arises in respect of the employer's special contribution payable or recoverable and there is no Employee's insurance Court having jurisdiction to try such question or dispute, the question or dispute shall be decided by such authority as the Central Government may specify in this behalf.

(*b*) The provisions of Sections 76 (1), 77 to 79 and 81 shall, so far as may be, apply in relation to a proceeding before any specified authority as they apply in relation to a proceeding before an Employees' Insurance Court.

3. Mode of Recovery of Employer's Special Contribution [Section 73D]

The employer's special contribution may be recovered as if it were an arrear of land revenue.

4. Power to Call for Additional Information or Return [Section 73E]

Without prejudice to the other provisions contained in this Act, the ESI Corporation may, for the purpose of determining whether the employer's special contribution is payable or for determining the amount thereof, by general or special order, require any principal or immediate employer or any other person to furnish such information or returns to such authority in such form and within such time as may be specified in the order.

5. Power to Exempt to be Exercised by Central Government alone in Respect of Employer's Special Contribution [Section 73F]

Notwithstanding anything contained in this Act, the Central Government may exempt having regard to size or location of, or the nature of the industry carried on, in any factory or establishment from the payment of the employer's special contribution and nothing contained in Sections 87 to 91 (inclusive) shall be deemed to authorise any State Government to grant any such exemption.

6. Provisions Cease to have Effect [Section 73-I]

The central Government may, by notification in the Official Gazette, direct that the above provisions shall cease to have effect on such date as may be specified in the notification, not being a date earlier than three months from the date of the notification.

Benefits under the ESI Schemes

The ESI Scheme guarantees a fair deal to members by providing medical facilities, besides adequate cash compensation to insured persons arising out of schemes and employment injuries. Under the ESI Scheme, an insured and his/her dependants become eligible from day one of entering the employment, full and free medical facilities, without any limit. Medical facilities may include OPD facilities, specialist and diagnostic services, hospitalisation, free supply of medicines and dressings etc. Besides, the insured person is also entitled for certain cash benefits which are payable through branch/local offices of the ESIC, against loss of wages or earning capacity caused by sickness, temporary disablement, occupational disease, maternity or death or permanent disablement of an insured person due to employment injury or an occupational disease. These benefits are payable after due medical certification by an authorised doctor or medical board.

Brief description of benefits is given below:

Benefit Under the ESI Scheme

S. No.	Benefit Type	Conditions	Permissible Benefit	Rate	To Whom Payable
1	(a) Sickness Benefit	If contribution paid for not less than 78 days in the corresponding contribution period (CP)	Not payable for more than 91 days in any two consecutive benefit periods (BP)	As per daily Standard Benefit Rate (SBR) 50% of wages (approx)	Only to insured person
	(b) Extended Sickness Benefit for longterm diseases like TB, Leprosy, etc.	Continuous employment for 2 years and contributions payable for 156 days in four consecutive contriution periods.	124 days extendable upto 2 years in the case of chronic cases during a period of 3 years.	25% SBR 70% of the wages (approx)	Only to the insured person
	(c) Enhanced Sickness Benefit for under going sterilization operation, etc.	If contributions paid for not less than 78 days in the corresponding contributions period	7 days for vasectomy and 14 days for tubectomy extendable in cases of post operative complications etc. Rate of payment is 100% of the wages.		Only to the insured person
2	Maternity Benefit	If contribution paid for not less than 70 days in the immediately preceding 2 consecutive contributions periods (i.e., one year)	(i) During a period of 12 weeks of which not more than 6 weeks shall precede the expected date of confinement. (ii) 6 weeks for miscarriage or for medical termination of pregnancy Additional	Twice the SBR subject to minimum of Rs. 20 per day. Medical bonus of Rs. 1000 on account of confinement expenses payable where ESI facility is not available.	Only to the insured woman

S. No.	Benefit Type	Conditions	Permissible Benefit	Rate	To Whom Payable
			payment for one month for pre or port complicat-ions arising out of pregnancy.		
3	Disablement Benefits	Available from day one of employment and irrespective of having paid contri-butions	As long as inca-pacity lasts in the case of tempo-rary disablement and for life time in the case of per-manent disable-ment.	(i) 70% above SBR in case of Temporary disablement (ii) specifi-ed in part I of 2nd sche-dule at the full rate of TDB in case of per-manent to-tal disable-m e n t. (iii) At such percentage of the full rate as spe-cified in the Part II of 2nd sche-dule being the percen-tage loss of e a r n i n g c a p a c i t y caused by the injury.	Only to i n s u r e d person
4	Dependant's Benefits	Payable to depen-dants	(i) Widow during life time until remarriage.	3/5 of the Full Rate	To Widow
			(ii) Legitimate or adopted son/ until attain the age of 18 years	2/5 of the Full Rate	To Legiti-mate or a d o p t e d son

S. No.	Benefit Type	Conditions	Permissible Benefit	Rate	To Whom Payable
			(*iii*) Legitimate or adopted unmarried daughter /daughters until attain the age of 18 years or until marriage whichever is earlier.	2/5 of the Full Rate	To each Legitimate or adopted unmarried daughters
			(*iv*) When the deceased does not leave a widow or legitimate or adopted child. Dependent Benefit in that case will be payable to:	3/10 of the Full Rate	Parent
			(*a*) Parent or grand Parent for life	2/10 of the Full Rate	Male dependent
			(*b*) Any other male dependent until attain the age of 18 yrs. (*c*) Any other female dependent until marriage or attain the age of 18 years which ever is earlier.	2/10 of the Full Rate	Female dependent
5	Medical Insured Benefit	No condition laid down	Benefit available from day one of his employment so long as he remains in the insurable employment and thereafter certain additional period also.	Full medical care including hospitalization facility	Insured person and his family

S. No.	Benefit Type	Conditions	Permissible Benefit	Rate	To Whom Payable
6	Funeral Expenses	No condition	Lump-sum payment	Up to Rs. 3000 w.e.f. 1-10-2007	To the eldest surviving member of the family of the deceased or to the person who actually incurs the expenses on the funeral of an insured person.
7	Medical Benefit to insured person who ceases employment on account of permanent disablement	(*i*) Production of proof by an insured person that he ceased to be in employment. (*ii*) Payment of contribution at the rate of Rs. 10 per month in lumsum for one year in advance every year.	Available till the date on which the insured person would have attained the age of superannuation.	At the rate prescribed under the Act	Insured person and spouse
8	Rehabilitation Allowance	No Condition	For each day of which the insured person remains admitted in Artificial Limb centre for fixation, repair or replacement of artificial limb	As per SBR up to Rs. 15 lakh for rehabilitation	Only to the insured person

Daily Rate Benefit or Standard Benefits Rate underthe ESI Act w.e.f. 1st October, 2006.

S. No.	Group of Employees whose Average Daily Wages are	Standard Benefit Rate Rs.
1	Below Rs. 28	14 or full average daily wage whichever is less
2	Rs. 28 and above but below Rs. 32	16
3	Rs. 32 and above but below Rs. 36	18
4	Rs. 36 and above but below Rs. 40	20
5	Rs. 40 and above but below Rs. 48	24
6	Rs. 48 and above but below Rs. 56	28
7	Rs. 56 and above but below Rs. 60	30
8	Rs. 60 and above but below Rs. 64	32
9	Rs. 64 and above but below Rs. 72	36
10	Rs. 72 and above but below Rs. 76	38
11	Rs. 76 and above but below Rs. 80	40
12	Rs. 80 and above but below Rs. 88	44
13	Rs. 88 and above but below Rs. 96	48
14	Rs. 96 and above but below Rs. 106	53
15	Rs. 106 and above but below Rs. 116	58
16	Rs. 116 and above but below Rs. 126	63
17	Rs. 126 and above but below Rs. 136	68
18	Rs. 136 and above but below Rs. 146	73
19	Rs. 146 and above but below Rs. 156	78
20	Rs. 156 and above but below Rs. 166	83
21	Rs. 166 and above but below Rs. 176	88
22	Rs. 176 and above but below Rs. 186	93
23	Rs. 186 and above but below Rs. 196	98
24	Rs. 196 and above but below Rs. 206	103
25	Rs. 206 and above but below Rs. 216	108
26	Rs. 216 and above but below Rs. 226	113
27	Rs. 226 and above but below Rs. 236	118
28	Rs. 236 and above but below Rs. 250	125
29	Rs. 250 and above but below Rs. 260	130
30	Rs. 260 and above but below Rs. 270	135
31	Rs. 270 and above but below Rs. 280	140

S. No.	Group of Employees whose Average Daily Wages are	Standard Benefit Rate Rs.
32	Rs. 280 and above but below Rs. 290	145
33	Rs. 290 and above but below Rs. 300	150
34	Rs. 300 and above but below Rs. 310	155
35	Rs. 310 and above but below Rs. 320	160
36	Rs. 320 and above but below Rs. 330	165
37	Rs. 330 and above but below Rs. 340	170
38	Rs. 340 and above but below Rs. 350	175
39	Rs. 350 and above but below Rs. 360	180
40	Rs. 360 and above but below Rs. 370	185
41	Rs. 370 and above but below Rs. 380	190
42	Rs. 380 and above but below Rs. 390	195
43	Rs. 390 and above but below Rs. 400	200
44	Rs. 400 and above but below Rs. 410	205
45	Rs. 410 and above but below Rs. 420	210
46	Rs. 420 and above but below Rs. 430	215
47	Rs. 430 and above but below Rs. 440	220
48	Rs. 440 and above but below Rs. 450	225
49	Rs. 450 and above but below Rs. 460	230
50	Rs. 460 and above but below Rs. 470	235
51	Rs. 470 and above but below Rs. 480	240
52	Rs. 480 and above but below Rs. 490	245
53	Rs. 490 and above but below Rs. 500	250
54	Rs. 500 and above but below Rs. 510	255
55	Rs. 510 and above but below Rs. 520	260
56	Rs. 520 and above but below Rs. 530	265
57	Rs. 530 and above but below Rs. 540	270
58	Rs. 540 and above but below Rs. 550	275
59	Rs. 550 and above but below Rs. 560	280
60	Rs. 560 and above but below Rs. 570	285
61	Rs. 570 and above but below Rs. 580	290
62	Rs. 580 and above but below Rs. 590	295
63	Rs. 590 and above but below Rs. 600	300
64	Rs. 600 and above but below Rs. 610	305
65	Rs. 610 and above but below Rs. 620	310

S. No.	Group of Employees whose Average Daily Wages are	Standard Benefit Rate Rs.
66	Rs. 620 and above but below Rs. 630	315
67	Rs. 630 and above but below Rs. 640	320
68	Rs. 640 and above but below Rs. 650	325
69	Rs. 650 and above but below Rs. 660	330
70	Rs. 660 and above but below Rs. 670	335
71	Rs. 670 and above but below Rs. 680	340
72	Rs. 680 and above but below Rs. 690	345
73	Rs. 690 and above but below Rs. 700	350
74	Rs. 700 and above but below Rs. 710	355
75	Rs. 710 and above but below Rs. 720	360
76	Rs. 720 and above but below Rs. 730	365
77	Rs. 730 and above but below Rs. 740	370
78	Rs. 740 and above but below Rs. 750	375
79	Rs. 750 and above but below Rs. 760	380
80	Rs. 760 and above but below Rs. 770	385
81	Rs. 770 and above but below Rs. 780	390
82	Rs. 780 and above but below Rs. 790	395
83	Rs. 790 and above but below Rs. 800	400
84	Rs. 800 and above but below Rs. 810	405
85	Rs. 810 and above but below Rs. 820	410
86	Rs. 820 and above but below Rs. 830	415
87	Rs. 830 and above but below Rs. 840	420
88	Rs. 840 and above but below Rs. 850	425
89	Rs. 850 and above but below Rs. 860	430
90	Rs. 860 and above but below Rs. 870	435
91	Rs. 870 and above but below Rs. 880	440
92	Rs. 880 and above but below Rs. 890	445
93	Rs. 890 and above but below Rs. 900	450
94	Rs. 910 and above but below Rs. 920	455
95	Rs. 920 and above but below Rs. 930	460
96	Rs. 930 and above but below Rs. 940	465
97	Rs. 940 and above but below Rs. 950	470
98	Rs. 950 and above but below Rs. 960	475
99	Rs. 950 and above	480

Adjudication of Dispute and Claims

Employees Insurance Court

The State Government constitutes Employees Insurance Court for such local area as may be specified in the Notification. The State Government may appoint the same Court for two or more local areas or two or more Courts for the same local areas and regulate the distribution of business between their.

The word 'Court' in Section 74 of ESI Act is used in a "contiguous sense" as has been held in a decided case "*Jiyajio Cotton Mills Ltd Gwalior* v *ESIC* AIR 1962 MP 340". When the constitution speaks of "Courts" in Articles 136, 227, 228 or 233 to 237, it interprets it as Courts of 'Civic Judicature' and not Tribunals which are constituted to decide controversies arising under certain special laws. Tribunals act in a judicial manner on evidence of oath but are not part of the ordinary Courts of civil judicature. Though Tribunals are very similar to courts but are not Courts in true sense. Broadly speaking, certain special matters go before Tribunals and the residue goes before the ordinary Courts of Civil Judicature.

Constitution [Section 74]

(a) State Government by notification in the Official Gazette constitutes an Employee's Insurance Court for such local areas as may be specified in the Notification.

(b) The Court shall consist of such number of Judges as the state government may think fit.

(c) Any person who is or has been a judicial officer or is legal practitioner of 5 years standing is qualified to be a Judge of ESI Court.

(d) No Civil Court has powers to decide the matters falling within the purview of ESI Court.

(e) ESI Court has jurisdiction to decide claims for recovery of contributions and other deposits.

Matters to be Decided by ESI Court [Section 75]

Following matters are to be decided by ESI Court:—

(a) Whether any person is an employee or whether any person is liable to pay the employee's contribution, or

(b) The rate of wages or average daily wages of an employee for the purpose of this Act, or

(c) The rate of contribution payable by a principal employer in respect of any employee.

(d) A person who is or was the principal employer in respect of any employee.

(e) The right of any person to any benefit and the amount and duration thereof.

(f) Any other matter which is in dispute between a principal employer and the

Corporation or between principal employer and an immediate employer, or between an employee and principal or immediate employer.

Following claims shall be decided by the ESI Court

(*i*)   Claim for the recovery of contributions from the principal employer.

(*ii*) Claim by a principal employer to recover contribution from any immediate employer.

(*iii*) Claim against a principal employer under Section 68 (where principal employer fails or neglects to pay any contribution)

(*iv*) Claim under Section 70 for the recovery of the value or amount of benefits received by a person when he is not lawfully entitled thereto, and

(*v*)   Any claim for the recovery of any benefit under the Act.

Judicial Interpretations/Case Example

Demand was raised against appellant consequent upon Inspector's report. No show-cause notice was issued and copy of inspection report not supplied to appellant. Held, it has become impossible for the appellant to respond to charge of having not calculated the wages properly in respect whereof contributions were required to be paid. Held, the Employees' Insurance Court has erred in rejecting plea of the employer challenging the validity of recovery by the ESI Authorities when no inspection report was supplied and also no proper calculation of contribution was made. Hence it is required to be re-examined. Impugned order was set aside and held that ESI Corporation, while exercising its powers under a statute, must furnish information to the affected party on the basis whereof the recovery from the employer is initiated.	*D.C.M. Shriram Consolidated Ltd* v *Employees' Insurance Court,* Delhi and Ors 2008 LLR 1018, (Delhi High Court).
ESI Court has jurisdiction to decide whether benefits availed of by employees prior to ESI scheme were more advantageous than those under ESI scheme.	*Regional Director ESIC* v *Narayan Chandra Raj Khowa,* (1997) 11 SCC 234: 1998 SCC (L&S) 127.
ESI Court cannot review its decision.	*Ved Prakash* v *ESIC,* (1962-63) 23 FJR 453 (Punj).
The claim petition filed before ESI Court is not a suit for the purpose of the Limitation Act.	*ESIC* v *APSEB* 1970 Lab IC 921 (AP).
An application under Section 75 is maintainable when the ESIC had to participate in the proceedings before the ESI Court without specific plea that the applicant had not approached the ESI Corp.	*ESIC* v *Super Tailors,* (2000) 1 Lab LJ 451 (Kant).
A dispute in respect of contributions payable under the Act is to be decided by the ESI Court. Writ jurisdiction cannot be invoked in such a case.	*ESIC* v *Hindustan Tile Works,* (2000) 1 Lab LJ 425 (Ker).

Contd...

No Civil Court has jurisdiction to decide or deal with any question or to adjudicate on any liability which by or under the Act is to be decided by a Medical Board, or by a Medical Appeal Tribunal or by the Employee's Insurance Court. It was held in this case that the provisions of this section are mandatory.	*Connemara Hotel, Spencer International Hotels Ltd.* v *Employees Insurance Court,* (2000) 2 Lab LJ 572 (Mad).
The Insurance Court cannot refuse to perform its mandatory duty even if the ESI Corporation had failed to perform its function.	*ESIC* v *Central Press,* (1977) 1 Lab LJ 479 SC.
ESI Corporation cannot approach ESI Court for resolving any difference or dispute with an employee.	*ESIC* v *F. Fibre Bangalore,* (1997) 1 SCC 625: 1997 SC (L&S) 190.
Order of ESI authorities can be challenged by filing application in ESI Court and not by filing writ petition.	*Mizar Govinda Annappa Pai* v *ESIC,* (1997) Lab IC 3262 (Kant).
Dispute between principal employer and ESI Corporation regarding former's liability under Sfection 45A can be decided by ESI Court.	*Royal Plastic Industries* v *ESIC,* (1997) Lab IC 3273: (1998) 1 LLJ 776 (Ori) (DB).

Institution of Proceedings, etc. [Section 76]

Subject to the provisions of this Act and any rules made by the State Government, all proceedings before the Employees' Insurance Court shall be instituted in the Court appointed for the local area in which the insured person was working at the time the question or dispute arose.

If the Court is satisfied that any matter arising out of any proceeding pending before it can be more conveniently dealt with by any other Employees' Insurance Court in the same State, it may, subject to any rules made by the State Government in this behalf, order such matter to be transferred to such other Court for disposal and shall forthwith transmit to such other Court the records connected with that matter.

The State Government may transfer any matter pending before any Employee' Insurance Court in the State to any such Court in another State with the consent of the State Government of that State.

The Court to which any matter is transferred under sub-section (2) or sub-section (3) shall continue the proceedings as if they had been originally instituted in it.

Commencement of Proceedings [Section 77]

The proceedings before an Employees' Insurance Court shall be commenced by application. Every such application shall be made within a period of three years from the date on which the cause of action arose.

For the purpose of this sub-section,—

(*a*) The cause of action in respect of claim for benefit shall not be deemed to arise unless the insured person or in the case of dependents' benefit, the dependents, of the insured person claims or claim that benefit in accordance with the regulations made in that behalf within a period of twelve months after the claim became due or within such further period as the Employee's Insurance Court may allow on grounds which appear to it to be reasonable.

(*b*) The cause of action in respect of a claim by the Corporation for recovering contributions (including interest and damages) from the principal employer shall be deemed to have arisen on the date on which such claim is made by Corporation for the first time. No claim shall be made by the Corporation after five years of the period to which the claim relates;

(*c*) The cause of action in respect of a claim by the principal employer for recovering contributions from an immediate employer shall not be deemed to arise till the date by which the evidence of contributions having been paid is due to be received by the Corporation under the regulations.

Every such application shall be in such form and shall contain such particulars and shall be accompanied by such fee, if any, as may be prescribed by rules made by the State Government in consultation with the Corporation.

Powers of Employee's Insurance Court [Section 78]

(*i*) The ESI Court shall have all the powers of a Civil Court within the meaning of Code of Criminal Procedure, 1973.

(*ii*) An order of the ESI Court shall be enforceable as if it were a decree passed in a suit by a Civil Court.

Judicial Interpretations/Case Example	
The ESI Court can issue an interim injunction.	*Modi Steel Unit-A* v *E.I. Court,* (1984) 2 LLN 655 (All).
An order of Employees Insurance Court is enforce-able as if it were a decree passed in a suit by a Civil Court.	*ESIC* v *C. Saseendran,* (2001) 9 SCC 349 (SC).
The ESI Court has no power to review its own judgment.	*ESIC* v *Surendra Sharma,* (2003) I CLR 947 (Gau HC).
ESI Court is not a court in strict sense. As such Section 5 of the Limitation Act is not applicable to a proceeding under Section 75 of the ESI Act.	*Kohinoor Tailoring Works* v *ESIC,* (2003) III CLR 839 (Cal HC).

Contd..

The ESI Court has jurisdiction to entertain an application for interim stay of the proceedings	*Aggarwal Hardware Industries* v *ESIC*, 80 CWN 848.
The jurisdiction of a civil court is ousted in respect of those matters over which a Medical Board or a Medical Appeal Tribunal or the ESI Court has exclusive jurisdiction under the Act. The ESI Act is a special Act which gives special forum of remedy different from remedy which exists in common law.	*ESIC* v *Nirmal Chemical Industries,* 1993 LLR 941 (Kar HC).
The ESI Court shall be deemed to be a Civil Court within the meaning of Section 195 of Code of Criminal Procedure, 1973. But, under the ESI Act, no power has been given to ESI Court to review its own earlier passed order.	*ESIC* v *Surendra Sharma,* 2003 LLR 522 (Gau HC).
Since the ESI Act is a self contained and independent code providing a forum of ESI Court a Writ petition in the High Court is not maintainable.	*ESIC* v *LML Karamchari Sangh,* 2000 LLR 289 (All HC).
Bus conductor failed to issue tickets despite receiving fare from the passengers. Disciplinary proceedings were initiated against him. Enquiry Officer favored the workman (the conductor) and disciplinary authority disagreed and punished the delinquent *i.e.* stoppage of his next due one increment without cumulative effect. There was no need to conduct any fresh enquiry. Show cause notice was given to the respondent and he was given an opportunity of being heard. High Court set aside the order of the Industrial Tribunal and restored the order passed by the disciplinary authority.	*Delhi Transport Corporation* v *Rajinder Parshad,* 2008 LLR 1117 (Delhi High Court).
If the petitioner is denied the opportunity of being heard, the conduct and action of ESI authorities will be violative of principles of natural justice and the Writ Court (High Court) will be within its jurisdiction to deal with the matter itself rather than remitting the matter under Section 5 of the ESI Act to the ESI Court.	*Power Tools and Appliances Ltd* v *Union of India,* 1995 LLR 239 (Cal HC) (DB).

Review against order of Employees Insurance Court

Review against order of Employees Insurance Court has to be filed within 30 days from the date of pronouncement of order of judgment.	*Regional Director ESIC* v *P K Sidhique,* 2006 Lab IC (NOC) 37 (Ker).

Appearance by Legal Practitioners, etc. [Section 79]

Any application, appearance or act required to be made or done by any person to or before an Employees' Insurance Court (other than appearance of a person required for the purpose of his examination as witness) may be made or done by a legal practitioner or by an officer of a registered trade union authorised in writing by such person or with the permission of the Court, by any other person so authorised.

Reference to High Court [Section 81]

An Employees' Insurance Court may submit any question of law for the decision of the High Court and if it does so, shall decide the question pending before it in accordance with such decision.

Appeal [Section 82]

The provisions are:

(*i*) An appeal shall lie to High Court from an order of ESI Court if it involves question of law

(*ii*) Save as expressly provided in this section, no appeal shall lie from an order of ESI Court if it does not involve a question of law.

Judicial Interpretations/Case Example	
The period of limitation for an appeal under this Section shall be 60 days	
An appeal shall lie to the High Court from an order of an E.S.I. Court if it involves a substantial question of law.	*ESIC v Radhas Printers,* (1996) 2 LLJ 1105: 1996 Lab IC 2388: (1997) 2 LLN 245 (Ker) (DB).
Application under Section 75 was dismissed by the EI Court. Appeal was allowed by learned Single Judge and the Order of coverage of establishment was set aside against which this letters patent appeal cannot be entertained since it will be barred by Section 100 A of the Civil Procedure Code.	*Employee's State Insurance Corporation v H. Fillunger and Co. Pvt. Ltd.,* 2009 LLR 109 (Bombay High Court).
The respondent filed an application under Section 75 of the Employees' State Insurance Act, 1948 challenging an order dated 28th September, 1983, passed by the appellant in exercise of powers under Section 45A of the said Act of 1948 by which a demand of Rs. 2,20,249.60 was made by the appellant towards the contribution. The said application under Section 75 was dismissed on 29th January, 1990. An appeal preferred against the said order by the respondent was dismissed by this Court. The respondent therefore paid the amount of Rs. 2,20,250. By an order dated 14th August, 2006, the appellant made a demand of Rs. 5,93,427 being the interest payable on the sum of Rs. 2,20,249.60. Another application under Section 75 of the said Act of 1948 was filed by the respondent for challenging the demand made by the said order dated 14th August, 2006. Held, an appeal in the High Court against the interim order by the Employees' Insurance Court is not maintainable against a procedural order since there is no final adjudication on the rights and liabilities of the parties. High Court will not entertain an appeal against interim order of the Employees' Insurance Court directing	*Employees' State Insurance Corporation, Pune v Force Motors Ltd. (Formally known as Bajaj Tempo Ltd), Pune* (Bombay HC, 2008 LLR 977).

Contd..

deposit of 50 per cent of the demanded amount by Employees' Insurance Court. Where an order was not otherwise appealable, a writ petition challenging it would also not be maintainable.	*Rainbow Industries v Regional Director ESIC*, (2001) 1 Lab LJ 1261 (Bom).
As appeal by an employer against the findings of the ESI court pertaining to the number of employees including casual employees will not lie because the findings pertained to the facts rather than law. Hence the appeal was dismissed.	*Ideal Trading Corporation v ESIC*, 2001 LLR 1055 (Gau HC).

Schedules

The First Schedule[1] [* * *]

The Second Schedule[2]

[*See* Sections 2(15A) and (15B)]

Part I

List of injuries deemed to result in permanent total disablement

Sl. No.	Description of Injury	Percentage of loss of earning capacity
1.	Loss of both hands or amputation at higher sites	100
2.	Loss of a hand and a foot	100
3.	Double amputation through leg or thigh, or amputation through leg or thigh on one side and loss of other foot.	100
4.	Loss of sight to such an extent as to render the claimant unable to perform any work for which eye sight is essential	100
5.	Very severe facial disfigurement	100
6.	Absolute deafness	100

---

1. *Omitted by the Employees' State Insurance (Amendment) Act, 1989, w.e.f. 1-2-1991. Earlier, it was amended by the Employees' State Insurance (Amendment) Act, 1984, w.e.f. 27-1-1985) and the Employees' State Insurance (Amendment) Act, 1975/1966/1951.*

2. *Substituted by the Employees' State Insurance (Amendment) Act, 1966. Earlier Second Schedule was amended by the Employees' State Insurance (Amendment) Act, 1951.*

Part II

List of injuries deemed to result in permanent partial disablement

Amputation—upper limbs (either arm)

Sl. No.	Description of Injury	Percentage of loss of earning capacity
7.	Amputation through shoulder joint	90
8.	Amputation below shoulder with stump less than 20.32 c.m. from tip of acromion.	80
9.	Amputation from 20.32 c.m. from tip of acromion to less than 11.43 c.m. below tip of olecranon	70
10.	Loss of a hand or of the thumb and four fingers of one hand or amputation from 11.43 c.m. below tip of olecranon	60
11.	Loss of thumb	30
12.	Loss of thumb and its metacarpal bone	40
13.	Loss of four fingers of one hand	50
14.	Loss of three fingers of one hand	30
15.	Loss of two fingers of one hand	20
16.	Loss of terminal phalanx of thumb	20
16A.	Guillotine amputation of the tip of the thumb without loss of bone	10
	Amputation—Lower limbs	
17.	Amputation of both feet resulting in end-bearing stumps	90
18.	Amputation through both feet proximal to the metatarsophalangeal joint	80
19.	Loss of all toes of both feet through the metatarso-phalangeal joint	40
20.	Loss of all toes of both feet proximal to the proximal interphalangeal joint	30
21.	Loss of all toes of both feet distal to the proximal interphalangeal joint	20
22.	Amputation at hip	90
23.	Amputation below hip with stump not exceeding 12.70 c.m. in length measured from tip of great trenchanter	80
24.	Amputation below hip with stump exceeding 12.70 c.m. in length measured from tip of great trenchanter but not beyond middle thigh	70

Sl. No.	Description of Injury	Percentage of loss of earning capacity
25.	Amputation below middle thigh to 8.89 c.m. below knee	60
26.	Amputation below knee with stump exceeding 8.89 c.m. but not exceeding 12.70 c.m.	50
27.	Amputation below knee with stump exceeding 12.70 c.m.	50
28.	Amputation of one foot resulting in end-bearing	50
29.	Amputation through one foot proximal to the metatarsophalangeal joint	50
30.	Loss of all toes of one foot through the metatarsophalangeal joint	20
	Other injuries	
31.	Loss of one eye, without complications, the other being normal	40
32.	Loss of vision of one eye without complications or disfigurement of eye-ball, the other being normal	30
32A.	Partial loss of vision of one eye	10
	Loss of—	
	A.—Fingers of right or left hand Index finger	
33.	Whole	14
34.	Two phalanges	11
35.	One phalanx	9
36.	Guillotine amputation of tip without loss of bone	5
	Middle finger	
37.	Whole	12
38.	Two phalanges	9
39.	One phalanx	7
40.	Guillotine amputation of tip without loss of bone	4
	Ring or little finger	
41.	Whole	7
42.	Two phalanges	6
43.	One phalanx	5
44.	Guillotine amputation of tip without loss of bone	2
	B.—Toes of right or left foot Great toe	
45.	Through metatarso-phalangeal joint	14
46.	Part, with some loss of bone	3

Sl. No.	Description of Injury	Percentage of loss of earning capacity
	Any other toe	
47.	Through metatarso-phalangeal joint	3
48.	Part, with some loss of bone	1
	Two toes of one foot, excluding great toe	
49.	Through metatarso-phalangeal joint	5
50.	Part, with some loss of bone	2
	Three toes of one foot, excluding great toe	
51.	Through metatarso-phalangeal joint	6
52.	Part, with some loss of bone	3
	Four toes of one foot, excluding great toe	
53.	Through metatarso-phalangeal joint	9
54.	Part, with some loss of bone	3

Note.—Complete and permanent loss of the use of any limb or member referred to in this Schedule shall be deemed to be the equivalent of the loss of that limb or member.

The Third Schedule

(*See* Section 52A)
List of occupational diseases

Sl. No.	Occupational disease	Employment
	Part A	
1.	Infectious and parasitic diseases contracted in an occupation where there is a particular risk of contamination	(*a*) All work involving exposure to health or laboratory work; (*b*) All work involving exposure to veterinary work; (*c*) Work relating to handling of such carcasses, or merchandise which may have been contaminated by animals or

Sl. No.	Occupational disease	Employment
		animal carcasses; animals, animal carcasses, part (d) Other work carrying a particular risk of contamination.
2.	Diseases caused by work in compressed air.	All work involving exposure to the risk concerned.
3.	Diseases caused by lead or its toxic compound	All work involving exposure to the risk concerned.
4.	Poisoning by nitrous fumes.	All work involving exposure to the risk concerned.
5.	Poisoning by organphosphorous compounds	All work involving exposure to the risk concerned.

Part B

Sl. No.	Occupational disease	Employment
1.	Diseases caused by phosphorus or its toxic compounds	All work involving exposure to the risk concerned.
2.	Diseases caused by mercury or its toxic compounds	All work involving exposure to the risk concerned.
3.	Diseases caused by benzene or its toxic homologues	All work involving exposure to the risk concerned.
4.	Diseases caused by nitro and amido toxic derivatives of benzene or its homologues	All work involving exposure to the risk concerned.
5.	Diseases caused by chromium or its toxic compounds	All work involving exposure to the risk concerned.
6.	Diseases caused by arsenic or its toxic Compounds	All work involving exposure to the risk concerned.
7.	Diseases caused by radioactive substance and ionising radiations.	All work involving exposure to the action of radioactive substances or ionising radiations.
8.	Primary epithelomatous cancer of the skin caused by tar, pitch, bitumen, mineral oil, anthracene, or the compounds, products of residues of these substances.	All work involving exposure to the risk concerned.

Sl. No.	Occupational disease	Employment
9.	Diseases caused by the toxic halogen derivatives of hydrocarbons (of the aliphatic and aromatice series).	All work involving exposure to the risk concerned.
10.	Diseases caused by the carbon disulphide.	All work involving exposure to the risk concerned.
11.	Occupational contract due to infra-red radiations.	All work involving exposure to the risk concerned.
12.	Diseases caused by manganese or its toxic compounds.	All work involving exposure to the risk concerned.
13.	Skin diseases caused by physical, chemical or biological agents not included in other items.	All work involving exposure to the risk concerned.
14.	Hearing impairment caused by noise.	All work involving exposure to the risk concerned.
15.	Poisoning by dinitrophenol or a homologue or by substituted dinitrophenol or by the salts of such substances.	All work involving exposure to the risk concerned.
16.	Diseases caused by beryllium or its toxic compounds.	All work involving exposure to the risk concerned.
17.	Diseases caused by cadmium or its toxic compounds.	All work involving exposure to the risk concerned.
18.	Occupational asthama caused by recognised sensitising agents inherent to the work process.	All work involving exposure to the risk concerned.
19.	Diseases caused by flourine or its toxic compounds.	All work involving exposure to the risk concerned.
20.	Diseases caused by nitroglycerine or other nitroacid esters.	All work involving exposure to the risk concerned.
21.	Diseases caused by alcohols and ketones.	All work involving exposure to the risk concerned.
22.	Diseases caused by asphyxiants: carbon monoxide, and its toxic derivatives, hydrogen sulfide.	All work involving exposure to the risk concerned.
23.	Lung cancer and mesotheliomas caused by asbestos.	All work involving exposure to the risk concerned.
24.	Primary neoplasm of the epithelial lining of the urinary bladder or the kidney or theureter.	All work involving exposure to the risk concerned.

Sl. No.	Occupational disease	Employment
	Part C	
1.	Pneumoconiosis caused by sclerogenic mineral dust (silicosis, anthralosilicosis asbestosis) and silico-tuberculosis provided that silicosis is an essential factor in causing the resultant incapacity or death.	All work involving exposure to the risk concerned.
2.	Bagassosis.	All work involving exposure to the risk concerned.
3.	Bronchopulmonary diseases caused by cotton, flax hemp and sisal dust (Byssinosis)	All work involving exposure to the risk concerned.
4.	Extrinsic allergic alveilitis caused by the inhalation of organic dusts.	All work involving exposure to the risk concerned.
5.	Bronchopulmonary diseases caused by hard metals.	All work involving exposure to the risk concerned.

Review Questions

1. Define the following terms as used in the Employees State Insurance Act 1948 :

    (a) Employment Injury
    (b) Factory
    (c) Manufacturing Process
    (d) Wages
    (e) Temporary Disablement
    (f) Permanent Partial Disablement
    (g) Permanent Total Disablement

2. State briefly short notes on the establishment and constitution of Employees State Insurance Corporation, the Standing Committee and the Medical Benefit Council and discuss briefly their powers and duties.

3. What is the effect of supersession of Employees State Insurance Corporation or the Standing Committee?

4. What is Employees State Insurance Fund? What are the purposes for which fund may be extended?

5. State the rules as to the employer and employees contributions as provided by Employees State Insurance Act 1948.

6. Describe the manner in which the contributions have been made payable and recoverable under Employees State Insurance Act 1948.

7. What are the different types of benefit provided by Employees State Insurance Act 1948?

8. Discuss the circumstances in which an employee, who suffers injury due to an accident, happening while acting in breach of regulations, will receive benefit.

9. How are the inspectors appointed under the Employees State Insurance Act 1948, and what are their functions and duties.

10. How does the Employees State Insurance Act 1948 provide for the adjudication of disputes and claims? To what extent is the jurisdiction of civil courts ousted in the act?

11. What are the provisions in regard to Employees State Insurance Corporation's right where the principal employer fails or neglects to pay any contribution?

12. What are the penalties prescribed by the Employees State Insurance Act 1948 for contravention of the provisions of the Act or the rules made there under?

13. Attempt the following. Each carries equal marks:

    (a) Discuss briefly various benefits provided under the ESI Act.

    (b) Deceased Purshothaman was milk vender for the distribution of milk by riding cycle. He sustained chest pain and fell down from his cycle on which he was carrying milk. While in hospital for treatment, he died of heart attack. He being servant of the milk society was an insured person under ESI Schemes. Decide if the deceased died on account of employment injury.

    (c) Loaders and unloaders are performing work for the corporation but engaged by the transporters (contractors) and coming at the premises of the principal employer for loading and unloading. When the employer corporation has given a contract to the transporter for loading and unloading of petroleum product manufactured by it, will the employer corporation be liable for covering the loaders and unloaders under the ESI Act?

14. Answer the following queries under the ESI Act, 1948 citing case law, if any:

    (a) Will an employee continue to be covered under the ESI Act even if he crosses the prescribed wage limit?

    (b) Who is to prove that 20 persons are not employed in the establishment?

    (c) If the number of employees at any time falls below the prescribed limit will the ESI Act continue to apply?

    (d) What is the difference between contribution period and benefit period?

    (e) If tapping the blood for purpose of diagnosis, storing it and conducting tests attracts ESI provisions?

(f) Whether construction workers/casual workers are treated employees under the ESI Act?

(g) Whether a partner of a firm being establishment under the ESI Act is covered?

(h) If the cinema enterprise is covered?

(i) Whether showroom employees are covered?

(j) Will a club which has a kitchen rendering catering services to its members is covered?

(k) Whether those working in workshop, laboratory or go down are covered under the ESI Act?

15. Attempt the following. Each carries equal marks:

(a) Explain the provisions of the Employees State Insurance Act, 1948 relating to the constitution ESI Corporation.

(b) The employee was assaulted at the bus stop while he was waiting for the bus to his house. Can the injury, which the employee in this case sustained due to the assault of strangers on his way to his house from the factory, be said to have its origin in the employment as per the ESI Act?

(c) Petitioner is a limited company engaged in manufacturing rain wears, air pillows, rubber canvas foot wear etc., in its small scale industrial unit. It is covered under the provision of the ESI Act. Petitioner offloads various work on piece rate basis to other units for stitching buttons hole fixing, taping, pasting, molding, mixing etc. The charges paid against such job work include the cost of job work and profit of the units who execute such job orders. Such units are independent and they do the job work of the petitioner as well as others at their own premises. Petitioner has no connection or control whatsoever on the said units. It has got no supervisory control over the day to day execution of the work. The said units submit their bills against such work and payment are made by cheque. Will a company manufacturing rainwear's and air pillows and covered under the ESI Act outsourcing various jobs on piece-rate basis to other units be liable to pay ESI contributions for such job work done for other establishments the job of which is neither supervised nor controlled by the company?

2

Workmen's Compensation Act, 1923

Historical Background

1855 **Fatal Accidents Act of 1855**

The origin of Labour welfare activity in India goes back to 1837, following the abolition of slavery in 1833. But the earliest legislative approach could be traced back to the passing of the Apprentices Act of 1850. The next Act was the Fatal Accidents Act of 1855 (effective from 27th March 1855) that aimed at providing compensation to the families of workmen who lost their life as a result of "actionable wrong". This Act extended to the whole of India except the State of Jammu and Kashmir. The Act had the Preamble "whereas no action or suit is now maintainable in any Court against a person who, by his wrongful act, neglect or default, may have caused the death of another person, and it is often-times right and expedient that the wrong-doer in such case should be answerable in damages for the injury so caused by him". Noteworthy provisions of the Fatal Accidents Act are as follows:

- Suit for compensation to the family of a person for loss occasioned to it by his death by actionable wrong. Whenever the death of a person shall be caused by wrongful act, neglect or default, and the act, neglect or default is such as would (if death had not ensued) have entitled the party injured to maintain an action and recover damages in respect thereof, the party who would have been liable if death had not ensued shall be liable to an action or suit for damages, notwithstanding the death of the person injured, and although the death shall have been caused under such circumstances as amount in law to felony or other crime.

- Every such action or suit shall be for the benefit of the wife, husband, parent and child, if any, of the person whose death shall have been so caused, and shall be brought by and in the name of the executor, administrator or representative of the person deceased; and in every such action the Court may give such damages as it may think proportioned to the loss resulting from such death to the parties respectively, for whom and for whose benefit such action shall be brought; and the amount so recovered, after deducting all costs and expenses, including the costs not recovered from the defendant, shall be divided amongst the before-mentioned parties.

It was way back in 1884 when the question of granting workmen's compensation for serious and fatal accidents was first raised in India and it took about 40 years for Government of India to frame a full fledged comprehensive Workmen's Compensation Act. Only towards the end of 1920-21, Government of India initiated steps for framing legislation by constituting a small committee, in June, 1922, comprising members of Legislative Assembly, employer's and worker's representatives and medical and insurance experts. The Committee's detailed recommendations for framing legislation were accepted and Workmen's Compensation Act was passed in 1923.

With slight changes here and there, the Workmen's Compensation Act, 1923, has been copied out from the English Act, 1906 and the Act of 1923. The English decisions even today continue to be a source of inspiration for our judges and they freely refer to these utterances as authorities for a particular interpretation of the provisions of our Act.

1923 : Enactment of the Workmen's Compensation Act, 1923

The Act came into force on 1st July 1924. The Act is considered to be one of the best pieces of social legislation assuring to the victims of industrial accidents and occupational diseases, the prescribed compensation as a sort of some immediate solace in the form of cash payments. The Act is a short one containing only 36 sections and 4 schedules. But the case law around these simple provisions has grown to such bulk that the short Act has become too voluminous and more complex. The Act applied in the first instance only to workers receiving monthly wages not exceeding Rs. 300, in factories, mines and ports, to those employed in the railways, tramways, on loading, unloading or coaling ships at docks, etc., where mechanical power was used in the building trade, bridge construction, telephone, telegraph and posts, brigade services. The compensation amount payable to the dependents was Rs. 2500 or 30 months wages whichever was less in the case of death of an adult and Rs. 200 in the case of minor's death. For permanent total disablement, the compensation payable to an adult was Rs. 3500 or 42 months wages, whichever was less and Rs. 3500 or 84 months wages whichever was less, in the case of a child.

Amendments from time to time	
1929	The Amendment Act enlarged the categories of workmen. Also, it altered the restrictions on distribution of compensation
1933	Act was amended extensively on the lines of recommendations of Royal Commission on Labour in India (1931). Amendment included enlargement in the coverage of workmen, increase in scales of compensation, etc.

Amendments from time to time	
1946	The wage limit of the workers was increased from Rs. 300 to Rs. 400.
1959	The Amendment Act removed the distinction between adult and a minor for the purpose of compensation, reduced waiting period from 7 to 3 days, and enlarged the scope of Schedule I, II and III
1962	Wage limit was raised from Rs. 400 to Rs. 500 and the rates of compensation for death was doubled
1976	Wage limit was raised from Rs. 500 to Rs. 1000 and compensation rates were substantially revised
1984	Wage limit was deleted altogether and substituted new schedule III and IV
1995	Keeping in view the general rise in prices and recommendations of Law Commission, the Amendment Act enhanced the minimum rates and amounts of compensation. In the case of death and total disablement, provision was made for lump sum payment towards funeral expenses in addition to compensation when workers die, and enhanced fines for certain offences.Certain categories of persons including employed in mechanised harvesting and threshing operations, spraying and dusting of insecticides/pesticides in agricultural operations, employed for outdoor duties in newspaper establishment, etc. have been added in Schedule II.

2000 : Workmen's Compensation (Amendment) Act, 2000

- ❏ The compensation amount in the case of death was raised from Rs 50,000 to Rs 80,000.
- ❏ The compensation amount in the case of permanent total disablement was raised from Rs 60,000 to Rs 90,000.

2008 : Workmen's Compensation (Amendment) Bill, 2008

The salient features of the Bill introduced in the Lok Sabha in September, 2008 are as follows:—

1. It provides for substitution of the word 'workman' with word 'employee' so that the Act is applicable to all classes of employees and to make the expression gender-neutral.
2. To re-name the Workmen's Compensation Act, 1923 as the Employee's Compensation Act, 1923.
3. To omit restrictive clauses in Schedule II of the Act, so as to make it more workers friendly.
4. Keeping in view the changing trend in the wage level of employees, it is proposed to have an enabling provision to revise the wage ceiling from time to time by the Central Government.

5. To enhance the funeral expenses of the deceased workman from Rs. 2500 to Rs. 3000 and also to empower the Central Government to enhance such expenses from time to time.

6. Provision is being made so that persons who have a minimum qualification of not less than five years as a member of a State Judicial Service or not less than five years of experience as an advocate or a pleader shall be eligible to become the Commissioner.

Objectives, Scope and Features of the Act

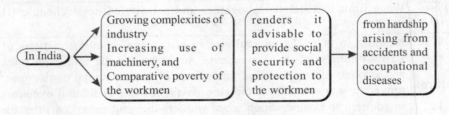

In India ↔ Growing complexities of industry Increasing use of machinery, and Comparative poverty of the workmen → renders it advisable to provide social security and protection to the workmen → from hardship arising from accidents and occupational diseases

To meet the said object, Workmen's Compensation Act was enacted in 1923.

Judicial Interpretation/Case Example

The Act has, true to its object, provided a separate, speedy and cheap forum to the workman or his dependent for claiming compensation and, for that purpose, has given wide powers to the Commissioner who is entrusted with adjudication of the claim.	*Samir U. Parikh* v *Sikandar Zahiruddin,* 1984 Lab IC (Bom) 521 P524.
While interpreting the provisions of Workmen's Compensation Act, liberal construction of provisions should be adopted for provisions and there is no reason for taking a narrow view.	*Oriental Insurance Company Ltd.* v *Nagaraj and Others* 2008 LLR 780 (Madras HC).
Workmen's Compensation Act is a beneficial legislation intended to give some security to workmen in certain types of employment. Therefore, the Act should be construed in a broad and liberal manner, lest its evident object is defeated.	*Zubeda Bano* v *Maharastra State Road Transport Corpn.,* (1991) 1 LLJ 66 (68) Bom (DB).
In a welfare legislation like the Workmen's Compensation Act, if any particular provision is capable of two interpretations, the one which is more favourable to the person for whose benefit the legislation has been made, should be adopted.	*Lipton (India) Ltd* v *Gokul Chandra Mondal,* 1981 Lab IC 1300, 1981 ACJ 453 (Cal).
The object behind the legislation being protection to the weaker section with a view to do social justice, the provisions of the Act have to be interpreted liberally. So that, other things being equal, the leaning of the Court has to be towards the person for whose benefit the Act is made.	*New India Assurance Co Ltd* v *Ajay Medhi and another,* 1996 (1) TCA 310 (Gau).

Contd..

Held, while disbursement of compensation, which is to be deposited by the employer, the Commissioner has to take utmost precautions that the interest of the claimant is protected under the benevolent legislation and the money will go to the right person and the middleman should not take advantage hence the guidelines as given by the High Courts are to be followed.	*New India Assurance Co. Ltd* v *Narsinh D. Harijan (Solanki) and Ors,* 2007 LLR 1085 (Gujarat HC).

Scope of the Act

Two criteria have been followed in the determination of the clauses to be included in schedule II

- (*i*) That the Act should be confined to industries which are more or less organised, and
- (*ii*) That only those workmen whose occupation is hazardous should be included.

Features of the Act

1. Act provides for cheaper and quicker mode of disposal of disputes through special proceedings than possible under Civil Laws
2. The Act provides compensation to workmen for injury caused by accident and occupational disease arising out of and in the course of employment
3. **Amount of Compensation**

> **Death**
> 50% of monthly wages multiplied by relevant factor
> or
> Rs. 80,000, whichever is more
> **Permanent total disablement**
> 60% of monthly wages multiplied by relevant factor
> or
> Rs. 90,000, whichever is more
> Permanent partial disablement
> **Part II of Schedule I specified injury**—Such percentage as payable in case of permanent total disablement
> **Part II of Schedule I unspecified injury**—proportionate to loss

4. The Act is applicable to apprentices also (during his training).
5. Procedure for settlement of claims is through Commissioners.
6. Workmen's compensation is not payable

- (*i*)   To persons insured under Employees State Insurance Act, 1948.
- (*ii*) If the workmen is under influence of drink or drugs.
- (*iii*) If the workmen wilfully disobeys instructions or rules framed or safety guards or other devices.
- (*iv*) If total or partial disablement does not exceed 3 days.

Comparison between Workmen's Compensation Act and ESI Act

Point of Comparison	Workmen's Compensation Act, 1923	ESI Act, 1948
Preamble	The WC Act is restricted to providing compensation to the workmen for injury caused to workmen arising out of and in the course of emp-loyment.	The ESI Act provides benefits to workmen in case of sickness, maternity and employment injury.
Coverage	Employment injury or death arising from accidents or occupational diseases is covered.	Employment injury or death arising from accidents or occupational diseases, sickness and maternity are covered.
Schemes	The Act offers non contributory set up wherein the employer has to pay the entire compensation which cannot be attached assigned or charged by the employer.	The Act offers contributory schemes where in both the employer and the employee contribute 4.75% and 1.75% of wages respectively.
Benefits	The Act provides only disablements benefit and dependent's benefit.	The Act provides for six benefits namely sickness benefit, medical benefit, maternity benefit, disablement benefit, death benefit and funeral expenses.
Payment Responsibility	The responsibility of payment lies with the employer.	The responsibility of payment lies on the ESIC.
Quantum of Compensation	Compensation is a one time lump sum cash payment.	Compensation is paid perio-dically.
Rehabilitation and Re-employment	No such provision under the Workmen's Compensation Act, 1923.	Section 19 provides for rehabilita-tion and reemployment of insured persons who have been disabled.
Claim Process	Process of getting claims/ redressal is too complex and time consuming.	Process is easy and convenient.
Supremacy of the Act	Workmen's Compensation Act, 1923 is not much attractive as it provides lesser compensation as compared to the ESIC Act.	Judicial pronouncements have upheld the supremacy of the ESI Act over the Workmen's Com-pensation Act, 1923 as held in *A. Trehan* v *Associated Electrical Agencies*, AIR 1996 SC 1990.

Definitions [Section 2]

■ *Dependent* [2 (1) (*d*)]

Means any of the relatives of a deceased workman specified in the list of relatives given under Section 2 (*d*)

Judicial Interpretations/Case Example	
In order to claim compensation, it is necessary for the claimants to prove that they were dependents on the deceased. A legal representative who is not dependent is not entitled to claim compensation for the death of the deceased under the Workmen's Compensation Act.	*I.S. Malik* v *Mohamadhu Sen Nabibbhai Shaikh*, 1984 LIC 70 (September).
The question of dependency is a question of fact and it must be proved to sustain a claim for compensation.	AIR 1939 Rang 369.
The law does not require that the widower should be wholly dependent on the earnings of the deceased wife. Partial dependence to whatever extent it may be, is sufficient to bring him within the purview of Section 2 (1) (*d*).	*Div. Manager New India Assurance Co. Ltd.* v *Rahidas Sabar*, 1998 Lab IC 2447 (Ori).
Widowed mother does not include 'widowed step-mother'.	*Munando Devi* v *Bengal Bone Mill*, 1940 (Cal) 285.
A widow after her re-marriage can claim compensation.	*R.B. Moondra and Co.* v *Bhanwari*, 1970 Lab IC 695 (Raj).
There is nothing in Workmen Compensation Act to prohibit a widow from remarrying. There is no provision in Workmen Compensation Act which debars a widow from claiming compensation solely on the ground that she has remarried. The Workmen Compensation Act clearly provides that a dependent, who was wholly dependent or partly dependent at the time of death of the deceased was entitled to receive compensation.	*Sohanbeer* v *Workmen's Compensation Commissioner, Muzaffarnagar and Ors*, 2007 LLR 791, (Allahabad HC).
Sister of mother of the deceased does not fall within the definition of 'dependant'.	*United India Insurance* v *Harinakshi*, 1998 Lab IC 2493 (Kant).
Held, real brother or the son of real brother would not come within the purview of 'dependent' under the Workmen's Compensation Act to claim compensation on an alleged accident. Also held, an adopted son is dependent for claiming compensation on the death of his father but when the adoption was neither proper nor there was any adoption ceremony of the real parents handing over the adopted or the parents receiving him, then it will not be deemed as adopted son for claiming compensation pertaining to death of his father.	*National Insurance Co. Ltd.* v *Mst. Param Pal Singh, through his father Sh. Santokh Singh*, 2007 LLR 984, (Delhi HC).

■ *Employer* [*Section* 2 (1) (e)]

Employer includes any body of persons whether incorporated or not including legal representative of a deceased employer.

Judicial Interpretations/Case Example	
It is a question of fact depending on the facts and circumstances of a particular case as to who is an employer within the meaning of Section 2(*e*). The general manager of railway is employer of its workers.	AIR 1960 All 362.
According to the Orissa High Court, the expression 'employer' does not include insurer who is the indemnifier in respect of any amount awarded against the insured	*Oriental Fire and General Insurance Co Ltd* v *Kamuran Bibi*, 1993 ACJ 172.

■ *Partial Disablement* [*Section* 2 (1) (g)]

If it is of temporary nature	Such disablement as reduces earning capacity of a workman in an employment in which he was engaged at the time of accident resulting in the disablement.
If it is of permanent nature	Such disablement as reduces earning capacity in every employment which the worker was capable of undertaking at that time. Every injury specified in Schedule I (Part II) shall be deemed to result in permanent partial disablement.

Judicial Interpretations/Case Example	
No compensation is granted for any physical disability unless there was loss of earning capacity. It is only in the case of scheduled injury that such loss is presumed. Where the injury is not scheduled injury, the loss of earning capacity must be proved.	*Calcutta Electric Supply Corp.* v *HC Das*, (1968) 2 LLJ 169.
Loss of earning capacity or its extent is a question of fact. It has to be determined by taking the destruction of physical capacity as disclosed by the medical evidence.	*Calcutta licensed Measures Bengal Chamber of Commerce* v *Md. Hassain*, AIR 1969 Cal 378 p 379.
The Act is not limited only to physical capacity of disablement, but extends to the reduction of earning capacity as well.	*Sukkai* v *Hukum Chand Jute Mills Ltd.*, AIR 1957 (Cal) 601.

■ *Total Disablement* [*Section* 2 (1) (l)]

Such disablement whether of a temporary or permanent nature as incapacitates a workman for all work which he was capable of performing at the time of accident resulting in such disablement and every injury specified in Part I of Schedule I or combination of injuries specified in Part II of Schedule I where to aggregate percentage, as specified in Part II against those injuries amounts to 100% or more.

Judicial Interpretations/Case Example	
'Partial disablement' concerns losses of earning capacity while 'total disablement' relates to total incapacitation for all work, the workman was capable of doing.	*Moti Lal* v *Thakurdas,* 1985, 2 LLN 951(All).
Where an employee becomes unfit for a particular class of job but is fit for another class which is offered to him by employer, held that the workman was entitled to claim compensation on the basis of partial disablement and not total disablement.	*General Manager GIP Railways* v *Shanker* AIR 1950 (Nag) 301.
Workman suffered injuries during course of employment. Held, he is entitled compensation on the basis of 100 % disablement particularly when he has not been able to perform the same duties which he was discharging prior to the injuries resulting into amputation of right leg upto knee level.	*Pamarthi Subba Rao* v *H. Rama Rao and Anr,* 2008 LLR 889 (AP HC).
Appellant tank driver met with an accident and was severely injured. His right leg amputated upto knee joint. Commissioner held it to be 100% disability and awarded compensation and interest. In appeal, based on the opinion of doctor, the High Court held it to be 65% disability. Relying upon the ratio laid down in the judgement of Pratap Narain Singh Deo v Srinivas Sabata and Another, the Apex Court held that appellant had suffered 100% disability and he was not in a position to work as a driver.Singh Deo v Srinivas Sabata and Another, the Apex Court held that appellant had suffered 100% disability and he was not in a position to work as a driver.	*K. Janardhan* v *United Insurance Company Ltd and Ors,* 2008 LLR 785 (Supreme Court).

■ Workmen [Section 2 (1) (n)]

Workman means any person (other than a person whose employment is of a casual nature and who is employed otherwise, then for the purposes of the employer's trade or business) who is—

(*i*) A railway servant as defined in clause 34 of Section 2 of Railway Act 1989, not permanently employed in any administrative district or sub-divisional office of a railway and not employed in any capacity as is specified in Schedule II, or

(*ii*) A master, seaman or other member of the crew of a ship.

(*iii*) A captain or other member of crew of an aircraft.

(*iv*) A person recruited as driver, helper, mechanic, cleaner, etc. in connection with a motor vehicle.

(*v*) A person recruited for work abroad by a company,

(*vi*) Employed in any such capacity specified in II Schedule.

But does not include any person working in the capacity of a member of the armed forces of the Union.

Judicial Interpretations/Case Example	
As per the definition of workman under Section 2 (n), a person whose employment is of a casual nature, is not covered by the definition unless he has been engaged for the trade or business of the employer. Also, a railway servant or a person specified in Schedule II is a workman, though all railway servants are not covered by the definition.	
The expression 'workman' as defined in the Workmen's Compensation Act, does not cover a casual worker. The claimant in the instant case was engaged as a casual worker who was not employed for the purposes of the employer's trade and business. Therefore his claim under the Act is not maintainable.	*Central Mine Planning and Design Institute Ltd* v *Ramu Passi and Anr.,* 2006 Lab IC 339 (SC).
Held, the definition of a 'workman' under Workman's Compensation Act is very wide hence it is not necessary that there should be a specific appointment letter given to an employee.	*United India Insurance Co. Ltd., Hyderabad* v *K. Anjaneyulu and Another,* 2007 LLR 1075, (AP HC).
A workman, sustaining injuries in an accident while operating the machine, cannot be deprived of compensation by the employer merely on the plea that he was not an employee but only a learner since if it was so; the employer should not have allowed him for operating machine.	*Hanil Era Textiles Ltd.* v *Namdev Mukund Deoghare,* 2007 LLR 1093, (Bombay HC).
In order to show that a person is not a workman within the definition of this section two things must be proved (*i*) his employment was of casual nature and (*ii*) his employment was otherwise than for the purpose of employer's trade or business.	*Mangala Ben* v *Dilip Motwani,* 1998 LLR 656.
A Khalasi employed for the purpose of loading or unloading a truck is a workman. The truck is a vehicle which is propelled by mechanical power and therefore, the Khalasi is covered by the description of workman in Schedule II.	*Orissa Coop Insurance Society Ltd.* v *Sarat Chandra Chaupati,* 1976 Lab IC 371 (Ori).
Held, a combined reading of the provisions of the definition "workman" in Section 2 (1) (*n*) and Sch. II of the Workman Compensation Act indicates that those who are employed in clerical or ministerial services in the factory or trade or other "avocations" are not covered by the Act.	*President/Secretary, Cheyyar Cooperative Primary Agricultural and Rural Development Bank, Ltd., Tiruvannamalai Taluk* v *R. Indirani.,* 2008 LLR 500, (Madras HC).
Mere designation given to a person as supervisor will not change his status as a workman if he is otherwise qualified for it.	*Managing Director J&K P.C.C.* v *Com-*

Contd...

	missioner (1996) 1 LLJ 65 (J&K).
A person employed in a factory where a manufacturing process has not commenced does not merely for that reason stand excluded from the definition of 'workman'.	*Juthi Devi* v *Pine Chemicals Ltd.*, 1989 Lab IC 2310: (1991) 2 LLJ 386 (J&K).
In view of Schedule II, a driver of a vehicle even if the vehicle belonged to the Government is a workman.	*Radhamony* v *Secretary Department of Home,* (1995) 1 LLN 370: 1995 Lab IC 812 (Ker).
A civil servant does not stand ipso facto excluded from the definition of 'workman'.	*State of Gujarat* v *R.K. Deshdia* (1991) 1 LLN 536: (1991) 1 Cur LR 582 (Guj).

Employer's Liability for Compensation [Section 3]

If personal injury is caused to a workman by an accident arising out of and in the course of an employment

(*i*) In case of personal injury ⟶ If personal injury is caused to a workman by an accident arising out of and in the course of an employment.

(*ii*) In case of occupational disease ⟶ If a workman, employed in any employment contracts any occu-pational disease, peculiar to that employment specified in Part A, B and C of Schedule III, the contracting of the disease shall be deemed to be an injury by accident within the meaning of this section.

Conditions

■ (*a*) *There must be Personal Injury*

Normally, injury implies physical or bodily injury caused by an accident. However, such personal injury shall also include nervous shock or break-down or mental strain. ⟶ *Facts of the case:* An electrician who had to go frequently to a heating room from cooling plant, contracted pneumonia which resulted in his death. It was held that the injury caused by an accident is not confined only to physical injury and the injury in the instant case was due to his working and going from a heating room to a cooling plant as it was the indispensable duty. The dependants of the deceased workman were entitled compensation. ⟶ *Indian News Chronicle* v *Mrs Lazarus* AIR 1961 (Punjab).

(b) *Personal Injury must be caused by Accident*

❑ Accident has not been defined in the Act but its meaning has been sufficiently explained in the following decided cases

In this case, the M.P. High Court has clarified the distinction between 'accident' and 'injury'. Accident means an untoward mishap which is not expected or designed by workman. "Injury" means physiological injury. Accident is an event happening externally to a man (workman falling from a ladder and suffers injuries). But injury may be an event happening internally to a man and in such cases accident and injury coincide -like, failure of heart.	*Smt. Sunderbai* v *The General Manager Ordinance Factory*, 1976, Jabalpur (MP).
A series of tiny accidents each cumulatively producing final injury constitutes together an accident within the meaning of this section.	*Chillu Kohar* v *Buru & Co. Ltd.,* AIR 1953 (Cal).

■ *Injury by Accident includes Occupational Disease*

The claimant was engaged as a Khalasi by the South-Eastern Railway in the year 1962. Later he was transferred to Diesel Shed M.T.B. as a Diesel Cleaner. The record of the claimant is unblemished. It is contended that the claimant developed an allergy of diesel and its fumes. Initially the claimant when he was young did not bother much but later he was required to take treatment and was not keeping well. The claimant had approached one Dr. B.D. Mehta for examination and he concluded that claimant was suffering from deformity which he has developed due to continuous contact with diesel. It was also found by the said doctor that he should not work in hot place and should work in cool place. This fact was communicated to the respondent but nothing was done. Applicant thereafter had contacted one Dr. Chiwhane but the condition did not improve. He even was referred by the Medical Officer of the Railways to their main hospital at Calcutta. It was found that he was having allergy of diesel. Due to this allergy it is alleged that he has suffered disfigurement of face and damage in liver as well as kidney that may be due to the allergy of diesel. The claimant's salary was Rs. 2150 p.m. He claimed Rs. 76,510 towards compensation. The Commissioner for Workmen's Compensation Act has not allowed the claim for compensation. Hence appeal was filed. Held, 'allergy of diesel and diesel fumes' cannot be termed as 'occupational disease' as contemplated under Workmen's Compensation Act. High Court held that except the appellant none other workman/employee has suffered similar kind of ailment (*i.e.*, allergy of diesel and diesel fumes) and therefore it cannot be construed an 'occupational disease' for awarding compensation.	*Shridhar Dhondiraj Kelapure, Nagpur* v *General Manager, South Eastern Railway, Calcutta & Ors.,* 2008 LLR 697 (Bombay HC).

Contd..

The claimants respondents had filed a petition seeking compensation in respect of the death of a driver, who had committed suicide. It was contended that after finishing his duty on a particular day the deceased had returned home and it is claimed that he was under extreme mental stress because of alleged harassment at work by his superiors. Therefore, it was urged that the death of the workman had a causal connection with his employment, in that; it arose out of his employment. The Labour Commissioner and Commissioner for Workmen's Compensation, Bijapur having awarded compensation in the face of the contest, the present appeal is filed. In this regard, Schedule III to the Workmen's Compensation Act, 1923 which lists out "occupational diseases" does not include mental stress or allied illnesses as being occupational diseases. Therefore, it cannot be accepted that the act of suicide was brought about by acute stress, which was the cause for the death. Held, the appeal succeeds and the impugned award of the Commissioner is set aside. The amount in deposit is to be refunded to the appellant.	*Maharashtra State Road Transport Corporation v Meenaxi Dhareppa Koli,* 2006 LLR 679 (Karnt. HC).

■ *(c) Accident Arising Out of and in the Course of Employment*

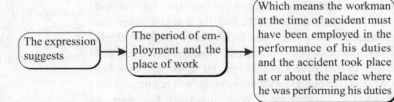

Judicial Interpretations/Case Example	
The burden of proving that accident arose out of employment is upon the workman.	
A workman may be in the course of employment not only when he is actually engaged in doing something in the discharge of his duties to his employer, but also when he is engaged in acts belonging to and arising out of it.	*Union of India* v *Noor Jahan,* 1979 Lab IC 652 (All).
Generally, if a workman is suffering from a particular disease and as a result of wear and tear of his employment he dies of that disease, employer is not liable. But, if the employment is the contributing cause or has accelerated the death, then the employer would be liable. The test is, 'was it part of the injured person's employment to hazard, to suffer or to do that which caused his injury? If yes, the accident arose out of his employment'. As observed by the Supreme Court, the expression "arising out of employment" is not confined to the mere nature to employment. The expression applies to employment, as such to its nature, its conditions, its obligations	*Mackinnon Mackenzie (P) Ltd.* v *Ibrahim Mohammad Issak,* AIR 1970 Goa 127: (1969) 2 SCC 607: 1970 Lab IC 1584.

Contd..

and its incidents. If by reason of any of these factors, the workman is brought within the zone of special danger, the injury would be one which arises out of employment."	
The applicant Fagua Sai being the father of the decreased Dhaneshwar Sai filed an application before the Lower Court for compensation. It is an admitted fact that Dhaneshwar Sai was working in the course of his employment when lighting struck at 4 p.m. Since Dhaneshwar Sai was working in the open field while it was raining, the nature of employment exposed Dhaneshwar to such hazards of lightning. The concept of liability under the Workmen's Compensation Act, 1923 is wide enough to cover a case of this nature since the accident had causal connection with the employment and arose out of it because if he had not been working in the open while it was raining the lightning could not have struck him. High Court upheld the award. Further held, copy of this order be sent forthwith to the Commissioner for Workmen's Compensation, Labour Court, Bilaspur for releasing the amount of compensation deposited by the appellant, in favour of the claimants.	*Divisional Forest Officer (Territorial)* v *Fagua Sai.,* 2008 LLR 276 (Chattisgarh HC).
Bipul Gogok was appointed as a driver of a vehicle bearing Registration No. AS-09/2289 by the third respondent. He reported to his duty at about 9.30 am on 9.10.1996. He was since then not heard by the members of his family or by his employer. The vehicle was not traced. No dead body was found. Whether the said Bipul Gogoi had died or still alive is not certain. Held, the legal heirs of the driver, who has absconded with the vehicle, will not be entitled to compensation in the absence of proof that there has been an accident which has arisen out of and during the course of employment. Hence the compensation as awarded by the Compensation Commissioner is liable to be quashed. Further held, that no presumption can be drawn upto a period of 7 years if a person is not heard. Therefore, the Commissioner under the Workmen's Compensation Act erred in drawing presumption awarding compensation to the dependents of the deceased prior to 7 years.	*Oriental Insurance Company Ltd.* v *Sorumai Gogoi and Others,* 2008 LLR 506, (Supreme Court).
The workman had been in service from 18.05.1990. On 25.12.1990, he suffered a cerebral stroke while at sea. He was therefore taken ashore and was treated in a hospital. Thereafter, in Jan 1991, he was repatriated to India and was admitted to hospital for further treatment. On 11.02.1991, respondent's son had discharged him from the hospital against the medical advice and returned to their native place. The respondent workman claims an amount of Rs 15 lakhs as compensation from the appellant shipper contending that he was suffered from an accident arising out of and in the course of employment. Held, the workman is not entitled to compensation as	*Dockendate Shipping Bombay and Anr* v *Jevanbhai Ramji Tandel,* 2006 Lab IC 896 (Bom HC).

Contd...

the respondent has been unable to show nexus between employment injury and the nature of work that he performed.	
Workman in this case was suffered from heart disease and died on account of strain of work by keeping continuously standing or working, High Court held that accident arose out of employment	*Laxmibai Atma Rami v Bombay Port Trust,* AIR 1954 Bom 180.
The employer went to the house of deceased workmen who was working as a stockmaker with the respondent employer at a salary of Rs. 4,000 p.m. The employer took the deceased on his scooter for some urgent work when on the route, the scooter met with a serious accident and the deceased succumbed to his injuries next day in the hospital. Held, the injury causing his death was sustained during course of employment and his heirs and defendants could file claim for compensation under the Motor Vehicles Act.	*New India Assurance Co Ltd v Jivram Jetha Samshamia (Dead) through his heirs Gita Sen and Others,* 2006 (109) FLR 900 (Guj-HC).
Deceased working as driver after loading his truck fell ill on his way and asked cleaner to drive his truck. On 20.05.94 at about 4.00 A.M, some army personnel stopped vehicle and asked the persons sitting inside the vehicle to come down. Due to illness, deceased driver took some time to come down which infuriated army personnel who fired at him resulting in his death. Held, the accident has occurred arising out of and in the course of his employment and the compensation is payable.	*United Insurance Co Ltd v Nirmal Kaur and Ors.,* 2006 Lab IC 612 (J&K HC).
A person appointed as a cleaner, drives the vehicle and the accident occurred. The question that requires to be answered in this appeal is whether the said accident and consequent injury or death can be said to be coming within the purview of expressions "accident arising out of and in the course of employment?" The grievance of the appellant-Insurance Company is that the deceased was not found to have been on duty as a "driver" at the time of the accident and therefore, the question of liability will not arise because the accident did not arise out of and in the course of the employment of the deceased as a "cleaner". The driving of the tractor by a cleaner cannot be brought within the fold of accident arising out of and in the course of employment. The Court held that the Commissioner for Workmen's was error in treating the accident as one arising out and in the course of employment and he lost sight of the fact that it was not the duty of the deceased Nagesh to drive to tractor. But on the other hand, he was only supposed to do the work of a cleaner and nothing else. As such the order of the Workmen's Compensation Commissioner putting the liability on the Insurance Company cannot be sustained in iaw and consequently the said portion of the order is set aside and the liability will be on the owner of the tractor to pay compensation to the claimants. In the results the appeal is allowed and the amount in deposit shall be refunded to the appellant.	*New India Assurance Company Ltd, Bangalore v K.S. Puttappa and Others,* 2008 LLR 327 (Karnataka HC).

Contd...

The deceased driver was entrusted the duty of driving the bus on a particular route. The deceased was free to go home after duty hours, yet he stayed back for rest on the terrace of the bus stand. In the morning while getting down from the terrace, the deceased tumble down resulting in his death. Held, the cause of accident is totally unconnected with the nature of employment and its attending hazard. The fact that accident occurred at work place is not a significant criteria for fastening liability on the employer. The manner of accident and cause of death cannot be deemed to be arising out of and in the course of employment. The employer therefore, is not liable to pay compensation.	*Divisional Contro- ller, North West Karnataka Road Transport Corpo- ration v Draksha- yani and Ors.,* 2006 Lab IC 492 (Karn HC).
Where a workman on duty was bitten by a scorpion and during operation therefore while under treatment as an indoor patient in the hospital, developed tetanus and ultimately died, compensation became payable.	*Divisional Rly Manager v Sham- sadi,* 1988 Lab IC 605 (Raj).

Accidents on Public Streets

The broad points in deciding as to whether in the case of an injury suffered by an employee on a public street while proceeding to or returning from his place of duty, he is entitled to compensation, are: 1. Whether at that moment he was obliged to be on that site by the express or implied terms of contract of his service 2. Whether he was there in his capacity as an employee or merely as a member of public 3. Whether he was at that time under the control or direction of the employer or was acting as a completely free person 4. Whether his presence on the spot was incidental to his employment 5. Whether there was a proximate connection between the employment and the accident	*Union of India* v *Noor Jahan,* 1979 (All).

Doctrine of Contributory Negligence (*Defence to the Employer*)

'Doctrine of Contributory Negligence' provides defence to the employer that the accident has occurred purely due to the negligence on the part of the workman. But such defence has been given no importance under the Workmen's Compensation Act. The main purpose of the Act is to safeguard the interest of the workman and not to deprive them of their rightful claim under the Act. This Doctrine was dealt in cases including like *Padma Devi* v *Raghunath Roy* 1950, *Orissa and Sunderdas Mudaliar* v *Muthamal* 1956.

Doctrine of Added Peril (*Work involves Extra Dangers*)

As per 'Doctrine of Added Peril', if a workman while doing his employer's work undertakes to do some thing which is not ordinarily called upon to do and which involves extra dangers, he cannot hold his employer liable for risks arising therefrom.

This Doctrine was dealt in number of cases including *Bharangya Coal Company Ltd* v *Sabebjan Main and another* 1956 Labour 128.

Doctrine of Notional Extension (*nexus between the time and place of accident and the employment.*). Means

- ❑ Workman is doing master's job, and
- ❑ There is nexus between the time and place of the accident and the employment.

> The expression 'employment' is wider than the actual work or duty which the workman has to do, is important here. It is enough if at the time of the accident the workman was in actual employment although he may not be actually doing the work at that time.

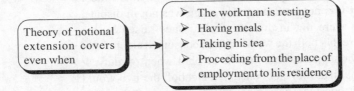

Theory of notional extension covers even when	➤ The workman is resting ➤ Having meals ➤ Taking his tea ➤ Proceeding from the place of employment to his residence

Judicial Interpretations/Case Example

Expression "arising out of and in the course of employment" under the Workmen's Compensation Act, 1923 for determining the nexus of accident would not mean in course of work and the workman. It is significant here that the expression says "in the course of employment" and not "in course of work". Hence there is notional extension of sphere of work of the workman.	*Divisional Manager M/s Oriental Insurance Co Ltd* v *Subhas Chandra Swain and another,* 2008 LLR 108 (Orissa HC).
A workman is in the course of his employment if he reaches the place of work or a point or an area which comes within the theory of notional extension outside of which the employer is not liable to pay compensation for accident.	*Dudhiben Dhoramshi* v *New Jahangir Vakil Mills,* 1977 Lab IC 10 (Guj).

When Employer is not Liable

Following defences are available to the employer:—

1. When injury does not result in disablement for a period exceeding 3 days
2. When the injury not resulting in death or permanent total disablement is due to any of the following reasons:
   - (a) Workman at the time of accident was under the influence of drink drugs or
   - (b) Workman wilfully disobeyed an instruction expressly given or disobeyed the rules of safety, or
   - (c) Workman wilfully disregards any safety of guards or devices provided for safety.

Judicial Interpretations/Case Example	
A sewer line belonging to NDMC but servicing the apartment owned by the appellant got choked. The service line had to be flushed for the reason domestic sewage including human excreta was not being flushed from the toilets in the buildings owned by the appellants or if flushed, was over flowing within the precincts of the complex. Ram Kumar and Ram Singh were made to clear and clean the sewer line. Without proper gear and tools or safety equipment, when the two entered the sewer line for flushing the same to remove the obstruction, both died inside the sewer line. The two inhaled the toxic gases. They were brought dead at RML Hospital. Their wife and children filed claim petition before the Commissioner Workmen Compensation. The employment under the appellant vas not in dispute. Their age was not in dispute. Their wages were not in dispute. Only issues raised by the appellant were that both the workmen had consumed alcohol and they were not supposed to consume alcohol when on duty. It was urged that had they not consumed alcohol, the two would not have lost consciousness when they encountered the toxic gases. Held, the High Court will not interfere with Order of the Commissioner under the Workmen's Compensation Act awarding compensation to the dependents of the deceased scavengers who died inside the sewer line due to toxic gases and plea of the employer that the deceased workmen were drunk will not be tenable, more . ɔ that if the workmen drunk, the Management should not have allowed them to carry their jobs.	*Sir Sobha Singh and Sons Pvt Ltd.* v *Sunita and Ors.,* 2008 LLR 532, (Delhi HC).

Suit for Damages Barred

- No compensation is payable under Workmen's Compensation Act, 1923 if workman has instituted in a Civil Court, a suit for damages against the employer or any other person.
- No suit for damages in any Court of Law is maintainable if a workman has instituted a compensation claim in respect of an injury before a Commissioner or if both workman and employer have entered into a agreement for the payment of compensation in accordance with provisions of Workmen's Compensation Act, 1923.

Compensation

■ *Amount of Compensation [Section 4]*

(*a*) Where death results from the Injury

> An amount equal to 50% of the monthly wages of the deceased workmen multiplied by relevant factor
> Or
> Rs. 80,000, which ever is more

(*b*) **Where permanent total disablement results from the Injury**

> 60% of monthly wages multiplied by relevant factor
> or
> Rs. 90,000, whichever is more

(*c*) **Where permanent partial disablement results from the Injury**

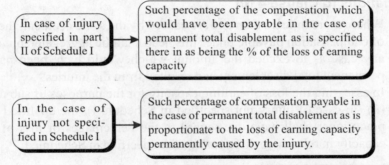

In case of injury specified in part II of Schedule I → Such percentage of the compensation which would have been payable in the case of permanent total disablement as is specified there in as being the % of the loss of earning capacity

In the case of injury not specified in Schedule I → Such percentage of compensation payable in the case of permanent total disablement as is proportionate to the loss of earning capacity permanently caused by the injury.

(*d*) **Where temporary disablements whether total or partial results from the injury**

> Half monthly payment of the sum equivalent to 25% of monthly wages to be paid in accordance with the following provisions:
>
> (*i*) Half monthly payment shall be payable on 16th day from the date of disablement where such disablement lasts for a period of 28 days or more
>
> OR
>
> (*ii*) Payable on 16th day, after the expiry of a waiting period of 3 days from the date of disablement where such disablement lasts for a period of less than 28 days and thereafter half monthly during the disablement or during a period of 5 years, whichever is shorter.

Explanations

1. For the purpose of Section 4 (*a*) and (*b*) relevant factor in relation to a workman means the factor specified in the 2nd column of Schedule IV. The

table given in schedule IV shows that relevant factor keeps on decreasing with the increase of workman's age, as is explained below:

Age	Relevant Factor
Not more than 16	228.54
17	227.49
—	
—	
—	
40	184.17
64	102.93
65 or more	99.37

2. Where the monthly wages of a workman exceed Rs. 2,000, his monthly wages for the purpose of 4 (*a*) and (*b*) shall be deemed to be Rs. 2,000 only.

Explanations to Clause 4 (c)

(*i*) Where more injuries than one are caused by the same accident, the amount of compensation payable under this head shall be aggregated but not so in any case as to exceed the amount which would have been payable if permanent total disablement had resulted from the injuries.

(*ii*) In assessing the loss of earning capacity for the purposes of sub clause 4c (*ii*) (in case of injury not specified in Schedule I), the qualified medical practitioner shall have due regard to the percentages of loss of earning capacity in relation to different injuries specified in Schedule I.

Judicial Interpretations/Case Example	
Compensation shall be calculated on the date of accident and not on the date of application or order. The rates which may be revised during proceedings will not apply retrospectively. Similarly, if a workman claims less compensation than what is admissible under Section 4 and the Schedule to the Act, the Commissioner may grant the compensation as prescribed under the provisions.	*Divisional Controller GSRTC* v *Ashok Kumar Kesharlal Parekh,* (1999) 11 LLJ 259 (Guj).
Held, certain distinction has to be made between the loss of earning and loss of earning capacity. The entitlement to compensation under the Act cannot be denied or postponed depending on the present or future earning. The total amount that a workman can get is fixed by the Act; the same depends upon the difference between his wage earning capacity before the accident and his wage earning capacity after the accident. The provisions of beneficent Legislation are to be constructed so as to advance the beneficent purpose. Held, the calculation of compensation for the injuries resulting from an accident will be in accordance with the Schedule as given under the Workman's Compensation Act and merely that the concerned workman though	*The General Manager, M/s Tungabadra Minerals Ltd.* v *Sri G Ameer,* 2007 LLR 1051, (Karnataka HC).

Contd..

rendered partially disabled has been employed with the same employer and also he has been given promotion to the senior electrician with higher scale of pay, he will not be deprived from claiming compensation.	
Where the management paid the ad-hoc amount immediately after the happening of the tragic accident in the course of employment, deduction of such amount from the compensation awarded under the Act was held to be wholly unjustified.	*Suchitra Devi V Laour Court,* (1996) 2 LLJ 712 (SC).
For non scheduled injuries *i.e.,* injuries outside Part I of Schedule II, the claim has to be accompanied by an assessment of a qualified medical practitioner.	*Bhag Narain Ram v Manik Sarkar* 2001 (Cal).
The deceased Jashubhai Rana expired in the accident while performing his duty in course of his employment. Employer ONGC given a job to wife of the deceased. Held, the fact that wife was given a job by ONGC cannot be considered for deducting the compensation. In the opinion of the Court, while the deceased was serving he was getting salary for the work done by him, after his death his wife is getting the salary for the work done by her. Whatever salary wife is receiving is on strength of the work done by her. It is neither gratuitous payment nor is an ex-gratia payment. The policy of compassionate appointment cannot be used as a sword to slash the compensation amount. The learned trial judge was unjustified in making a deduction of 1/3rd amount from the compensation amount. The approach of the trial court was erroneous, unjustified and contrary to the provisions of law. Findings of the trail court were set aside and the court held, no deductions should be made from the ascertained amount of compensation.	*Ushaben J. Rana and Ors v Project Manager, ONGC and Ors,* 2006 Lab IC 1209 (Guj HC).
The rates for calculating the compensation must be the rates given in Schedule IV prevalent on the day of the accident. The claimant must be awarded the full amount of compensation under Section 4 even if claimed a lesser amount.	*New India Assurance Co. Ltd. v Abidabai and Others,* 1996 (MP).
The workmen's compensation commissioner has jurisdiction to award compensation higher than what is claimed.	*Shivlal v Punjab State Electricity Board* 1989 (P&H). *Radhamony v Secretary, Deptt. of Home Affairs,* 1995 (Kerala).
Physical disability is not the same as loss in earning capacity and the two cannot be equated.	*Commrs for Port of Calcutta v S.K. Mushim* 1983 (Cal).

■ Time of Payment of Compensation [Section 4A]

1. In cases, where the employer does not accept the liability for compensation to the extent claimed, he shall be bound to make provisional payment based on the extent of liability which he accepts and such provisional payment shall be deposited with the Commissioner or made to the workman, as the case may be.

2. Where the employer is in default in paying the compensation due under this Act within one month of the date, the Commissioner shall direct the employer. (*a*) To pay simple interest @ 12% p.a. or such higher rate as specified by Central Government. (*b*) To pay further sum not exceeding 50% of such amount (dues + interest) as penalty.

Judicial Interpretations/Case Example

Section 3 of the Act mandates payment of compensation by employer immediately when injury occurs to a workman in the course of employment arising out of employment. Held, the date of accident is the date when compensation fell due. Unlike Motor Vehicle Act, under Workmen's Compensation Act, it is mandatory that the interest is to be paid on the compensation from the date when it fell due for payment. Section 4A (1) casts liability to pay compensation as soon as it falls due. Section 4A (3) casts liability to pay interest if it is not paid within one month from the date of compensation amount fell due. Further held, the term "fell due" under Workmen's Compensation Act means that the compensation for an accident has to be calculated with reference to the provisions of the Act as on the date of accident as compensation fell due on that date itself hence the relevant date for determining the rights and liabilities of parties concerned is the date of accident and not the date of adjudication of the claim.	*National Insurance Co. Ltd v Rekha,* 2008 LLR 5 (Kerala HC).
The interest payable shall be paid to the workman or his dependent as the case may be, but the penalty shall be credited to the State Government.	
Compensation becomes payable on the date of accident and not on the date of determination of the amount thereof.	*Pratap Narain Singh Deo* v *Srinivas Sabata* (1976) 1 SCC 289:
No interest is payable on the penalty imposed u/s 4A(3).	*C. Rajan* v *P.M. Subramanian* 1992 (Ker).

■ Calculation of Wages [Section 5]

(a) Where the workman is in continuous service of not less than 12 months immediately preceding the accident	Monthly Wages is calculated as follows Monthly wages shall be 1/12th of the total wages due in the last 12 months.
(b) Where the whole of continuous service was less than one month	Monthly wages shall be average monthly amount earned during 12 months by any workman employed.
(c) In other cases including cases in which it is not possible to calculate the monthly wages under clause (b) for want of information	Monthly wages shall be 30 times of the total wages earned in respect of the last continuous service preceding the accident divided by number of days comprising such period of work.

> Continuous service means any service which has not been interrupted by a period of absence from the work exceeding 14 days.

■ Distribution of Compensation [Section 8]

If injury Resulted in Death

(a) No payment of compensation (including to a woman or disable person) otherwise than by deposit with the Commissioner, provided that in the case of deceased workman, advances on account of compensation can be made.

(b) Any other sum amounting to not less than Rs. 10 (as compensation) may be deposited with Commissioner.

(c) The receipt of the commissioner shall be a sufficient discharge in respect of deposited compensation.

(d) On the deposit of compensation money, the Commissioner shall issue notice to be published/served on each dependent, to appear before him on date fixed and the Commissioner after inquiry, shall return the amount to employer if no dependent exists.

(e) The deposited compensation shall be apportioned among the dependents.

(f) Where any lumpsum deposited is payable to a woman/disabled person, such sum may be invested or applied in such manner as the Commissioner may direct.

(g) In case of fraud/impersonation/or other improper means, amount may be recovered.

Judicial Interpretations/Case Example	
The provisions of Section 8 prohibit an employer from making any payment of compensation in respect of the death of a workman directly to his heirs and legal representatives or any of them. The employer shall deposit the amount of compensation with the commissioner. Any direct payment made shall be no payment.	*Samuben* v *Patel Industries*, 1995 ACJ 75 pg78 (Guj).

Contd..

The object of the provisions of Section 8 is that a manipulator or unscrupulous type of employer should not take undue advantage of the ignorance of the employee. Therefore, the section safeguards the interest of the workman by providing that any private payment will not discharge the statutory obligation.	*May-field Estate Nalhollah Nilgiris v Krishna*, 1984 (48) FLR 483 (Mad).
Where the deceased workman had only one heir, the compensation amount deposited with the Commissioner became the property of such dependent and if that sole dependent died prior to allotment of that compensation, the said amount devolved on the heirs of the dependent and not on the heirs of the deceased workman.	*Commissioner for Workmen's Compensation v P. Mohanan*, 1989 Lab IC 1072: (1988) 1 Cur LR 238: (1988) 2 LLJ 177 (Ker) (DB).
In the case of minor dependants and illiterate widows, the Commissioner should order the amount of compensation to be invested in long term fixed deposits with Nationalised Banks enabling the claimants to get interest monthly and to make withdrawals for emergencies	*Vrajlal Laximidas Ladani v Fatimaben*, (1986) 1 LLN 642 (Guj) (DB).
Where a dependent dies during the pendency of the claim filed by him, his or her legal heirs can prosecute the claim for compensation.	*Kaveri Structurals Ltd. v Bhagyam*, (1978) 36 HR 31 (Kar).

■ Compensation not to be Assigned, Attached or Charged [Section 9]

No payment payable under this Act shall in any way be capable of being assigned, or charged or liable to be attached or pass to any person other than the workman by operation of law, nor shall any claim be set-off against the same.

Notice and Claim [Sec 10] Notice of accident in the prescribed manner be given as soon as practicable after the occurrence of accident

Claim within 2 years of the accident or death be filed.

Power to Require from Employers Statements Regarding Fatal Accidents [Section 10A]

1. Where a Commissioner receives information from any source that a workman has died as a result of an accident arising out of and in the course of his employment, he may send by registered post a notice to the workman's employer requiring him to submit, within thirty days of the service of the notice, a statement, in the prescribed form, giving the circumstances attending

the death of the workman, and indicating whether, in the opinion of the employer, he is or is not liable to deposit compensation on account of the death.

2. If the employer is of opinion that he is liable to deposit compensation, he shall make the deposit within thirty days of the service of the notice.

3. If the employer is of opinion that he is not liable to deposit compensation, he shall in his statement indicate the grounds on which he disclaims liability.

4. Where the employer has so disclaimed liability, the Commissioner, after such inquiry as he may think fit, may inform any of the dependants of the deceased workman that it is open to the dependants to prefer a claim for compensation, and may give them such other further information as he may think fit.

Reports of Fatal Accidents and Serious Bodily Injuries [Section 10B]

1. Where, by any law for the time being in force, notice is required to be given to any authority, by or on behalf of an employer, of any accident occurring on his premises which results in death or serious bodily injury, the person required to give the notice shall, within seven days of the death or serious bodily injury send a report to the Commissioner giving the circumstances attending the death or serious bodily injury:

   Provided that where the State Government has so prescribed the person required to give the notice may instead of sending such report to the Commissioner send it to the authority to whom he is required to give the notice.

   Explanation.— "Serious bodily injury" means an injury which involves, or in all probability will involve the permanent loss of the use of, or permanent injury to, any limb, or the permanent loss of or injury to the sight or hearing, or the fracture of any limb, or the enforced absence of the injured person from work for a period exceeding twenty days.

2. The State Government may, by notification in the Official Gazette, extend the provisions of sub-section (1) to any class of premises other than those coming within the scope of that sub-section, and may, by such notification, specify the persons who shall send the report to the Commissioner.

3. Nothing in this section shall apply to factories to which the Employees State Insurance Act, 1948 (34 of 1948), applies.

Medical Examination [Section 11]

❑ Before the expiry of 3 days of service of notice, the workman should offer himself for medical examination by a qualified medical practitioner. This medial examination is done at the cost of employer.

Contracting

■ *Principal Employer's Liability when a Contractor is Engaged Contracting* [*Section* 12]

This section envisages the employer's liability to pay compensation to a contractor if an injury is caused by an accident to any of the workers engaged by a contractor who is appointed by the principal employer. Normally the principal employer is not held liable because such workers are not employed by him.

→

The principal employer's liability under Section 12(1) is in the following circumstances:

(*a*) The contractor is engaged to do a work which is part of the trade or business of the principal employer.

(*b*) The workmen were engaged in the course of or for the purpose of his trade or business.

(*c*) The accident occurred in or about the premises on which the principal employer undertakes to execute the work.

■ *Indemnified by the Contractor* [*Section* 12(2)]

(*a*) The principal employer shall be entitled to be indemnified by the contractor or any other person from whom the workman could have recovered compensation.

(*b*) All questions as the right to and the amount of any such indemnity shall in the absence of agreement, be settled by the Commissioner

(*c*) Above provisions, however, do not prevent a workman from recovering compensation from the contractor instead of the principal employer.

(*d*) Section (12(2)) shall not apply in any case where the accident occurred elsewhere than on in or about the premises on which the principal employer has undertaken or usually undertakes the work or which are otherwise under his control or management.

Judicial Interpretations/Case Example	
Under Section 12, a right is given to the workman to claim compensation either from the contract being the immediate employer or from the principal or from both: The object behind the provision of Section 12 is to secure compensation to the poor workman who cannot otherwise fight out his battle for compensation by a speedy process.	*Koli Mansukh Rana* v *Patel Natha Ramji,* (1995) II LLJ (Supp) 669 (Guj).
Under Section 12, the principal employer is made liable even in respect of the workman engaged under the contractor, if the work entrusted with the contractor is connected with the trade and business of the principal employer.	*Asstt. Director of Horticulture Division Anna Pannai* v *Andi,* (1997) 2 LLJ 568 (Mad).

Contd..

The object of Section 12 is to protect the workman and secure compensation for him from persons in a better position to pay.	*Bhutabhai Angadbhai* v *Gujarat Electricity* Board, (1987) 1 LLN 156 (Guj) (DB).
The principal's liability under Section 12(1) does not extend to interest and penalty.	*Sarjero Unkar Jhadav* v *Gurinder Singh* (1990) 2 LLN 921 (Bom).

Commissioners

Appointment of Commissioners [Section 20]

(*i*) State Government may, by notification in the Official Gazette, appoint any person to be a Commissioner for Workmen's Compensation for the specified areas.

(*ii*) If more than one Commissioner has been appointed for any area, the State Government may by general or specific order, regulate the business between them.

(*iii*) Every Commissioner shall be deemed to be a public servant within the meaning of the Indian Penal Code (IPC) 1860.

(*iv*) Any Commissioner may choose one or more persons possessing special knowledge to assist him in holding the inquiry.

Jurisdiction of Commissioners [Section 19]

(*i*) The Commissioner has jurisdiction over following matters:

  (*a*) Liability of any person to pay compensation,
  (*b*) Whether a person injured is or is not a workman?
  (*c*) The nature and extent of disablement
  (*d*) The amount or duration of compensation.

(*ii*) **Jurisdiction of Civil Court Barred:** No Civil Court has jurisdiction to settle, decide or deal with any question which is under this Act, required to be settled, decided or dealt by a Commissioner.

However, where the Commissioner has no jurisdiction and even fails to decide any matter when raised thereby leaving a party without any defence, the Civil Court has jurisdiction to entertain such suits.	*Madina Saheb* v *Province of Madras* 1946 (Mad).

Judicial Interpretations/Case Example	
Commissioner under this Act is not a Court within the meaning of Section 115 of CPC and an order passed by him under Section 19 of the Workmen Compensation Act, is not revisable by the High Court under Section 115 of CPC.	*New India Assurance Co. Ltd* v *Joseph,* (2000) 1 Lab LJ 1063 (Ker).
However, Commissioner's order has been held to be revisable.	*Mohanlal* v *Fine Knitting Mills Co. Ltd.,* AIR 1960 Bombay.

Venue of Proceedings and Transfer [Section 21]

Where any matter is under the Act to be done by or before a Commissioner, the same shall be done for the area in which the accident took place which resulted in the injury.

Judicial Interpretations/Case Example	
Deceased Md. Rajik Ahmed was an employee of the respondent-company. He died on 14th July, 2000. A petition for claiming compensation under the Workmen's Compensation Act was filed by the father and mother of the deceased before the Commissioner, Workmen's Compensation, Zone-III, Tezpur. In the said petition, the learned, Commissioner, Tezpur awarded compensation of Rs. 2,20,520. Aggrieved against the said order passed by the Commissioner, Workmen's Compensation, Tezpur, the resident-company preferred an appeal before the High Court of Guahati. Two arguments were raised before the High Court on behalf of the respondent-company (appellant in the High Court), (1) that the Commissioner, Workmen's Compensation, Tezpur had no jurisdiction to entertain the claim petition, and (2) the death of the deceased did not occur during the course of employment. As per the territorial jurisdiction for filling of compensation claim, petition can be filed where claimant ordinarily resides. It is not necessary that it should be filed where accident has taken place. Section 21(1) (*b*) read with proviso is a beneficial legislation for the welfare of the workmen. It has to be interpreted to advance the cause of the workmen for whom the enactment is made. Held, even when the dependents of the deceased dieing in accident have shifted from the place of accident and residing with the son-in-law, they can raise the claim at the place where they have started residing and not at the place of accident.	*Morgina Begam* v *Managing Director, Hanuma plantation Ltd,* 2008 LLR 386, (Supreme Court).
Where any proceeding pending before the Commissioner is sought to be transferred before any other Commissioner, such transfer cannot be ordered by the Commissioner himself unless prior sanction of the State Government is obtained. If the second Commissioner works for another State, then prior approval of the Government of the State is required to be obtained for transfer.	*United India Insurance Co. Ltd.* v *Sasikala Sahoo,* (1995) 2 LLJ 1235 (Ori).

Powers and Duties of Commissioners: The powers and duties of commissioners are:

    (*i*)   Deposit and distribution of compensation (Section 8)

    (*ii*)   Powers to require from employers statement regarding fatal accident (Section 10A)

    (*iii*) Power of settlement of disputes [Section 19(1)]

    (*iv*) Power of transfer [Section 21 (2)]

(*v*)　Power to require further deposit in cases of fatal accident [Section 22A]

(*vi*)　Power of Civil Court [Section 23]

(*vii*)　Power to order costs [Section 26]

(*viii*)　Power to submit cases [Section 27]

(*ix*)　Power to withhold certain payments pending decisions of an appeal [Section 30A]

(*x*)　Power of recovery [Section 31]

(*xi*)　Power and duty to record evidence

Procedure of Commissioners Powers [Section 23]

(*i*)　The Commissioner shall have all the powers of a Civil Court under the Code of Civil Procedure 1908 for the following purposes:

　　(*a*)　Taking evidence on oath.

　　(*b*)　Enforcing the attendance of witnesses, and

　　(*c*)　Compelling the production of documents and material objects.

(*ii*)　Further, for the purposes of Section 195 and of Chapter XXVI of the Code of Criminal Procedure 1973, the Commissioner shall be deemed to be a Civil Court.

Judicial Interpretations/Case Example	
Commission while awarding compensation under Workmen's Compensation Act is not required conducting elaborate inquiry. The commissioner is required to find out prima facie as to whether the accident has arisen out of the use of a motor vehicle and it has resulted in permanent disablement or death of the person concerned and as such an elaborate inquiry is not required to dispose of the application. Similar views were expressed by Supreme Court in the case of *Shivaji Dayanu Patil* v *Vatschata Uttam More*, AIR 1991 SC 1769.	*National Insurance Company Ltd* v *Bidashi Kalo and Others*, 2006 Lab IC 1395 (Orissa HC).
The Commissioner has no inherent power to review his earlier judgement on the ground of illegality.	*Basudeo Roi* v *Jagarnath Singh* 1987 (Pat).
It is not for the medical practitioner to certify as to loss of earning power while certifying percentage of disability. It is the Commissioner to assess and fix the percentage of disability.	*United Insurance Co.* v *Sethumadavan* (1993) 1 LLJ 142 (AP) (Ker).

Judicial Interpretations/Case Example	
The Commissioner has jurisdiction for appointment and issue of orders for recording evidence of a workman who is injured and practically unable to come to the Court of Commissioner.	*Jeewabhai R. Tandel* v *Dockendaie Shipping* (1996) 2 Cur LR 639 (Bom) (DB)

Appearance of Parties [Section 24]

Any appearance, application or act required to be made by any person before a Commissioner, may be made or done on behalf of such person by a legal practitioner or by an official of insurance company or a registered trade union or by an Inspector appointed under Factories Act or under Mines Act or any other officer authorised by State government.

Judicial Interpretations/Case Example	
This section permits an office bearer of registered Trade Union to make an application on behalf of an injured employee	*Bhagwandas* v *Pyarelal,* AIR 1954 MB 59.
A manager of a Joint Hindu Family without any authorisation in writing is competent to make application.	*Nanak Chand Shadiram* v *Mahabir,* AIR 1935 (All) 408.

Method of Recording Evidence [Section 25]

This Section provides that the Commissioner shall make a brief memorandum of the substance of the evidence of every witness and such memorandum shall be written and signed by the Commissioner with his own hand and shall form part of the record.

Judicial Interpretations/Case Example	
Without examining the medical officer, the medical certificate ought not to be made the basis of award.	*MSN Co.Ltd.* v *Mohd. Kunjee* AIR 1956 Tra Co. 935

Appeals [Section 30]

An appeal lies to High Court from the following orders of a Commissioner:

(a) An order awarding lump sum compensation.

(b) An order awarding interest or penalty.

(c) An order refusing to allow redemption of a half monthly payment.

(d) An order providing for the distribution of compensation among the dependents.

(e) An order allowing or disallowing any claim for the amount of indemnity under the provisions of Section 12(2).

(f) An order refusing to register a memorandum of agreement or registering the same or providing for the registration of the same subject to conditions.

The period of limitation for an appeal under this Section is 60 days.

No Appeal

❑ No appeal lies against any order unless a substantial question of law is involved in the appeal.

❑ No appeal lies in any case in which the parties have agreed to abide by the decision of the Commissioner or in which the order of the Commissioner gives effect to an agreement came to by the parties.

Judicial Interpretations/Case Example	
Compensation was claimed on account of death of an employee in an accident in factory of petitioner. Application by the petitioner to summon persons and certain documents was rejected by Commissioner. Held, merely because the Compensation Commissioner under the Workmen's Compensation Act has declined to accept the application for summoning certain persons, the appeal for such interlocutory order will not be tenable in the High Court.	*Vaibhav Castings (P.) Ltd. v Workmen's Compensation Commissioner, Kanpur and Others,* (Allahabad HC, 2008 LLR 1007).
Appeal filed by the Delhi Jal Board against the respondent workman on the ground that the employee was neither on duty nor sustained any injury. No evidence led before the Commissioner' Court by the appellant. Held, the High Court will not interfere with the Award of the Compensation Commissioner awarding compensation for injuries as sustained in an accident even by a casual workman while he was performing his duty.	*Delhi Jal Board v Nayanga Singh,* (Delhi HC, 2008 LLR 960).
Appeal was filed by the employer against the award. Held, for the purpose of preferring an appeal, statutory deposit of amount means principal sum and not interest or penalty. Held, for filing an appeal against award of the Workmen's Compensation Commissioner, the employer has to deposit the amount awarded and not the interest or penalty.	*Indo Aromatic Pvt. Ltd. v Smt. Sarvesh Devi and Others,* (Allahabad HC, 2008 LLR 910).
The appeal is directed against the judgement and order dated 5th December 2006 passed by the Learned Single Judge (Chief Justice) of the High Court by which the High Court has dismissed the appeal on technical ground that the appeal was not maintainable under Section 30(1) of the Workmen's Compensation Act, 1923 and the memorandum of appeal was not accompanied by the certificate issued by the Commissioner, to show that the appellant has deposited with him the amount payable under the order which was appealed. Held, the High Court should not have rejected the appeal of the employer filed against the Commissioner by depositing the amount of compensation as determined by way of demand draft along-with covering letter since there is no prescribed format in the Act or the Rules. Hence the Supreme Court set aside the order of the High Court.	*EMM Tex Synthetics v Om Prakash and Anr,* 2008 LLR 872 (Supreme Court).
The proviso to Section 30 (1) states that no appeal shall lie against any order unless a substantial question of law is involved. This provision has been incorporated into the section with the object that the workers shall not be dragged into unending litigation.	*Raveedran v Somavally,* (1996) 1 LLJ 325: 1995 Lab IC 2765: 1995 LLR 903 (Ker) (DB).

Contd...

The phrase 'substantial question of law' must be given a wider construction than under Section 110 of Civil Procedure Code. It should cover even cases in which the Commissioner has clearly misdirected himself on question of law such as awarding compensation without giving notice to the employer.	AIR 1958 (All) 564.
Where compensation claimed was less than what the claimant was entitled to and the Commissioner granted the compensation as claimed, the claimant can subsequently file an appeal against the Commissioner's order for availing the compensation as permissible under the Act.	*Chhatia Devi* v *Ruplal Sao,* 1978 Lab IC 1368 (Pat).
Depositing the amount of interest or penalty imposed u/s 4A is not a condition precedent for preferring an appeal against the same. Further, the period of limitation for an appeal u/s 30 is to be computed from the date of pronouncement of the impugned order and not from the date of communication thereof.	*Kap Steel* v *R. Sasikala,* (1990) 2 LLN 738: (1990) Lab IC 1144: (1992) 1 LLJ 61 (Kant) (DB).
If a finding is recorded without any evidence whatsoever, the question is one of law and therefore an appeal under Section 30 (1) is maintainable.	*Forbes Forbes Co-mpbell & Co. Ltd.* v *Mohanand Sharma,* (1965) 2 LLJ 455 (HC).
The question whether a workman has or has not retired after obtaining full wages and petitionary benefits is question of fact on which no appeal lies.	*Chandametta Co-lliery Western Coalfields Ltd.* v *Mangloo,* 1997 ACJ 544 (MP).
The question of condonation of delay in presenting the appeal can be considered only after the certificate of deposit is filed.	*New India Assurance Co. Ltd.* v *Manorama Sahu* (1994) 1 LLN 819 (Ori).
Where subsequent to the passing of an order by the Commissioner, the workman died, the dependents could prefer an appeal against the order even without getting themselves impleaded.	*Kunhipathumma* v *Div Personnel Officer* (1984) 1 LLN 699 (Ker)(DB): 1984 Lab IC 107.

Schedules

The First Schedule

[*See* Sections 2 (1) and (4)]

Part I

List of Injuries Deemed to Result in Permanent Total Disablement

Sl. No.	Description of injury	Percentage of loss of earning capacity
1.	Loss of both hands or amputation at higher sites	100
2.	Loss of a hand and a foot	100
3.	Double amputation through leg or thigh, or amputation through leg or thigh on one side and loss of other foot	100
4.	Loss of sight to such an extent as to render the claimant unable to perform any work for which eye-sight is essential	100
5.	Very severe facial disfigurement	100
6.	Absolute deafness	100

Part II

List of Injuries Deemed to Result in Permanent Partial Disablement

Amputation cases-upper limbs (*either arm*)

Sl. No.	Description of injury	Percentage of loss of earning capacity
1.	Amputation through shoulder joint	90
2.	Amputation below shoulder with stump less than 20.32 cms. from tip of acromion	80
3.	Amputation from 20.32 cms. from tip of acromion to less than 11.43 cms. below tip of olecranon	70
4.	Loss of a hand or of the thumb and four fingers of one hand or amputation from 11.43 cms. below tip of olecranon	60
5.	Loss of thumb	30
6.	Loss of thumb and its metacarpal bone	40
7.	Loss of four fingers of one hand	50
8.	Loss of three fingers of one hand	30
9.	Loss of two fingers of one hand	20
10.	Loss of terminal phalanx of thumb	20
	Amputation cases — lower limbs	
10A	Guillotine amputation of tip of thumb without loss of bone	10

Sl. No.	Description of injury	Percentage of loss of earning capacity
11	Amputation of both feet resulting in end bearing stumps	90
12	Amputation through both feet proximal to the metatarso-phalangeal joint	80
13	Loss of all toes of both feet through the metatarso-phalangeal joint	40
14	Loss of all toes of both feet proximal to the proximal inter-phalangeal joint	30
15	Loss of all toes of both feet distal to the proximal inter-phalangeal joint	20
16	Amputation at hip	90
17	Amputation below hip with stump not exceeding 12.70 cms. in length measured from tip of great trenchanter	80
18	Amputation below hip with stump exceeding 12.70 cms. in length measured from tip of great trenchanter but not beyond middle thigh	70
19	Amputation below middle thigh to 8.89 cms. below knee	60
20	Amputation below knee with stump exceeding 8.89 cms. but not exceeding 12.70 cms.	50
21	Amputation below knee with stump exceeding 12.70 cms.	50
22	Amputation of one foot resulting in end bearing	50
23	Amputation through one foot proximal to the metatarso-phalangeal joint	50
24	Loss of all toes of one foot through the metatarsophalangeal joint	20
	Other injuries	
25	Loss of one eye, without complications, the other being normal	40
26	Loss of vision of one eye, without complications or dis-figurement of eye-ball, the other being normal	30
26A	Loss of partial vision of one eye	10

Loss of—

	A — Fingers of right or left hand Index finger	
27	Whole	14
28	Two phalanges	11
29	One phalanx	9
30	Guillotine amputation of tip without loss of bone	5
	Middle finger	
31	Whole	12
32	Two phalanges	9

Sl. No.	Description of injury	Percentage of loss of earning capacity
33	One Phalanx	7
34	Guillotine amputation of tip without loss of bone	4
	Ring or little finger	
35	Whole	7
36	Two phalanges	6
37	One phalanx	5
38	Guillotine amputation of tip without loss of bone	2
	B — Toes of right or left foot Great toe	
39	Through metatarso-phalangeal joint	14
40	Part, with some loss of bone	3
	Any other toe	
41	Through metatarso-phalangeal joint	3
42	Part with some loss of bone	1
	Two toes of one foot, excluding great toe	
43	Through metatarso-phalangeal joint	5
44	Part, with some loss of bone	2
	Three toes of one foot, excluding great toe	
45	Through metatarso-phalangeal joint	6
46	Part, with some loss of bone	3
	Four toes of one foot, excluding great toe	
47	Through metatarso-phalangeal joint	9
48	Part-with some loss of bone	3

Note.—Complete and permanent loss of the use of any limb or member referred to in this Schedule shall be deemed to be the equivalent to the loss of that limb or member.

The Second Schedule

[*See* Section 2(1)(*n*)]

List of Persons Who, Subject to the Provisions of Section 2 (1) (*n*), are Included in the Definition of Workmen

The following persons are workmen within the meaning of Section 2(1) (*n*) and subject to the provisions of that section, that is to say, any person who is—

(*i*) Employed, otherwise than in a clerical capacity or on a railway, in connection with the operation, repair or maintenance of a lift or a vehicle propelled by steam or other mechanical power or by electricity or in connection with the loading or unloading of any much vehicle; or

(*ii*) Employed, otherwise than in a clerical capacity, in any premises wherein or within the precincts whereof a manufacturing process as defined in clause (*k*) of Section 2 of the Factories Act, 1948 (63 of 1948), is being carried on, or in any kind of work whatsoever incidental to or connected with any such manufacturing process or with the article made, whether or not employment in any such work is within such premises or precincts and steam, water or other mechanical power or electrical power is used; or

(*iii*) Employed for the purpose of making, altering, repairing, ornamenting, finishing or otherwise adapting for use, transport, or sale any article or part of an article in any premises wherein or within the precincts whereof twenty or more persons are so employed;

Explanation: For the purposes of this clause, persons employed outside such premises or precincts but in any work incidental to, or connected, with, the work relating to making, altering, repairing, ornamenting, finishing or otherwise adapting for use, transport or sale any article or part of an article shall be deemed to be employed within such premises or precincts; or

(*iv*) Employed in the manufacture of handling of explosives in connection with the employer's trade or business; or

(*v*) Employed, in any mine as defined in clause (*j*) of Section 2 of the Mines Act, 1952 (35 of 1952), in any mining operation or in any kind of work other than clerical work, incidental to or connected with any mining operation or with the mineral obtained, or in any kind of work whatsoever below ground; or

(*vi*) Employed as the master or as a seaman of—

    (*a*) Any ship which is propelled wholly or in part by steam or other mechanical power or by electricity or which is towed or intended to be towed by a ship so propelled; or

    (*b*) Any ship not included in sub-clause (*a*), of twenty-five tons net tonnage or over; or

    (*c*) Any sea going ship not included in sub-clause (*a*) or sub-clause (*b*) provided with sufficient area for navigation under sails alone; or

(*vii*) Employed for the purpose of:

    (*a*) Loading, unloading, fuelling, constructing, repairing, demolishing, cleaning or painting any ship of which he is not the master or a member of the crew, or handling or transport within the limits of any port subject to the Indian Ports Act, 1908 (15 of 1908), or the Major Port Trusts Act, 1963 (38 of 1963)], of goods which have been discharged from or are to be loaded into any vessel; or

(b) Warping a ship through the lock; or

(c) Mooring and unmooring ships at harbour wall berths or in pier; or

(d) Removing or replacing dry dock caisoons when vessels are entering or leaving dry docks; or

(e) The docking or undocking of any vessel during an emergency; or

(f) Preparing splicing coir springs and check wires, painting depth marks on locksides, removing or replacing fenders whenever necessary, landing of gangways, maintaining lifebuoys up to standard or any other maintenance work of a like nature; or

(g) Any work on jolly-boats for bringing a ships line to the wharf; or

(viii) Employed in the construction, maintenance, repair or demolition of:

(a) Any building which is designed to be or is or has been more than one storey in height above the ground or twelve feet or more from the ground level to the apex of the roof; or

(b) Any dam or embankment which is twelve feet or more in height from its lowest to its highest point; or

(c) Any road, bridge, tunnel or canal; or

(d) Any wharf, quay, sea wall or other marine work including any moorings of ships; or

(ix) Employed in setting up, maintaining repairing or taking down any telegraph or telephone line or post or any overhead electric line or cable or standard or fittings and fixtures for the same; or

(x) Employed, otherwise than in a clerical capacity, in the construction, working, repair or demolition of any aerial ropeway, canal, pipeline or sewer; or

(xi) Employed in the service of any fire brigade; or

(xii) Employed upon a railway as defined in clause (31) of Section 2 and sub-section (1) of Section 197 of the Railways Act, 1989 (24 of 1989), either directly or through a sub-contractor, by a person fulfilling a contract with the railway administration; or

(xiii) Employed as an inspector, mail guard, sorter or van peon in the Railway Mail Service or as a telegraphist or as a postal or railway signaller, or employed in any occupation ordinarily involving outdoor work in the Indian Posts and Telegraphs Department; or

(xiv) Employed, otherwise than in a clerical capacity, in connection with operations for winning natural petroleum or natural gas; or

(xv) Employed in any occupation involving blasting operations; or

(xvi) Employed in the making of any excavation in which on any one day of the preceding twelve months more than twenty-five persons have been employed or explosives have been used, or whose depth from its highest to its lowest point exceeds twelve feet; or (*xvii*)   Employed in the operation of any ferry boat capable of carrying more than ten persons; or

(*xviii*)   Employed, otherwise than in a clerical capacity, on any estate which is maintained for the purpose of growing cardamom, cinchona, coffee, rubber or tea, and on which on any one day in the preceding twelve months twenty-five or more persons have been so employed; or

(*xix*)   Employed, otherwise than in a clerical capacity, in the generating, transforming, transmitting or distribution of electrical energy or in generation or supply of gas; or

(*xx*)   Employed in a lighthouse as defined in clause (*d*) of Section 2 of the Indian Lighthouse Act, 1927 (17 of 1927); or

(*xxi*)   Employed in producing cinematograph pictures intended for public exhibition or in exhibiting such pictures; or

(*xxii*)   Employed in the training, keeping or working of elephants or wild animals; or

(*xxiii*)   Employed in the tapping of palm-trees or the felling or logging of trees, or the transport of timber by inland waters, or the control or extinguishing or forests fires; or

(*xxiv*)   Employed in operations for the catching or hunting of elephants or other wild animals; or

(*xxv*)   Employed as a diver; or

(*xxvi*)   Employed in the handling or transport of goods in, or within the precincts of,:

    (*a*)   Any warehouse or other place in which goods are stored, and in which on any one day of the preceding twelve months ten or more persons have been so employed, or

    (*b*)   Any market in which on any one day of the preceding twelve months fifty or more persons have been so employed; or

(*xxvii*)   Employed in any occupation involving the handling and manipulation of radium or X-rays apparatus, or contact with radioactive substances; or

(*xxviii*)   Employed in or in connection with the construction, erection, dismantling operation or maintenance of an aircraft as defined in Section 2 of the Indian Aircraft Act, 1934 (22 of 1934); or

(*xxix*)   Employed in horticultural operations, forestry, bee-keeping or farming by tractors or other contrivances driven by steam or other mechanical power or by electricity; or

(*xxx*)   Employed, otherwise than in a clerical capacity, in the construction, working, repair or maintenance of a tube, well; or

(*xxxi*)   Employed in the maintenance, repair or renewal of electric fittings in any building; or

(*xxxii*)   Employed in a circus.

(*xxxiii*) Employed as watchman in any factory or establishment; or

(*xxxiv*) Employed in any operation in the sea for catching fish; or

(*xxxv*) Employed in any employment which requires handling of snakes for the purpose of extraction of venom or for the purpose of looking after snakes or handling any other poisonous animal or insect; or

(*xxxvi*) Employed in handling animals like horses, mules and bulls; or

(*xxxvii*) Employed for the purpose of loading or unloading any mechanically propelled vehicle or in the handling or transport of goods which have been loaded in such vehicles; or

(*xxxviii*) Employed in cleaning of sewerlines or septic tanks within the limits of a local authority; or

(*xxxix*) Employed on surveys and investigation, exploration or gauge or discharge observation of rivers including drilling operations, hydrological observations and flood forecasting activities, ground water surveys and exploration; or

(*xl*) Employed in cleaning of jungles or reclaiming land or ponds in which on any one day of the preceding twelve months more than twenty-five persons have been employed; or

(*xli*) Employed in cultivation of land or rearing and maintenance of livestock or forest operations or fishing in which on any one day of the preceding twelve months more than twenty-five persons have been employed; or

(*xlii*) Employed in installation, maintenance or repair of pumping equipment used for lifting of water from wells, tube-wells, ponds, lakes, streams and the like; or

(*xliii*) Employed in the construction, boring or deepening of an open well or dug well, bore well, bore-*cum*-dug well, filter point and the like; or

(*xliv*) Employed in spraying and dusting or insecticides or pesticides in agricultural operations or plantations; or

(*xlv*) Employed in mechanised harvesting and threshing operations; or

(*xlvi*) Employed in working or repair or maintenance of bulldozers, tractors, power tillers and the like; or

(*xlvii*) Employed as artists for drawing pictures on advertisement boards at a height of 3.66 meters or more from the ground level; or

(*xlviii*) Employed in any newspaper establishment as defined in the Working Journalists and Other Newspaper Employees (Conditions of Service) and Miscellaneous Provisions Act, 1955 (45 of 1955) and engaged in outdoor work.

(*xlix*) Employed as dones for work under water.

Explanation: In this Schedule, "the preceding twelve months" relates in any particular case to the twelve months ending with the day on which the accident in such case occurred.

The Third Schedule

(*See* Section 3)

List of Occupational Diseases

Sl. No.	Occupational Disease	Employment
	Part A	
1.	Infectious and parasitic diseases contracted in any occupation where there is a particular risk of contamination	(*a*) All work involving exposure to health or laboratory work; (*b*) All work involving exposure to veterinary work; (*c*) Work relating to handling animals, animal carcasses, part of such carcasses or merchandise which may have been contaminated by animals or animal carcasses; (*d*) Other work carrying a particular risk of contamination.
2.	Diseases caused by work in compressed the risk concerned	All work involving exposure to air.
3.	Diseases caused by lead or its toxic the risk concerned.	All work involving exposure to compounds.
4.	Poisoning by nitrous fumes.	All work involving exposure to the risk concerned.
5.	Poisoning by organo phosphorus the risk concerned.	All work involving exposure to compounds.
	Part B	
1.	Diseases caused by phosphorus or its toxic compounds.	All work involving exposure to the risk concerned.
2.	Diseases caused by mercury or its toxic compounds.	All work involving exposure to the risk concerned.
3.	Diseases caused by benzene or its toxic homologues.	All work involving exposure to the risk concerned.
4.	Diseases caused by nitro and amino toxic derivatives of benzene or its homologues	All work involving exposure to the risk concerned.
5.	Diseases caused by chromium, or its toxic compounds.	All work involving exposure to the risk concerned.

Sl. No.	Occupational Disease	Employment
6.	Diseases caused by arsenic, or its toxic the compounds.	All work involving exposure to the risk concerned.
7.	Diseases caused by radioactive substances and ionising radiations substances or ionising radiations.	All work involving exposure to the action of radioactive.
8.	Primary epitheliomatous cancer of the skin, caused by tar, pitch, bitumen, mineral oil, anthracene, or the compounds, products or residues of these substances.	All work involving exposure to the risk concerned.
9.	Diseases caused by the toxic halogen derivatives of hydrocarbons (of the aliphatic and aromatic series).	All work involving exposure to the risk concerned
10.	Diseases caused by carbon disulphide.	All work involving exposure to the risk concerned
11.	Occupational cataract due to infrared radiations.	All work involving exposure to the risk concerned.
12.	Diseases caused by manganese or its toxic compounds.	All work involving exposure to the risk concerned.
13.	Skin diseases caused by physical, chemical or bio-logical agents not included in other items.	All work involving exposure to the risk concerned.
14.	Hearing impairment caused by noise.	All work involving exposure to risk concerned.
15.	Poisoning by dinitrophenal or a homologue or by substituted dinitrophenol or by the salts or such substances.	All work involving exposure to the risk concerned.
16.	Diseases caused by beryllium or its toxic compounds.	All work involving expsure to the risk concerned.
17.	Diseases caused by cadmium or its toxic compounds.	All work involving exposure to the risk concerned.
18.	Occupational asthma caused by recognised sensitizing agents inherent to the work process.	All work involving exposure to the risk concerned.
19.	Diseases caused by fluorine or its toxic compounds.	All work involving exposure to the risk concerned.
20.	Diseases caused by nitroglycerin, or other nitro-acid esters.	All work involving exposure to the risk concerned.
21.	Diseases caused by alcohols and ketones.	All work involving exposure to the risk concerned.
22.	Diseases caused by asphyxiants, carbonmonoxide, and its toxic derivatives, hydrogen sulphide.	All work involving exposure to the risk concerned.

Sl. No.	Occupational Disease	Employment
23.	Lung cancer and mesotheliomas caused by asbestos.	All work involving exposure to the risk concerned.
24.	Primary neoplasm of the epithelial lining of the urinary bladder of the kidney or the ureter.	All work involving exposure to the risk concerned.
25.	Snow blindness in snow bound areas.	All work involving exposure to risk concerned.
26.	Disease due to effect of heat in extreme hot climate.	All work involving exposure to the risk concerned.
27.	Disease due to effect of cold in extreme cold climate.	All work involving exposure to the risk concerned.
	Part C	
1.	Pneumoconioses caused by sclerogenic mineral dust (silicosis, anthraoosilicosis, asbestosis) and silico tuberculosis provided that silicosis is an essential factor in causing the resultant incapacity or death.	All work involving exposure to the risk concerned.
2.	Bagassosis	All work involving exposure to the risk concerned.
3.	Bronchopulmonary diseases caused by cotton, flax hemp and sisal dust (Byassionsis).	All work involving exposure to the risk concerned.
4.	Extrinsic allergic alveelitis caused by the inhalation of organic dusts.	All work involving exposure to the risk concerned.
5.	Bronchopulmonary diseases caused by hard metals.	All work involving exposure to the risk concerned.
6.	Acute Pulmonary Oedema of High Altitude	All work involving exposure to the risk concerned.

The Fourth Schedule

(*See* Section 4)

Factors for Working out Lump Sum Equivalent of Compensation Amount in case of Permanent Disablement and Death.

Completed years of age on the last birthday of the workman immediately preceding the date on which the compensation fell due	Factors
Not more than 16	228.54
17	227.49
18	226.38

19	225.22
20	224.00
21	222.71
22	221.37
23	219.95
24	218.47
25	216.91
26	215.28
27	213.57
28	211.79
29	209.92
30	207.98
31	205.95
32	203.85
33	201.66
34	199.40
35	197.06
36	194.64
37	192.14
38	189.56
39	186.90
40	184.17
41	181.37
42	178.49
43	175.54
44	172.52
45	169.44
46	166.29
47	163.07
48	159.80
49	156.47
50	153.09
51	149.67
52	146.20
53	142.68
54	139.13
55	135.56
56	131.95
57	128.33
58	124.70
59	121.05

60	117.41
61	113.77
62	110.14
63	106.52
64	102.93
65 or more	99.37

Review Questions

1. Define the following terms as used in the Workmen Compensation Act 1923 :
   - (*i*) Dependent,
   - (*ii*) Employer
   - (*iii*) Partial Disablement
   - (*iv*) Total Disablement
   - (*v*) Workmen
   - (*vi*) Personal Injury
   - (*vii*) Injury by accident includes occupational disease
   - (*viii*) Accident arising out of and in the Course of Employment

2. How far is an employer liable for the compensation to a workmen injured by an accident arising out and in the course of employment?

3. What are the defences available to an employer against a claim for compensation made by workmen under the Workmen Compensation Act 1923?

4. How the amount of compensation is payable to an injured workman is calculated under Workmen Compensation Act 1923?

5. State the rules regarding the notice of an accident and its proper manner.

6. Under what circumstances is the order of the Commissioner under the Workmen Compensation Act 1923, appealable?

7. Will the employer be liable in the following cases, to give compensation under the Workmen's Compensation Act, 1923? Cite cases, if any.

   - (*a*) Where a workman suffering from heart disease died on account of strain of work by keeping continuously standing.
   - (*b*) A watchman in the course of his duty lifts G.I. pipe in order to keep it in safe place and receives injuries.
   - (*c*) Where a workman on duty was bitten by a scorpion and during operation therefore while under treatment as an indoor patien in the hospital developed tetanus and ultimately died.

8. Describe the provisions of the Workmen Compensation Act 1923 relating to:
   - (*i*) Commutation of half monthly payments
   - (*ii*) Distribution of compensation

9. Attempt the following. Each carries equal marks:

(*i*)   The employer went to the house of deceased workmen who was working as a stock maker with the respondent employer at a salary of Rs. 4,000 p.m. The employer took the deceased on his scooter for some urgent work when on the route, the scooter met with a serious accident and the deceased succumbed to his injuries next day in the hospital. Decide, if the injury causing his death was sustained during course of employment and his heirs and defendants could file claim for compensation under the Workmen's Compensation Act and Motor Vehicles Act?

(*ii*)   The deceased working as driver after loading his truck fell ill on his way and asked cleaner to drive his truck. In the early morning hours, some army personnel stopped vehicle and asked the persons sitting inside the vehicle to come down. Due to illness, deceased driver took some time to come down which infuriated army personnel who fired at him resulting in his death. Decide, if the accident has occurred arising out of and in the course of his employment and the compensation is payable to the dependents?

(*iii*)   Where a workman suffering from heart disease died on account of strain of work by keeping continuously standing. Will the employer be liable to give compensation under the Workmen's Compensation Act, 1923? Cite cases, if any.

(*iv*)   An electrician, who had to go frequently to a heating room from cooling plant, contracted pneumonia, which resulted in his death. If the dependants of the deceased workman were entitled compensation under the Workmen's Compensation Act?

(*v*)   The workman had been in service from 18.05.1990. On 25.12.1990, he suffered a cerebral stroke while at sea. He was therefore taken ashore and was treated in a hospital. Thereafter, in Jan 1991, he was repatriated to India and was admitted to hospital for further treatment. On 11.02.1991, respondent's son has discharged him from the hospital against the medical advice and returned to their native place. The respondent workman claims an amount of Rs 15 lakhs as compensation from the appellant shipper contending that he was suffered from an accident arising out of and in the course of employment. Decide, if the workman is entitled to compensation?

(*vi*)   The deceased driver was entrusted the duty of driving the bus on a particular route. The deceased was free to go home after duty hours, yet he stayed back for rest on the terrace of the bus stand.

In the morning while getting down from the terrace, the deceased tumble down resulting in his death. Decide if the cause of accident is connected with the nature of employment and the employer is liable to pay compensation.

(*vii*) Where a workman on duty was bitten by a scorpion and during operation therefore while under treatment as an indoor patient in the hospital developed tetanus and ultimately died. Will the employer be liable to give compensation under the Workmen's Compensation Act, 1923? Cite cases, if any.